Structural
Anthropology

CLAUDE LÉVI-STRAUSS

Structural
Anthropology

Translated from the French by Claire Jacobson
and Brooke Grundfest Schoepf

BASIC BOOKS, Inc., *Publishers, New York*

May an inconstant disciple dedicate this book which appears in 1958, the year of Émile Durkheim's centenary, to the memory of the founder of *Année Sociologique:* that famed workshop where modern anthropology fashioned part of its tools and which we have abandoned, not so much out of disloyalty as out of the sad conviction that the task would prove too much for us.

Χρυσεον μεν πρωτιστα γενος.

Author's Preface
to the French Edition

IN A RECENT STUDY, Jean Pouillon wrote a sentence which, with his permission, I shall cite at the beginning of this work, since it corresponds perfectly to all that I hoped to accomplish in the scientific realm, though often doubtful of having been successful: "Lévi-Strauss is certainly not the first nor the only one to have emphasized the structural character of social phenomena, but his originality consists in taking that character seriously and in serenely deriving all the consequences from it." * My hopes would be fulfilled if this book could induce other readers to share this judgment.

One will find here a collection of seventeen of some one hundred papers written during the past thirty years. A few have been lost; others can profitably remain in oblivion. Among those which seemed to me less unworthy of survival, I have made a choice, rejecting works of purely ethnographic and descriptive character, as

* Jean Pouillon, "L'Oeuvre de Claude Lévi-Strauss," *Les Temps Modernes,* XII (1956), 158.

well as others of theoretical scope, but the substance of which has been incorporated into my book, *Tristes Tropiques*. Two papers (chapters V and XVI) are published here for the first time in conjunction with fifteen others that seem to me to elucidate the structural method in anthropology. . . .

Translator's Preface

For the past decade and a half, Claude Lévi-Strauss has been the most influential anthropological theorist in France. He has attracted a large following in Europe and evoked wide interest in the United States. Standing in the mainstream of the French sociological school, he has carried Durkheim's and Mauss's theories to a totally new level of conceptualization.

This book, first published in France in 1958, is a collection of papers, written between 1944 and 1957, which constitute what Lévi-Strauss regards as his most representative work. More than any of his other writings, *Structural Anthropology* offers a comprehensive view of Lévi-Strauss's theories.

Each of these papers is a self-contained whole in which he applies the structural method to particular problems and data. Lévi-Strauss is primarily concerned with universals, that is, basic social and mental processes of which cultural institutions are the concrete external projections or manifestations. Anthropology should be a science of general principles; the theories which the anthropologist formulates should be applicable to all societies and valid for all possible observers.

Lévi-Strauss has long been one of the chief exponents of the structural method; he considers the relations among phenomena, rather than the nature of the phenomena themselves, and the systems into which these relations enter. He persuasively argues that the attainment of a general science of man is contingent on structural considerations, which must include unconscious as well as conscious social processes, and he time and again develops his thesis in dealing with some of the major aspects of culture—language, kinship, social organization, magic, religion, and art.

How does structural analysis proceed? The first step is the definition of the constituent units of an institution; these are conceptually equivalent to the phonemes or morphemes of a language and, therefore, comparable cross-culturally. Once the various aspects of culture have been reduced to their structural elements, relationships of opposition and correlation and permutation and transformation among these elements can be defined. Homologies between institutions within the same society or among various societies can be explained, not in terms of a mechanical causality, but rather in dialectical terms. Correspondences or isomorphisms should be sought, not between empirical data pertaining to different institutions, but between systematized forms, or models, which are abstracted on different levels and which can be compared either intra- or cross-culturally. To Lévi-Strauss, the building of such models is the basic aim of anthropology.

The author proposes bold and at times frankly speculative hypotheses, in which he attempts to relate aspects of culture which no one has previously thought to connect in this particular manner. His originality lies in the emphasis on form, on the primacy of relations over entities, and on the search for constant relationships among phenomena at the most abstract level. His generalizations, however, always depart from empirical observation and return to it. To document his hypotheses, he sifts masses of data pertinent to various aspects of culture and to various societies. Though he deals with the major world areas, his use of ethnographic source materials is highly selective; he employs only those monographs which provide a thorough, intensive, and reliable coverage of a society. In addition, he draws on his own field work in central Brazil, as well as on observations of life in contemporary Western society.

Lévi-Strauss's anthropology emphasizes the close relationship between field work and theory, between the description of social phenomena and structural analysis, as two phases of the same process. The ethnographic study of societies must have a concrete, almost microscopic character; fluid, uncrystallized attitudes, the subjective aspects of institutions, must be observed and described with the same care as institutionalized and sanctioned norms and behavior. At the same time, a systematic, comparative, and generalizing perspective must complement the close-range view, so that the patterns which underlie the various manifestations of social life may be uncovered.

Lévi-Strauss's approach is holistic and integrative. In this sense, he has not deviated from the major concerns of Boas, Lowie, Kroeber, and other pioneering figures in the field to whom he often refers. He conceives of anthropology in the broadest sense, as the study of man, past and present, in all his aspects—physical, linguistic, cultural, conscious, and unconscious. In his elaboration of Mauss's concept of "the total social phenomenon," he is concerned with relating the synchronic to the diachronic, the individual to the cultural, the physiological to the psychological, the objective analysis of institutions to the subjective experience of individuals.

In Chapter I, Lévi-Strauss outlines his position; he defines the aims, scope, and methods of anthropology and discusses the complementary role of history in providing a perspective to the study of social life. According to him, anthropology has in the past suffered from a surfeit of empiricism on the one hand and culture-bound theorizing on the other. Rejecting the atomistic and mechanistic interpretations of evolutionism and diffusionism, as well as the naturalistic and empirical approach of British functionalism, the author formulates a critique of arbitrary concepts and classifications and exposes fallacious generalizations and truisms extant in much anthropological theory. He returns to this critique in other parts of the book, apropos of specific problems whose analysis and interpretation, he thinks, were misconstrued by his predecessors.

In chapters II through V, Lévi-Strauss emphasizes the revolutionary role of structural linguistics with respect to the social sciences. He reviews the goals and methods of linguistics and argues that it provides a model of scientific method for anthropology. Its approach is objective and rigorous; it has defined constituent units, studied their interrelations, and isolated constants; finally, language is susceptible of mathematical analysis. Both language and culture are built of oppositions, correlations, and logical relations. Language can, therefore, be treated as a conceptual model for other aspects of culture; these aspects can also be regarded as systems of communication.

In Chapter II, the author deals with the dialectical nature of the relationship between kinship terminology and prescribed attitudes toward kin. He shows, for a variety of societies, the systematic character of the relations among four prescribed attitudes within the basic unit of kinship, that is, the oppositions, correlations, and possible combinations among them. By the same process, he sheds new light on the significance of the avunculate in primitive society, which can only be understood if it is treated as a single relationship within a larger system.

In Chapter III, Lévi-Strauss compares the structural properties of a variety of kinship systems in various geographical areas to basic features of the linguistic stocks found in those areas. If such a comparison is successful—that is, if kinship systems and preferential marriage rules, on the one hand, and linguistic structures, on the other, could be formulated in the same terms—we would be one step closer to an understanding of the unconscious processes which underlie the various manifestations of social life.

In Chapter IV, the author attempts to define the levels at which correlations can be established between language and culture; he cautions against unwarranted correlations between intensively analyzed linguistic materials and empirical behavioral data. He compares the Indo-European and Sino-Tibetan language areas with respect to marriage rules, social organization, and kinship terminology; he finds structural contrasts between these areas which he believes have linguistic parallels. He expresses a need for a much closer collaboration between linguists and anthropologists, so as to pave the way for a truly integrated science of man.

Chapter V, written especially for this volume, is a rejoinder by Lévi-Strauss to criticisms which were addressed to him with respect to previous publications (here chapters III and IV). This chapter provides a clarification and amplification of the positions initially formulated. The reader will be especially interested in the author's highly original and suggestive comparison of the cuisine of various societies, which he shows is susceptible of the same type of structural analysis as other parts of culture. He examines the relationship between semantic content and linguistic form, which he argues is not so arbitrary as has been heretofore supposed.

In Chapter VI, the author examines the historical position of some of the more primitive societies of South America, by bringing to bear both distributional evidence and internal structural principles. The so-called archaism of these peoples is called into question, and they are shown to have regressed from a higher level of culture.

Chapters VII and VIII are devoted to an examination of the problem of dual organization in North and South America, Melanesia, and Indonesia. The author shows that, notwithstanding native theories as to the importance of this form of social organization, its role is secondary, if not actually contradictory to reality. Lévi-Strauss's study of the spatial projection of their institutions exposes gaps and contradictions in the natives' conception of these institutions and permits him to uncover the real social structure, which departs considerably from the natives' idea. These chapters offer a convincing demonstration of the author's oft-repeated point that, although informants' accounts of institutions must be taken into consideration, they are rationalizations and reinterpretations, not to be confused with the actual social organization.

Chapter IX deals with the nature of the shamanistic complex: the relationship between sorcerer or shaman and the group, the factors involved in the acquisition of supernatural power, and the social bases of the religious practitioner's effectiveness or failure. Shamanistic curing permits the articulation into a system of diffuse and disorganized emotions. Shamanism and psychoanalysis, considered as two forms of psychotherapy, are contrasted with respect to the roles ascribed to the healer, the patient, and the group.

Chapter X is an analysis of a strictly psychological shamanistic cure for difficult childbirth. This chapter concludes with an illuminating comparison of the shamanistic and psychoanalytic techniques in which the role of symbols in bringing about a cure, whether of a psychological or a physiological disturbance, is cogently demonstrated.

Chapter XI offers a fundamental contribution to the theory of myth. In analyzing the Oedipus story and a series of North American myths, Lévi-Strauss sheds new light on the logical development and structure of myth. He shows that the intellectual process involved in mythical thought is as rigorous as that of scientific thinking—an important theme which he develops at great length in his recent book, *La Pensée sauvage*.

Chapter XII illustrates the close connection between structural analysis and the dialectical method. What is examined here is the nature of the relationship between myth and ritual, once these are reduced to their structural elements. Myth and ritual are not only compared within the confines of one society, but within the context of the beliefs and practices of neighboring societies. As the author convincingly demonstrates, the structural properties of myth and ritual may be shared by several tribes within a culture area, just as, in language, phonetic and grammatical features may diffuse and areas of affinity be formed.

In Chapter XIII, a comparative study of primitive and prehistoric art, the author attempts to account for thematic and stylistic resemblances which cannot be explained on historical grounds in terms of their relationships to structurally similar forms of social organization and religion.

In Chapter XIV, Lévi-Strauss points out, on the basis of South American evidence, striking parallels between art and mythology in societies which are widely separated in time and space. He suggests that the structural analysis of contemporary ethnographic data can contribute to the elucidation of historical problems raised by the syncretism characteristic of South American cultures.

Chapter XV is the author's systematic presentation of the structural approach. Here, he formulates requirements for the construction of models which are to account for various aspects of empirical social reality. He provides a typology of models, showing how they can be employed and their formal properties compared. He discusses the spatial, temporal, numerical, and other properties or correlates of social structures. Lévi-Strauss considers the various forms of communication (exchange of women, goods, and messages) among groups and individuals in a society and calls for a greater consolidation of kinship studies, economics, and linguistics within a general science of communication. He deals with problems of change in social structure, whether associated with socialization, internal contradictions within the structure, or the dynamic properties of hierarchical social relations. A formal mathematical method is proposed as one approach to the study of the integration of hierarchical and communication structures. Here, as elsewhere, Lévi-Strauss makes a strong case for the role of mathematics in providing the tools and methods to consolidate various types of anthropological research. Finally, he considers the "order of orders," that is, the manner in which institutional structures are themselves interrelated and can be integrated within a total structure, as well as the relationship between the "order of orders" as it actually functions and is reconstructed by the anthropologist and the way in which the society itself, through myth and religion, conceives of its ordering.

Chapter XVI answers objections of his French critics to points raised in his article "Social Structure," first published in *Anthropology Today* (Chapter XV of the present volume). The author reexamines the concepts of cultural relativity, evolution, progress, and other perennial concerns of anthropology and shows their differential validity within the primitive and current Western contexts.

Chapter XVII offers a significant early discussion of the relationship of anthropology to cognate fields and the problems involved in teaching it. Preceding by almost a decade the recent memoir of the American Anthropological Association, *The Teaching of Anthropology*, this chapter reviews the organizational contexts of teaching and exposes ambiguities in the position of anthropology in traditional curriculums, both in the United States and abroad. Lévi-Strauss discusses basic principles in the teaching of the subject to anthropology students and to specialists in other disciplines; desirable curriculum content and methods; training for teaching and research; and the role of field work, museums, and applied anthropology. Thus, this chapter anticipates, in many ways, some of the ideas expressed in the memoir. The author also returns to a theme developed in Chapter I and recurrent throughout the book—the call for new modes of thinking in the anthropological profession. He insists on the need to evolve new categories and concepts which will be cross-culturally valid.

Acknowledgments

The translation might never have been successfully completed were it not for the encouragement and assistance of Brooke G. Schoepf, who translated chapters II, VII, VIII, and IX and who helped me revise other parts of the book. I am responsible for the translation of chapters I, V, VI, X, XII, XIII, XIV, and XVI and for the preparation of four chapters originally written and published in English—III, IV, XI, and XV—as well as of Chapter XVII, written in French and published simultaneously in French and English. Many of the figures were ably redrawn for this edition by Claude Schoepf.

My thanks go to Professors Joseph H. Greenberg and Morton H. Fried for reading a few chapters relating to their respective fields of specialization and for their useful advice on several questions of terminology. I am indebted to Esther V. Banks and Dana Raphael Jacobson for their willing and able editing of several chapters. Finally, I wish to acknowledge particular gratitude to Ariane Brunel. One of our difficulties was in attempting to convey the author's vivid French into English, and special credit must be given to Miss Brunel, whose gifted ear for style in both languages was of invaluable help.

All those mentioned here contributed to the successful completion of the work, but final responsibility for the translation rests with Mrs. Schoepf and me.

Claire Jacobson

October 1963

Contents

Part Three MAGIC AND RELIGION

Part Four ART

Part Five PROBLEMS OF METHOD AND TEACHING

List of Figures

List of Plates

between pages 250-251

Structural
Anthropology

CHAPTER I

Introduction:
History and Anthropology

MORE THAN A HALF-CENTURY has elapsed since Hauser and Simiand formulated and contrasted the principles and methods which seemed to them to distinguish history from sociology. These differences stemmed primarily from the comparative nature of the sociological method, on the one hand, and the documentary and functional character of the historical method, on the other.[1] While the two authors agreed on the contrasting nature of these disciplines, they diverged in evaluating the respective merits of each method.

What has happened since then? We must acknowledge that history has confined itself to its original modest and lucid program and that it has prospered by adhering to it closely. From the vantage point of history, problems of principle and method appear to have been definitely resolved. What has happened to sociology, however, is another matter. Those branches of sociology with which we shall be particularly concerned here, ethnography and ethnology, have, during the last thirty years, produced a great number of theoretical and descriptive studies. This productivity, however, has been achieved at the price of conflicts, cleavages, and confusions which duplicate, within anthropology itself, the traditional and far more clear-cut dispute that set off ethnology as a discipline separate from history. Just as paradoxically, the historians' theories have been taken over literally by anthropologists, and particularly by those anthropologists who proclaim their opposition to the historical method. This situation will be more easily understood if we briefly trace its origins and, for the sake of clarity, sketch some preliminary definitions.

In this discussion we shall not use the term *sociology*, which has never come to stand, as Durkheim and Simiand hoped it would, for a general science of human behavior. If *sociology* is taken to mean examination of the principles of social life and the ideas which men either have entertained or now entertain with respect to it—and this interpretation is still current in several European countries—then sociology can be equated with social philosophy and thus it falls outside our scope. If, on the other hand, sociology is considered, as it is in the Anglo-Saxon countries, as the corpus of all the empirical research bearing on the structure and functioning of the more complex societies, it becomes a branch of ethnography. In the latter case, precisely because of the complexity of its subject matter, it cannot yet aspire to findings so concrete and varied as those of ethnography, which, at least from a methodological standpoint, have greater value.

We have yet to define ethnography itself and ethnology. Let us distinguish them briefly and tentatively—this being sufficient at the outset—by stating that ethnography consists of the observation and analysis of human groups considered as individual entities (the groups are often selected, for theoretical and practical reasons unrelated to the nature of the research involved, from those societies that differ most from our own). Ethnography thus aims at recording as accurately as possible the respective modes of life of various groups. Ethnology, on the other hand, utilizes for comparative purposes (the nature of which will be explained below) the data provided by the ethnographer. Thus, *ethnography* has the same meaning in all countries, and *ethnology* corresponds approximately to what is known in Anglo-Saxon countries—where the term *ethnology* has become obsolete—as social or cultural anthropology.

Social anthropology is devoted especially to the study of institutions considered as systems of representations,[2] cultural anthropology, to the study of techniques which implement social life (and, sometimes also, to the study of institutions considered as such techniques). Finally, it is obvious that if the data resulting from the objective study of both complex societies and so-called primitive societies should ever be successfully integrated to provide universally valid conclusions from a synchronic or diachronic point of view, then sociology, having attained its positivistic form, would automatically acquire the crowning position among the social sciences that its scholars have always coveted. But we have not yet reached that point.

After these preliminary remarks and definitions, we can formulate the problem of the relationship between the anthropological sciences and history as follows: Either anthropology is focused on the diachronic dimension of phenomena, that is, on their temporal order, and thus is unable to trace their history; or anthropologists attempt to apply the method of the historian, and the time dimension escapes them. The problem of reconstructing a past whose history we are incapable of grasping confronts ethnology more particularly; the problem of writing the history of a present without a past confronts ethnography. That is, at any rate, the dilemma which has too often halted the development of these sciences in the course of the last fifty years.

This contradiction has not been stated here in terms of the classical opposition between evolutionism and diffusionism, because from this point of view the two schools converge. The evolutionist interpretation in anthropology clearly derives from evolutionism in biology.[3] Western civilization thus appears to be the most advanced expression of the evolution of societies, while primitive groups are "survivals" of earlier stages, whose logical classification reflects their order of appearance in time. But the task is not so simple. The Eskimo, while excellent technicians, are poor sociologists; the reverse is true of the natives of Australia. One could cite many such examples. With an unlimited choice of criteria an unlimited number of evolutionary sequences could be constructed, all of them different. Nor does Leslie White's neo-evolutionism[4] seem able to overcome this difficulty. Although the criterion which he suggests, namely, the amount of energy harnessed per capita in each society, corresponds to an ideal found in certain historical periods and valid for certain aspects of Western civilization, it does not apply to the great majority of human societies, for which the proposed standard would seem to entirely lack significance.

An alternative approach is to break down cultures into abstract elements and to establish, between elements of the same type in different cultures, rather than between cultures themselves, the same kind of relationships of historical descent and progressive differentiation which the paleontologist sees in the evolution of species. For the ethnologist, Tylor says:

> The bow and arrow is a species, the habit of flattening children's skulls is a species, the practice of reckoning numbers by tens is a species. The geographical distribution of these things, and their transmission from region to region, have to be studied as the naturalist studies the geography of his botanical and zoological species.[5]

But nothing is more dangerous than this analogy. For even if the concept of species should be discarded once and for all in the development of genetics, what made—and still makes—the concept valid for the natural historian is the fact that a horse indeed begets a horse and that, in the course of a sufficient number of generations, *Equus caballus* is the true descendant of *Hipparion*. The historical validity of the naturalist's reconstructions is guaranteed, in the final analysis, by the biological link of reproduction. An ax, on the contrary, does not generate another ax. There will always be a basic difference between two identical tools, or two tools which differ in function but are similar in form, because one does not stem from the other; rather, each of them is the product of a system of representations. Thus the European fork and the Polynesian fork (which is used in ritual meals) do not constitute a species, any more than do the straws through which one sips lemonade at a café, the "bombilla" to drink maté, and the drinking tubes used for ritual purposes by some American Indian tribes. The same is true of institutions. We cannot classify under the same rubric the custom of killing the old for economic reasons and that of hastening their entrance into the joys of the other world.

Therefore when Tylor writes, "When a general law can be inferred from a group of facts, the use of detailed history is very much superseded. When we see a magnet attract a piece of iron, having come by experience to the general law that magnets attract iron, we do not take the trouble to go into the history of the particular magnet in question," [6] he is really forcing us into a blind alley. For, unlike the physicist, the anthropologist is still uncertain which of the objects of his study correspond to the magnet and which to the iron, and, furthermore, whether it is possible to identify objects which at first appear to be two magnets or two pieces of iron. Only a "detailed history" would enable the anthropologist to overcome his doubts in each case. The critical evaluation of the concept of totemism has long provided an excellent example of this difficulty. If one limits the application of the totemic concept to irrefutable cases where the institution appears with all its characteristics, these cases are too special to permit the formulation of a law of religious evolution. If, on the other hand, one extrapolates only from certain constituent elements, it becomes impossible to know, without a "detailed history" of the religious ideas of each group, whether animal or plant names and practices or beliefs referring to animal or plant species can be explained as vestiges of an earlier totemic system or in terms of entirely different causes, such as, for example, the logico-aesthetic tendency of the human mind to classify into categories the physical, biological, and social entities which constitute its universe. (A classic study by Durkheim and Mauss has demonstrated the universality of this mode of thinking.[7])

Actually, the evolutionist and diffusionist interpretations have a great deal in common. Tylor, indeed, formulated and applied them side by side. Both approaches differ from the historian's methods. The historian always studies individuals, whether these be persons, events, or groups of phenomena individualized by their location in space and time. The diffusionist breaks down the species developed in the comparative method in order to reconstruct individuals with fragments borrowed from different categories. But he never succeeds in building more than a pseudo-individual, since the spatial and temporal coordinates are the result of the way the elements were chosen and assembled, instead of being the reflection of a true unity in the object. The "cycles" or cultural "complexes" of the diffusionist, like the "stages" of the evolutionist, are the product of an abstraction that will always lack the corroboration of empirical evidence. Their history remains conjectural and ideological. This qualification applies even to the more modest and rigorous studies—such as those by Lowie, Spier, and Kroeber—of the distribution of certain cultural traits in limited areas of North America.[8] This is true not so much because we can never conclude that events actually occurred in the way suggested by the proposed reconstruction—for it is always legitimate to formulate hypotheses, and, at least in some instances, the points of origin and the extent of diffusion which are postulated hold a high degree of probability; such studies deceive us because they do not teach us anything about the conscious and unconscious processes in concrete individual or collective experiences, by means of which men who did not possess a certain institution went about acquiring it, either by inventing it, by modifying previous institutions, or by borrowing from the outside. This kind of research seems to us to be one of the essential goals of the ethnographer as well as of the historian.

No one has contributed more than Boas toward exposing these contradictions. Thus, a brief analysis of his major tenets will enable us to find out to what extent he himself was able to escape such dilemmas and whether they are inherent in the nature of all ethnographic research.

Referring to history, Boas begins with a proclamation of humility: "As a matter of fact, all the history of primitive peoples that any ethnologist has ever developed is reconstruction and cannot be anything else." [9] And to those who object that he has not studied the history of this or that aspect of a civilization to which he has, nevertheless, devoted the greater part of his life, he gives this heroic answer: "Unfortunately we have not found any data that throw light on its development." [10] But once these limitations are recognized, it becomes possible to define a method whose application, though no doubt limited in scope by the exceptionally unfavorable conditions under which the anthropologist works, may still yield findings. The detailed study of customs and of their place within the total culture of the tribe which practices them, together with research bearing on the geographical distribution of those customs among neighboring tribes, enables us to determine, on the one hand, the historical factors which led to their development and, on the other, the psychological processes which made them possible.[11]

To be legitimate, such research should be restricted to a small region with clearly defined boundaries, and comparisons should not be extended beyond the area selected for study. Actually, the recurrence of similar customs or institutions cannot be held as a proof of contact unless there is a continuous chain of traits of the same type which allows us to relate the polar traits through a series of intermediaries.[12] We shall probably never achieve chronological certainty, but it is possible to obtain high probabilities with reference to phenomena, or groups of phenomena, of limited distribution in time and space. The evolution of secret societies among the Kwakiutl was traced over a period of a half-century. Hypotheses bearing on the relationship between the cultures of northern Siberia and the Northwest Coast have been formulated; and the itineraries followed by one or another mythical theme of North America have been reasonably reconstructed.

Nevertheless, such thorough inquiry rarely reaches the point of truly recreating history. In the entire work of Boas the result appears to be rather negative. Among the Pueblo Indians of the Southwest, as well as among the tribes of Alaska and British Columbia, it has been noted that social organization takes extreme and contrasting forms at the two ends of the territory under consideration and that the intermediary regions present a series of transitional forms. Thus, the western Pueblo have matrilineal clans without moieties and the eastern Pueblo patrilineal moieties without clans. The northern part of the Pacific Coast is characterized by few clans and a large number of local groups with clearly defined privileges, while the southern part has a bilateral organization and local groups without marked privileges.

Can we draw the conclusion that one type has evolved from the other? For such a hypothesis to be legitimate we should have to be able to prove that one type is more primitive than the other; that the more primitive type evolves necessarily toward the other form; and, finally, that this law operates more rigorously in the center of the region than at its periphery. Failing this threefold and impossible demonstration, any theory of survivals is futile, and in this particular case the facts support no reconstruction tending, for example, to assert the historical priority of matrilineal over patrilineal institutions: "All that can be said is that fragments of earlier historical stages are bound to exist and are found." [13] While it is possible and even likely that the instability inherent in matrilineal institutions often leads to their transformation into patrilineal or bilateral institutions, it can by no means be concluded that, always and everywhere, matrilineal descent represents the primitive form.[14]

Such a critical analysis is conclusive. Nevertheless, if it were carried to an extreme, it would lead to complete historical agnosticism. For Boas, however, this kind of analysis is directed against the alleged universal laws of human development and generalizations based on what he once called "a 40 per cent possibility," [15] not against modest and conscientious effort at historical reconstruction within the bounds of precise and limited objectives. What are, according to Boas, the conditions necessary for such effort? He recognizes that in ethnology ". . . evidence of change can be inferred only by indirect methods," that is, as in comparative linguistics, by analysis of static phenomena and study of their distribution.[16] But we should not forget that Boas, a geographer by training and a disciple of Ratzel, became aware of his anthropological vocation during the course of his first field work, as a result of a flash of insight into the originality, uniqueness, and spontaneity of social life in each human group. These social experiences and these constant interactions between the group and the individual can never be inferred; they must be observed. As he once said, "In order to understand history it is necessary to know not only how things are, but how they have come to be." [17]

We are now in a position to explore the character of Boas' thought and to bring out its paradoxical quality. By university training a physicist as well as a geographer, he ascribes a scientific aim and universal scope to anthropological research. "He himself often said that the problem was the relation between the objective world and man's subjective world as it had taken form in different cultures." [18]

But while he aspired to apply to this subjective world the rigorous methodology that he had learned in the natural sciences, he recognized the infinite variety of historical processes which shapes it in each case. Knowledge of social facts must be based on induction from individualized and concrete knowledge of social groups localized in time and space. Such specific knowledge, in turn, can be acquired only from the history of each group. Yet such is the nature of the subject-matter of ethnographic studies that in the vast majority of cases history lies beyond reach. Boas introduces the standards of the physicist in tracing the history of societies for which we possess only documents that would discourage the historian. When Boas is successful, his reconstructions amount to true history—but this is a history of the fleeting moment, the only kind of history that can be captured immediately —in other words, a *microhistory*, which can no more be related to the past then can the *macrohistory* of evolutionism and diffusionism.[19]

In this demanding enterprise to overcome contradictory requirements with rigor, toil, and genius, the work of Boas continues, and will long continue, to dominate from its monumental heights all subsequent developments. In any event, the developments of recent years can only be understood as efforts to escape the dilemma which he himself formulated without recognizing its inevitable character. Thus, Kroeber tried to loosen somewhat the rigid criteria of validity which Boas imposed for historical reconstructions, justifying his method with the observation that, after all, the historian, who with a wealth of documents to help him occupy a much more secure position than the anthropologist, is far from being so exacting.[20] Malinowski and his school, along with most of the contemporary American school, chose the opposite direction. Since Boas' work itself demonstrated the extent to which it was deceptive to seek knowledge about "how things have come to be," they renounced "understanding history" in order to convert the study of cultures into a synchronic analysis, in the present, of relationships between their constituent elements. The whole question is to know whether, as Boas so profoundly observed, even the most penetrating analysis of a unique culture—which includes description of its institutions and their functional interrelations, as well as study of the dynamic processes by which culture and the individual interact—can attain full significance without knowledge of the historical development underlying the present patterns.[21] This essential point will become clearer from the discussion of a specific problem.

The term *dual organization* has been ascribed to a type of social structure frequently found in America, Asia, and Oceania and characterized by the division of the social group—whether tribe, clan, or village—into two moieties, whose respective members have relationships which may range from the most intimate cooperation to latent hostility, and which generally contain both types of behavior. Sometimes the purpose of moieties seems to be the control of marriage, in which case they are termed exogamous. Sometimes their role is confined to activities of a religious, political, economic, ceremonial, or merely recreational character, or even to one or another of these activities only. Membership in a moiety is transmitted in some instances by matrilineal descent, in others by patrilineal descent. The division into moieties may or may not coincide with clan organization. It may be simple or complex, in which case several pairs of moieties will cross-cut one another, each pair having different functions. In short, almost as many kinds of dual organization are known as peoples possessing it. Where then does it begin and where does it end?

Let us immediately rule out evolutionist and diffusionist interpretations. The evolutionist, who tends to consider dual organization as a necessary stage of social development, would first have to define a simple form whose actually observed forms would be concrete manifestations, survivals, or vestiges. He would then have to postulate the presence, at a remote time, of this form among peoples where nothing demonstrates that a moiety division ever existed. The diffusionist, in turn, would select one of the observed types, usually the most developed and complex, as representing the archaic form of the institution and would attribute its origin to that region of the world where it is best documented, all other forms being considered the product of migrations and borrowings from the common cradle. In both cases, one arbitrarily selects a type from all those provided by experience and makes of this type the model from which one attempts, through speculation, to derive all the others.

Are we then compelled to carry Boasian nominalism to its limit and study each of the cases observed as so many individual entities? We should be aware, first, that the *functions* assigned to dual organization do not coincide, and, second, that the *history* of each social group demonstrates that the division into moieties stems from the most different origins.[22] Thus, depending on the case, dual organization may be the result of the invasion of a population by an immigrant group; of fusion between two neighboring groups, for any of several reasons (economic, demographic, or ceremonial); of the crystallization, in institutional form, of empirical norms designed to insure marriage exchanges within a given group; of the distribution within the group—over two parts of the year, two types of activities, or two segments of the population—of two sets of antithetical behavior, each of which is considered equally indispensable for the maintenance of social equilibrium; and so forth. We are therefore forced to reject the concept of dual organization as a spurious category and, if we extend this line of reasoning to all other aspects of social life, to reject *institutions* exclusively, in favor of *societies*. Ethnology and ethnography—the former thus reduced to the latter—would be no more than history reduced to such a level, owing to the lack of written or graphic documents, that it would no longer be worthy of the name.

Malinowski and his followers have rightly protested against this abdication. But we might ask them whether, by banning all history on the premise that ethnologists' history is not worthy of consideration, they have not gone to too great extremes. For one of two things will occur: The functionalists may proclaim that all anthropological research must be based on painstaking study of concrete societies and their institutions—including the interrelations of those institutions, their relationships with custom, belief, and technology, and the interrelations between the individual and the group and among individuals within the group. In this case, they are merely doing what Boas recommended in these same terms in 1895 and what the French school, under Durkheim and Mauss, also advised in those days—in other words, sound ethnography. Malinowski at the beginning of his career did some admirable ethnography, especially in his *Argonauts of the Western Pacific*. But we fail to see in what way he transcended Boas' theoretical position.

Or the functionalists may find salvation in their asceticism and, by an unheard-of miracle, do what every good ethnographer must do and does; but they stubbornly refuse to consider any historical information regarding the society under study or any comparative data borrowed from neighboring or remote societies. In this way they claim to achieve, through inner meditation, those general truths whose possibility Boas never denied, but which he placed at the end of an undertaking so vast that all primitive societies will no doubt have disappeared long before appreciable progress has been made. Such, indeed, is Malinowski's attitude. His belated cautiousness[23] cannot temper his many ambitious proclamations. This is also the attitude of many an anthropologist of the younger generation who disdains study of any source materials or regional bibliographies before going into the field. He does this in order not to spoil the wonderful intuition that will enable him to grasp eternal truths on the nature and function of social institutions through an abstract dialogue with his little tribe, over and beyond a context of highly differentiated norms and customs, each of which possesses, nevertheless, countless variants among neighboring or remote peoples. But did not Malinowski label "herodotage" the curiosity for "primitive eccentricities of man"? [24]

When one confines oneself to the study of a single society, one may do valuable work. Experience shows that the best monographs are generally produced by investigators who have lived and worked in one particular region. But they must forgo conclusions about other regions. When, in addition, one completely limits study to the present period in the life of a society, one becomes first of all the victim of an illusion. For everything is history: What was said yesterday is history, what was said a minute ago is history. But, above all, one is led to misjudge the present, because only the study of historical development permits the weighing and evaluation of the interrelationships among the components of the present-day society. And a little history—since such, unfortunately, is the lot of the anthropologist—is better than no history at all. How shall we correctly estimate the role, so surprising to foreigners, of the *apéritif* in French social life if we are ignorant of the traditional prestige value ascribed to cooked and spiced wines ever since the Middle Ages? How shall we analyze modern dress without recognizing in it vestiges of previous customs and tastes? To reason otherwise would make it impossible to establish what is an essential distinction between primary function, which corresponds to a present need of the social body, and secondary function, which survives only because the group resists giving up a habit. For to say that a society functions is a truism; but to say that everything in a society functions is an absurdity.

The danger of the truism, which threatens functionalist interpretations, was aptly pointed out by Boas: ". . . the danger is ever present that the widest generalizations that may be obtained by the study of cultural integration are commonplaces." [25] Because such general characteristics *are* universal, they pertain to biology and psychology. The ethnographer's task is to describe and analyze the different ways in which they are manifested in various societies; the ethnologist's task is to explain them. But what have we learned about the "institution of gardening" when we are told that it is "universally found wherever the environment is favorable to the cultivation of the soil and the level of culture sufficiently high to allow it"? [26] Or about the outrigger canoe, its multiple forms, and its peculiar distribution, when it is defined as a canoe whose "arrangement gives the greatest stability, seaworthiness and manageability, considering the limitations in material and in technical handicraft of the Oceanic cultures"? [27] Or about the nature of society in general and the infinite variety of manners and customs, when we are confronted by this statement: "The organic needs of man [Malinowski lists nutrition, defense and comfort, mating and propagation] form the basic imperatives leading to the development of culture . . ."? [28] Yet these needs are common to both man and animals. It might also be submitted that one of the essential tasks of the ethnographer is to describe and analyze the complicated marriage rules and associated customs in various societies. Malinowski rejects this: "To put it bluntly, I should say that the symbolic, representative or ceremonial contents of marriage are of secondary importance to the anthropologist. . . . The real essence of the marriage act is that by means of an extremely simple or highly complicated ceremony it gives a public, tribally recognized, expression to the fact that two individuals enter the state of marriage." [29] Why then bother going to distant places? And, according to this point of view, would the 603 pages of *The Sexual Life of Savages in Northwestern Melanesia* be worth very much? In the same way, should we dismiss the fact that some tribes permit premarital sexual freedom while others require chastity, on the premise that these customs can be reduced to one function, that of insuring permanent marriage? [30] What interests the anthropologist is not the universality of the function—which is far from definitely established, and which cannot be asserted without a careful study of all the customs of this type *and their historical development*—but, rather, the fact that the customs are so varied. It is true that a discipline whose main, if not sole, aim is to analyze and interpret differences evades all problems when it takes into account only similarities. But at the same time it thus loses the means of distinguishing between the general truths to which it aspires and the trivialities with which it must be satisfied.

It may be said, perhaps, that these unfortunate incursions into the field of comparative sociology are exceptions in Malinowski's work. But the idea that empirical observation of a single society will make it possible to understand universal motivations appears continually in his writings, weakening the significance of data whose vividness and richness are well known.

The ideas held by the Trobriand Islanders concerning the value and respective function of each sex in the society are highly complex. They take pride in numbering in their clans more women than men, and are unhappy when there are fewer women. At the same time, they hold male superiority as an accepted fact: Men possess an aristocratic virtue which their wives lack. Why should such subtle observations be blunted by the brutal and contradicting introductory statement that "For the continuation and very existence of the family, woman as well as man is indispensable; therefore both sexes are regarded by the natives as being of equal value and importance"? [31] The first part of this statement is a truism, and the second is not consistent with the facts reported. Few topics have attracted Malinowski's attention as much as that of magic, and throughout his whole work one finds reiterated constantly the argument that all over the world,[32] as well as in the Trobriand Islands, magic is used for "all important activities and enterprises in which man has not the issue firmly and safely in hand. . . ." [33] Let us set aside the general thesis to consider its application to the specific case.

The men of the Trobriand Islands, we are told, employ magic for gardening, fishing, hunting, canoe-building, safety at sea, woodcarving, sorcery, and weather; women use magic for abortion, toothache, and skirtmaking.[34] These activities represent only a small fraction of those "in which man has not the issue firmly and safely in hand"; but even from this point of view they are not comparable. Why the making of straw skirts and not the preparation of dried gourds or pottery, which has an equally uncertain outcome? Can one arbitrarily state that a better knowledge of the history of religious thought in Melanesia, or of data from other tribes (both of which reveal the role often attributed to plant fiber as the symbol of a change of status),[35] would not throw some light on the reasons why these specific activities are carried out with the aid of magic? Let us cite two other examples which illustrate the flaws in this intuitive method. In Malinowski's book on the sexual life of Melanesians, we learn that one of the principal reasons for marriage, here as elsewhere, is ". . . the natural inclination of a man past his first youth to have a house and a household of his own . . . and . . . a natural longing for [children]." [36] But in *Sex and Repression in Savage Society*, in which a theoretical commentary is added to the field-work account, we read the following: "In man this need for an affectionate and interested protector of pregnancy still remains. That the innate mechanism has disappeared we know from the fact that in most societies . . . the male refuses to take any responsibility for his offspring unless compelled to do so by society." [37] An odd natural longing, indeed!

The followers of Malinowski are unfortunately not exempt from the curious combination of dogmatism and empiricism that weakens his entire system. When Margaret Mead, for instance, characterizes three neighboring societies of New Guinea in terms of the different and complementary combinations of relationship between the sexes (passive man, passive woman; aggressive man, aggressive woman; aggressive woman, passive man), we admire the elegance of this construction.[38] But our suspicion of oversimplification and *a priori* thinking is confirmed by other observations, such as those that stress the existence of a specifically female piracy among the Arapesh.[39] And when the same author classifies North American tribes as competitive, cooperative, and individualistic,[40] she remains as far removed from a true taxonomy as a zoologist who would define species by grouping animals as solitary, gregarious, and social.

We really wonder whether all these hasty constructions,

which only result in making the peoples studied "reflections of our own society," [41] of our categories and our problems, do not proceed, as Boas profoundly perceived, from an overestimation of the historical method, rather than from the opposite attitude. For, after all, it was the historians who formulated the functionalist method. After enumerating the complex of traits that characterized a certain stage of Roman society, Hauser wrote in 1903: "All this constitutes an irreducible complex; all these traits are mutually explanatory to a much greater extent than the evolution of the Roman family can be explained in terms of the Semitic, or Chinese, or Aztec family." [42] This statement could have been written by Malinowski, with the one exception that Hauser added events to institutions. And, undoubtedly, his statement requires a double qualification: For what is true of *process* is not so true of *structure*, and for the anthropologist comparative studies compensate to some extent for the absence of written documents. But the paradox remains, nevertheless: The criticism of evolutionist and diffusionist interpretations has showed us that when the anthropologist believes he is doing historical research, he is doing the opposite; it is when he thinks that he is not doing historical research that he operates like a good historian, who would be limited by the same lack of documents.

What are the differences then between historical method and ethnographic method, if we use these terms in the strict sense defined at the beginning of this essay? Both history and ethnography are concerned with societies *other* than the one in which we live. Whether this *otherness* is due to remoteness in time (however slight), or to remoteness in space, or even to cultural heterogeneity, is of secondary importance compared to the basic similarity of perspective. What constitutes the goal of the two disciplines? Is it the exact reconstruction of what has happened, or is happening, in the society under study? To assert this would be to forget that in both cases we are dealing with systems of representations which differ for each member of the group and which, on the whole, differ from the representations of the investigator. The best ethnographic study will never make the reader a native. The French Revolution of 1789 lived through by an aristocrat is not the same phenomenon as the Revolution of 1789 lived through by a *sans-*

culotte, and neither would correspond to the Revolution of 1789 as conceived by Michelet or Taine. All that the historian or ethnographer can do, and all that we can expect of either of them, is to enlarge a specific experience to the dimensions of a more general one, which thereby becomes accessible *as experience* to men of another country or another epoch. And in order to succeed, both historian and ethnographer must have the same qualities: skill, precision, a sympathetic approach, and objectivity.

How do they proceed? Here the difficulty begins. For history and ethnography have often been contrasted on the grounds that the former rests on the critical study of documents by numerous observers, which can therefore be compared and cross-checked, whereas the latter is reduced, by definition, to the observations of a single individual.

To this criticism we reply that the best way to overcome this obstacle in ethnography is to increase the number of ethnographers. Certainly we shall not reach this goal by discouraging prospective ethnographers with tendentious objections. Furthermore, this criticism has been rendered obsolete by the very development of ethnography. Today there are indeed few peoples who have not been studied by numerous investigators and observed from different points of view over a period of several generations, sometimes even several centuries. Moreover, what does the historian do when he studies documents if not to surround himself with the testimony of amateur ethnographers, who were often as far removed from the culture they described as is the modern investigator from the Polynesians or Pygmies? Would the historian of ancient Europe have made less progress if Herodotus, Diodorus, Plutarch, Saxo Grammaticus, and Nestorius had been professional ethnographers, familiar with the difficulties of field-work and trained in objective observation? Far from distrusting ethnographers, the historian concerned about the future of his discipline should heartily welcome them.

But the methodological parallels which are sought between ethnography and history, in order to contrast them, are deceptive. The ethnographer is someone who collects data and (if he is a good ethnographer) presents them in conformity with requirements that are the same as those of the historian. The historian's role is to utilize these studies when the observations extend over a sufficient period of time. The ethnologist also draws upon the ethnographer's observations when they include a sufficient number of different regions. At any rate, the ethnographer furnishes documents which the historian can use. And if documents already exist and the ethnographer chooses to integrate their contents into his study, should not the historian—provided, naturally, that the ethnographer has a sound historical method—envy him the privilege of writing the history of a society which he has experienced as a living reality?

The issue can thus be reduced to the relationship between history and ethnology in the strict sense. We propose to show that the fundamental difference between the two disciplines is not one of subject, of goal, or of method. They share the same subject, which is social life; the same goal, which is a better understanding of man; and, in fact, the same method, in which only the proportion of research techniques varies. They differ, principally, in their choice of complementary perspectives: History organizes its data in relation to conscious expressions of social life, while anthropology proceeds by examining its unconscious foundations.

The principle that anthropology draws its originality from the unconscious nature of collective phenomena stems (though in a still obscure and ambiguous manner) from a statement made by Tylor. Having defined anthropology as the study of "Culture or Civilization," he described culture as "that complex whole which includes knowledge, belief, art, morals, law, custom, and any other capabilities and habits acquired by man as a member of society." [43] We know that among most primitive peoples it is very difficult to obtain a moral justification or a rational explanation for any custom or institution. When he is questioned, the native merely answers that things have always been this way, that such was the command of the gods or the teaching of the ancestors. Even when interpretations are offered, they always have the character of rationalizations or secondary elaborations. There is rarely any doubt that the unconscious reasons for practicing a custom or sharing a belief are remote from the reasons given to justify them. Even in our own society, table manners, social etiquette, fashions of dress, and many of our moral, political, and religious attitudes are scrupulously observed by everyone, although their real origin and function are not often critically examined. We act and think according to habit, and the extraordinary resistance offered to even minimal departures from custom is due more to inertia than to any conscious desire to maintain usages which have a clear function. There is no question that the development of modern thought has favored the critical examination of custom. But this phenomenon is not something extraneous to anthropological study. It is, rather, its direct result, inasmuch as its main origin lies in the tremendous ethnographic self-consciousness which the discovery of the New World aroused in Western thought. And even today, secondary elaborations tend to acquire the same unconscious quality as soon as they are formulated. With surprising rapidity—which shows that one is dealing with an intrinsic property of certain modes of thinking and action—collective thought assimilates what would seem the most daring concepts, such as the priority of mother-right, animism, or, more recently, psychoanalysis, in order to resolve automatically problems which by their nature seem forever to elude action as well as thought.

Boas must be given credit for defining the unconscious nature of cultural phenomena with admirable lucidity. By comparing cultural phenomena to language from this point of view, he anticipated both the subsequent development of linguistic theory and a future for anthropology whose rich promise we are just beginning to perceive. He showed that the structure of a language remains unknown to the speaker until the introduction of a scientific grammar. Even then the language continues to mold discourse beyond the consciousness of the individual, imposing on his thought conceptual schemes which are taken as objective categories. Boas added that "the essential difference between linguistic phenomena and other ethnological phenomena is, that the linguistic classifications never rise to consciousness, while in other ethnological phenomena, although the same unconscious origin prevails, these often rise into consciousness, and thus give rise to secondary reasoning and to reinterpretations." [44] But this difference, which is one of degree, does not lessen their basic identity or the high value of linguistic method when it is used in ethnological research. On the contrary:

> The great advantage that linguistics offers in this respect is the fact that, on the whole, the categories which are formed always

remain unconscious, and that for this reason the processes which lead to their formation can be followed without misleading and disturbing factors of secondary explanations, which are so common in ethnology, so much so that they generally obscure the real history of the development of ideas entirely.[45]

In the light of modern phonemics we can appreciate the immense scope of these propositions, which were formulated eight years before the publication of *Cours de linguistique générale* by Ferdinand de Saussure, which marked the advent of structural linguistics. But anthropologists have not yet applied these propositions to their field. Boas was to use them fully in laying down the foundations of American linguistics and they were to enable him to refute theories theretofore undisputed.[46] Yet with respect to anthropology he displayed a timidity that still restrains his followers.

Actually Boasian ethnographic analysis, which is incomparably more honest, solid, and methodical than that of Malinowski, remains, like Malinowski's, on the level of individual conscious thought. Boas of course refused to consider the secondary rationalizations and reinterpretations, which retained so much hold over Malinowski that he managed to discard those offered by the natives only by substituting his own. But Boas continued to utilize the categories of individual thought. His scientific scruples only deprived it of its human overtones. He restricted the scope of the categories that he compared, but he did not re-create them on a new level. When the work of fragmentation seemed to him impossible, he refrained from making comparisons. And yet linguistic comparison must be supported by something more than a mere fragmentation—namely, a real analysis. From words the linguist extracts the phonetic reality of the phoneme; and from the phoneme he extracts the logical reality of distinctive features.[47] And when he has found in several languages the same phonemes or the use of the same pairs of oppositions, he does not compare individually distinct entities. It is the same phoneme, the same element, which will show at this new level the basic identity of empirically different entities. We are not dealing with two similar phenomena, but with one and the same. The transition from conscious to unconscious is associated with progression from the specific toward the general.

In anthropology as in linguistics, therefore, it is not comparison that supports generalization, but the other way around. If, as we believe to be the case, the unconscious activity of the mind consists in imposing forms upon content, and if these forms are fundamentally the same for all minds—ancient and modern, primitive and civilized[48] (as the study of the symbolic function, expressed in language, so strikingly indicates)—it is necessary and sufficient to grasp the unconscious structure underlying each institution and each custom, in order to obtain a principle of interpretation valid for other institutions and other customs, provided of course that the analysis is carried far enough.

How are we to apprehend this unconscious structure? Here anthropological method and historical method converge. It is unnecessary to refer here to the problem of diachronic structures, for which historical knowledge is naturally indispensable. Certain developments of social life no doubt require a diachronic structure. But the example of phonemics teaches anthropologists that this study is more complex and presents other problems than the study of synchronic structures,[49] which they are only beginning to consider. Even the analysis of synchronic structures, however, requires constant recourse to history. By showing institutions in the process of transformation, history alone makes it possible to abstract the structure which underlies the many manifestations and remains permanent throughout a succession of events. Let us return to the problem of dual organization. If we do not wish to conceive it either as a universal stage in social development or as a system devised in a single place and at one particular time, and if, on the other hand, we are too well aware of what all dual institutions have in common to consider them as totally unrelated products of unique and dissimilar historical development, we must analyze each dual society in order to discover, behind the chaos of rules and customs, a single structural scheme existing and operating in different spatial and temporal contexts. This scheme will correspond neither to a particular model of the institution nor to the arbitrary grouping of characteristics common to several variants of the institution. It may be reduced to certain relationships of correlation and opposition, which undoubtedly operate unconsciously among peoples who possess dual organization, but which, because they are unconscious, should also be found among peoples who have never known this institution.

Thus the Mekeo, Motu, and Koita of New Guinea, whose social evolution Seligman was able to reconstruct over a considerable period of time, have a highly complex organization constantly troubled by various factors. Warfare, migrations, religious schisms, demographic pressures, and quarrels over prestige bring about the destruction of whole clans and villages or the emergence of new groups. And yet these units, whose identity, number, and distribution are constantly varying, remain linked by relationships whose content is equally variable but whose formal character is maintained through the vicissitudes in their history. Whether economic, jural, matrimonial, religious, or ceremonial, the *ufapie* relationship links, two by two, at the level of the clan, subclan, or village, social units bound by reciprocal gift exchange. In some villages of Assam chronicled by Von Fürer-Haimendorf, marriage exchanges are frequently threatened by quarrels between boys and girls of the same village or by antagonism between neighboring villages. These dissensions are expressed by the withdrawal, or sometimes the extermination, of one or another group; but the cycle is restored in each case, either through a reorganization of the exchange structure or through the admission of new partners. Finally, the Mono and Yokut of California, some of whose villages possess dual organization while others do not, enable us to study how an identical social structure can be expressed with or without a defined and concrete institutional form. In every case, something is preserved which may be gradually isolated through observation—by means of a kind of straining process which allows the "lexicographical" content of institutions and customs to filter through—in order to retain only the structural elements. In the case of dual organization, these elements appear to be three in number: the need for a rule; the concept of reciprocity, providing immediate resolution of the opposition between the self and the other; and the synthetic nature of the gift. These factors are found in all the societies considered; at the same time, they explain the less differentiated usages and customs which fulfill the same functions among peoples who do not have dual organization.[50]

Thus, anthropology cannot remain indifferent to historical processes and to the most highly conscious expressions of social phenomena. But if the anthropologist brings to them the same scrupulous attention as the historian, it is in order to eliminate, by a kind of backward course, all that they owe to the historical process and to conscious thought. His goal is to grasp, beyond the conscious and always shifting images which men hold, the complete range of unconscious possibilities. These are not unlimited, and the relationships of compatibility or incompatibility which each maintains with all the others provide a logical framework for historical developments, which, while perhaps unpredictable, are never arbitrary. In this sense, the famous statement by Marx, "Men make their own history, but they do not know that they are making it," justifies, first, history and, second, anthropology. At the same time, it shows that the two approaches are inseparable.

Although the anthropologist applies his analysis primarily to the unconscious elements of social life, it would be absurd to suppose that the historian remains unaware of them. The historian no doubt intends, first of all, to explain social phenomena in terms of the events in which they are embodied and the way in which individuals have thought about and lived them. But in his progress in grasping and explaining that which appears to men as the consequence of their representations and actions (or of the representations and actions of some of them), the historian knows quite well, and to an increasing degree, that he must call to his aid the whole apparatus of unconscious elaborations. We are no longer satisfied with political history which chronologically strings dynasties and wars on the thread of secondary rationalizations and reinterpretations. Economic history is, by and large, the history of unconscious processes. Thus any good history book (and we shall cite a great one) is saturated with anthropology. In his *Le Problème de l'incroyance au XVIe siècle*, Lucien Febvre constantly refers to psychological attitudes and logical structures which can be grasped only indirectly because they have always eluded the consciousness of those who spoke and wrote—for example, the lack of terminology and standards of measurement, vague representation of time, traits common to several different techniques, and so forth.[51] All these pertain to anthropology as well as to history, for they transcend documents and informants' accounts, none of which deals with this level, and rightly so.

It would be inaccurate, therefore, to say that on the road toward the understanding of man, which goes from the study of conscious content to that of unconscious forms, the historian and the anthropologist travel in opposite directions. On the contrary, they both go the same way. The fact that their journey together appears to each of them in a different light—to the historian, transition from the explicit to the implicit; to the anthropologist, transition from the particular to the universal—does not in the least alter the identical character of their fundamental approach. They have undertaken the same journey on the same road in the same direction; only their orientation is different. The anthropologist goes forward, seeking to attain, through the conscious, of which he is always aware, more and more of the unconscious; whereas the historian advances, so to speak, backward, keeping his eyes fixed on concrete and specific activities from which he withdraws only to consider them from a more complete and richer perspective. A true two-faced Janus, it is the solidarity of the two disciplines that makes it possible to keep the whole road in sight.

One final remark will clarify our thinking. Traditionally we distinguish history from anthropology by the presence or absence of written documents in the societies studied. This distinction is not incorrect; but we do not think it essential, since it stems from, rather than explains, those fundamental characteristics which we have attempted to define. Beyond question, the absence of written documents in most so-called primitive societies forced the anthropologist to develop methods and techniques appropriate to the study of activities which remain, for that reason, imperfectly conscious on all the levels where they are expressed. But, apart from the fact that this limitation is often overcome by oral tradition (so rich among certain African and Oceanian peoples), we should not regard it as a rigid barrier. Anthropology is equally concerned with populations which possess writing, such as those of ancient Mexico, the Arab world, and the Far East. And it is also possible to reconstruct the history of peoples who have never known writing, as, for example, the Zulu. Here again, the question is one of a difference in orientation, not in subject matter, and of two ways of organizing data which are more alike than they first appear. The anthropologist is above all interested in unwritten data, not so much because the peoples he studies are incapable of writing, but because that with which he is principally concerned differs from everything men ordinarily think of recording on stone or on paper.

Until now, a division of labor, justified by ancient tradition and the needs of the moment, has contributed to the confusion of the theoretical and practical aspects of the distinction, and thus to an undue separation of anthropology from history. If anthropology and history once begin to collaborate in the study of contemporary societies, it will become apparent that here, as elsewhere, the one science can achieve nothing without the help of the other.

NOTES

1. H. Hauser, *L'Enseignement des sciences sociales* (Paris: 1903); F. Simiand, "Méthode historique et science sociale," *Revue de Synthèse* (1903).
[2. *Translator's note:* In the Durkheimian sense of beliefs, sentiments, and norms common to the members of a society.]
3. This became true at the end of the nineteenth century. But it should not to be forgotten that, historically, sociological evolutionism preceded biological evolutionism.
4. Leslie A. White, "Energy and the Evolution of Culture," *American Anthropologist*, n.s., XLV (1943); "History, Evolutionism, and Functionalism: Three Types of Interpretation of Culture," *Southwestern Journal of Anthropology*, I (1945); "Evolutionary Stages, Progress, and the Evaluation of Cultures," *Southwestern Journal of Anthropology*, III (1947).
5. E. B. Tylor, *Primitive Culture* (London: 1871), I, 7.
6. E. B. Tylor, *Researches into the Early History of Mankind and the Development of Civilization* (London: 1865), p. 3.
7. Émile Durkheim and Marcel Mauss, "De quelques formes primitives de classification," *L'Année sociologique*, VI (1901-2).
8. R. H. Lowie, *Societies of the Hidatsa and Mandan Indians*, Anthropological Papers of the American Museum of Natural History, XI (1913); L. Spier, *The Sun-Dance of the Plains Indians*, Anthropological Papers of the American Museum of Natural History, XVI (1921), A. L. Kroeber, "Salt, Dogs, Tobacco," *Anthropological Records*, VI (1941).
9. F. Boas, "History and Science in Anthropology: a Reply," *American Anthropologist*, n.s., XXXVIII (1936), p. 139.
10. *Ibid.*, p. 140.
11. F. Boas, "The Limitations of the Comparative Method of Anthropology" (1896) in *Race, Language, and Culture* (New York: 1940), p. 276.

12. *Ibid.*, p. 277.
13. F. Boas, "Evolution or Diffusion?" *American Anthropologist*, n.s., XXVI (1924), p. 342.
14. *Loc. cit.*
15. F. Boas, "History and Science in Anthropology . . . ," *op. cit.*, p. 139.
16. F. Boas, "The Methods of Ethnology," *American Anthropologist*, n.s., XXII (1920), pp. 314-15.
17. *Ibid.*, p. 314.
18. Ruth Benedict, "Franz Boas as an Ethnologist," in *Franz Boas: 1858-1942*, Memoirs of the American Anthropological Association, n.s., No. 61 (1943), p. 27.
19. We are not criticizing here Boas' archaeological work, which belongs to archaeology and not ethnology, or his research on the diffusion of mythological themes, which constitutes historical research based on ethnographic data. Similarly, Paul Rivet, when he formulates his hypotheses on the primitive peopling of America, uses archaeological, linguistic, and ethnographic data for an investigation which is properly historical. These undertakings must, therefore, be examined from a historical viewpoint. The same may be said about some of Rivers' studies.
20. A. L. Kroeber, "History and Science in Anthropology," *American Anthropologist*, n.s., XXXVII (1935), pp. 539-69.
21. F. Boas, "History and Science in Anthropology . . . , *op. cit.*
22. R. H. Lowie, "American Culture History," *American Anthropologist*, n.s., XLII (1940).
23. B. Malinowski, "The Present State of Studies in Culture Contact," *Africa*, XII (1939), p. 43.
24. B. Malinowski, "Culture as a Determinant of Behavior," in *Factors Determining Human Behavior*, Harvard Tercentenary Publications (Cambridge: 1937), p. 155. On the following page he also speaks of "these queer and sordid customs," which have, however, "a core of rational and practical principle." This constitutes a return to the eighteenth century, but to its worst aspect.
25. F. Boas, "Some Problems of Methodology in the Social Sciences," in Leonard D. White (ed.), *The New Social Science* (Chicago: 1930), pp. 84-98.
26. B. Malinowski, "Culture," in *Encyclopaedia of the Social Sciences* (New York: 1935), IV, 625.
27. *Ibid.*, p. 627.
28. *Loc. cit.* For Malinowski, furthermore, it seems that no distinction is necessary when a transition is made from the general to the particular: "Thus culture, as we find it among the Masai, is an apparatus for the satisfaction of the elementary needs of the human organism." And, referring to the Eskimo, ". . . towards sex they have the same attitude as the Masai. They have also a somewhat similar type of political system. . . ." ("Culture as a Determinant of Behavior," *op. cit.*, pp. 136 and 140.)
29. B. Malinowski, "Introduction" to H. I. Hogbin, *Law and Order in Polynesia* (London: 1934), pp. 48-9.
30. B. Malinowski, "Culture," *op. cit.*, p. 630.
31. B. Malinowski, *The Sexual Life of Savages in Northwestern Melanesia* (London-New York: 1929), I, 29.

32. B. Malinowski, "Culture," *op. cit.*, p. 634 ff.
33. B. Malinowski, *The Sexual Life* . . . , *op. cit.*, p. 40.
34. *Ibid.*, pp. 43-5.
35. F. Boas, *The Social Organization and the Secret Societies of the Kwakiutl Indians* (Washington: 1895); M. Griaule, *Masques Dogons* (Paris: 1938), and "Mythe de l'organisation du monde chez les Dogons," *Psyché*, II (1947).
36. B. Malinowski, *The Sexual Life* . . . , *op. cit.*, p. 81.
37. B. Malinowski, *Sex and Repression in Savage Society* (London-New York: 1927), p. 204.
38. Margaret Mead, *Sex and Temperament in Three Primitive Societies* (New York: 1935), p. 279.
39. R. F. Fortune, "Arapesh Warfare," *American Anthropologist*, n.s., XLI (1939), pp. 22-41.
40. Margaret Mead (ed.), *Competition and Cooperation among Primitive Peoples* (London-New York: 1937), p. 461.
41. F. Boas, "History and Science . . . ," *op. cit.*
42. H. Hauser, *op. cit.*, p. 414.
43. E. B. Tylor, *Primitive Culture*, I, 1.
44. F. Boas (ed.), *Handbook of American Indian Languages*, Bureau of American Ethnology, Bulletin 40, 1911 (1908), Part I, p. 67.
45. *Ibid.*, pp. 70-1.
46. At a time when students of Indo-European linguistics still firmly believed in the theory of the "proto-language," Boats demonstrated that certain traits common to several American Indian languages may be the result of the secondary formation of areas of affinity just as well as of a common origin. The application of the same hypothesis to Indo-European data had to await Troubetzkoy.
47. R. Jakobson, "Observations sur le classement phonologique des consonnes," in *Proceedings of the Third International Congress of Phonetic Sciences* (Ghent: 1938).
48. See "The Effectiveness of Symbols," Chapter X of this volume.
49. R. Jakobson, "Principien der historischen Phonologie," in *Travaux du Cercle Linguistique de Prague*, IV.
50. C. Lévi-Strauss, *Les Structures élémentaires de la parenté* (Paris: 1949), Chapters VI and VII.
51. Lucien Febvre, *Le Problème de l'incroyance au XVIe siècle*, Second Edition (Paris: 1946). (First edition: 1942.)

PART ONE

Language and Kinship

CHAPTER II

Structural Analysis in Linguistics and in Anthropology

LINGUISTICS OCCUPIES a special place among the social sciences, to whose ranks it unquestionably belongs. It is not merely a social science like the others, but, rather, the one in which by far the greatest progress has been made. It is probably the only one which can truly claim to be a science and which has achieved both the formulation of an empirical method and an understanding of the nature of the data submitted to its analysis. This privileged position carries with it several obligations. The linguist will often find scientists from related but different disciplines drawing inspiration from his example and trying to follow his lead. *Noblesse oblige.* A linguistic journal like *Word* cannot confine itself to the illustration of strictly linguistic theories and points of view. It must also welcome psychologists, sociologists, and anthropologists eager to learn from modern linguistics the road which leads to the empirical knowledge of social phenomena. As Marcel Mauss wrote already forty years ago: "Sociology would certainly have progressed much further if it had everywhere followed the lead of the linguists. . . ." [1] The close methodological analogy which exists between the two disciplines imposes a special obligation of collaboration upon them.

Ever since the work of Schrader[2] it has been unnecessary to demonstrate the assistance which linguistics can render to the anthropologist in the study of kinship. It was a linguist and a philologist (Schrader and Rose)[3] who showed the improbability of the hypothesis of matrilineal survivals in the family in antiquity, to which so many anthropologists still clung at that time. The linguist provides the anthropologist with etymologies which permit him to establish between certain kinship terms relationships that were not immediately apparent. The anthropologist, on the other hand, can bring to the attention of the linguist customs, prescriptions, and prohibitions that help him to understand the persistence of certain features of language or the instability of terms or groups of terms. At a meeting of the Linguistic Circle of New York, Julien Bonfante once illustrated this point of view by reviewing the etymology of the word for uncle in several Romance languages. The Greek Θεῖος corresponds in Italian, Spanish, and Portuguese to *zio* and *tio;* and he added that in certain regions of Italy the uncle is called *barba.* The "beard," the "divine" uncle—what a wealth of suggestions for the anthropologist! The investigations of the late A. M. Hocart into the religious character of the avuncular relationship and the "theft of the sacrifice" by the maternal kinsmen immediately come to mind.[4] Whatever interpretation is given to the data collected by Hocart (and his own interpretation is not entirely satisfactory), there is no doubt that the linguist contributes to the solution of the problem by revealing the tenacious survival in contemporary vocabulary of relationships which have long since disappeared. At the same time, the anthropologist explains to the linguist the bases of etymology and confirms its validity. Paul K. Benedict, in examining, as a linguist, the kinship systems of Southeast Asia, was able to make an important contribution to the anthropology of the family in that area.[5]

But linguists and anthropologists follow their own paths independently. They halt, no doubt, from time to time to communicate to one another certain of their findings; these findings, however, derive from different operations, and no effort is made to enable one group to benefit from the technical and methodological advances of the other. This attitude might have been justified in the era when linguistic research leaned most heavily on historical analysis. In relation to the anthropological research conducted during the same period, the difference was one of degree rather than of kind. The linguists employed a more rigorous method, and their findings were established on more solid grounds; the sociologists could follow their example in "renouncing consideration of the spatial distribution of contemporary types as a basis for their classifications." [6] But, after all, anthropology and sociology were looking to linguistics only for insights; nothing foretold a revelation.[7]

The advent of structural linguistics completely changed this situation. Not only did it renew linguistic perspectives; a transformation of this magnitude is not limited to a single discipline. Structural linguistics will certainly play the same renovating role with respect to the social sciences that nuclear physics, for example, has played for the physical sciences. In what does this revolution consist, as we try to assess its broadest implications? N. Troubetzkoy, the illustrious founder of structural linguistics, himself furnished the answer to this question. In one programmatic statement,[8] he reduced the structural method to four basic operations. First, structural linguistics shifts from the study of *conscious* linguistic phenomena to study of their *unconscious* infrastructure; second, it does not treat *terms* as independent entities, taking instead as its basis of analysis the *relations* between terms; third, it introduces the concept of *system*—"Modern phonemics does not merely proclaim that phonemes are always part of a system; it *shows* concrete phonemic systems and elucidates their structure" [9]—; finally, structural linguistics aims at discovering *general laws*, either by induction "or . . . by logical deduction, which would give them an absolute character." [10]

Thus, for the first time, a social science is able to formulate necessary relationships. This is the meaning of Troubetzkoy's last point, while the preceding rules show how linguistics must proceed in order to attain this end. It is not for us to show that Troubetzkoy's claims are justified. The vast majority of modern linguists seem sufficiently agreed on this point. But when an event of this importance takes place in one of the sciences of man, it is not only permissible for, but required of, representatives of related disciplines immediately to examine its consequences and its possible application to phenomena of another order.

New perspectives then open up. We are no longer dealing with an occasional collaboration where the linguist and the anthropologist, each working by himself, occasionally communicate those findings which each thinks may interest the other. In the study of kinship problems (and, no doubt, the study of other problems as well), the anthropologist finds himself in a situation which formally resembles that of the structural linguist. Like phonemes, kinship terms are elements of meaning; like phonemes, they acquire meaning only if they are integrated into systems. "Kinship systems," like "phonemic systems," are built by the mind on the level of unconscious thought. Finally, the recurrence of kinship patterns, marriage rules, similar prescribed attitudes between certain types of relatives, and so forth, in scattered regions of the globe and in fundamentally different societies, leads us to believe that, in the case of kinship as well as linguistics, the observable phenomena result from the action of laws which are general but implicit. The problem can therefore be formulated as follows: Although they belong to *another order of reality*, kinship phenomena are *of the same type* as linguistic phenomena. Can the anthropologist, using a method analogous *in form* (if not in content) to the method used in structural linguistics, achieve the same kind of progress in his own science as that which has taken place in linguistics?

We shall be even more strongly inclined to follow this path after an additional observation has been made. The study of kinship problems is today broached in the same terms and seems to be in the throes of the same difficulties as was linguistics on the eve of the structuralist revolution. There is a striking analogy between certain attempts by Rivers and the old linguistics, which sought its explanatory principles first of all in history. In both cases, it is solely (or almost solely) diachronic analysis which must account for synchronic phenomena. Troubetzkoy, comparing structural linguistics and the old linguistics, defines structural linguistics as a "systematic structuralism and universalism," which he contrasts with the individualism and "atomism" of former schools. And when he considers diachronic analysis, his perspective is a profoundly modified one: "The evolution of a phonemic system at any given moment is directed by the *tendency toward a goal.* . . .

This evolution thus has a direction, an internal logic, which historical phonemics is called upon to elucidate." [11] The "individualistic" and "atomistic" interpretation, founded exclusively on historical contingency, which is criticized by Troubetzkoy and Jakobson, is actually the same as that which is generally applied to kinship problems.[12] Each detail of terminology and each special marriage rule is associated with a specific custom as either its consequence or its survival. We thus meet with a chaos of discontinuity. No one asks how kinship systems, regarded as synchronic wholes, could be the arbitrary product of a convergence of several heterogeneous institutions (most of which are hypothetical), yet nevertheless function with some sort of regularity and effectiveness.[13]

However, a preliminary difficulty impedes the transposition of the phonemic method to the anthropological study of primitive peoples. The superficial analogy between phonemic systems and kinship systems is so strong that it immediately sets us on the wrong track. It is incorrect to equate kinship terms and linguistic phonemes from the viewpoint of their formal treatment. We know that to obtain a structural law the linguist analyzes phonemes into "distinctive features," which he can then group into one or several "pairs of oppositions." [14] Following an analogous method, the anthropologist might be tempted to break down analytically the kinship terms of any given system into their components. In our own kinship system, for instance, the term *father* has positive connotations with respect to sex, relative age, and generation; but it has a zero value on the dimension of collaterality, and it cannot express an affinal relationship. Thus, for each system, one might ask what relationships are expressed and, for each term of the system, what connotation—positive or negative—it carries regarding each of the following relationships: generation, collaterality, sex, relative age, affinity, etc. It is at this "microsociological" level that one might hope to discover the most general structural laws, just as the linguist discovers his at the infraphonemic level or the physicist at the infra-molecular or atomic level. One might interpret the interesting attempt of Davis and Warner in these terms.[15]

But a threefold objection immediately arises. A truly scientific analysis must be real, simplifying, and explanatory. Thus the distinctive features which are the product of phonemic analysis have an objective existence from three points of view: psychological, physiological, and even physical; they are fewer in number than the phonemes which result from their combination; and, finally, they allow us to understand and reconstruct the system. Nothing of the kind would emerge from the preceding hypothesis. The treatment of kinship terms which we have just sketched is analytical in appearance only; for, actually, the result is more abstract than the principle; instead of moving toward the concrete, one moves away from it, and the definitive system—if system there is—is only conceptual. Secondly, Davis and Warner's experiment proves that the system achieved through this procedure is infinitely more complex and more difficult to interpret than the empirical data.[16] Finally, the hypothesis has no explanatory value; that is, it does not lead to an understanding of the nature of the system and still less to a reconstruction of its origins.

What is the reason for this failure? A too literal adherence to linguistic method actually betrays its very essence. Kinship terms not only have a sociological existence; they are also elements of speech. In our haste to apply the methods of linguistic analysis, we must not forget that, as a part of vocabulary, kinship terms must be treated with linguistic methods in direct and not analogous fashion. Linguistics teaches us precisely that structural analysis cannot be applied to words directly, but only to words previously broken down into phonemes. *There are no necessary relationships at the vocabulary level.*[17] This applies to all vocabulary elements, including kinship terms. Since this applies to linguistics, it ought to apply *ipso facto* to the sociology of language. An attempt like the one whose possibility we are now discussing would thus consist in extending the method of structural linguistics while ignoring its basic requirements. Kroeber prophetically foresaw this difficulty in an article written many years ago.[18] And if, at that time, he concluded that a structural analysis of kinship terminology was impossible, we must remember that linguistics itself was then restricted to phonetic, psychological, and historical analysis. While it is true that the social sciences must share the limitations of linguistics, they can also benefit from its progress.

Nor should we overlook the profound differences between the phonemic chart of a language and the chart of kinship terms of a society. In the first instance there can be no question as to function; we all know that language serves as a means of communication. On the other hand, what the linguist did not know and what structural linguistics alone has allowed him to discover is the way in which language achieves this end. The function was obvious; the system remained unknown. In this respect, the anthropologist finds himself in the opposite situation. We know, since the work of Lewis H. Morgan, that kinship terms constitute systems; on the other hand, we still do not know their function. The misinterpretation of this initial situation reduces most structural analyses of kinship systems to pure tautologies. They demonstrate the obvious and neglect the unknown.

This does not mean that we must abandon hope of introducing order and discovering meaning in kinship nomenclature. But we should at least recognize the special problems raised by the sociology of vocabulary and the ambiguous character of the relations between its methods and those of linguistics. For this reason it would be preferable to limit the discussion to a case where the analogy can be clearly established. Fortunately, we have just such a case available.

What is generally called a "kinship system" comprises two quite different orders of reality. First, there are terms through which various kinds of family relationships are expressed. But kinship is not expressed solely through nomenclature. The individuals or classes of individuals who employ these terms feel (or do not feel, as the case may be) bound by prescribed behavior in their relations with one another, such as respect or familiarity, rights or obligations, and affection or hostility. Thus, along with what we propose to call the *system of terminology* (which, strictly speaking, constitutes the vocabulary system), there is another system, both psychological and social in nature, which we shall call the *system of attitudes*. Although it is true (as we have shown above) that the study of systems of terminology places us in a situation analogous, but opposite, to the situation in which we are dealing with phonemic systems, this difficulty is "inversed," as it were, when we examine systems of attitudes. We can guess at the role played by systems of attitudes, that is, to insure group cohesion and equilibrium, but we do not understand the nature of the interconnections between the various attitudes, nor do we perceive their necessity.[19] In other words, as in the case of language, we know their function, but the system is unknown.

Thus we find a profound difference between the *system of terminology* and the *system of attitudes*, and we have to disagree with A. R. Radcliffe-Brown if he really believed, as has been said of him, that attitudes are nothing but the expression or transposition of terms on the affective level.[20] The last few years have provided numerous examples of groups whose chart of kinship terms does not accurately reflect family attitudes, and vice versa.[21] It would be incorrect to assume that the kinship system constitutes the principal means of regulating interpersonal relationships in all societies. Even in societies where the kinship system does function as such, it does not fulfill that role everywhere to the same extent. Furthermore, it is always necessary to distinguish between two types of attitudes: first, the diffuse, uncrystallized, and non-institutionalized attitudes, which we may consider as the reflection or transposition of the terminology on the psychological level; and second, along with, or in addition to, the preceding ones, those attitudes which are stylized, prescribed, and sanctioned by taboos or privileges and expressed through a fixed ritual. These attitudes, far from automatically reflecting the nomenclature, often appear as secondary elaborations, which serve to resolve the contradictions and overcome the deficiencies inherent in the terminological system. This synthetic character is strikingly apparent among the Wik Munkan of Australia. In this group, joking privileges sanction a contradiction between the kinship relations which link two unmarried men and the theoretical relationship which must be assumed to exist between them in order to account for their later marriages to two women who do not stand themselves in the corresponding relationship.[22] There is a contradiction between two possible systems of nomenclature, and the emphasis placed on attitudes represents an attempt to integrate or transcend this contradiction. We can easily agree with Radcliffe-Brown and assert the existence of "real relations of interdependence between the terminology and the rest of the system." [23] Some of his critics made the mistake of inferring, from the absence of a rigorous parallelism between attitudes and nomenclature, that the two systems were mutually independent. But this relationship of interdependence does not imply a one-to-one correlation. The system of attitudes constitutes, rather, a dynamic integration of the system of terminology.

Granted the hypothesis (to which we whole-heartedly subscribe) of a functional relationship between the two systems, we are nevertheless entitled, for methodological reasons, to treat independently the problems pertaining to each system. This is what we propose to do here for a problem which is rightly considered the point of departure for any theory of attitudes—that of the maternal uncle. We shall attempt to show how a formal transposition of the method of structural linguistics allows us to shed new light upon this problem. Because the relationship between nephew and maternal uncle appears to have been the focus of significant elaboration in a great many primitive societies, anthropologists have devoted special attention to it. It is not enough to note the frequency of this theme; we must also account for it.

Let us briefly review the principal stages in the development of this problem. During the entire nineteenth century and until the writings of Sydney Hartland,[24] the importance of the mother's brother was interpreted as a survival of matrilineal descent. This interpretation was based purely on speculation, and, indeed, it was highly improbable in the light of European examples. Furthermore, Rivers' attempt[25] to explain the importance of the mother's brother in southern India as a residue of cross-cousin marriage led to particularly deplorable results. Rivers himself was forced to recognize that this interpretation could not account for all aspects of the problem. He resigned himself to the hypothesis that *several* heterogeneous customs which have since disappeared (cross-cousin marriage being only one of them) were needed to explain the existence of a *single* institution.[26] Thus, atomism and mechanism triumphed. It was Lowie's crucial article on the matrilineal complex[27] which opened what we should like to call the "modern phase" of the problem of the avunculate. Lowie showed that the correlation drawn or postulated between the prominent position of the maternal uncle and matrilineal descent cannot withstand rigorous analysis. In fact, the avunculate is found associated with patrilineal, as well as matrilineal, descent. The role of the maternal uncle cannot be explained as either a consequence or a survival of matrilineal kinship; it is only a specific application "of a very general tendency to associate definite social relations with definite forms of kinship regardless of maternal or paternal side." In accordance with this principle, introduced for the first time by Lowie in 1919, there exists a general tendency to *qualify attitudes*, which constitutes the only empirical foundation for a theory of kinship systems. But, at the same time, Lowie left certain questions unanswered. What exactly do we call an avunculate? Do we not merge different customs and attitudes under this single term? And, if it is true that there is a tendency to qualify all attitudes, why are only certain attitudes associated with the avuncular relationship, rather than just any possible attitudes, depending upon the group considered?

A few further remarks here may underline the striking analogy between the development of this problem and certain stages in the evolution of linguistic theory. The variety of possible attitudes in the area of interpersonal relationships is almost unlimited; the same holds true for the variety of sounds which can be articulated by the vocal apparatus—and which are actually produced during the first months of human life. Each language, however, retains only a very small number among all the possible sounds, and in this respect linguistics raises two questions: Why are certain sounds selected? What relationships exist between one or several of the sounds chosen and all the others? [28] Our sketch of the historical development of the avuncular problem is at precisely the same stage. Like language, the social group has a great wealth of psychophysiological material at its disposal. Like language too, it retains only certain elements, at least some of which remain the same throughout the most varied cultures and are combined into structures which are always diversified. Thus we may wonder about the reason for this choice and the laws of combination.

For insight into the specific problem of the avunculate we should turn to Radcliffe-Brown. His well-known article on the maternal uncle in South Africa[29] was the first attempt to grasp and analyze the modalities of what we might call the "general principle of attitude qualification." We shall briefly review the fundamental ideas of that now-classic study.

According to Radcliffe-Brown, the term *avunculate* covers two antithetical systems of attitudes. In one case, the maternal uncle represents family authority; he is feared and obeyed, and possesses certain rights over his nephew. In the other case, the nephew holds privileges of familiarity in relation to his uncle and can treat him more or less as his victim. Second, there is a correlation between the boy's attitude toward his maternal uncle and his attitude toward his father. We find the two systems of attitudes in both cases, but they are inversely correlated. In groups where familiarity characterizes the relationship between father and son, the relationship between maternal uncle and nephew is one of respect; and where the father stands as the austere representative of family authority, it is the uncle who is treated with familiarity. Thus the two sets of attitudes constitute (as the structural linguist would say) two pairs of oppositions. Radcliffe-Brown concluded his article by proposing the following interpretation: In the final analysis, it is descent that determines the choice of oppositions. In patrilineal societies, where the father and the father's descent group represent traditional authority, the maternal uncle is considered a "male mother." He is generally treated in the same fashion, and sometimes even called by the same name, as the mother. In matrilineal societies, the opposite occurs. Here, authority is vested in the maternal uncle, while relationships of tenderness and familiarity revolve about the father and his descent group.

It would indeed be difficult to exaggerate the importance of Radcliffe-Brown's contribution, which was the first attempt at synthesis on an empirical basis following Lowie's authoritative and merciless criticism of evolutionist metaphysics. To say that this effort did not entirely succeed does not in any way diminish the homage due this great British anthropologist; but we should certainly recognize that Radcliffe-Brown's article leaves unanswered some fundamental questions. First, the avunculate does not occur in all matrilineal or all patrilineal systems, and we find it present in some systems which are neither matrilineal nor patrilineal.[30] Further, the avuncular relationship is not limited to two terms, but presupposes four, namely, brother, sister, brother-in-law, and nephew. An interpretation such as Radcliffe-Brown's arbitrarily isolates particular elements of a global structure which must be treated as a whole. A few simple examples will illustrate this twofold difficulty.

The social organization of the Trobriand Islanders of Melanesia is characterized by matrilineal descent, free and familiar relations between father and son, and a marked antagonism between maternal uncle and nephew.[31] On the other hand, the patrilineal Cherkess of the Caucasus place the hostility between father and son, while the maternal uncle assists his nephew and gives him a horse when he marries.[32] Up to this point we are still within the limits of Radcliffe-Brown's scheme. But let us consider the other family relationships involved. Malinowski showed that in the Trobriands husband and wife live in an atmosphere of tender intimacy and that their relationship is characterized by reciprocity. The relations between brother and sister, on the other hand, are dominated by an extremely rigid taboo. Let us now compare the situation in the Caucasus. There, it is the brother-sister relationship which is tender—to such an extent that among the Pschav an only daughter "adopts" a "brother" who will play the customary brother's role as her chaste bed companion.[33] But the relationship between spouses is entirely different. A Cherkess will not appear in public with his wife and visits her only in secret. According to Malinowski, there is no greater insult in the Trobriands than to tell a man that he resembles his sister. In the Caucasus there is an analogous prohibition: It is forbidden to ask a man about his wife's health.

When we consider societies of the Cherkess and Trobriand types it is not enough to study the correlation of attitudes between *father / son* and *uncle / sister's son*. This correlation is only one aspect of a global system containing four types of relationships which are organically linked, namely: *brother / sister, husband / wife, father / son,* and *mother's brother / sister's son*. The two groups in our example illustrate a law which can be formulated as follows: In both groups, the relation between maternal uncle and nephew is to the relation between brother and sister as the relation between father and son is to that between husband and wife. Thus if we know one pair of relations, it is always possible to infer the other.

Let us now examine some other cases. On Tonga, in Polynesia, descent is patrilineal, as among the Cherkess. Relations between husband and wife appear to be public and harmonious. Domestic quarrels are rare, and although the wife is often of superior rank, the husband ". . . is nevertheless of higher authority in all domestic matters, and no woman entertains the least idea of rebelling against that authority." [34] At the same time there is great freedom between nephew and maternal uncle. The nephew is *fahu,* or above the law, in relation to his uncle, toward whom extreme familiarity is permitted. This freedom strongly contrasts with the father-son relationship. The father is *tapu;* the son cannot touch his father's head or hair; he cannot touch him while he eats, sleep in his bed or on his pillow, share his food or drink, or play with his possessions. However, the strongest *tapu* of all is the one between brother and sister, who must never be together under the same roof.

Although they are also patrilineal and patrilocal, the natives of Lake Kutubu in New Guinea offer an example of the opposite type of structure. F. E. Williams writes: "I have never seen such a close and apparently affectionate association between father and son. . . ." [35] Relations between husband and wife are characterized by the very low status ascribed to women and "the marked separation of masculine and feminine interests. . . ." [36] The women, according to Williams, "are expected to work hard for their masters . . . they occasionally protest, and protest may be met with a beating." [37] The wife can always call upon her brother for protection against her husband, and it is with him that she seeks refuge. As for the relationship between nephew and maternal uncle, it is ". . . best summed up in the word 'respect' . . . tinged with apprehensiveness," [38] for the maternal uncle has the power to curse his nephew and inflict serious illness upon him (just as among the Kipsigi of Africa).

Although patrilineal, the society described by Williams is structurally of the same type as that of the Siuai of Bougainville, who have matrilineal descent. Between brother and sister there is ". . . friendly interaction and mutual generosity. . . ." [39] As regards the father-son relationship, Oliver writes, ". . . I could discover little evidence that the word 'father' evokes images of hostility or stern authority or awed respect." [40] But the relationship between the nephew and his mother's brother "appears to range between stern discipline and genial mutual dependence. . . ." However, ". . . most of the informants agreed that all boys stand in some awe of their mother's brothers, and are more likely to obey them than their own fathers. . . ." [41] Between husband and wife harmonious understanding is rare: ". . . there are few young wives who remain altogether faithful . . . most young husbands

are continually suspicious and often give vent to jealous anger
. . . marriages involve a number of adjustments, some of them apparently difficult. . . ." [42]

The same picture, but sharper still, characterizes the Dobuans,
who are matrilineal and neighbors of the equally matrilineal Tro-
brianders, while their structure is very different. Dobuan marriages
are unstable, adultery is widespread, and husband and wife constantly fear death induced by their spouse's witchcraft. Actually,
Fortune's remark, "It is a most serious insult to refer to a woman's
witchcraft so that her husband will hear of it" [43] appears to be a
variant of the Trobriand and Caucasian taboos cited above.

In Dobu, the mother's brother is held to be the harshest of all
the relatives. "The mother's brother may beat children long after
their parents have ceased to do so," and they are forbidden to utter
his name. There is a tender relationship with the "navel," the
mother's sister's husband, who is the father's double, rather than
with the father himself. Nevertheless, the father is considered "less
harsh" than the mother's brother and will always seek, contrary to
the laws of inheritance, to favor his son at the expense of his uterine
nephew. And, finally, "the strongest of all social bonds" is the one
between brother and sister. [44]

What can we conclude from these examples? The correlation
between types of descent and forms of avunculate does not exhaust
the problem. Different forms of avunculate can coexist with the
same type of descent, whether patrilineal or matrilineal. But we
constantly find the same fundamental relationship between the four
pairs of oppositions required to construct the system. This will
emerge more clearly from the diagrams which illustrate our examples. The sign + indicates free and familiar relations, and the
sign — stands for relations characterized by hostility, antagonism, or reserve (Figure 1). This is an oversimplification, but we
can tentatively make use of it. We shall describe some of the indispensable refinements farther on.

The synchronic law of correlation thus suggested may be
validated diachronically. If we summarize, after Howard, the evolution of family relationships during the Middle Ages, we find approximately this pattern: The brother's authority over his sister
wanes, and that of the prospective husband increases. Simultane-

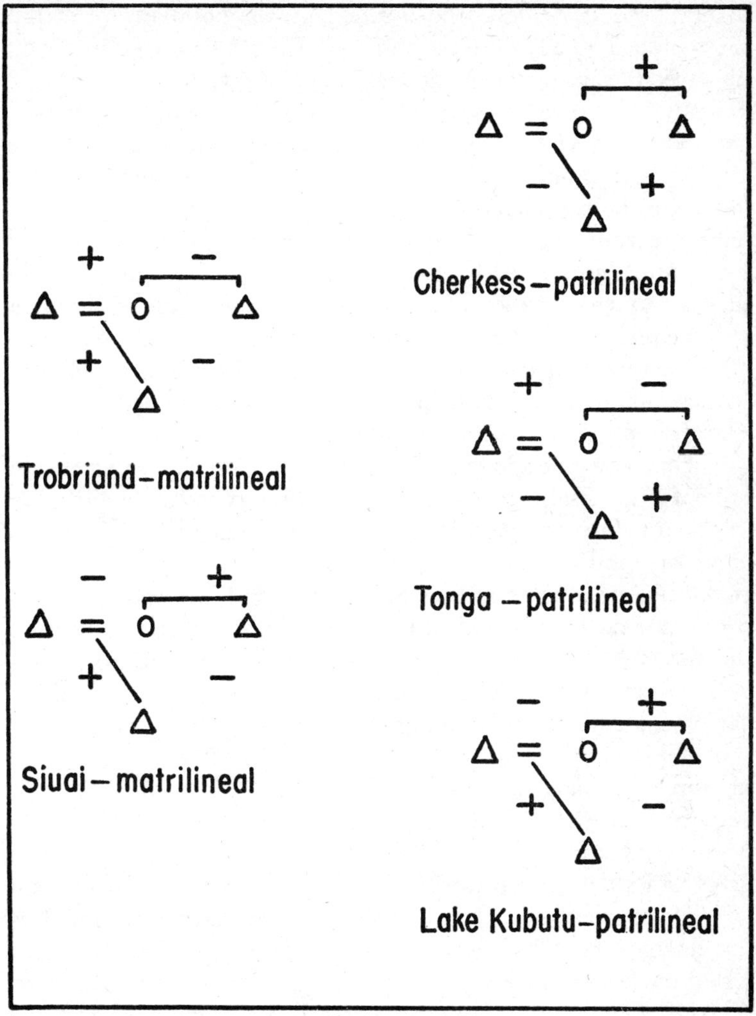

FIGURE I

ously, the bond between father and son is weakened and that between maternal uncle and nephew is reinforced.[45]

This evolution seems to be confirmed by the documents
gathered by Léon Gautier, for in the "conservative" texts (Raoul

de Cambrai, Geste des Loherains, etc.),[46] the positive relationship is established chiefly between father and son and is only gradually displaced toward the maternal uncle and nephew.[47]

Thus we see[48] that in order to understand the avunculate we must treat it as one relationship within a system, while the system itself must be considered as a whole in order to grasp its structure. This structure rests upon four terms (brother, sister, father, and son), which are linked by two pairs of correlative oppositions in such a way that in each of the two generations there is always a positive relationship and a negative one. Now, what is the nature of this structure, and what is its function? The answer is as follows: This structure is the most elementary form of kinship that can exist. It is, properly speaking, *the unit of kinship*.

One may give a logical argument to support this statement. In order for a kinship structure to exist, three types of family relations must always be present: a relation of consanguinity, a relation of affinity, and a relation of descent—in other words, a relation between siblings, a relation between spouses, and a relation between parent and child. It is evident that the structure given here satisfies this threefold requirement, in accordance with the scientific principle of parsimony. But these considerations are abstract, and we can present a more direct proof for our thesis.

The primitive and irreducible character of the basic unit of kinship, as we have defined it, is actually a direct result of the universal presence of an incest taboo. This is really saying that in human society a man must obtain a woman from another man who gives him a daughter or a sister. Thus we do not need to explain how the maternal uncle emerged in the kinship structure: He does not emerge—he is present initially. Indeed, the presence of the maternal uncle is a necessary precondition for the structure to exist. The error of traditional anthropology, like that of traditional linguistics, was to consider the terms, and not the relations between the terms.

Before proceeding further, let us briefly answer some objections which might be raised. First, if the relationship between "brothers-in-law" is the necessary axis around which the kinship structure is built, why need we bring in the child of the marriage when considering the elementary structure? Of course the child here may be either born or yet unborn. But, granting this, we must understand that the child is indispensable in validating the dynamic and teleological character of the initial step, which establishes kinship on the basis of and through marriage. Kinship is not a static phenomenon; it exists only in self-perpetuation. Here we are not thinking of the desire to perpetuate the race, but rather of the fact that in most kinship systems the initial disequilibrium produced in one generation between the group that gives the woman and the group that receives her can be stabilized only by counter-prestations in following generations. Thus, even the most elementary kinship structure exists both synchronically and diachronically.

Second, could we not conceive of a symmetrical structure, equally simple, where the sexes would be reversed? Such a structure would involve a sister, her brother, brother's wife, and brother's daughter. This is certainly a theoretical possibility. But it is immediately eliminated on empirical grounds. In human society, it is the men who exchange the women, and not vice versa. It remains for further research to determine whether certain cultures have not tended to create a kind of fictitious image of this symmetrical structure. Such cases would surely be uncommon.

We come now to a more serious objection. Possibly we have only inverted the problem. Traditional anthropologists painstakingly endeavored to explain the origin of the avunculate, and we have brushed aside that research by treating the mother's brother not as an extrinsic element, but as an immediate *given* of the simplest family structure. How is it then that we do not find the avunculate at all times and in all places? For although the avunculate has a wide distribution, it is by no means universal. It would be futile to explain the instances where it is present and then fail to explain its absence in other instances.

Let us point out, first, that the kinship system does not have the same importance in all cultures. For some cultures it provides the active principle regulating all or most of the social relationships. In other groups, as in our own society, this function is either absent altogether or greatly reduced. In still others, as in the societies of the Plains Indians, it is only partially fulfilled. The kinship system is a language; but it is not a universal language, and a society may prefer other modes of expression and action. From the viewpoint of the anthropologist this means that in dealing with a specific culture we must always ask a preliminary question: Is the system systematic? Such a question, which seems absurd at first, is absurd only in relation to language; for language is the semantic system par excellence; it cannot but signify, and exists only through signification. On the contrary, this question must be rigorously examined as we move from the study of language to the consideration of other systems which also claim to have semantic functions, but whose fulfillment remains partial, fragmentary, or subjective, like, for example, social organization, art, and so forth.

Furthermore, we have interpreted the avunculate as a characteristic trait of elementary structure. This elementary structure, which is the product of defined relations involving four terms, is, in our view, the true *atom of kinship*.[49] Nothing can be conceived or given beyond the fundamental requirements of its structure, and, in addition, it is the sole building block of more complex systems. For there are more complex systems; or, more accurately speaking, all kinship systems are constructed on the basis of this elementary structure, expanded or developed through the integration of new elements. Thus we must entertain two hypotheses: first, one in which the kinship system under consideration operates through the simple juxtaposition of elementary structures, and where the avuncular relationship therefore remains constantly apparent; second, a hypothesis in which the building blocks of the system are already of a more complex order. In the latter case, the avuncular relationship, while present, may be submerged within a differentiated context. For instance, we can conceive of a system whose point of departure lies in the elementary structure but which adds, at the right of the maternal uncle, his wife, and, at the left of the father, first the father's sister and then her husband. We could easily demonstrate that a development of this order leads to a parallel splitting in the following generation. The child must then be distinguished according to sex—a boy or a girl, linked by a relation which is symmetrical and inverse to the terms occupying the other peripheral positions in the structure (for example, the dominant position of the father's sister in Polynesia, the South African *nhlampsa*, and inheritance by the mother's brother's wife). In this type of structure the avuncular relationship continues to prevail, but it is no longer the predominant one. In structures of still greater complexity, the avunculate may be obliterated or may merge with other relationships. But precisely because it is part of the elementary structure, the avuncular relationship re-emerges unmistakably and tends to become reinforced each time the system under consideration reaches a crisis—either because it is undergoing rapid transformation (as on the Northwest Coast), or because it is a focus of contact and conflict between radically different cultures (as in Fiji and southern India), or, finally, because it is in the throes of a mortal crisis (as was Europe in the Middle Ages).

We must also add that the positive and negative symbols which we have employed in the above diagrams represent an oversimplification, useful only as a part of the demonstration. Actually, the system of basic attitudes comprises at least four terms: an attitude of affection, tenderness, and spontaneity; an attitude which results from the reciprocal exchange of prestations and counterprestations; and, in addition to these bilateral relationships, two unilateral relationships, one which corresponds to the attitude of the creditor, the other to that of the debtor. In other words there are: mutuality ($=$), reciprocity ($\pm$), rights ($+$), and obligations ($-$). These four fundamental attitudes are represented in their reciprocal relationships in Figure 2.

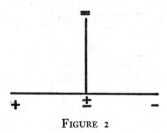

FIGURE 2

In many systems the relationship between two individuals is often expressed not by a single attitude, but by several attitudes which together form, as it were, a "bundle" of attitudes (as in the Trobriands, where we find both mutuality *and* reciprocity between husband and wife). This is an additional reason behind the difficulty in uncovering the basic structure.

We have tried to show the extent to which the preceding analysis is indebted to outstanding contemporary exponents of the sociology of primitive peoples. We must stress, however, that in its most fundamental principle this analysis departs from their teachings. Let us cite as an example Radcliffe-Brown:

> The unit of structure from which a kinship is built up is the group which I call an "elementary family," consisting of a man and his wife and their child or children. . . . The existence of the elementary family creates three special kinds of social relationship, that between parent and child, that between children of the same parents (siblings), and that between husband and wife as parents of the same child or children. . . . The three relationships that exist within the elementary family constitute what I call the first order. Relationships of the second order are those which depend on the connection of two elementary families through a common member, and are such as father's father, mother's brother, wife's sister, and so on. In the third order are such as father's brother's son and mother's brother's wife. Thus we can trace, if we have genealogical information, relationships of the fourth, fifth or n^{th} order.[50]

The idea expressed in the above passage, that the biological family constitutes the point of departure from which all societies elaborate their kinship systems, has not been voiced solely by Radcliffe-Brown. There is scarcely an idea which would today elicit greater consensus. Nor is there one more dangerous, in our opinion. Of course, the biological family is ubiquitous in human society. But what confers upon kinship its socio-cultural character is not what it retains from nature, but, rather, the essential way in which it diverges from nature. A kinship system does not consist in the objective ties of descent or consanguinity between individuals. It exists only in human consciousness; it is an arbitrary system of representations, not the spontaneous development of a real situation. This certainly does not mean that the real situation is automatically contradicted, or that it is to be simply ignored. Radcliffe-Brown has shown, in studies that are now classic, that even systems which are apparently extremely rigid and artificial, such as the Australian systems of marriage-classes, take biological parenthood carefully into account. But while this observation is irrefutable, still the fact (in our view decisive) remains that, in human society, kinship is allowed to establish and perpetuate itself only through specific forms of marriage. In other words, the relationships which Radcliffe-Brown calls "relationships of the first order" are a function of, and depend upon, those which he considers secondary and derived. The essence of human kinship is to require the establishment of relations among what Radcliffe-Brown calls "elementary families." Thus, it is not the families (isolated terms) which are truly "elementary," but, rather, the relations between those terms. No other interpretation can account for the universality of the incest taboo; and the avuncular relationship, in its most general form, is nothing but a corollary, now covert, now explicit, of this taboo.

Because they are symbolic systems, kinship systems offer the anthropologist a rich field, where his efforts can almost (and we emphasize the "almost") converge with those of the most highly developed of the social sciences, namely, linguistics. But to achieve this convergence, from which it is hoped a better understanding of man will result, we must never lose sight of the fact that, in both anthropological and linguistic research, we are dealing strictly with symbolism. And although it may be legitimate or even inevitable to fall back upon a naturalistic interpretation in order to understand the emergence of symbolic thinking, once the latter is given, the nature of the explanation must change as radically as the newly appeared phenomenon differs from those which have preceded and prepared it. Hence, any concession to naturalism might jeopardize the immense progress already made in linguistics, which is also beginning to characterize the study of family structure, and might drive the sociology of the family toward a sterile empiricism, devoid of inspiration.

NOTES

1. Marcel Mauss, "Rapports réels et pratiques de la psychologie et de la sociologie," *Journal de Psychologie Normale et Pathologique* (1924); reprinted in *Sociologie et Anthropologie* (Paris: 1951), p. 299.
2. O. Schrader, *Prehistoric Antiquities of the Aryan Peoples*, trans. F. B. Jevons (London: 1890), Chapter XII, Part 4.
3. *Ibid*. See also H. J. Rose, "On the Alleged Evidence for Mother-Right in Early Greece," *Folklore*, XXII (1911), and the more recent studies by George Thomson, which support the hypothesis of matrilineal survivals.
4. A. M. Hocart, "Chieftainship and the Sister's Son in the Pacific,"

American Anthropologist, n.s., XVII (1915); "The Uterine Nephew," *Man*, XXIII, No. 4 (1923); "The Cousin in Vedic Ritual," *Indian Antiquary*, LIV (1925); etc.

5. Paul K. Benedict, "Tibetan and Chinese Kinship Terms," *Harvard Journal of Asiatic Studies*, VI (1942); "Studies in Thai Kinship Terminology," *Journal of the American Oriental Society*, LXIII (1943).
6. L. Brunschvicg, *Le Progrès de la conscience dans la philosophie occidentale* (Paris: 1927), II, p. 562.
7. Between 1900 and 1920 Ferdinand de Saussure and Antoine Meillet, the founders of modern linguistics, placed themselves determinedly under the wing of the anthropologists. Not until the 1920's did Marcel Mauss begin—to borrow a phrase from economics—to reverse this tendency.
8. N. Troubetzkoy, "La Phonologie actuelle," in *Psychologie du langage* (Paris: 1933).
9. *Ibid.*, p. 243.
10. *Loc. cit.*
11. *Ibid.*, p. 245; Roman Jakobson, "Principien der historischen Phonologie," *Travaux du Cercle linguistique de Prague*, IV (1931); and also Jakobson, "Remarques sur l'évolution phonologique du russe," *ibid.*, II (1929).
12. W. H. R. Rivers, *The History of Melanesian Society* (London: 1914), *passim*; *Social Organization*, ed. W. J. Perry (London: 1924), Chapter IV.
13. In the same vein, see Sol Tax, "Some Problems of Social Organization," in Fred Eggan (ed.), *Social Anthropology of North American Tribes* (Chicago: 1937).
14. Roman Jakobson, "Observations sur le classement phonologique des consonnes," *Proceedings of the Third International Congress of Phonetic Sciences* (Ghent: 1938).
15. K. Davis and W. L. Warner, "Structural Analysis of Kinship," *American Anthropologist*, n.s., XXXVII (1935).
16. Thus at the end of the analysis carried out by these authors, the term *husband* is replaced by the formula:
$$C^{2a}/2^d/0\ S\ U^{1a\ 8}/Ego\ (Ibid.)$$
There are now available two works which employ a much more refined logical apparatus and offer greater interest in terms both of method and of results. See F. G. Lounsbury, "A Semantic Analysis of the Pawnee Kinship Usage," *Language*, XXXII, No. 1 (1956), and W. H. Goodenough, "The Componential Analysis of Kinship," *ibid.*
17. As will be seen in Chapter V, I have now refined this formulation.
18. A. L. Kroeber, "Classificatory Systems of Relationship," *Journal of the Royal Anthropological Institute*, XXXIX (1909).
19. We must except the remarkable work of W. L. Warner, "Morphology and Functions of the Australian Murngin Type of Kinship," *American Anthropologist*, n.s., XXXII-XXXIII (1930-1931), in which his analysis of the system of attitudes, although fundamentally debatable, nevertheless initiates a new phase in the study of problems of kinship.
20. A. R. Radcliffe-Brown, "Kinship Terminology in California," *American Anthropologist*, n.s., XXXVII (1935); "The Study of Kinship Systems," *Journal of the Royal Anthropological Institute*, LXXI (1941).
21. M. E. Opler, "Apache Data Concerning the Relationship of Kinship Terminology to Social Classification," *American Anthropologist*, n.s.,

XXXIX (1937); A. M. Halpern, "Yuma Kinship Terms," *American Anthropologist*, n.s., XLIV (1942).

22. D. F. Thomson, "The Joking Relationship and Organized Obscenity in North Queensland," *American Anthropologist*, n.s., XXXVII (1935).
23. Radcliffe-Brown, "The Study of Kinship Systems," *op. cit.*, p. 8. This later formulation seems to us more satisfactory than his 1935 statement that attitudes present "a fairly high degree of correlation with the terminological classification" (*American Anthropologist*, n.s., XXXVII [1935], p. 53).
24. Sydney Hartland, "Matrilineal Kinship and the Question of its Priority," *Memoirs of the American Anthropological Association*, No. 4 (1917).
25. W. H. R. Rivers, "The Marriage of Cousins in India," *Journal of the Royal Asiatic Society* (July, 1907).
26. *Ibid.*, p. 624.
27. R. H. Lowie, "The Matrilineal Complex," *University of California Publications in American Archaeology and Ethnology*, XVI, No. 2 (1919).
28. Roman Jakobson, *Kindersprache, Aphasie und allgemeine Lautgesetze* (Uppsala: 1941).
29. A. R. Radcliffe-Brown, "The Mother's Brother in South Africa," *South African Journal of Science*, XXI (1924).
30. As among the Mundugomor of New Guinea, where the relationship between maternal uncle and nephew is always familiar, although descent is alternately patrilineal or matrilineal. See Margaret Mead, *Sex and Temperament in Three Primitive Societies* (New York: 1935), pp. 176-185.
31. B. Malinowski, *The Sexual Life of Savages in Northwestern Melanesia* (London: 1929), 2 vols.
32. Dubois de Monpereux (1839), cited in M. Kovalevski, "La Famille matriarcale au Caucase," *L'Anthropologie*, IV (1893).
33. *Ibid.*
34. E. W. Gifford, "Tonga Society," *Bernice P. Bishop Museum Bulletin*, No. 61 (Honolulu: 1929), pp. 16-22.
35. F. E. Williams, "Group Sentiment and Primitive Justice," *American Anthropologist*, n.s., XLIII, No. 4, Part 1 (1941), p. 523.
36. F. E. Williams, "Natives of Lake Kutubu, Papua," *Oceania*, XI (1940-1941), p. 266.
37. *Ibid.*, p. 268.
38. *Ibid.*, p. 280. See also *Oceania*, XII (1941-1942).
39. Douglas L. Oliver, *A Solomon Island Society: Kinship and Leadership among the Siuai of Bougainville* (Cambridge, Mass.: 1955), p. 255.
40. *Ibid.*, p. 251.
41. *Ibid.*, p. 257.
42. *Ibid.*, pp. 168-9.
43. R. F. Fortune, *The Sorcerers of Dobu* (New York: 1932), p. 45.
44. *Ibid.*, pp. 8, 10, 62-4.
45. G. E. Howard, *A History of Matrimonial Institutions*, 3 vols. (Chicago: 1904).
[46. *Translator's note:* The "Chansons de Geste," which survive in manuscript versions of the twelfth to the fifteenth century, are considered to be remodelings of much earlier originals, dating back to the age of

Charlemagne. These poems of heroic and often legendary exploits also constitute a source of information on the family life of that period.]

47. Léon Gautier, *La Chevalerie* (Paris: 1890). See also: F. B. Gummere, "The Sister's Son," in *An English Miscellany Presented to Dr. Furnivall* (London: 1901); W. O. Farnsworth, *Uncle and Nephew in the Old French Chanson de Geste* (New York: 1913).

48. The preceding paragraphs were written in 1957 and substituted for the original text, in response to the judicious remark by my colleague Luc de Heusch of the Université Libre of Brussels that one of my examples was incorrect. I take this opportunity to thank him.

49. It is no doubt superfluous to emphasize that the atomism which we have criticized in Rivers refers to classical philosophy and has nothing to do with the structural conception of the atom developed in modern physics.

50. A. R. Radcliffe-Brown, "The Study of Kinship Systems," *op. cit.*, p. 2.

CHAPTER III

Language and the Analysis of Social Laws

In a recent work, whose importance from the point of view of the future of the social sciences can hardly be overestimated, Wiener poses, and resolves in the negative, the question of a possible extension to the social sciences of the mathematical methods of prediction which have made possible the construction of the great modern electronic machines. He justifies his position by two arguments.[1]

In the first place, he maintains that the nature of the social sciences is such that it is inevitable that their very development have repercussions on the object of their investigation. The coupling of the observer with the observed phenomenon is well known to contemporary scientific thought, and, in a sense, it illustrates a universal situation. But it is negligible in fields which are ripe for the most advanced mathematical investigation; as, for example, in astrophysics, where the object has such vast dimensions that the influence of the observer need not be taken into account, or in atomic physics, where the object is so small that we are interested only in average mass effects in which the effect of bias on the part of the observer plays no role. In the field of the social sciences, on the contrary, the object of study is necessarily affected by the intervention of the observer, and the resulting modifications are *on the same scale* as the phenomena that are studied.

In the second place, Wiener observes that the phenomena subjected to sociological or anthropological inquiry are defined within our own sphere of interests; they concern questions of the life, education, career, and death of individuals. Therefore the statistical runs available for the study of a given phenomenon are always far too short to lay the foundation of a valid induction. Mathematical analysis in the field of social science, he concludes, can bring results which should be of as little interest to the social scientist as those of the statistical study of a gas would be to an individual about the size of a molecule.

These objections seem difficult to refute when they are examined in terms of the investigations toward which their author has directed them, the data of research monographs and of applied anthropology. In such cases, we are dealing with a study of individual behavior, directed by an observer who is himself an individual; or with a study of a culture, a national character, or a pattern, by an observer who cannot dissociate himself completely from his culture, or from the culture out of which his working hypotheses and his methods of observation, which are themselves cultural patterns, are derived.

There is, however, at least one area of the social sciences where Wiener's objections do not seem to be applicable, where the conditions which he sets as a requirement for a valid mathematical study seem to be rigorously met. This is the field of language, when studied in the light of structural linguistics, with particular reference to phonemics.

Language is a social phenomenon; and, of all social phenomena, it is the one which manifests to the greatest degree two fundamental characteristics which make it susceptible of scientific study. In the first place, much of linguistic behavior lies on the level of unconscious thought. When we speak, we are not conscious of the syntactic and morphological laws of our language. Moreover, we are not ordinarily conscious of the phonemes that we employ to convey different meanings; and we are rarely, if ever, conscious of the phonological oppositions which reduce each phoneme to a bundle of distinctive features. This absence of consciousness, moreover, still holds when we do become aware of the grammar or the phonemics of our language. For, while this awareness is the privilege of the scholar, language, as a matter of fact, lives and develops only as a collective construct; and even the scholar's linguistic knowledge always remains dissociated from his experience as a speaking agent, for his mode of speech is not affected by his ability to interpret his language on a higher level. We may say, then, that insofar as language is concerned we need not fear the influence of the observer on the observed phenomenon, because the observer cannot modify the phenomenon merely by becoming conscious of it.

Furthermore, as regards Wiener's second point, we know that language appeared very early in human history. Therefore, even if we can study it scientifically only when written documents are available, writing itself goes back a considerable distance and furnishes long enough runs to make language a valid subject for mathematical analysis. For example, the series we have at our disposal in studying Indo-European, Semitic, or Sino-Tibetan languages is about four or five thousand years old. And, where a comparable temporal dimension is lacking, the multiplicity of coexistent forms furnishes, for several other linguistic families, a spatial dimension that is no less valuable.

We thus find in language a social phenomenon that manifests both independence of the observer and long statistical runs, which would seem to indicate that language is a phenomenon fully qualified to satisfy the demands of mathematicians for the type of analysis Wiener suggests.

It is, in fact, difficult to see why certain linguistic problems could not be solved by modern calculating machines. With knowledge of the phonological structure of a language and the laws which govern the groupings of consonants and vowels, a student could easily use a machine to compute all the combinations of phonemes constituting the words of n syllables existing in the vocabulary, or even the number of combinations compatible with the structure of the language under consideration, such as previously defined. With a machine into which would be "fed" the equations regulating the types of structures with which phonemics usually deals, the repertory of sound which human speech organs can emit, and the minimal differential values, determined by psycho-physiological methods, which distinguish between the phonemes closest to one another, one would doubtless be able to obtain a computation of the totality of phonological structures for n oppositions (n being as high as one wished). One could thus construct a sort of periodic table of linguistic structures that would be comparable to the table of elements which Mendeleieff introduced into modern chemistry. It would then remain for us only to check the place of known languages in this table, to identify the positions and the relationships of the languages whose first-hand study is still too imperfect to give us a proper theoretical knowledge of them, and to discover the place of languages that have disappeared or are unknown, yet to come, or simply possible.

To add a last example: Jakobson has suggested that a language may possess several coexisting phonological structures, each of which may intervene in a different kind of grammatical operation.[2] Since there must obviously be a relationship between the different structural modalities of the same language, we arrive at the concept of a "metastructure" which would be something like the law of the group (*loi du groupe*) consisting of its modal structures. If all of these modalities could be analyzed by our machine, established mathematical methods would permit it to construct the "metastructure" of the language, which would in certain complex cases be so intricate as to make it difficult, if not impossible, to achieve on the basis of purely empirical investigation.

The problem under discussion here can, then, be defined as follows. Among all social phenomena, language alone has thus far been studied in a manner which permits it to serve as the object of truly scientific analysis, allowing us to understand its formative process and to predict its mode of change. This results from modern researches into the problems of phonemics, which have reached beyond the superficial conscious and historical expression of linguistic phenomena to attain fundamental and objective realities consisting of systems of relations which are the products of unconscious thought processes. The question which now arises is this: Is it possible to effect a similar reduction in the analysis of other forms of social phenomena? If so, would this analysis lead to the same result? And if the answer to this last question is in the affirmative, can we conclude that all forms of social life are substantially of the same nature—that is, do they consist of systems of behavior that represent the projection, on the level of conscious and socialized thought, of universal laws which regulate the unconscious activities of the mind? Obviously, no attempt can be made here to do more than to sketch this problem by indicating certain points of reference and projecting the principal lines along which its orientation might be effective.

Some of the researches of Kroeber appear to be of the greatest importance in suggesting approaches to our problem, particularly his work on changes in the styles of women's dress.[3] Fashion actually is, in the highest degree, a phenomenon that depends on the unconscious activity of the mind. We rarely take note of why a particular style pleases us or falls into disuse. Kroeber has demonstrated that this seemingly arbitrary evolution follows definite laws. These laws cannot be reached by purely empirical observation, or by intuitive consideration of phenomena, but result from measuring some basic relationships between the various elements of costume. The relationship thus obtained can be expressed in terms of mathematical functions, whose values, calculated at a given moment, make prediction possible.

Kroeber has thus shown how even such a highly arbitrary aspect of social behavior is susceptible of scientific study. His method may be usefully compared not only with that of structural linguistics, but also with that of the natural sciences. There is a remarkable analogy between these researches and those of a contemporary biologist, G. Teissier, on the growth of the organs of certain crustaceans.[4] Teissier has shown that, in order to formulate the laws of this growth, it is necessary to consider the relative dimensions of the component parts of the claws, and not the exterior forms of those organs. Here, relationships allow us to derive constants—termed parameters—from which it is possible to derive the laws which govern the development of these organisms. The object of a scientific zoology, in these terms, is thus not ultimately concerned with the forms of animals and their organs as they are usually perceived, but with the establishment of certain abstract and measurable relationships, which constitute the basic nature of the phenomena under study.

An analogous method has been followed in studying certain features of social organization, particularly marriage rules and kinship systems.[5] It has been shown that the complete set of marriage regulations operating in human societies, and usually classified under different headings, such as incest prohibitions, preferential forms of marriage, and the like, can be interpreted as being so many different ways of insuring the circulation of women within the social group or of substituting the mechanism of a sociologically determined affinity for that of a biologically determined consanguinity. Proceeding from this hypothesis, it would only be necessary to make a mathematical study of every possible type of exchange between *n* partners to enable one almost automatically to arrive at every type of marriage rule actually operating in living societies and, eventually, to discover other rules that are merely possible; one would also understand their function and the relationships between each type and the others.

This approach was fully validated by the demonstration, reached by pure deduction, that the mechanisms of reciprocity known to classical anthropology—namely, those based on dual organization and exchange-marriage between two partners or partners whose number is a multiple of two—are but a special instance of a wider kind of reciprocity between any number of partners. This fact has tended to remain unnoticed, because the partners in those matings, instead of giving and receiving from each other, do not give to those from whom they receive and do not receive from those to whom they give. They give to and receive from different partners to whom they are bound by a relationship that operates only in one direction.

This type of organization, no less important than the moiety system, has thus far been observed and described only imperfectly and incidentally. Starting with the results of mathematical study, data had to be compiled; thus, the real extension of the system was shown and its first theoretical analysis offered.[6] At the same time, it became possible to explain the more general features of marriage rules such as preferential marriage between bilateral cross-cousins or with only one kind of cross-cousin, on the father's side (patrilateral), or on that of the mother (matrilateral). Thus, for example, though such customs had been unintelligible to anthropologists,[7] they were perfectly clear when regarded as illustrating different modalities of the laws of exchange. In turn, these were reduced to a still more basic relationship between the rules of residence and the rules of descent.[8]

Now, these results can be achieved only by treating marriage regulations and kinship systems as a kind of language, a set of processes permitting the establishment, between individuals and groups, of a certain type of communication. That the mediating factor, in this case, should be the *women of the group*, who are *circulated* between clans, lineages, or families, in place of the *words of the group*, which are *circulated* between individuals, does not at all change the fact that the essential aspect of the phenomenon is identical in both cases.

We may now ask whether, in extending the concept of communication so as to make it include exogamy and the rules flowing from the prohibition of incest, we may not, reciprocally, achieve insight into a problem that is still very obscure, that of the origin of language. For marriage regulations, in relation to language, represent a much more crude and archaic complex. It is generally recognized that words are signs; but poets are practically the only ones who know that words were also once values. As against this, women are held by the social group to be values of the most essential kind, though we have difficulty in understanding how these values become integrated in systems endowed with a significant function. This ambiguity is clearly manifested in the reactions of persons who, on the basis of the analysis of social structures referred to,[9] have laid against it the charge of "anti-feminism," because women are referred to as objects.[10] Of course, it may be disturbing to some to have women conceived as mere parts of a meaningful system. However, one should keep in mind that the processes by which phonemes and words have lost—even though in an illusory manner—their character of value, to become reduced to pure signs, will never lead to the same results in matters concerning women. For words do not speak, while women do; as producers of signs, women can never be reduced to the status of symbols or tokens. But it is for this very reason that the position of women, as actually found in this system of communication between men that is made up of marriage regulations and kinship nomenclature, may afford us a workable image of the type of relationships that could have existed at a very early period in the development of language, between human beings and their words. As in the case of women, the original impulse which compelled men to exchange words must be sought for in that split representation that pertains to the symbolic function. For, since certain terms are simultaneously perceived as having a value both for the speaker and the listener, the only way to resolve this contradiction is in the exchange of complementary values, to which all social existence is reduced.

These speculations may be judged utopian. Yet, if one considers that the assumptions made here are legitimate, a very important consequence follows, one that is susceptible of immediate verification. That is, the question may be raised whether the different aspects of social life (including even art and religion) cannot only be studied by the methods of, and with the help of concepts similar to those employed in linguistics, but also whether they do not constitute phenomena whose inmost nature is the same as that of language. That is, in the words of Voegelin, we may ask whether there are not only "operational" but also "substantial comparabilities" between language and culture.[11]

How can this hypothesis be verified? It will be necessary to develop the analysis of the different features of social life, either for a given society or for a complex of societies, so that a deep enough level can be reached to make it possible to cross from one to the other; or to express the specific structure of each in terms of a sort of general language, valid for each system separately and for all of them taken together. It would thus be possible to ascertain if one had reached their inner nature and to determine if this pertained to the same kind of reality. In order to develop this point, an experiment can be attempted. It will consist, on the part of the anthropologist, in translating the basic features of the kinship systems from different parts of the world into terms general enough to be meaningful to the linguist, and thus be equally applicable by the linguist to the description of languages from the same regions. Both could thus ascertain whether or not different types of communication systems in the same societies—that is, kinship and language—are or are not caused by identical unconscious structures. Should this be the case, we could be assured of having reached a truly fundamental formulation.

If then, a substantial identity were assumed to exist between language structure and kinship systems, one should find, in the following regions of the world, languages whose structures would be of a type comparable to kinship systems in the following terms:

(1) *Indo-European:* As concerns the *kinship systems*, we find that the marriage regulations of our contemporary civilization are entirely based on the principle that, a few negative prescriptions being granted, the density and fluidity of the population will achieve by itself the same results which other societies have sought in more complicated sets of rules; i.e., social cohesion obtained by marriage in degrees far removed or even impossible to trace. This statistical solution has its origin in a typical feature of most ancient Indo-European systems. These belong, in the author's terminology, to a simple formula of generalized reciprocity (*formule simple de l'échange généralisé*).[12] However, instead of prevailing between lineages, this formula operates between more complex units of the *bratsvo* type, which actually are clusters of lineages, each of which enjoys a certain freedom within the rigid framework of general reciprocity effective at the cluster level. Therefore, it can be said that a characteristic feature of Indo-European kinship structure lies in the fact that a problem set in simple terms always admits of many solutions.

Should the linguistic structure be homologous with the kinship structure it would thus be possible to express the basic feature of Indo-European languages as follows: The languages have simple structures, utilizing numerous elements. The opposition between the *simplicity of the structure* and the *multiplicity of elements* is expressed in the fact that several elements compete to occupy the same positions in the structure.

(2) *Sino-Tibetan kinship systems* exhibit quite a different type of complexity. They belong to or derive directly from the simplest form of general reciprocity, namely, mother's brother's daughter marriage, so that, as has been shown,[13] while this type of marriage insures social cohesion in the simplest way, at the same time it permits this to be indefinitely extended so as to include any number of participants.

Translated into more general terms applicable to language that would correspond to the following linguistic pattern, we may say that the structure is complex, while the elements are few, a feature that may be related to the tonal structure of these languages.

(3) The typical feature of *African kinship systems* is the extension of the bride-wealth system, coupled with a rather frequent prohibition on marriage with the wife's brother's wife. The joint result is a system of general reciprocity more complex than the mother's brother's daughter system, while the types of unions resulting from the circulation of the marriage-price approaches, to some extent, the statistical mechanism operating in our own society.

Therefore one could say that African languages have several modalities corresponding in general to a position intermediate between (1) and (2).

(4) The widely recognized features of *Oceanic kinship systems* seem to lead to the following formulation of the basic characteristics of the linguistic pattern: simple structure and few elements.

(5) The originality of *American Indian kinship systems* lies in the so-called Crow-Omaha type, which should be carefully distinguished from other types showing the same disregard for generation levels.[14] The important point with the Crow-Omaha type is not that two kinds of cross-cousins are classified in different generation levels, but rather that they are classified with consanguineous kin instead of with affinal kin (as is the case, for instance, in the Miwok system). But systems of the Miwok type belong equally to the Old and the New World; while the differential systems just referred to as Crow-Omaha are, apart from a few exceptions, typical only for the New World. It can be shown that this quite exceptional feature of the Crow-Omaha system resulted from the simultaneous application of the two simple formulas of reciprocity, both special and general (*échange restreint* and *échange généralisé*),[15] which elsewhere in the world were generally considered to be incompatible. It thus became possible to achieve marriage within remote degrees by using simultaneously two simple formulas, each of which independently applied could have led only to different kinds of cross-cousin marriages.

The linguistic pattern corresponding to this situation is that certain of the American Indian languages offer a relatively high number of elements which succeed in becoming organized into relatively simple structures by the structures' assuming asymmetrical forms.

It should be kept in mind that in the above highly tentative experiment the anthropologist proceeds from what is known to him to what is unknown: namely, from kinship structures to linguistic structures. Whether or not the differential characteristics thus outlined have a meaning insofar as the respective languages are concerned remains for the linguist to decide. The author, being a social anthropologist and not a linguist, can only try to explain briefly to which specific features of kinship systems he is referring in this attempt toward a generalized formulation. Since the general lines of his interpretation have been fully developed elsewhere,[16] short sketches were deemed sufficient for the purpose of this paper.

If the general characteristics of the kinship systems of given geographical areas, which we have tried to bring into juxtaposition with equally general characteristics of the linguistic structures of those areas, are recognized by linguists as an approach to equivalences of their own observations, then it will be apparent, in terms of our preceding discussion, that we are much closer to understanding the fundamental characteristics of social life than we have been accustomed to think.

The road will then be open for a comparative structural analysis of customs, institutions, and accepted patterns of behavior. We shall be in a position to understand basic similarities between forms of social life, such as language, art, law, and religion, that on the surface seem to differ greatly. At the same time, we shall have the hope of overcoming the opposition between the collective nature of culture and its manifestations in the individual, since the so-called "collective consciousness" would, in the final analysis, be no more than the expression, on the level of individual thought and behavior, of certain time and space modalities of the universal laws which make up the unconscious activity of the mind.

NOTES

1. N. Wiener, *Cybernetics, or Control and Communication in the Animal and the Machine* (Paris-Cambridge-New York: 1948).
2. Roman Jakobson, "The Phonemic and Grammatical Aspects of Language in Their Interrelations," *Actes du VIᵉ Congrès International des Linguistes* (Paris: 1948).
3. J. Richardson and A. L. Kroeber, "Three Centuries of Women's Dress Fashions. A Quantitative Analysis," *Anthropological Records*, V, No. 2 (1940).

4. G. Teissier, "La Description mathématique des faits biologiques," *Revue de Métaphysique et de Morale* (January, 1936).

5. C. Lévi-Strauss, *Les Structures élémentaires de la parenté* (Paris: 1949), *passim*.

6. *Ibid.*, pp. 278-380.

7. *Ibid.*, pp. 558-66.

8. *Ibid.*, pp. 547-50.

9. *Ibid.*, p. 616.

10. *Ibid.*, p. 45 ff.

11. "Language and Culture: Substantial and Operational Comparabilities" was the title given by C. F. Voegelin to the symposium held at the Twenty-ninth International Congress of Americanists, New York, September 5-12, 1949, where these comments were first offered.

12. Lévi-Strauss, *op. cit.*, pp. 583-91.

13. *Ibid.*, pp. 291-380.

14. From this point of view, G. P. Murdock's suggestion (*Social Structure* [New York: 1949], pp. 224, 340) that the Crow-Omaha type be merged with the Miwok type should be categorically rejected.

15. Lévi-Strauss, *op. cit.*, pp. 228-33.

16. *Op. cit.*

CHAPTER IV

Linguistics and Anthropology[1]

P ROBABLY FOR THE FIRST TIME, anthropologists and linguists have come together on a formal basis and for the specific purpose of confronting their respective disciplines. However, the problem was not a simple one, and it seems to me that some of the many difficulties which we have met with can be referred to the fact we were not only trying to make a confrontation of the theme of linguistics and of anthropology, but that this confrontation itself could be and had to be undertaken on several different levels, and it was extremely difficult to avoid, in the midst of the same discussion, shifting from one level to another. I shall try first of all to outline what these different levels are.

In the first place, we have spoken about the relation between *a* language and *a* culture. That is, how far is it necessary, when we try to study a culture, to know the language, or how far is it necessary to understand what is meant by the population, to have some knowledge of the culture besides the language.

There is a second level, which is not the relationship between *a* language and *a* culture, but the relationship between *language* and *culture*. And though there are also many important problems on this level, it seems to me that our discussions have not so often been placed on the second level as on the first one. For instance, I am rather struck by the fact that at no moment during our discussions has any reference been made to the behavior of culture as a whole toward language as a whole. Among us, language is used in a rather reckless way—we talk all the time, we ask questions about many things. This is not at all a universal situation. There are cultures—and I am inclined to say most of the cultures of the world —which are rather thrifty in relation to language. They don't believe that language should be used indiscriminately, but only in certain specific frames of reference and somewhat sparingly. Problems of this kind have, to be sure, been mentioned in our discussions, but certainly they have not been given the same importance as the problems of the first type.

And there is a third level, which has received still less attention. It is the relation, not between *a* language or *language* and *a* culture or *culture*, but the relation between linguistics as a scientific discipline and anthropology. And this, which to my mind would be probably the most important level, has remained somewhat in the background during our discussions.

Now how can this be explained? The relationship between language and culture is an exceedingly complicated one. In the first place, language can be said to be a result of culture: The language which is spoken by one population is a reflection of the total culture of the population. But one can also say that language is a *part* of culture. It is one of those many things which make up a culture —and if you remember Tylor's famous definition of culture, culture includes a great many things, such as tools, institutions, customs, beliefs, and also, of course, language. And from this point of view the problems are not at all the same as from the first one. In the third place, language can be said to be a *condition* of culture, and this in two different ways: First, it is a condition of culture in a diachronic way, because it is mostly through the language that we learn about our own culture—we are taught by our parents, we are scolded, we are congratulated, with language. But also, from a much more theoretical point of view, language can be said to be a condition of culture because the material out of which language is built is of the same type as the material out of which the whole culture is built: logical relations, oppositions, correlations, and the like. Language, from this point of view, may appear as laying a kind of foundation for the more complex structures which correspond to the different aspects of culture.

This is how I see our problem from an objective point of view. But there is also a subjective point of view, which is no less important. During the discussion it appeared to me that the reasons for anthropologists' and linguists' being so eager to get together are of an entirely different nature, and that their motivations are practically contradictory. Linguists have told us over and over again during these sessions that they are somewhat afraid of the trend which is becoming predominant in their discipline—that they have felt more and more unrelated; that they have been dealing more and more with abstract notions, which many times have been very difficult to follow for the others; and that what they have been mainly concerned with, especially in structural linguistics, has no relation whatsoever to the whole culture, to the social life, to the history, of the people who speak the language; and so on. And the reason, it seems to me, for the linguists' being so eager to get closer to the anthropologists is precisely that they expect the anthropologists to be able to give back to them some of this concreteness which seems to have disappeared from their own methodological approach. And now, what about the anthropologists? The anthropologists are in a very peculiar situation in relation to linguistics. For many years they have been working very closely with the linguists, and all of a sudden it seems to them that the linguists are vanishing, that they are going on the other side of the borderline which divides the exact and natural sciences on the one hand from the human and social sciences on the other. All of a sudden the linguists are playing their former companions this very nasty trick of doing things as well and with the same sort of rigorous approach that was long believed to be the privilege of the exact and natural sciences. Then, on the side of the anthropologist there is some, let us say, melancholy, and a great deal of envy. We should like to learn from the linguists how they succeeded in doing it, how we may ourselves in our own field, which is a complex one—in the field of kinship, in the field of social organization, in the field of religion, folklore, art, and the like—use the same kind of rigorous approach which has proved to be so successful for linguistics.

And I should like to elaborate—since the point of view that I am expected to explain here is the point of view of the anthropologist—how important this is to us. I have learned a great deal during this Conference, but it was not only during the sessions of the Conference: I was extremely impressed, as a non-linguist anthropologist, in attending some of the classes in field work, led by C. F. Voegelin and Henry L. Smith, to witness the precision, the care, the rigor which is used in a field that, after all, belongs to the social sciences to the same extent as the other fields of anthropology. And this is not all. During the past three or four years we have been impressed not only by the theoretical but by the practical connection which has been established between linguistics and communication engineering—by the fact that now, when you have a problem, it is possible not only to use a method more rigorous than our own to solve it, but to have a machine built by an engineer and to make a kind of experiment, completely similar to a natural-science experiment, and to have the experiment tell you if the hypothesis is worthwhile or not. For centuries the humanities and the social sciences have resigned themselves to contemplating the world of the natural and exact sciences as a kind of paradise which they will never enter. And all of a sudden there is a small door which is being opened between the two fields, and it is linguistics which has done it. So you may see that the motivations of the anthropologists, insofar as I am able to interpret them correctly, are rather contradictory to the motivations of the linguists. The linguists try to join the anthropologists in order to make their study more concrete, while the anthropologists are trying to rejoin the linguists precisely because the linguists appear to show them a way to get out of the confusion resulting from too much acquaintance and familiarity with concrete and empirical data. Sometimes it seems to me this has resulted, during this Conference, in a somewhat—shall I call it—unhappy merry-go-round, where the anthropologists were running after the linguists while the linguists were running after the anthropologists, each group trying to get from the other precisely what it was trying itself to get rid of. And this, I think, deserves some kind of attention. Why this basic misunderstanding? In the first place, because the task is extremely difficult.

I was particularly struck by the session where Mary Haas tried to write on the board formulas to analyze a problem as apparently simple as that of bilingualism—very simple, since it might seem from the outside that there are only two terms, two languages, though the number of possible permutations was enormous. And enormous as it was, during the discussion new types of permutation were discovered. It was also admitted that, besides these permutations, other dimensions could be introduced which would complicate the problem still more. This is what I believe to be one of the main lessons of this Conference—that whenever we try to express in the same language linguistic problems and cultural problems, the situation becomes tremendously complicated, and we shall always have to keep this in mind.

In the second place, we have been behaving as if there were only two partners—language on the one hand, culture on the other —and as if the problem should be set up in terms of the causal relations: "Is it language which influences culture? Is it culture which influences language?" But we have not been sufficiently aware of the fact that *both* language and culture are the products of activities which are basically similar. I am now referring to this uninvited guest which has been seated during this Conference beside us and which is *the human mind*. The fact that the psychologist C. E. Osgood is here and the many occasions when he was literally compelled to intervene in order to call our attention to this basic fact are the best proofs of the point I am trying to make.

If we try to formulate our problem in purely theoretical terms, then it seems to me that we are entitled to affirm that there should be some kind of relationship between language and culture, because language has taken thousands of years to develop, and culture has taken thousands of years to develop, and both processes have been taking place side by side within the same minds. Of course, I am leaving aside for the moment cases where a foreign language has been adopted by a society that previously spoke another language. We can, for the sake of argument, consider only those cases where, in an undisturbed fashion, language and culture have been able to develop together. Is it possible to conceive of the human mind as consisting of compartments separated by rigid bulkheads without anything being able to pass from one bulkhead to the other? Though, when we try to find out what these connections or correlations are, we are confronted with a very serious problem, or, rather, with two very serious problems.

The first problem has to do with *the level* at which to seek the correlations between language and culture, and the second one, with *the things* we are trying to correlate. I shall now give some attention to these basic distinctions.

I remember a very striking example which was given to us by F. G. Lounsbury, about the use of two different prefixes for womankind among the Oneida. Lounsbury was telling us he paid great attention to what was going on on the social level, but he could find no correlation whatsoever. Indeed, no correlation can be found on the level of behavior, because behavior, on the one hand, and categories of thought, on the other (such as would be called for to explain the use of these two different prefixes), belong to two entirely different levels. It would not be possible to try to correlate one with the other.

But I can hardly believe it a pure coincidence that this strange dichotomy of womankind should appear precisely in a culture where the maternal principle has been developed in such an extreme way as among the Iroquois. It is as if the culture had to pay a price for giving women an importance elsewhere unknown, the price being an inability to think of women as belonging to only one logical category. To recognize women, unlike most other cultures of the world, as full social beings would thus compel the culture, in exchange, to categorize that part of womankind as yet unable to play the important maternal role—such as young girls—as animals and not as humans. However, when I suggest this interpretation, I am not trying to correlate language and behavior, but two parallel ways of categorizing the same data.

Let me now give you another example. We reduce the kinship structure to the simplest conceivable element, the atom of kinship, if I may say so, when we have a group consisting of a husband, a woman, a representative of the group which has given the woman to the man—since incest prohibitions make it impossible in all societies for the unit of kinship to consist of one family, it must always link two families, two consanguineous groups—and one offspring. Now it can be shown that, if we divide all the possible behavior between kin according to a very simple dichotomy, positive behavior and negative behavior (I know this is very unsatisfactory, but it will help me to make my point), it can be shown that a great many different combinations can be found and illustrated by specific ethnographical observations. When there is a positive relationship between husband and wife and a negative one between brother and sister, we note the presence of two correlative attitudes: positive between father and son, negative between maternal uncle and nephew. We may also find a symmetrical structure, where all the signs are inverted. It is therefore common to find arrangements of the type $\left(\frac{+}{-}\frac{-}{}\right)$ or $\left(\frac{-}{}\frac{+}{-}\right)$, that is, two permutations. On the other hand, arrangements of the type $\left(\frac{+}{-}\frac{-}{+}\right)$, $\left(\frac{-}{+}\frac{+}{-}\right)$ occur frequently but often are poorly developed, while those of the type $\left(\frac{+}{-}\frac{+}{-}\right)$, $\left(\frac{-}{+}\frac{-}{+}\right)$ are rare, or perhaps impossible, because they would lead to the breakdown of the group, diachronically in the first case, synchronically in the second.[2]

Now, what connections are possible with linguistics? I cannot see any whatsoever, except only one, that when the anthropologist is working in this way he is working more or less in a way parallel to that of the linguist. They are both trying to build a structure with constituent units. But, nevertheless, no conclusions can be drawn from the repetition of the signs in the field of behavior and the repetition, let us say, of the phonemes of the language, or the grammatical structure of the language; nothing of the kind—it is perfectly hopeless.

Now let us take a somewhat more elaborate way of approaching a problem of that kind, Whorf's approach, which has been discussed so many times and which certainly must have been at the back of our minds during this discussion.[3] Whorf has tried to establish a correlation between certain linguistic structures and certain cultural structures. Why is it that the approach is unsatisfactory? It is, it seems to me, because the linguistic level as he considers it is the result of a rather sophisticated analysis—he is not at all trying to correlate an empirical impression of the language, but, rather, the result of true linguistic work (I don't know if this linguistic work is satisfactory from the point of view of the linguists, I'm just assuming it for the sake of argument)—what he is trying to correlate with this linguistic structure is a crude, superficial, empirical view of the culture itself. So he is really trying to correlate things which belong to entirely different levels.

When we now turn to study the communication system, there

are two statements that can be made. The first is that in order to build a model of the Hopi kinship system one has to use a block model, tri-dimensional. It is not possible to use a two-dimensional model. And this, incidentally, is characteristic of all the Crow-Omaha systems. Now, why is that so? Because the Hopi system makes use of three different time continuums. We have the first one, which corresponds to the mother's line (female Ego), which is a kind of time dimension that we use ourselves, that is, progressive and continuative: We have the grandmother, mother, Ego, daughter, granddaughter, and so on; it is really genealogical. (See Figure 3.) Now, when we consider other lines, there is a different

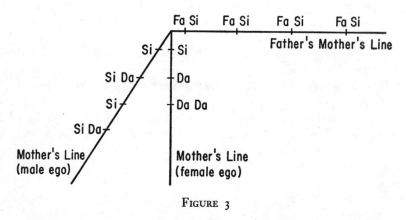

FIGURE 3

time dimension: For instance, if we take the father's mother's line, we find that, although people do belong to generations which are consecutive to each other, the same terms are consistently applied to them—that is, a woman is called "father's sister" and her daughter is still "father's sister," and so on indefinitely; this is a kind of empty time, with no change taking place whatsoever. And there is also a third dimension, which is found in the mother's line for male Ego, where individuals are alternately called "sibling" and "nephew."

Now if we consider the Zuni kinship system, these three dimensions still exist, but they are considerably reduced; they have a somewhat abortive form. And what is important is that the "straight" time framework that we have in the mother's line is replaced by a kind of "circular" framework, where we have only three terms, a term which equally means "grandmother" and "grand-daughter," and then a term for "mother" and a term for "daughter"—a woman would call by the same term her grandmother and her granddaughter.

If we look now at another Pueblo system, let us say Acoma or Laguna, which are Keresan and belong to a different linguistic stock, then we find a completely new picture: the development of symmetrical terms. Two individuals who occupy symmetrical positions in relation to a third individual will call each other by the same term. This is usually called a "self-reciprocal" terminology.

When we pass from Hopi to Acoma, we have a change from a block model to a flat model, but we have other significant changes. We have a change from a time framework which has a threefold quality, through the Zuni, which is intermediate, to something quite different; it is no longer a time continuum, it is a time-space continuum, since in order to conceive of the system one individual has to think of the other individual through the intermediary of a third one.

This can be very well correlated with the different aspects of the same myths among the Hopi, Zuni, and Acoma. When we consider one myth, let us say the emergence myth, the very striking thing is that among the Hopi the entire structure of the myth is organized in a genealogical way. The different gods are conceived as husband, wife, father, grandfather, daughter, and so on, to one another, more or less as it occurs in the Greek pantheon. Among the Zuni we do not find such a developed genealogical structure. Instead we find a kind of cyclical historical structure. The history is divided into periods, and each period repeats to some extent the preceding period. Now, with the Acoma the striking fact is that most of the characters which among the Hopi or the Zuni are conceived as one person are dichotomized into different persons with antithetic attributes. This is made clear by the fact that the emergence scene, which is so obvious in the first two cases, is preceded, and to some extent replaced, by a dual operation, in which the power from above and the power from below cooperate to create mankind. It is no longer a progressive linear movement, it is a system of polar oppositions, such as we find in the kinship system. Now if it is true that these features of the kinship system can be correlated with systems belonging to a completely different field, the field of mythology, we are entitled to ask the linguist whether or not something of the same kind does not show up in the field of language. And it would be very surprising if something—I do not know exactly what, because I am not a linguist—could not be found to exist, because if the answer should be in the negative, we should have to assume that, while fields that are so wide apart as kinship and mythology nevertheless succeed in remaining correlated, language and mythology, which are much more closely related, show no connection or no communication whatsoever.

This new formulation of the problem is, it seems to me, on a level with what the linguists are doing. The linguists are dealing in grammar with the time aspect. They discover the different ways of expressing the idea of time in a language. And we might try to compare the way of expressing time on a linguistic level with the way of expressing time on the kinship level. I do not know what the answer will be, but it is possible to discuss the problem, and it is possible in a meaningful way to answer it by "yes" or "no."

Permit me to give you another, and much more elaborate, example of the kind of analysis the anthropologist could perform to try to find common ground with the linguist. I am going to consider two social developments which have taken place in widely different parts of the world, the first in an area extending roughly from India to Ireland, the second in an area extending from Manchuria to Assam. I am certainly not saying that each of these two areas has shown exactly one kind of development, and only one. I am saying only that the developments I am referring to are well illustrated within these very vague boundaries, which, as you are well aware, correspond to some extent to the boundaries of the Indo-European languages on the one hand and the Sino-Tibetan languages on the other.

I propose to consider from three different points of view what has taken place. First, the marriage rules; next, social organization; and third, the kinship system.

Now let us consider first the marriage rules, for the sake of clarity. What we find in the Indo-European area are various systems, which in order to be properly interpreted have to be referred to a very simple type of marriage rule called the generalized form of exchange, or circular system, because any number of groups can be connected by using this rule. This corresponds roughly to what the anthropologists have called marriage with mother's brother's daughter: Group *A* is taking wives from Group *B*, Group *B* from Group *C*, and Group *C* again from Group *A*; so it is a kind of circle; you can have two groups, three groups, four, five, any number of groups; they can always be organized according to this system. This does not mean that Indo-European-speaking groups have necessarily, at one time or another, practiced marriage with mother's brother's daughter, but that most of the marriage systems in their area of occupancy belong directly or indirectly to the same family as the simpler type.

	INDO-EUROPEAN AREA	SINO-TIBETAN AREA
MARRIAGE RULES	Circular systems, either resulting directly from explicit rules or indirectly from the fact that the choice of a mate is left to probability	Circular systems, present in juxtaposition with systems of symmetrical exchange
SOCIAL ORGANIZATION	Numerous social units, with a complex structure (extended family type)	Few social units, with a simple structure (clan or lineage type)
KINSHIP SYSTEM	(1) subjective (2) few terms	(1) objective (2) numerous terms

Now, in the field of social organization, what do we have? We have, as distinctive of the Indo-European area, something we know by the name of "extended family." What is an extended family? An extended family consists of several collateral lines; but the collateral lines should remain to some extent distinguished from one another, because if they did not—if, for instance, Extended Family *A* were marrying into *B*, and Extended Family *B* into *C*, then there would be no distinction whatsoever between an extended family and a clan. The extended family would become a kind of clan. And what keeps the different collateral lines distinct in an extended family is that there cannot exist a rule of marriage applicable to all the lines. Now this has been followed up in Indo-European kinship systems in many different ways. Some systems, which are still working in India, state that it is only the senior line which follows a rule, and that all the other lines can marry exactly as they wish within the sole limitation of prohibited degrees. When one studies certain curious features of the old Slavic kinship system, the interpretation is somewhat different: It seems that what may be called the "exemplary line" was more or less diagonal to the main one; that is, if a man married according to a given rule, then at the next generational level it would be a man of a different line, and then in the next generation a man of another different line. This does not matter. The point is that with an extended family system it is not possible for all the groups to marry according to the same rule and that a great many exceptions to any conceivable rule should take place.

Now the kinship system itself calls for very few terms and it is a subjective system. This means that all the relatives are described in relation to the subject, and the further the relative is from the subject the vaguer the terms are. We can accurately describe our relationship to our father, mother, son, daughter, brother, and sister, but even aunt or uncle is slightly vague; and when it comes to more distant relationships, we have no terms at all at our disposal; it is an egocentric system.

Let us now compare some features in the Sino-Tibetan area. Here we find two types of marriage rules: one which is the same as the one previously described, generalized exchange; and another one, which is a special form of exchange, usually called "exchange marriage," a special form because, instead of making it possible to organize any number of groups, it can work only with two, four, six, eight—an even number—the system could not work with an odd number. And these two rules exist side by side within the area.

Now about the social organization. We do not have extended families in our second area, but we do find very simple types of the clan system, which can become complicated quantitatively (when the clan system divides into lineages), but never qualitatively, as is the case with the extended family.

As regards the kinship system, the terms are very numerous. You know, for instance, that in the Chinese kinship system the terms number several hundreds, and it is even possible to create an indefinite number of terms; any relationship can be described with accuracy, even if it is very far away from the subject. And this makes the system completely objective; as a matter of fact, Kroeber a long time ago noticed that no kinship systems are so completely different from each other as the Indo-European on the one hand and the Chinese on the other.

If we try to interpret this picture, what do we find? We find that in the Indo-European case we have a very simple structure (marriage rules), but that the elements (social organization) which must be arranged in this structure are numerous and complicated, whereas in the Sino-Tibetan case the opposite prevails: We have a very complicated structure (marriage rules), with two different sets of rules, and the elements (social organization) are few. And to the separation between the *structure* and the *elements* correspond, on the level of terminology—which is a linguistic level— antithetic features as to the framework (*subjective* versus *objective*) and to the terms themselves (*numerous* versus *few*). Now it seems to me that if we formulate the situation in these terms, it is at least possible to start a useful discussion with the linguists. While I was making this chart, I could not but remember what R. Jakobson said at yesterday's session about the structure of the Indo-European language: a great discrepancy between form and substance, a great many irregularities in relation to the rules, and considerable freedom regarding the choice of means to express the same idea. Are not all of these traits similar to those we have singled out with respect to social structure?

Finally, I would say that between culture and language there cannot be *no* relations at all, and there cannot be 100 per cent correlation either. Both situations are impossible to conceive. If there were no relations at all, that would lead us to assume that the human mind is a kind of jumble—that there is no connection at all between what the mind is doing on one level and what the mind is doing on another level. But, on the other hand, if the correlation were 100 per cent, then certainly we should know about it and we should not be here to discuss whether it exists or not. So the conclusion which seems to me the most likely is that some kind of correlation exists between certain things on certain levels, and our main task is to determine what these things are and what these levels are. This can be done only through a close cooperation between linguists and anthropologists. I should say that the most important results of such cooperation will not be for linguistics alone or for anthropology alone, or for both; they will mostly be for an anthropology conceived in a broader way—that is, a knowledge of man that incorporates all the different approaches which can be used and that will provide a clue to the way according to which our uninvited guest, the human mind, works.

NOTES

1. Transcribed from a tape recording of a paper read at the Conference of Anthropologists and Linguists, Bloomington, Indiana, 1952, and first published in *Supplement to International Journal of American Linguistics*, XIX, No. 2.
2. For examples and a more intensive analysis, see Chapter II of this book.
3. Benjamin L. Whorf, *Collected Papers on Metalinguistics* (Washington: 1952); *Language, Thought, and Reality*, ed. John B. Carroll (New York: 1956).

CHAPTER V

Postscript to
Chapters III and IV

IN THE SAME ISSUE of *Cahiers internationaux de Sociologie* containing an article by Gurvitch partly devoted to me, there is an article written by Haudricourt and Granai, whose data are more substantial and whose thought is more precise.[1] It would be easier for me to agree with them if, before writing their article, they had become acquainted with both my papers on the relationship between language and society, instead of limiting themselves to the first one. These two articles form a whole, since the second answers objections raised in the United States by the publication of the first. For this reason, they have been brought together in this volume.[2]

Furthermore, I concede to Haudricourt and Granai that, since these two articles are in English—the first one written, and the second a transcription of a tape recording—they are sometimes less accurate in expression than I should like. More than my opponents, perhaps, I am responsible for some of their errors with regard to my thinking. But on the whole, it seems to me their main error lies in their adoption of an extraordinarily timorous position.

Apparently disturbed by the rapid development of structural linguistics, they are trying to distinguish between the *science of language* and *linguistics*. The former, they say, "is more general than linguistics, yet does not include it; it develops on a different level; it does not utilize the same concepts or, consequently, the same methods as linguistics." This is true up to a certain point. But this distinction would give the anthropologist the right—which does not seem to be contested here—to directly refer to the science of language when he studies, as these authors well express it, "the indefinite whole of real or possible systems of communication," that is, those "symbolic systems other than the system of language," which comprise "the realms of myth, ritual, and kinship, which may actually be considered as so many special languages." [3] And then the authors continue: "Thus, and in varying degrees, these systems are amenable to a structural analysis which is analogous to that applied to the system of language. In this vein, we are acquainted with the remarkable studies by Lévi-Strauss of 'kinship systems,' which have unquestionably refined and clarified these highly complex problems." [4] I might, therefore, merely acknowledge this approval, for I have never attempted to do anything else or to extend the method to areas other than those listed.

The authors concede, nevertheless, in the one instance what they deny in the other by questioning my intentions. They state that "to interpret global society in terms of a general theory of communication" amounts "implicitly (and sometimes admittedly) to reducing society or culture to language." [5] Such criticism, which is expressed anonymously here, becomes explicitly directed toward me later: "Claude Lévi-Strauss clearly states the problem of the identity between language and society and seems to resolve it in the affirmative." [6] But the adjective *inmost* which I used means "the deepest," and does not exclude the possibility of other areas of application of lesser explanatory value. Haudricourt and Granai are guilty here of the same error as Gurvitch. They assume that the structural method, when applied to anthropology, is aimed at acquiring an exhaustive knowledge of societies. This is patently absurd. We simply wish to derive constants which are found at various times and in various places from an empirical richness and diversity that will always transcend our efforts at observation and description. In proceeding this way we work as does the linguist, and Haudricourt and Granai's attempt to maintain a distinction between the study of a particular idiom and the study of language seems quite weak. As Jakobson and Halle put it:

> . . . the ever increasing number of detected laws moves into the foreground the problem of the universal rules underlying the phonemic patterning of languages . . . of the world. . . . The supposed multiplicity of features proves to be largely illusory. . . . The same laws of implication underlie the languages of the world both in their static and dynamic aspects.[7]

Not only does the study of one language, therefore, lead inevitably to general linguistics, but it also involves us in the study of all forms of communication: "Like musical scales, phonemic patterning is an intervention of culture in nature, an artifact imposing logical rules upon the sound continuum." [8]

Without reducing society or culture to language, we can initiate this "Copernican revolution" (as Haudricourt and Granai call it), which will consist of interpreting society as a whole in terms of a theory of communication. This endeavor is possible on three levels, since the rules of kinship and marriage serve to insure the circulation of women between groups, just as economic rules serve to insure the circulation of goods and services, and linguistic rules the circulation of messages.

These three forms of communication are also forms of exchange which are obviously interrelated (because marriage relations are associated with economic prestations, and language comes into play at all levels). It is therefore legitimate to seek homologies between them and define the formal characteristics of each type considered independently and of the transformations which make the transition possible from one to another.

This formulation of the problem, to which I have always subscribed,[9] points up the tenuous basis of Gurvitch's criticism. According to him, I take the position that "communication, considered as the origin of social life, is first of all speech." [10] To derive from language a logical model which, being more accurate and better known, may aid us in understanding the structure of other forms of communication, is in no sense equivalent to treating the former as the origin of the latter.

But society includes many things besides marriage, economic, and linguistic exchanges. We also find in society other kinds of languages, whose analogy to *language* itself Haudricourt and Granai recognize. There are, for instance, art, myth, ritual, and religion, all of which I have considered at one time or another.[11] Finally, there are a large number of elements which do not lend themselves to structuring at present, either because of their nature or our own inadequate knowledge. These are the ones invoked by Haudricourt and Granai for the sake of some sort of mystical goal, for I believe these authors to be, despite appearances, bound to some metaphysical view of history. It seems to me more fruitful to retain, as an immediate focus of our studies, those strategic levels which I mentioned, not because they are the only ones or because the other levels can be identified with them, but because, in the present state of science, they alone permit the introduction of rigorous modes of reasoning into our disciplines.

I reject, therefore, the dilemma formulated by these writers, that either society does not exist as an entity and is then made up of the juxtaposition of irreducible systems, or that all the systems considered are equivalent and express, each in its own language, the whole of social life.[12] To this dilemma I had anticipated a reply in my 1953 article, which my critics did not read:

> . . . I would say that between culture and language there cannot be *no* relations at all, and there cannot be 100 per cent correlation either. Both situations are impossible to conceive. . . . So the conclusion which seems to me the more likely is that some kind of correlation exists between certain things on certain levels, and our main task is to determine what these things are and what these levels are.[13]

If we wished to establish a series of correlations, term for term, between language and culture (the latter considered as the totality of data pertaining to a specific society), we should be committing a logical error which would provide a simpler and more forceful argument than those formulated by Haudricourt and Granai. But, actually the whole is not equivalent to one of its parts. Is this flaw in reasoning at times characteristic of American metalinguistics, with which Haudricourt and Granai associate me? This is possible. But if I am not mistaken, both term and subject-matter became fashionable in the United States after my address to the International Congress of Americanists, held in New York in

1949,[14] which derived its inspiration from other sources.[15] The objections which, as far back as 1952, I raised with respect to so-called metalinguistics are of a more technical nature and pertain to another level. The error of Whorf and his followers stems from their attempt to compare highly elaborate linguistic data, which are the product of a preliminary analysis, with ethnographic observations based on an empirical level or on the level of an ideological analysis that implies an arbitrary breakdown of social reality. Thus they compare objects of dissimilar nature and run the risk of achieving nothing but truisms or weak hypotheses.

But Haudricourt and Granai are guilty of the same mistake when they write:

> The subject matter of linguistics is language (in the usual sense of the word: French language, English language, etc.). In sociology, comparable entities would be what we call societies or global structures (nation, people, tribe, etc.). The entity whose characteristics we wish to study must necessarily be as independent as possible from other entities.[16]

If this be true, our cause is indeed lost and criticism is fully justified. However, in the two studies which constitute Chapters III and IV of this volume, I propose something entirely different. The object of comparative structural analysis is not the French or English language, but rather a certain number of structures, which the linguist can derive from these empirical entities, such as, for instance, the phonemic structure of French, its grammatical or lexical structure, or even the structure of discourse, which is not altogether random. I do not compare French society or even the structure of French society with those structures, as Gurvitch might think (for he believes that a society as such possesses a structure); I compare, rather, a certain number of structures which I seek where they may be found, and not elsewhere: in other words, in the kinship system, political ideology, mythology, ritual, art, code of etiquette, and—why not?—cooking. I look for common properties by examining these structures, which are all partial expressions, though especially well suited to scientific study, of this entity called French, English, or any other society. For even in this case, the question is not to substitute one particular content for another or to reduce one to the other, but, rather, to discover whether the formal properties present homologies, and what kinds of homologies; contradictions, and what kind of contradictions; or dialectical relationships that may be expressed as transformations. Finally, I do not assert that such comparisons will always be fruitful, but that where they are fruitful, convergences will be extremely important in understanding the position of a society in relation to others of the same type, as well as the laws which govern its evolution in time.

Let us take an example different from the ones presented in the articles under discussion. Like language, it seems to me, the cuisine of a society may be analyzed into constituent elements, which in this case we might call "gustemes," and which may be organized according to certain structures of opposition and correlation. We might then distinguish English cooking from French cooking by means of three oppositions: *endogenous / exogenous* (that is, national versus exotic ingredients); *central / peripheral* (staple food versus its accompaniments); *marked / not marked* (that is, savory or bland). We should then be able to construct a chart, with + and − signs corresponding to the pertinent or nonpertinent character of each opposition in the system under consideration.

	ENGLISH CUISINE	FRENCH CUISINE
endogenous / exogenous	+	−
central / peripheral	+	−
marked / not marked	−	+

In other words, in English cuisine the main dishes of a meal are made from endogenous ingredients, prepared in a relatively bland fashion, and surrounded with more exotic accompaniments, in which all the differential values are strongly marked (for example, tea, fruitcake, orange marmalade, port wine). Conversely, in French cuisine the opposition *endogenous / exogenous* becomes very weak or disappears, and equally marked gustemes are combined together in a central as well as in a peripheral position.

Can this scheme also be applied to Chinese cooking? Yes, if we restrict ourselves to the preceding oppositions; no, if others are introduced (such as *sweet / sour*) which are mutually exclusive in French cuisine, in contrast to Chinese (or German), or if one also takes into account the fact that French cooking is diachronic (the same oppositions do not come into play in different parts of the meal). Thus French hors-d'oeuvres are built around the oppositions *maximal transformation / minimal transformation* of the type "charcuterie" [17] / raw foods, which does not recur synchronically in subsequent dishes, whereas Chinese cooking is conceived synchronically, that is, the same oppositions are suitable for all parts of the meal (which, for this reason, may be served all at one time). We must call upon other oppositions in order to account for all the properties of the structure; in order to account, for example, for the opposition between roast and stew, which plays such an important role in the native cooking of the interior of Brazil (roasting being the sensual way, and boiling the nutritive way— and they are mutually exclusive—of preparing meats). There are, finally, certain incompatibilities which are consciously maintained by the social group and which possess a normative value: *hot food / cold food; milky drink / alcoholic drink; fresh fruit / fermented fruit*, etc.

Once we have defined these differential structures, there is nothing absurd about inquiring whether they belong strictly to the sphere considered or whether they may be encountered (often in transformed fashion) in other spheres of the same society or in different societies. And, if we find these structures to be common to several spheres, we have the right to conclude that we have reached a significant knowledge of the unconscious attitudes of the society or societies under consideration.

I have intentionally selected this somewhat flimsy example because it is borrowed from contemporary societies. Haudricourt and Granai, who seem at times ready to concede the value of my method for the so-called primitive societies, attempt to differentiate these radically from the more complex societies. In the case of the latter, they say that a perception of the total society is impossible. Now I have shown that it is never a question of grasping the total society (an enterprise which cannot, strictly speaking, ever be successful), but rather of discerning the levels which are comparable and thus meaningful. I agree that these levels are more numerous, and that each, in itself, is more difficult to study in our gigantic modern societies than in small primitive tribes. Nevertheless, the difference is one of degree and not of kind. It is also true that in the modern Western world linguistic boundaries rarely coincide with cultural boundaries; however, the difficulty is not insuperable. Instead of comparing certain aspects of language with certain aspects of culture, we shall compare the differential aspects of language and culture in two societies, or subsocieties, which have language *or* culture in common, but not both. Thus, for instance, we might ask ourselves whether a correlation exists between the Swiss or Belgian way of speaking French and other characteristics that seem peculiar to these societies when we compare them to the corresponding characteristics of French language and society.

Nor do I agree with the assertion that social phenomena have a spatial dimension, whereas a language is unaffected by the number of its speakers. On the contrary, it seems to me possible to assume a priori that the "major" languages and the "minor" languages must express, in their structure and evolutionary development, not only the size of the area they cover, but also the presence at their boundaries of linguistic areas of different sizes than theirs.

The many misunderstandings in Haudricourt and Granai's article can be reduced to two central errors—first, overemphasizing the contrast between the diachronic and synchronic viewpoints; second, building a gap between language, which is seemingly arbitrary at all levels, and other social phenomena, which do not have the same character. It is striking that in making these assertions the authors chose to ignore Roman Jakobson's article, "Principes de phonologie historique," [18] and the equally important article in which Émile Benveniste examined Saussure's principle of the arbitrary nature of the linguistic sign.[19]

As to the first point, the authors assert that structural analysis confines the linguist or anthropologist to synchronic studies. Thus, it would inevitably lead, "at each stage considered, to the construction of a system irreducible to others," and, therefore, "to the denial of the history and evolution of language." A purely synchronic perspective would lead to the indefensible view that two phonemic interpretations of the same phonetic reality must be considered as equally valid.

We may address this criticism to certain neo-positivists in the United States, but not to European structuralists. Here Haudricourt and Granai are guilty of serious confusion. It is a healthy attitude, at certain stages of scientific investigation, to believe that, in the present state of knowledge, two interpretations of the same facts are equally valid. Until the twentieth century, physics was (and in many respects it still is) in this position. The error consists, not in recognizing this state of affairs when it exists, but in being satisfied with it and in not seeking to transcend it. Structural analysis already offers a way out of this situation, through the principle of parsimony, which Jakobson among others has constantly utilized, after borrowing it from the physicists: *Frustra fit per plura quod fieri potest per pauciora.* This principle leads us in a direction opposite to that of pragmatism, formalism, and neo-positivism, since the assertion that the most parsimonious explanation also comes closest to the truth rests, in the final analysis, upon the identity postulated between the laws of the universe and those of the human mind.

But, above all, we know since Jakobson's article that the opposition between synchronic and diachronic is to a large extent illusory and useful only in the preliminary stages of research. The following citation demonstrates this point:

> It would be a serious error to consider statics and the synchronic as synonymous. The static cross-section is a fiction: it is only a helpful scientific device, and not a particular mode of being. We can consider the perception of a film not only diachronically but also synchronically; however, the synchronic aspect of a film is not identical to an isolated image extracted from the film. Movement is also perceived in the synchronic aspect as well. The same is true of language.[20]

And the following statement by Jakobson applies directly to the comments, in themselves very interesting, made by the authors on the evolution of spoken French:

> Attempts to identify the *synchronic,* the *static,* and the area of application of *teleology,* on the one hand, and the *diachronic,* the *dynamic,* and the sphere of *mechanical causality,* on the other, unjustifiably restrict the scope of the synchronic, make historical linguistics an agglomeration of disconnected facts, and create the illusion, which is both superficial and dangerous, of a chasm between the synchronic and the diachronic.[21]

Haudricourt and Granai's second error consists in rigidly contrasting language—which "offers us a twofold arbitrary relation," that between word and concept and that between the meaning of the concept and the physical object which it denotes—and society, which "is directly related . . . to nature . . . in a large number of cases"; [22] in so doing, they restrict society's symbolic function.

I could be satisfied with the qualification "a large number of cases" and reply that I am concerned precisely with the other cases. But since the implicit assertion of the authors seems to me one of the most dangerous possible, I shall dwell on it for a moment.

As early as 1939, Benveniste speculated whether the linguist might one day be able to solve the metaphysical problem of the congruence between mind and universe. While he might be better advised to relinquish it for the moment, still he ought to realize that "to formulate this relationship as arbitrary is for the linguist a means of evading the question. . . ." [23] Haudricourt, since he is the linguist of the team, remains on the defensive. And yet, as an ethnographer and a technologist, he knows that technology is not so natural, or language so arbitrary, as he declares.

Not even the linguistic arguments put forth in support of this contrast are satisfactory. Does the term *pomme de terre* [potato] really stem from an arbitrary convention "denoting an object that is not an apple and does not lie in the earth"? And is the arbitrary character of the concept made clearer when we note that in English the *pomme de terre* is called *potato*? Actually the French term inspired to a large extent by didactic considerations, reflects the specific technical and economic conditions which prevailed when this food was finally accepted in France. It also reflects the verbal forms current in those countries from which the plant was imported. Finally, *pomme de terre*, if not inevitable, was at least one of the likely names, because the word *pomme*, which originally meant any rounded fruit with stone or seeds, had already provided a number of functional variants established in previous usage, such as *pomme de pin* [pine cone], *pomme de chêne* [acorn], *pomme de coing* [quince], *pomme de grenade* [pomegranate], *pomme d'orange* [orange], etc. Can a choice which has historical, geographical, and sociological connotations, as well as strictly linguistic ones, really be considered arbitrary? Let us say, rather, that the French *pomme de terre* was not prescribed, but existed as a possible solution (and resulted, moreover, by contrast, in *pomme de l'air*, which is so common in the language of chefs and which replaces the expression *pomme vulgaire*, frequent in archaic French for the fruit of the apple tree, since the latter is endowed with stronger connotations of vulgarity). The solution is the result of a choice among pre-existing possibilities.

In addition to being arbitrary on the conceptual level, language is also claimed by the authors to be arbitrary on the phonemic level: "There is . . . no intelligible relationship between the pronunciation of a word and the concept it represents. What possible relationship, for example, can exist betwen the closure of the lips at the beginning and the end of the word *pomme* and the rounded fruit which it denotes?" [24]

The Saussurean principle here invoked by the authors cannot be disputed if we are concerned only with the level of linguistic description. This principle has played an important role in the science of language by permitting the liberation of phonetics from naturalistic metaphysical interpretations. Nevertheless, it represents only one phase in the evolution of linguistic thought, and when we attempt to perceive things from a more general viewpoint, its scope becomes limited and its precision blunted.

To simplify my argument, I will say that the linguistic sign is arbitrary a priori, but ceases to be arbitrary a posteriori. Nothing existing a priori in the nature of certain preparations made of fermented milk requires the sound-form *fromage* [cheese], or rather, *from-* (since the ending is shared with other words). It is sufficient to compare the French *froment* [wheat], whose semantic content is entirely different, to the English *cheese*, which means the same thing as *fromage*, though it utilizes different phonemic material. So far, the linguistic sign appears to be arbitrary.

On the other hand, it is in no way certain that these phonemic options, which are arbitrary in relation to the *designatum*, do not, once the choice has been made, imperceptibly affect, perhaps not the general meaning of words, but their position within a semantic environment. This a posteriori influence works on two levels, the phonemic and the lexical.

On a phonemic level, phenomena of synesthesia have often been described and studied. Practically all children and a good many adults—though for the most part adults will deny it—spontaneously associate sounds, whether phonemes or the timbre of musical instruments, with colors and forms. These associations also exist on the level of vocabulary in such highly structured areas as calendar terminology. Although the associated colors may not always be the same for each phoneme, it would appear that individuals construct, with variable terms, a system of relations which corresponds, analogically and on another level, to the structural phonemic properties of the language considered. Thus an individual whose mother tongue is Hungarian sees vowels in the following fashion: *i, í*, white; *e*, yellow; *é*, a shade darker; *a*, tan; *á*, a shade darker; *o*, dark blue; *ó*, black; *u, ú*, both red, as fresh blood. And Jakobson remarks, in connection with the preceding observation:

> The ascending chromatism of the colors parallel to the gradation from high to low vowels and the contrast of light and dark parallel to the opposition of front and back vowels are consistent except for the *u* vowels which show a deviating perception. The ambivalent character of the rounded front vowels is clearly indicated: *ö, ő* very dark blue base with light blurred spots spread on it; *ü, ű* a very red base with pinkish spots on it.[25]

It is, therefore, not a question of peculiarities which can be explained through the personal history and predilections of each individual. Not only may the study of these phenomena disclose, as stated by the authors we have just cited, "much of importance to the psychological and theoretical aspects of linguistics," [26] but it leads us directly to a consideration of the "natural bases" of the phonemic system, that is, the structure of the brain. Re-examining this question in a later issue of the same journal, D. I. Mason concludes his analysis as follows: ". . . there probably exists in the human brain a map of colors part of which is similar topologically to a map of sound frequencies there. If there is, as suggested by Martin Joos, a map, in the brain, of mouth shapes . . . then this would appear to be the *inverse*, in one sense, of both the frequency map and the color map. . . ." [27]

If we admit, therefore, in accordance with the Saussurean principle, that nothing compels, a priori, certain sound-clusters to denote certain objects, it appears probable, nonetheless, that once they are adopted, these sound-clusters transmit particular shadings to the semantic content with which they have become associated. It has been pointed out that high-frequency vowels (from *i* to *e*) are preferred in English poetry to suggest pale or dim colors, whereas low-frequency vowels (from *u* to *a*) refer to rich or dark colors.[28] Mallarmé complained that the phonemic values of the French words *jour* and *nuit* were the opposite of their respective meanings. As soon as French and English ascribe heterogeneous phonemic values to words denoting the same food, the semantic positions of the terms are no longer entirely the same. As for myself, who has spoken English exclusively during certain periods of my life without, however, becoming bilingual, *fromage* and *cheese* mean the same thing, but with different shadings. *Fromage* evokes a certain heaviness, an oily substance not prone to crumble, and a thick flavor. This term is especially suitable for denoting what [French] dairymen call *pâtes grasses* [high in butter-fat content], whereas *cheese*, which is lighter, fresher, a little sour, and which crumbles in the mouth (compare the shape of the mouth) reminds me immediately of the French *fromage blanc* [a variety of cottage cheese]. The "archetypal cheese," therefore, is not always the same for me, according to whether I am thinking in French or in English.

When we consider vocabulary a posteriori, that is, after it has been constructed, words lose a good deal of their arbitrary character, for the meaning that we give them is no longer solely a function of convention. The meaning of a word depends on the way in which each language breaks up the realm of meaning to which the word belongs; and it is a function of the presence or absence of other words denoting related meanings. Thus *time* and *temps* cannot mean the same thing in French and English, if only because English also has the term *weather*, which French lacks. Conversely, *chair* and *armchair* belong, retrospectively, to a more restricted semantic environment than *chaise* and *fauteuil*. Words are also contaminated by their homophones, despite differences in meaning. If a large number of Frenchmen were asked to provide free associations to the series: *quintette* [quintet], *sextuor* [sextet], *septuor* [septet], I would be very much surprised if these associations were related only to the number of musical instruments and if the meaning of *quintette* were not influenced to some extent by *quinte* (*de toux*) [coughing spell] and the meaning of *sextuor* by *sexe*.[29] *Septuor* suggests a feeling of duration, owing to the hesitant modulation of the first syllable which the second then resolves, as if by a majestic chord. Michel Leiris, in his literary works, has initiated a study of this unconscious structuring of vocabulary, but a scientific theory still remains to be constructed. We would be mistaken in seeing this as a poetic game, rather than as the perception, as through a telescope, of phenomena which—though they are quite remote from lucid consciousness and rational thought—play a vital role in our growing understanding of the nature of linguistic phenomena.[30]

The arbitrary character of the linguistic sign is thus only provisional. Once a sign has been created its function becomes explicit, as related, on the one hand, to the biological structure of the brain and, on the other, to the aggregate of other signs—that is, to the linguistic universe, which always tends to be systematic.

Traffic regulations have also arbitrarily assigned differential semantic values to the red and green traffic signals. The opposite choice could have been made. And yet, if it had, the emotional and symbolic overtones of red and green would not simply be reversed thereby. In the current system, red evokes danger, violence, and blood, whereas green is associated with hope, serenity, and the placid unfolding of a natural process such as that of vegetation. But what would happen if red were to stand for "go" and green for "stop"? Red would no doubt be perceived as an expression of human warmth and communication and green as an icy and venomous symbol. Red, then, would not merely replace green, and vice versa. The choice of the sign may be arbitrary, but it retains an inherent value—an independent content—which becomes associated with its semantic function and modulates it. If the opposition *red/green* is inverted, its semantic content shifts perceptibly, for red remains red and green green, not only as sensory stimuli in their own right, each endowed with its own inherent value, but also because they constitute the supports of a traditional symbolism which, once it has come into historical existence, can no longer be manipulated with complete freedom.

When we shift from language to other social phenomena, we are surprised that Haudricourt permitted himself to be influenced by an empirical and naturalistic conception of the relations between the geographical environment and society, when he himself has done so much to prove the artificial character of such a relationship. I have just demonstrated that language is not really such an arbitrary thing, but the relationship between nature and society is far more arbitrary than the article cited would lead us to believe. Need I recall that all mythical thought and ritual consist in a reorganization of sensory experience within the context of a semantic system? And that the reasons why different societies choose to utilize or reject certain natural products and, if they do utilize them, the modes of employment they choose depend not only upon the intrinsic properties of the products but also on the symbolic values ascribed to them? I shall not list examples that can be found in any textbook; I shall limit myself to a single authority, one who cannot be suspected of idealism—Karl Marx. In the *Contribution to a Critique of Political Economy*, he examines the reasons which have led humanity to select precious metals as standards of value. He enumerates several factors which refer to the "natural properties" of gold and silver: homogeneity, uniform quality, divisibility into any number of fractions which can always be recombined by melting, high specific weight, scarcity, portability, and durability. He then comments:

> Furthermore, gold and silver are not only negatively superfluous, i.e., dispensable articles, but their aesthetic properties make them the natural material of luxury, ornamentation, splendor, festive occasions, in short, the positive form of abundance and wealth. They appear, in a way, as spontaneous light brought out from the underground world, since silver reflects all rays of light in their original combination, and gold only the color of highest intensity, viz., red light. The sensation of color is, generally speaking, the most popular form of aesthetic sense. The etymological connection between the names of the precious metals, and the relations of colors, in the different Indo-Germanic languages has been established by Jacob Grimm. . . .[31]

Marx himself, therefore, suggests that we uncover the symbolic systems which underlie both language and man's relationship with the universe. "It is only through the habit of everyday life that we come to think it perfectly plain and commonplace, that a social relation of production should take on the form of a thing. . . ."[32]

But as soon as the various aspects of social life—economic, linguistic, etc.—are expressed as relationships, anthropology will become a general theory of relationships. Then it will be possible to analyze societies in terms of the differential features character-istic of the systems of relationships which define them.

NOTES

1. A. G. Haudricourt and G. Granai, "Linguistique et sociologie," *Cahiers internationaux de Sociologie*, n.s., XIX (1955) pp. 114-29. Regarding Gurvitch's article, see Chapter XVI of this volume.
2. Chapters III and IV.
3. A. G. Haudricourt and G. Granai, "Linguistique et sociologie," *op. cit.*, p. 127
4. *Loc. cit.*
5. *Ibid.*, p. 114.
6. *Ibid.*, p. 126.
7. Roman Jakobson and M. Halle, *Fundamentals of Language* (The Hague: 1956) pp. 27, 28, 17, and *passim*.
8. *Ibid.*, p. 17. And, as the authors declare, farther on, "the study of inva-riants within the phonemic pattern of one language must be supple-mented by a search for universal invariants in the phonemic pattern-ing of language" (*ibid.*, p. 28).
9. See Chapter XV of this volume.
10. G. Gurvitch, "Le Concept de structure sociale," *Cahiers internationaux de Sociologie*, n.s., XIX (1955), p. 11.
11. See, for art, Chapter XIII of this volume; for myth, Chapters X and XI; for ritual, Chapter XII.
12. Haudricourt and Granai, "Linguistique et sociologie," *op. cit.*, p. 128.
13. See Chapter IV.
14. Chapter III, above.
15. For example, certain articles by E. Sapir. See E. Sapir, *Selected Writ-ings in Language, Culture and Personality*, ed. by D. Mandelbaum (Berkeley: 1949).
16. Haudricourt and Granai, "Linguistique et sociologie," *op. cit.*, p. 126.
[17. *Translator's note:* "Charcuterie" refers to cold meats, sausages, patés, etc., which make up a major part of hors-d'oeuvres.]
18. In N. Troubetzkoy, ed., *Principes de phonologie* (French translation; Paris: 1949), pp. 315-6.
19. E. Benveniste, "Nature du signe linguistique," *Acta Linguistica*, I, (1939), p. 1.
20. R. Jakobson, "Principes de phonologie historique," *op. cit.*, pp. 333-4.
21. *Ibid.*, pp. 335-6.
22. Haudricourt and Granai, "Linguistique et sociologie," *op. cit.*, pp. 126-7.
23. E. Benveniste, "Nature du signe linguistique," *op. cit.*, p. 26.
24. Haudricourt and Granai, *loc. cit.*
25. G. A. Reichard, R. Jakobson, and E. Werth, "Language and Synes-thesia," *Word*, V, No. 2 (1949), p. 226.
26. *Ibid.*, p. 224.
27. D. I. Mason, "Synesthesia and Sound Spectra," *Word*, VIII, No. 1 (1952), p. 41, citing Martin Joos, *Acoustic Phonetics* (supplement to *Language:* Language Monographs, II, No. 23 (April-June 1948), p. 46.

28. *Ibid.*, p. 40, citing M. M. McDermott, *Vocal Sounds in Poetry* (1940).

29. This is so true for me that I have difficulty in not using the term *sextette* in French (which would be an Anglicism), perhaps because of its feminine inflection.

30. M. Leiris, *La Règle du jeu*: Vol. I, *Biffures* (Paris: 1948), Vol. II, *Fourbis* (Paris: 1955).

31. K. Marx, *A Contribution to the Critique of Political Economy*, trans. N. I. Stone (Chicago: 1911), p. 211.

32. *Ibid.*, p. 30.

PART TWO

Social Organization

CHAPTER VI

The Concept of
Archaism in Anthropology

D ESPITE ALL ITS IMPERFECTIONS, and the de-
served criticism which it has received, it seems that *primitive*, in the
absence of a better term, has definitely taken hold in the contemporary anthropological and sociological vocabulary. We thus study
"primitive" societies. But what do we mean by this? Taken in its
broad sense, the expression is clear enough. First, we know that
"primitive" denotes a vast array of non-literate peoples, who are
thus not accessible through the research methods of the conventional historian. Second, they have only recently been affected by
the expansion of industrial civilization and, because of their social
structure and world view, the concepts of economics and political
philosophy regarded as basic to our own society are inapplicable to
them. But where shall we draw the line of demarcation? Ancient
Mexico fulfills the second criterion, but hardly the first. Archaic
Egypt and China are open to anthropological research, certainly
not because writing was unknown to them, but because the scope
of preserved documents is not sufficient for us to dispense with

other methods. Furthermore, neither lies outside the area of industrial civilization; rather, they precede it in time. Conversely, the fact that the folklorist works in the present and within an industrial civilization does not cut him off from the anthropologist. The last twenty-five years in the United States have witnessed tremendous progress in social science research—progress which clearly expresses a crisis in the values of contemporary American society (whose boundless self-confidence has begun to wane and which seeks a measure of self-understanding through examination by detached professional observers). But this progress, which has opened to anthropologists industry, the agencies of national and municipal government, and sometimes even the armed forces, implicitly proclaims that the difference between anthropology and the other sciences of man is one of method rather than of subject matter.

It is only the subject matter, however, that we wish to consider here. It is striking to note that, in losing awareness of its particular subject matter, American anthropology is permitting a disintegration of the method—too narrowly empirical, but precise and scrupulous—with which it was endowed by its founders, in favor of a social metaphysics which is often simplistic and which uses dubious techniques of investigation. This method cannot be consolidated, much less refined, except through an increasingly exact knowledge of its own subject matter, its specific characteristics, and its distinctive elements. We are far from having achieved this. To be sure, the term *primitive* now seems to be safe from the confusion inherent in its etymological meaning and reinforced by an obsolete evolutionism. A primitive people is not a backward or retarded people; indeed it may possess, in one realm or another, a genius for invention or action that leaves the achievements of civilized peoples far behind. One might cite as illustrations the true "sociological planning" evident in the study of family organization among Australian societies; the integration of emotional life within a complex system of rights and obligations in Melanesia; and, almost everywhere, the utilization of religious feeling to establish a viable, if not always harmonious, synthesis of individual aspirations and the social order.

Nor do primitive peoples lack history, although its development often eludes us. The work of Seligman on the natives of New Guinea[1] shows how a seemingly systematic social structure evolved and has been maintained through a succession of contingent events: wars, migrations, rivalries, and conquests. Stanner has described the upheaval resulting from the enactment in a contemporary society of new marriage and kinship regulations: The "Young Turks," reformers converted to the doctrines of a neighboring people, successfully introduced a more refined system in place of the simpler ancient institutions. And natives absent from their tribe for several years are no longer able, upon their return, to adapt themselves to the new order.[2] In North America, for example, the number, distribution, and reciprocal relations of Hopi clans were not the same two centuries ago as they are today.[3]

All this we know, but what have we learned from it? A distinction, theoretically ambiguous and in fact impracticable, between the so-called primitives as conventionally designated (including almost all the peoples studied by anthropologists) and a few rare "true primitives"—a term which, according to Marcel Mauss,[4] could include only the Australians and Fuegians. We have just seen how the Australians should be regarded. Would the Fuegians (and a few other South American tribes mentioned by other authors)[5] be the only ones, therefore, along with certain Pygmy groups, to enjoy the peculiar distinction of having endured without possessing any history? This curious assertion rests on a twofold argument. First of all, the history of these peoples is completely unknown to us, and on account of the lack or paucity of oral traditions and archaeological remains, it is forever beyond our reach. From this we cannot conclude that it does not exist. Second, owing to the archaic nature of their techniques and institutions, these peoples recall what we have been able to reconstruct about the social organization of peoples that lived ten or twenty thousand years ago. Hence the conclusion that they remain today just as they were in that remote period. We leave it to philosophy to explain why in some cases something happened and why in other cases nothing happened.

Once the problem is advanced to this philosophical level, it seems insoluble. Let us suppose, as a theoretical possibility, that certain ethnic fragments were for some reason left behind in the uneven forward march of humanity. Since then they have been evolving at a hardly perceptible pace, preserving until now the greater part of their primeval traits; or, on the other hand, let us suppose that their evolutionary momentum met an untimely end and left them frozen in a state of permanent inertia. But the real problem cannot be stated in these terms. When we look today at one or another seemingly archaic people, can we establish certain criteria whose presence or absence would permit us to make a decision, not, to be sure, in the affirmative—we saw that the hypothesis is ideological and not subject to demonstration—but in the negative? If this negative demonstration could be applied to each known case, the question would be settled practically, if not theoretically. But then a new problem would have to be resolved. If consideration of the past is excluded, what formal structural characteristics would differentiate the so-called primitive societies from those we call modern or civilized?

These are questions we might profitably bear in mind when considering those South American societies for which the hypothesis of original archaism has recently been revived.

Ever since Martius,[6] anthropologists have been in the habit of dividing the indigenous cultures of tropical America into two major categories. The cultures of the coast and the Orinoco-Amazon system are characterized by either a forest habitat or a river-bank habitat in close proximity to the forest, an agriculture which is rudimentary in technique but characterized by extensive clearings, with many species of plants under cultivation, a clearly differentiated social organization that suggests or emphasizes an unmistakable social hierarchy, and a complex of collective houses testifying to the level of native craftsmanship as well as to the degree of integration of the society. The Arawak, Tupi, and Carib share these characteristic traits in various degrees and with regional variations. On the other hand, the peoples of central Brazil have a more rudimentary culture. Sometimes nomadic, and unfamiliar with the construction of permanent dwellings and pottery, they live by food-gathering or, when they are sedentary, by individual or group hunting rather than by raising crops, which they consider to be a secondary occupation. Martius believed that he could group into a single cultural and linguistic family, to which he gave the name Ge, peoples that actually differ in language and other aspects of culture. He considered them the descendants of the Tapuya savages, described by sixteenth-century travelers as the traditional enemies of the coastal Tupi. The Tupi were assumed to have driven the Tapuya into the interior in the course of migrations which led to the Tupi occupation of the coast and the Amazon Valley. These migrations ended only in the seventeenth century, and there are even more recent examples of them.

Within the last thirty years this apparently likely hypothesis was shaken by the investigations of the late Curt Nimuendajú among several tribes of the so-called Ge family living in the savanna between the coastal escarpment and the Araguaia Valley in eastern and northeastern Brazil. Among the Ramcocamecra, Cayapó, Sherente, and Apinayé, Nimuendajú found, first of all, a more original agriculture than had been supposed: Some of these tribes cultivate species (*Cissus sp.*) which are unknown elsewhere. But, above all, in the area of social organization, these so-called primitives had devised systems of an astonishing complexity: exogamous moieties cross-cutting recreational or ceremonial moieties, secret societies, men's clubs, and age grades. These structures are ordinarily associated with much higher cultural levels. We may conclude either that these structures are not restricted to higher cultures or that the archaism of the so-called Ge is less indisputable than it appears. Interpreters of Nimuendajú's findings, especially Lowie and Cooper, inclined toward the first explanation. Thus Lowie writes that ". . . the appearance of matrilineal moieties on the Bororo-Canella level indicates the local origin of such institutions among hunter-gatherers or at best incipient farmers." [7] But do the Ge and their parallels on the western plateau, the Bororo and Nambicuara, deserve such an unqualified definition? Is it not also possible to see them as a regressive people, that is, one that descended from a higher level of material life and social organization and retained one trait or another as a vestige of former conditions? To this hypothesis, suggested to him in the course of private correspondence, Lowie replied that this alternative was admissible, but that it would remain dubious ". . . until a particular model is produced of which the Bororo-Canella organization is the demonstrably attenuated replica. . . ." [8]

There are many ways of meeting this requirement, and the first is no doubt deceptive in its simplicity. Yet the pre-Columbian cultures of Peru and Bolivia had something resembling dual organization: The inhabitants of the Inca capital were divided into two groups, Upper Cuzco and Lower Cuzco, and the significance of the division was not merely geographic, for at the ceremonies the mummies of the ancestors were solemnly placed in two parallel rows, as was done in Chou China.[9] And Lowie himself, commenting on my description of a Bororo village laid out according to a plan that reflected its complex social structure, refers in this connection to the layout of Tiahuanaco as it was reconstructed by Bandelier.[10] The same dualism, or at any rate its fundamental themes, may be observed also in Central America, in the ritual antagonism of the Aztec Eagle and Jaguar societies. The two animals play a role in the mythology of the Tupi and other South American tribes, as seen in the motif of the "Sacred Jaguar" and the ritual capture of a harpy-eagle in native villages on the Xingu and Machado rivers. These resemblances between the Tupi and Aztec societies extend to other aspects of religious life. Is the concrete model, of which the primitive cultures of the tropical savanna present an attenuated replica, then to be found in the Andean highlands?

This would be an oversimplified explanation. Between the great civilizations of the highlands and the barbarians of the savanna and forest, contacts have undoubtedly been in the form of trading, military reconnaissance, and forays. The natives of the Chaco knew by hearsay of the existence of the Incas and described that amazing kingdom to the first explorers. Orellana found gold objects in the middle Amazon region; and metal axes of Peruvian origin have been excavated as far as the São Paulo coast. Yet the rapid cycles of expansion and decline of the Andean civilizations allowed for only sporadic exchanges of short duration. On the other hand, the social organization of the Aztecs and Incas reached us through the accounts of conquerors who were enamored of their discovery, and who ascribed to it a systematic character that it probably did not possess. In both cases, we witness the ephemeral union of highly varied cultures, often quite ancient and heterogeneous. From the pre-eminent position temporarily occupied by one tribe among so many others, we cannot conclude that that tribe's particular customs were observed throughout the whole region where its influence was felt, even if its dignitaries had an interest in giving that impression, especially to the European newcomers. Neither in Peru nor in Mexico was there ever actually an empire whose colonized peoples, whether willing borrowers or merely dazzled witnesses, attempted to copy the model on a more modest scale. The analogies between high and low cultures stem from more basic facts.

Dual organization is actually only one trait among several which are common to both types. These traits are distributed in the most sporadic fashion. They disappear and reappear irrespective of geographical distance or of the cultural level considered, as though they were scattered at random over the entire continent. We find them present here, absent there, now grouped, now isolated, richly developed in a high civilization, or meagerly preserved in the lowest. How could we possibly account for each of these occurrences as the result of diffusion? In each case it would be necessary to find a historical contact, to set its date, and to trace an itinerary of migration. Not only would the task be impossible to carry out, but it would not correspond to reality, which presents us with a global picture that should be understood as such. We are dealing with a vast syncretic phenomenon, whose historical and local causes antecede by many years the beginnings of what we call the pre-Columbian history of America. Sound method compels us to accept this syncretism as the starting point from which the higher cultures of Mexico and Peru sprang and expanded.

Is it possible to find a reflection of this starting point in the present low cultures of the savanna? Actually there is no conceivable transition; it is impossible to reconstruct stages between, let us say, the cultural level of the Ge and the beginnings of the Maya culture or the archaic levels of the Valley of Mexico. Thus, all these cultures undoubtedly derive from a common foundation, which must be sought on a level intermediate between the present cultures of the savanna and the ancient civilizations of the highlands.

Numerous facts support this hypothesis. It was archaeology that first discovered centers of a relatively developed civilization that existed until the recent past throughout tropical America: in the Antilles, on Marajó island, on the Cunani river, on the Lower Amazon, at the mouth of the Tocantins, on the Mojos plain, and at Santiago del Estero. The large petroglyphs of the Orinoco Valley and other regions presuppose collective work, of which we still find striking evidence today in the clearing and cultivation of garden plots among the Tapirapé.[11] At the beginning of the historic period, Orellana observed a large variety of cultivated crops along the Amazon. Can we not assume that at the height of their development the inferior tribes participated, at least to some extent, in the vitality whose manifestations we have just recalled?

Dual organization itself is not a differential characteristic of the populations of the savanna. It was reported among the Parintintin and the Mundurucú; it may have existed among the Tembe and Tucuna, and certainly occurred at the two extremities of Brazil, among Arawak cultures of such high development as the Palikur and the Terena. We ourselves found it, as a survival, among the Tupi-Cawahib of the Upper Machado. We may thus delineate, in either matrilineal or patrilineal form, an area of dual organization which extends from the right bank of the Tocantins to the Madeira River. It is impossible to define dual organization in South America as a trait typical of the most primitive tribes, since they share it with their forest neighbors, who are expert horticulturists and head-hunters with a much higher level of culture.

One should not separate the social organization of the peoples of the savanna from that of their neighbors in forested valleys and on river banks. On the other hand, one sometimes places on so-called archaic levels tribes which actually have quite different cultures. The Bororo offer a particularly striking example of such false analogies. In order to make them into "true primitives" or an approximation thereof, a text by Von den Steinen is invoked: "The women, accustomed to digging up wild roots in the jungle, began to cut down the young (*manioc*) plants by carefully turning over the soil in the hope of finding edible roots. This tribe of hunters lacked any true agriculture and, especially, the patience to wait for the tubers to develop." [12] From this it is concluded that prior to their contact with the expeditionary corps which was to subjugate them, the Bororo lived exclusively by hunting and food-gathering. What is overlooked is the fact that the observation referred to the garden plots of Brazilian soldiers, not those of the natives, and that, according to the same author, "the Bororo did not in the least care for the gifts of civilization." [13] It is sufficient to place these remarks in their context, which provides a vivid picture of the disintegration of Bororo society under the influence of its so-called pacifiers, in order to grasp their anecdotal character. What do such comments teach us? That at that time the Bororo did not till the soil? (But for more than fifty years they had been ruthlessly hunted down and exterminated by the colonists.) Or that the natives found it more profitable to loot the gardens of the military posts than to clear the land themselves?

A few years later, in 1901, Cook observed "fields of small yellow maize" among the Bororo of the Ponte de Pedra River (then a little known tributary of the São Lourenço River).[14] Concerning the villages of the Rio Vermelho, which retained their independence, Radin wrote in 1905: "The Bororo plant very little in the Colonia Theresa Christina and for that reason, perhaps, Professor Von den Steinen, who only saw them plow under compulsion, believed that they had never been an agricultural nation. Frič, visiting those still in a wild state, discovered many plantations carefully kept."[15] Furthermore, the same author describes an agrarian rite: "A ceremony of blessing; to taste the corn before the ceremony would mean certain death. . . ."[16] This ritual consists in washing the barely ripe corn husk, which is then placed before the *aroetorrari* (or shaman), who dances and sings for several hours at a stretch, smokes continuously, and thus enters a kind of hypnotic ecstasy. Trembling all over, ". . . he bites into the husk, uttering shrieks from time to time. A similar ceremony is repeated whenever a large animal . . . or fish . . . is taken. It is the firm belief of the Bororo that should anyone touch unconsecrated meat or maize . . . he and his entire tribe would perish."[17] If we remember that except for the villages on the Rio Vermelho, Bororo society had completely disintegrated between 1880 and 1910, we can hardly believe that the natives found the time and took the trouble, in so short and tragic a period of time, to dignify their newly adopted agriculture with a complicated agrarian ritual—unless they already possessed the ritual, which of course would imply the traditional character of agriculture.

Can we ever speak, then, of true hunters and gatherers in South America? Certain tribes seem today very primitive, such as the Guayaki of Paraguay, the Siriono of Bolivia, the Nambicuara of the Tapajoz head-waters, and the food-gatherers of the Orinoco Valley. Yet those who are completely unfamiliar with horticulture are rare, and they are all found isolated among groups of a higher level. The history of each of these tribes, if we only had the knowledge, would better account for their special characteristics than does the hypothesis of an archaic level of which they are claimed to be a survival. In most cases, these tribes practice rudimentary horticulture, which does not replace hunting, fishing, or collecting. This is not enough to prove that they are newcomers to horticulture rather than horticulturists who regressed owing to new living conditions which were imposed upon them.

The late Father J. M. Cooper suggested a division of the tribes of tropical America into two main groups, which he called "silval" and "marginal." The marginal is subdivided in turn into "savannal" and "intrasilval." [18] We shall consider only the main distinction, which is perhaps of practical utility, but which should not be thought of as a true representation of the facts. Nothing proves, or even suggests, that the savanna was permanently settled in the earliest times. On the other hand, it seems that even in their present habitat the "savannal" tribes seek to preserve the remnants of a forest mode of life.

No geographical distinction is clearer and more fundamental to the thinking of the South American native than that between savanna and forest. The savanna is unsuitable not only for horticulture but also for the gathering of wild products, since vegetation and animal life are scanty. The Brazilian forest, by contrast, is prodigal in fruit and game, and the soil is rich and fertile so long as it is barely scratched. The contrast between the forest cultivators and the savanna hunters may have a cultural significance, but it has no natural basis. In tropical Brazil, the forest and the river banks are the most favorable environments for horticulture, hunting, and fishing, *as well as* for collecting and gathering. And if the savanna is poor, it is poor from all these points of view. We cannot distinguish between the pre-horticultural mode of life retained by the peoples of the savanna and the superior culture of the forest, based on slash-and-burn horticulture, since the forest peoples are not only the better horticulturists but also the better collectors and gatherers. The reason for this is quite simple: There are many more things to gather in the forest than outside it. Horticulture and food-gathering co-exist in the two environments, but both these modes of life are better developed in the one than in the other.

The greater mastery of forest societies over the natural environment is manifested with respect to wild species as well as to cultivated species. The plant environment varies from east to west in the tropical forest, but the way of life varies less than the species used. Thus the craft of basketry is identical, though the baskets may be made from different types of palm; and narcotic drugs play the same ritual role, although they are prepared from different plants. The products change, while the customs remain. On the other hand, the savanna exercises a negative influence; it does not open up new possibilities but, rather, restricts those of the forest. There is no such thing as a "savannal culture." What is called by this name is an attenuated replica, a weak echo, an impotent imitation, of forest culture. The food-gathering peoples would have chosen a forest habitat just as the horticulturists did; or, more accurately, they would have remained in the forest if they had been able to do so. If they are not there, it is not because they belong to a so-called "savannal culture," but because they have been driven from the forest. Thus the Tapuya were pushed into the interior by the great Tupi migrations.

Having clarified this matter, we readily admit that in any particular case the new habitat may have exerted a positive influence. The hunting skill of the Bororo was no doubt stimulated or fostered by forays into the game-filled marshes of the middle course of the Paraguay. And the place which fishing occupies in the economy of the Xingu region is undoubtedly more important than it was in the northern regions from which the Auetö and Camayura came. But whenever they have the opportunity, the tribes of the savanna cling to the forest and to the conditions of forest life. All the horticulture is carried out in the narrow bands of forest which, even in the savanna, fringe the major rivers. In fact, it would be impossible to cultivate elsewhere, and the Bacairi deride the legendary deer who stupidly planted his manioc in the bush.[19] The natives travel far to reach the forest and to find certain products necessary to their technology, such as thick bamboo stems, river shells, and seeds. Even more striking are the elements involved in the utilization of wild plants, to which the forest tribes dedicate a wealth of knowledge and techniques, for example, the extraction of starch from the pith of certain palm trees, the alcoholic fermentation of stored seeds, and the use of poisonous plants as food. Among the peoples of the savanna this amounts to large-scale gathering followed by immediate consumption, as

though the need had suddenly arisen to compensate for the disappearance of a differently balanced diet. Even collecting and gathering, among them, are impoverished and limited techniques.[20]

The preceding considerations apply only to tropical America.
But if they are correct, they permit us to establish more broadly
valid criteria, which may be employed whenever a hypothesis of
authentic archaism is advanced. There seems to be no doubt that
the same conclusion would be reached in each case, namely, that
true archaism is the realm of the archaeologist and the prehistorian,
but that the social anthropologist who studies contemporary societies should not forget that, in order to be such, *they must have
lived, endured, and, therefore, changed.* Actually a change, if it
brings conditions of life and organization so elementary that they
suggest an archaic state, only amounts to regression. Is it possible to
distinguish, through an internal analysis, pseudo-archaism from real
archaism?

The problem of the primitiveness of a society is usually raised
by the contrast which the society offers in relation to its neighbors, near or remote. A difference in cultural level is observed
between this society and those to which it may be most easily compared. Its culture is poorer, owing to the absence or inadequacy of
those features—permanent dwellings, horticulture, animal hus-
bandry, techniques of stone-polishing, weaving, and pottery—
the habitual use, if not always the invention of which, dates back
to the Neolithic period. With these traits we generally associate—
though in this case the induction is less certain—a differentiated
social organization. There is no doubt that in certain regions of
the world these contrasts exist and even persist in modern times.
Yet, in the pseudo-archaic instances considered here, they are not
exclusive. These societies do not differ from their more highly
evolved neighbors in all respects, but only in some, while in other
respects numerous analogies exist.

The most striking example, which we have already noted, is
that of dual organization. In South America, this institution (or,
more accurately, this structural pattern) is a trait common to several societies, including the most primitive as well as the most advanced and a whole series of intermediate ones. The Bororo and
Nambicuara languages also show affinities with dialects lying out-

side the geographical area of those tribes and characteristic of higher civilizations. The physical types, so different in the two groups, suggest a southern origin in one case, a northern origin in the other. The same applies to social organization, certain kinship institutions, political institutions, and mythology—all of which recall one or another trait whose most developed expression must be sought outside the area. If, therefore, the problem of archaism is raised by the differences between certain societies, we shall immediately observe that in the case of pseudo-archaic societies these differences never extend to the whole society: Some resemblances remain to offset the contrasts.

Let us now consider the internal structure of a so-called "archaic" society, rather than its relationship to other societies. A strange sight awaits us, for this structure is full of incongruities and contradictions. The example of the Nambicuara is particularly illuminating in this respect, since the peoples of this linguistic family, which is scattered over a territory half as large as France, present one of the most primitive cultural levels now to be found in the world. At least some of their bands are completely unfamiliar with the construction of permanent dwellings and pottery; weaving and horticulture are reduced to their simplest forms; and the nomadic groups of five or six families, which are joined under the leadership of a chief who possesses no real authority, seem to be motivated entirely by the requirements of food-gathering and the ever-present threat of famine. Yet, instead of the absolute simplicity one would expect from such rudimentary skills and such sketchy organization, Nambicuara culture is full of riddles.

Let us recall the contrast among the Bororo between a developed agrarian ritual and the apparent absence of agriculture, whose existence, however, is disclosed by a more careful investigation. The Nambicuara present, in a related realm, an analogous but reversed situation. The Nambicuara are highly skilled poisoners. (In tropical America, where manioc is eaten, food and poison are not mutually exclusive categories.) Curare is one of the toxic substances used by the Nambicuara; this is the southernmost point in its area of distribution. Among the Nambicuara, the manufacture of curare is not associated with any ritual, magical operation, or secret procedure, as is the case everywhere else. The formula for curare involves merely the basic material, and the method of manufacture is a purely secular activity. And yet, the Nambicuara possess a theory of poisons which includes all sorts of mystical considerations and is based on a metaphysics of nature. But by a curious contrast, this theory is not applied to the manufacture of real poisons; it merely explains their effectiveness. Yet the theory is of primary importance in the making, manipulation, and utilization of other products, which are called by the same name and to which the same power is attributed by the natives, though these are innocuous substances of a purely magical character.

This example deserves further examination, for it holds a wealth of implications. First, it fulfills the two criteria we proposed for the detection of pseudo-archaism. The presence of curare, so far from its present area of diffusion and among a people of a culture so inferior to the groups among which it is ordinarily found, constitutes an *external coincidence*. But the empirical character of its preparation—in a society which also uses magical poisons, which merges all its poisons under one and the same term, and which also interprets their effects metaphysically—is an *internal discrepancy*, whose value is even more significant. The presence among the Nambicuara of curare which is reduced to its basic material and which is prepared without any ritual strikingly raises the question as to whether the apparently archaic traits of their culture are original traits or vestiges in an impoverished culture. In the matter of poisons, it is much more plausible to interpret the contradiction between theory and practice in terms of the loss of complex rituals which are associated farther north with the manufacture of curare, than to explain how a supernatural complex could have evolved on the basis of a purely experimental treatment of the strychnos root.

This is not the only discrepancy. The Nambicuara still possess polished stone axes of excellent workmanship. But while they are still capable of hafting them, they no longer know how to make them. The stone tools that they manufacture from time to time are limited to irregular, scarcely trimmed flakes. During the greater part of the year they depend on food-gathering for their sustenance. But in the preparation of wild products they either lack the refined techniques of the forest peoples or use them only in a rudimentary form. All Nambicuara groups engage in a little horticulture during the rainy season, all of them practice basketry, and some of them manufacture a shapeless though serviceable pottery.

And yet, despite the terrible food shortage during the dry season, they preserve their manioc crops only by burying cakes of pulp, which are practically rotten when they are unearthed after several weeks or months. The demands of nomadic life and the absence of permanent dwellings prevent them from using their pots and baskets for conservation. On the one hand, a pre-horticultural economy is not associated with any of the techniques characteristic of this mode of life; on the other hand, knowledge of various types of containers fails to transform horticulture into a stable occupation. We could borrow other examples from social organization. That of the Apinayé resembles Australian institutions only superficially.[21] Its extreme surface complexity conceals very crude differentiations, and the functional value of the system is actually very low.

We find therefore that the criterion of pseudo-archaism consists in the simultaneous presence of what we have called external coincidences and internal discrepancies. But we can go even further: In pseudo-archaic cultures those correspondences and discrepancies are contrasted through an additional feature which characterizes each form as considered separately.

Let us turn again to the Nambicuara and briefly examine the pattern of their external coincidences. These have not been established with any neighboring culture whose influence—due to geographical proximity or to an overwhelming technical, political, or psychological superiority—might have been exerted on a miraculously preserved archaic island. The points of correspondence tie the Nambicuara to a number of peoples, some of whom are neighbors and others remote, some closely related on a cultural level, others very advanced. The physical type reminds us of ancient Mexico, and especially of the Atlantic coast. The language has some similarities with those of the Isthmus of Panama and the northern part of South America. The concept of family organization and the religious themes, together with the vocabulary associated with them, recall the southern Tupi. The manufacture of poisons and the customs of warfare (which are independent, since curare is used only in hunting) point to the Guianas. Finally, the marriage customs stir Andean echoes. The same is true for the Bororo, whose physical type is southern, political organization western, and mode of life eastern, in relation to their present area of settlement.

Thus, the coincidences have a scattered distribution. Inversely, discrepancies are concentrated in the heart of the culture; they affect its fundamental structure, its unique essence. We might even say they confer upon it its individuality. All, or almost all, the elements of the Neolithic complex are present among the Nambicuara. They cultivate gardens, spin cotton, weave legbands, plait fibers, and mold clay. But these elements are not organized; a synthesis is lacking. And in parallel fashion, even the food-gathering obsession fails to blossom into specialized techniques. The natives are thus paralyzed before an impossible choice. The dualism of their mode of life permeates their daily activities and extends to all their psychological attitudes, to their social organization, and to their metaphysical thinking. The opposition between male activity, defined by hunting and gardening—which are equally productive and equally intermittent—and female activity, based on food-gathering—whose results are constant but mediocre—is turned into an opposition between the sexes according to which women are actually cherished, but ostensibly depreciated; an opposition between the seasons—that of nomadic wandering and that of more durable settlement; an opposition between two modes of existence —the one defined by what we might call temporary shelter and permanent basket, which is rich in trials and adventures, and the other by the tedious repetition of agricultural processes, which creates a dull security. This whole complex, finally, is expressed on a metaphysical level by the different fates which await the souls of men—eternally reincarnated, just as the slash-and-burn holdings of their owners will be cultivated over and over again after long fallow periods—and the souls of women—after death scattered to the winds, rains, and thunderstorms, destined to the same precarious fate as female food-gathering.[22]

The hypothesis of a survival of archaic societies, which is based on the discovery of external discrepancies between their culture and that of neighboring societies, faces, in the case of pseudo-archaism, two great obstacles. First, the external discrepancies are never sufficiently numerous to eliminate completely the coincidences, which are also external. The external coincidences are *atypical* as well: Instead of having been established with a society or aggregate of societies, culturally well defined and geographically localized, they point in all directions and recall heterogeneous societies. Second, the analysis of a pseudo-archaic culture as an autonomous system reveals internal discrepancies which are, in this case, *typical*, in that they affect the basic structure of the society and irremediably jeopardize its specific equilibrium. For pseudo-archaic societies are condemned societies. This should be obvious, owing to their precarious position in the environment, where they struggle to survive and to overcome the pressures of their neighbors.

It is easy to understand that these intimate traits might elude the historian and the sociologist, who study documents. But a good field-worker cannot overlook them. Our theoretical conclusions are based upon a body of data from South America which was gathered by direct observation. It remains for the specialists on Malaya and Africa to say whether their experiences confirm these theories in their areas, where the same problems have been raised. If we can reach agreement, great progress will have been made in the definition of the subject matter of anthropological research. For this research consists in a complex of investigational techniques required, not so much by the character of those societies over which no special doom hangs, as by the specific circumstances *in which we find ourselves* in relation to them. In this sense, anthropology might be defined as the *technique du dépaysement*.[23]

For the moment, the important thing is to help anthropology to disengage itself from the philosophical residue surrounding the term *primitive*. A true primitive society should be harmonious, a society, so to speak, at one with itself. We have seen, on the contrary, that in a large part of the world—outstanding in many other respects for anthropological study—societies which appear the most authentically archaic are completely distorted by discrepancies that bear the unmistakable stamp of *time elapsed*. A cracked bell, alone surviving the work of time, will never give forth the ring of bygone harmonies.

NOTES

1. C. G. Seligman, *The Melanesians of British New Guinea* (London: 1910).
2. W. E. H. Stanner, "Murinbata Kinship and Totemism," *Oceania*, VII, No. 2 (1936-1937).
3. R. H. Lowie, "Notes on Hopi Clans," *Anthropological Papers of the American Museum of Natural History*, XXX (1929), p. 6.

4. See the summary of his lecture notes, collected and published by his students: Marcel Mauss, *Manuel d'Ethnographie* (Paris: 1947), p. 1, *n* 1.

5. J. M. Cooper, "The South American Marginal Cultures," *Proceedings of the 8th American Scientific Congress* (Washington, D.C.: 1940), II, 147-60.

6. C. F. P. Von Martius, *Beiträge zur Ethnographie und Sprachenkunde Amerikas zumal Brasiliens* (Leipzig: 1867).

7. R. H. Lowie, "A Note on the Northern Ge Tribes of Brazil," *American Anthropologist*, n.s., XLIII (1941), p. 195.

8. *Loc. cit.*

9. Garcilaso de La Vega, *Histoire des Incas*, trans. into French (Paris: 1787), I, 167; H. Maspero, *La Chine antique* (Paris: 1927), pp. 251-52.

10. C. Nimuendajú and R. H. Lowie, "The Dual Organization of the Ramkokamekran (Canella) of Southern Brazil," *American Anthropologist*, n.s., XXIX (1927), p. 578.

11. H. Baldus, "Os Tapirapé," *Revista do Arquivo Municipal* (São Paulo: 1944-1946).

12. K. Von den Steinen, *Unter den Naturvölkern Zentral-Brasiliens*, Second Edition (Berlin: 1897); p. 581 of the Portuguese translation (São Paulo: 1940).

13. *Ibid.*, p. 580.

14. W. A. Cook, "The Bororo Indians of Matto Grosso, Brazil," *Smithsonian Miscellaneous Collection*, Vol. L (Washington, D.C.: 1908).

15. V. Frič and P. Radin, "Contributions to the Study of the Bororo Indians," *Journal of the Royal Anthropological Institute*, XXXVI (1906), p. 391.

16. *Ibid.*, p. 392.

17. *Loc. cit.*

18. J. M. Cooper, "The South American Marginal Cultures," *op. cit.*

19. K. Von den Steinen, *op. cit.*, p. 488.

20. C. Lévi-Strauss, "On Dual Organization in South America," *America Indígena*, (Mexico: 1944), IV; "The Tupi-Cawahib," in *Handbook of South American Indians*, Vol. III (Washington, D.C.: Smithsonian Institution, 1948). This reconstruction has been ingeniously criticized by M. I. Pereira de Queiroz. She refers to several important elements of Sherente mythology and ritual which suggest that the natives have lived in the savanna for a prolonged period. I am ready to admit that this presents a problem, although it is risky to interpret—as do the Sherente themselves—certain mythical themes which are distributed in the New World from Canada to Peru in terms of the economic history of a specific tribe. Cf. M. I. Pereira de Queiroz, "A noção de arcaismo em etnologia e a organização social dos Xerente," *Revista de Antropologia*, I, No. 2 (1953), pp. 99-108.

21. C. Nimuendajú, "The Apinayé," *The Catholic University of America Anthropological Series*, No. 8 (Washington, D.C.: 1939); see also Chapter VII of the present volume.

22. C. Lévi-Strauss, *La Vie familiale et sociale des Indiens Nambikwara* (Paris: 1948); *Tristes Tropiques* (Paris: 1955).

[23. *Translator's note:* This expression defies translation. Literally, *dépaysement* means "homelessness" or "uprooting." As used here, it is better rendered as "marginality." When the author defines social anthropology

as the *technique du dépaysement*, he is referring to the conscious cultivation by the anthropologist of an attitude of marginality toward all
cultures, including his own, to the point where this becomes second
nature to him.]

CHAPTER VII

Social Structures of Central and Eastern Brazil

D URING RECENT YEARS our attention has been focused on the institutions of certain tribes of central and eastern Brazil which had been classed as very primitive because of their low level of material culture. These tribes are characterized by highly complex social structures which include several systems of criss-crossing moieties, each with specific functions, clans, age grades, recreational or ceremonial associations, and other types of groups. The most striking examples are furnished by the Sherente, who have exogamous patrilineal moieties subdivided into clans; the Canella and the Bororo, with exogamous matrilineal moieties and other types of groups; and finally, the Apinayé, with non-exogamous matrilineal moieties. The most complex types, such as a double system of moieties subdivided into clans, and a triple system of moieties lacking clan subdivisions, are found among the Bororo and the Canella, respectively. (These tribes have been described by Colbacchini, Nimuendajú, and the present author, as well as earlier observers.)

The general tendency of observers and theorists has been to interpret these complex structures on the basis of dual organization, which seemed to represent the simplest form.[1] This followed the lead of native informants, who focused their descriptions on the dual forms. I do not differ from my colleagues in this respect. Nevertheless, a long-standing doubt led me to postulate the residual character of dual structures in the area under consideration. As we shall see, this hypothesis later proved inadequate.

We propose to show here that the description of indigenous institutions given by field-workers, ourselves included, undoubtedly coincides with the natives' image of their own society, but that this image amounts to a theory, or rather a transmutation, of reality, itself of an entirely different nature. Two important consequences stem from this observation, which until now had been applied only to the Apinayé: The dual organization of the societies of central and eastern Brazil is not only adventitious, but often illusory; and, above all, we are led to conceive of social structures as entities independent of men's consciousness of them (although they in fact govern men's existence), and thus as different from the image which men form of them as physical reality is different from our sensory perceptions of it and our hypotheses about it.

Our first example will be the Sherente, described by Nimuendajú. This tribe, which belongs to the central Ge linguistic family, is distributed in villages, each composed of two exogamous patrilineal moieties subdivided into four clans. Three of these clans are considered by the natives as the original Sherente clans; the fourth is attributed by legend to a foreign "captured" tribe. The eight clans, four in each moiety, are differentiated by ceremonial functions and privileges; but neither these clans, nor the two athletic teams, nor the four men's clubs and the related women's association, nor the six age grades function in the regulation of marriage, which depends exclusively upon the moiety system. We would expect, then, to find the usual corollaries of dual organization, namely, distinction between parallel-cousins and cross-cousins; merging of patrilateral and matrilateral cross-cousins; and preferential marriage between bilateral cross-cousins. This, however, is only rarely the case.

In another work whose conclusions we shall review briefly,[2] we have distinguished three fundamental types of marriage exchange; these are expressed, respectively, by preferential bilateral cross-cousin marriage, marriage between sister's son and brother's daughter, and marriage between brother's son and sister's daughter. We have called the first type *restricted exchange*, implying the division of the group into two sections, or a multiple of two, while the term *generalized exchange*, which includes the two remaining types, refers to the fact that marriage can take place between an unspecified number of partners. The difference between matrilateral and patrilateral cross-cousin marriage arises from the fact that the former represents the richest and most complete form of marriage exchange, the partners finding themselves oriented once and for all in an open-ended global structure. Patrilateral cross-cousin marriage, on the contrary, is a "borderline" form of reciprocity, links groups *only* in pairs, and implies a total reversal of all the cycles with each succeeding generation. It follows that matrilateral marriage is normally accompanied by a kinship terminology which we have called "consecutive": Since the position of the descent groups in relation to one another is unchanging, their successive members tend to be merged under the same term, and differences of generation are ignored. Patrilateral marriage, on the other hand, is associated with an "alternating" terminology, which expresses the opposition of consecutive generations and the identification of alternating generations. A son marries in the direction opposite from his father—yet in the same direction as his father's sister—and in the same direction as his father's father—yet in the opposite direction from that of his father's father's sister. For daughters, the situation is exactly the reverse. A second result follows. In matrilateral marriage, we find two separate and distinct terms for two types of affinal relatives: "sisters' husbands" and "wives' brothers." In patrilateral marriage, this dichotomy is transposed into the descent group itself, in order to distinguish first-degree collateral relatives according to sex. Brother and sister, who always follow opposite paths in marriage, are distinguished by what F. E. Williams, in Melanesia, described as "sex affiliation"; each receives a fraction of the status of the ascendant whose matrimonial destiny he or she follows or complements, that is, the son receives the status of his mother, and the daughter that of her father—or vice versa according to the situation.

When we apply these definitions to the Sherente, we immediately perceive certain anomalies. Neither the kinship terminology nor the marriage rules coincide with the requirements of a dual system or a system of restricted exchange. Rather, they contradict one another, each pattern being associated with one of the two fundamental types of generalized exchange. Thus the kinship vocabulary offers several examples of consecutive terms, as, for instance:

> father's sister's son = sister's son
> wife's brother's son = wife's brother
> father's sister's husband = sister's husband = daughter's husband

The two types of cross-cousins are also distinguished. However, marriage (for male Ego) is permitted only with the patrilateral cousin and is prohibited with the matrilateral cousin, which should imply an alternating terminology, and not a consecutive one—as is precisely the case. At the same time, several terminological identifications of individuals belonging to different moieties (mother and mother's sister's daughter; brother, sister, and mother's brother's children; father's sister's children and brother's children; etc.) suggest that this moiety division does not represent the most essential aspect of the social structure. Thus, even a superficial examination of the kinship terminology and marriage rules leads to the following observations: Neither the terminology nor the rules of marriage coincide with an exogamous dual organization. The terminology, on the one hand, and the marriage rules, on the other, belong to two mutually exclusive patterns, both of which are incompatible with dual organization.

On the other hand we find indices of matrilateral marriage which contradict the patrilateral pattern, the only one for which we have evidence. These are: (1) plural union—a form of polygyny usually associated with matrilateral marriage and matrilineal descent, although in this case the descent is actually patrilineal; (2) the presence of two reciprocal terms among affinal kin, *aimapli* and *izakmu*, which leads us to believe that affines maintain a unidimensional relationship with one another, that is, that they are sisters' husbands or wives' brothers, but not both at the same time; (3) finally, and above all, there is the role of the bride's maternal uncle, which is unusual for a moiety system.

Dual organization is characterized by reciprocal services between moieties which are, at the same time, associated and opposed. This reciprocity is expressed in the set of special relationships between a nephew and his maternal uncle, who belong to different moieties regardless of type of descent. But among the Sherente, these relations, restricted in their classic form to the special *narkwa* bond, seem to be transposed to the husband or bridegroom, on the one hand, and to the *bride's* maternal uncle, on the other. Let us examine this point further.

The bride's maternal uncle performs the following functions: He organizes and carries out the abduction of the bridegroom as a preliminary to the marriage; he takes in his niece in the event of a divorce and protects her against her husband; if the niece's husband dies, he forces her brother-in-law to marry her; together with her husband, he avenges his niece if she is raped. In other words, he is his niece's protector with, and if necessary against, her husband. If, however, the moiety system had a truly functional value, the bride's maternal uncle would be a classificatory "father" of the bridegroom, rendering his role as abductor (and as protector of the wife of one of his "sons," thus hostile to the latter) absolutely incomprehensible. There must, therefore, always be at least three distinct descent groups—Ego's group, Ego's wife's group, and the group of Ego's wife's mother—and this is incompatible with a pure moiety system.

On the other hand, members of the same moiety often reciprocate services. At the occasion of female name-giving, ceremonial exchanges take place between the alternate moiety to that of the girls and their maternal uncles who belong to the officiants' moiety. The boys' initiation is performed by their paternal uncles who belong to the same moiety; at the giving of the name *Wakedi* to two boys (a privilege reserved to the women's association), the maternal uncles of the boys accumulate game that is then taken by the women of the opposite moiety, which is therefore the moiety of the uncles as well. In short, everything happens as though there were a dual organization, but in reverse. Or, more accurately, the role of the moieties is lost. Instead of moieties exchanging services, the services are exchanged within the same moiety, *on the occasion* of a special activity held by the other moiety. Three partners, therefore, are always involved instead of two.

Given these conditions, it is significant to discover, at the level of the associations, a formal structure which corresponds exactly to a law of generalized exchange. The four men's societies are organized in a circuit. When a man changes his association he must do it in a prescribed and immutable order. This order is the same as the one governing the transfer of feminine names, which is a privilege of the men's societies. Finally, this order

krara → krieriekmū → akemhā → annōrowa → (krara)

is the same, although inverted, as that of the mythical origin of the societies and of the transfer, from one society to another, of the obligation to celebrate the Padi rite.

Another surprise awaits us when we turn to the myth. The myth actually presents the associations as *age grades*, created in a succession from youngest to oldest. For mask-making, however, the four associations are grouped in pairs linked by reciprocal services, as though they formed moieties, and these pairs consist of age grades which are not consecutive but alternate, as though each moiety were composed of two marriage classes in a system of generalized exchange. (See Figure 4.) We find the same order in the rules of *aikmā*—the commemoration of the deaths of illustrious men.

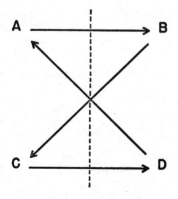

FIGURE 4

The following outline sketches the main features of the preceding discussion:

1. There are no rigid barriers between exogamous moieties, associations, and age grades. The associations function as marriage classes. They fulfill the requirements of the marriage rules and kinship terminology better than the moieties do. On the level of myth, the associations appear as age grades, and in ceremonial life they are grouped within a theoretical moiety system. Only the clans appear extraneous and seemingly indifferent to this organic whole. Everything functions as if the moieties, associations, and age grades were awkward and fragmentary expressions of an underlying reality.

2. The only possible historical evolution that could account for these contradictory characteristics would be:

a. Originally, three patrilineal and patrilocal descent groups with generalized exchange (marriage with mother's brother's daughter);

b. the introduction of matrilineal moieties, leading to

c. the formation of a fourth patrilocal descent group (the fourth clan of each present moiety, or the "captured tribe"; the origin myth of the associations likewise affirms that there were originally three clans);

d. a conflict arising between the rule of descent (matrilineal) and the rule of residence (patrilocal), resulting in

e. the conversion of the moieties to patrilineal descent, with

f. the concomitant loss of the functional role of the descent groups, which are changed into associations through the phenomenon of "masculine resistance" which appeared with the introduction of the original matrilineal moieties.

The Bororo head the list of our other examples, which we shall sketch more briefly. First, we must note the remarkable symmetry between Sherente and Bororo social organization. Both tribes have circular villages divided into exogamous moieties, each with four clans and a central men's house. This parallelism goes even further, despite the opposition of terms that is due to the patrilineal or matrilineal character of the two societies. Thus the Bororo men's house is open to married men and that of the Sherente is reserved for bachelors; it is the scene of sexual license among the Bororo, while chastity is imperative in the Sherente men's house; Bororo bachelors drag in girls or women with whom they then have extra-conjugal sexual relations, whereas the Sherente girls enter only to capture husbands. A comparison between the two tribes is therefore certainly justified.

Recent studies have provided new information concerning social organization and kinship. For the latter, the rich documents published by Father Albisetti show that although the dichotomy between "cross" and "parallel" relatives exists (as we should expect in a system of exogamous moieties), it does not coincide with the moiety division but, rather, cross-cuts it, since identical terms occur in both moieties. We shall limit ourselves to a few striking examples. Ego equates brother's children and sister's children, although they belong to different moieties. Although in the grandchildren's generation we find the expected dichotomy between "sons and daughters" (terms theoretically limited to grandchildren of the moiety opposite Ego's own) on the other hand and "sons-in-law" and "daughters-in-law" (terms theoretically restricted to grandchildren of Ego's moiety) on the other, the actual distribution of these terms does not correspond to the moiety division.

We know that in other tribes—for example, the Miwok of California—such anomalies indicate the presence of groupings different from, and more important than, the moieties. Furthermore, in the Bororo system, we note certain striking terminological equivalents, such as:

> mother's brother's son's son is called: daughter's husband, grandson; father's sister's daughter's daughter is called: wife's mother, grandmother;

and especially:

> mother's mother's brother's son and mother's mother's mother's brother's son's son are called: son.

These equivalents immediately bring to mind kinship structures of the Bank-Ambrym-Easter Island type. The similarities are corroborated by the possibility of marriage with the mother's brother's daughter's daughter in both cases.[3]

Regarding social organization, Father Albisetti specifies that each matrilineal moiety always consists of four clans and that there is preferential marriage not only between certain clans but between certain sections of these clans. According to him, each clan is actually divided into three matrilineal sections: Upper, Middle, and Lower. Given two clans linked by preferential marriage, unions can take place only between Upper and Upper, Middle and Middle, and Lower and Lower section members. If this description were correct (and the observations of the Salesian Fathers have always been trustworthy), we see that the classic picture of Bororo institutions would collapse. Whatever the marriage preferences linking certain clans, the clans themselves would lose all functional value (as we have already observed for the Sherente), and thus Bororo society would be reduced to three endogamous groups— Upper, Middle, and Lower—each divided into two exogamous sections. As there are no kinship relationships between the three principal groups, these would really constitute three sub-societies (Figure 5).

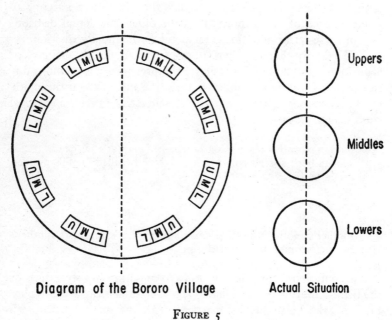

Diagram of the Bororo Village   Actual Situation

FIGURE 5

Since the kinship terminology seems explicable only in terms of three theoretical descent groups, ultimately split into six—wife's father, mother, daughter's husband—and linked by a system of generalized exchange, we are led to postulate an original triadic system transformed by the addition of a dual system, as among the Sherente.

To regard the Bororo as an endogamous society is so startling that we should hesitate even to consider this possibility had not an analogous conclusion already been drawn for the Apinayé by three different authors working independently with documents collected by Nimuendajú.

We know that the Apinayé moieties are non-exogamous and that marriage is regulated by the division of the group into four *kiyé*, as follows: a man *A* marries a woman *B*, a man *B* marries a woman *C*, a man *C* marries a woman *D*, etc. Since boys belong to the *kiyé* of their fathers and girls to that of their mothers, the apparent division into four exogamous groups masks a real division into four endogamous groups: men of *A* and women of *B*, who are related; men of *B* and women of *C*, also related; men of *C* and women of *D*; men of *D* and women of *A*. The men and women grouped into the same *kiyé*, on the other hand, are not related at all. This is exactly the situation we have described among the Bororo, based on information currently available, except that the latter would have only three endogamous groups instead of four. Certain clues suggest the same type of groups among the Tapirapé. Under these conditions we may ask ourselves if the Apinayé marriage rule that prohibits cousin marriage and the endogamous privileges of certain Bororo clans (whose members may contract marriages, although they belong to the same moiety) do not aim, by antithetical means, to counteract the division of the group, either by incestuous exceptions or by marriages contrary to the rules, which the remoteness of kinship ties makes it difficult to distinguish.

Unfortunately, gaps and obscurities in Nimuendajú's work on the Eastern Timbira do not allow us to carry the analysis to this point. At any rate, we can be certain that here again we are in the presence of the same elements of a complex common to the entire culture area. The Timbira have a systematically consecutive terminology in which:

father's sister's son = father
father's sister's daughter = father's sister
mother's brother's son = brother's son
daughter's daughter = sister's daughter

And the prohibition of cross-cousin marriage (as among the Apinayé) despite the presence of exogamous moieties; the role of the bride's maternal uncle as the protector of his niece against her husband, a situation already encountered among the Sherente; the rotating cycle of age grades, analogous to that of the Sherente associations and the Apinayé marriage classes; and, finally, the regrouping of alternate pairs of age grades in athletic contests, like that of the Sherente associations in ceremonies—all this leads us to assume that the problems raised would be quite similar.

Three conclusions emerge from this schematic presentation:

1. The study of social organization among the populations of central and eastern Brazil must be thoroughly re-examined in the field—first, because the actual functioning of these societies is quite different from its superficial appearance, which is all that has been observed until now; and second, and more important, because this study must be carried out on a comparative basis. Undoubtedly the Bororo, the Canella, the Apinayé, and the Sherente have, each in their own way, created real institutions which are strikingly similar to one another and, at the same time, simpler than their explicit formulation. Furthermore, the various types of groupings found in these societies—specifically, three forms of dual organization, clans, sub-clans, age grades, associations, etc.—do not represent, as they do in Australia, so many functional groups. They are, rather, a series of expressions, each partial and incomplete, of the same underlying structure, which they reproduce in several copies without ever completely exhausting its reality.

2. Field-workers must learn to consider their research from two different perspectives. They are always in danger of confusing the natives' theories about their social organization (and the superficial form given to these institutions to make them consistent with theory) with the actual functioning of the society. Between the two there may be as great a difference as that between the physics of Epicurus or Descartes, for example, and the knowledge derived from contemporary physics. The sociological representations of the natives are not merely a part or a reflection of their social or-

ganization. The natives may, just as in more advanced societies, be unaware of certain elements of it, or contradict it completely.

3. We have seen that, in this respect, the native representations of central and eastern Brazil, as well as the institutional language in which these are expressed, constitute an effort to regard as basic a type of structure (moieties or exogamous classes) whose true role is quite secondary, if not totally illusory.

Behind the dualism and the apparent symmetry of the social structure we perceive a more fundamental organization which is asymmetrical and triadic;[4] the requirements of a dualist formulation lead to insuperable difficulties in the harmonious functioning of the organization.

Why do societies affected by a high degree of endogamy so urgently need to mystify themselves and see themselves as governed by exogamous institutions, classical in form, of whose existence they have no direct knowledge? This problem (to which we have elsewhere sought a solution) belongs to general anthropology. Raising it in a technical discussion and with respect to a limited geographical area at least shows the contemporary trend of anthropological research and demonstrates that henceforth in the social sciences, theory and research are indissolubly linked.

NOTES

1. By 1940, however, Lowie had cautioned against drawing false analogies to the Australian systems.
2. See C. Lévi-Strauss, *Les Structures élémentaires de la parenté* (Paris: 1949).
3. Among the Bororo, however, marriage remains possible with the mother's brother's daughter, which indicates that we must not push the comparison too far.
4. This triadic organization had already been pointed out by A. Métraux among the Aweikoma, but it was disputed because it would have been "unique to Brazil." (For the authors cited in this argument, see the bibliography at the end of the book.)

CHAPTER VIII

Do Dual Organizations Exist?

THE SCHOLAR whom we are honoring here has divided his attention between America and Indonesia. Perhaps this twofold interest has fostered the daring and fruitfulness of Professor J. P. B. de Josselin de Jong's theoretical ideas, for the road which he has charted seems to me rich in promise for anthropological theory, which often suffers from the difficulties involved in defining and circumscribing comparative studies. Either the facts to be compared are so closely related, geographically and historically, that one cannot be sure one is dealing with several phenomena rather than only one phenomenon superficially diversified, or the facts are so heterogeneous that comparison ceases to be legitimate, since the things themselves are not comparable.

America and Indonesia offer an escape from this dilemma. The anthropologist who examines the beliefs and institutions of these two areas will become convinced that the facts in this case are of the same nature. Some investigators have tried to find a common substratum to account for this affinity. I shall not discuss here their provocative but doubtful hypotheses. From my point of view, it might just as well be a case of structural similarity between societies that have made related choices from the spectrum of institutional possibilities, whose range is probably not unlimited. Leaving aside the question of whether the affinity is to be explained by a common origin or by an accidental resemblance between the structural principles which govern the social organization and religious beliefs in both areas, we all acknowledge that this affinity does exist. And I think there is no better way to honor Professor J. P. B. de Josselin de Jong than to follow the direction implied in his work, that is, to show how a comparative analysis of certain institutional forms can shed light on a fundamental problem in the life of societies. We know the remarkably widespread distribution of what is generally referred to as *dual organization.* It is to this type of organization that I shall now devote attention, drawing upon some Amerindian and Indonesian examples.

A remark by Paul Radin in his classic monograph devoted to a Great Lakes tribe, the Winnebago,[1] will furnish my point of departure.

We know that the Winnebago were formerly divided into two moieties, called, respectively, *wangeregi,* or "those who are above," and *manegi,* or "those who are on earth" (hereafter, for greater convenience, we shall call the latter "those who are below"). These moieties were exogamous, and they also had clear reciprocal rights and duties. Thus the members of each moiety were required to hold funerals for deceased members of the opposite moiety.

When he examined the influence of moiety division upon the village structure, Radin noted a curious discrepancy among the answers of the old people who were his informants. They described, for the most part, a circular village plan in which the two moieties were separated by an imaginary diameter running northwest and southeast (Figure 6). However, several informants vigorously denied that arrangement and outlined another, in which the lodges of the moiety chiefs were in the center rather than on the periphery (Figure 7). According to Radin, the first pattern was always described by informants of the upper phratry and the second by informants of the lower phratry.[2]

Thus for some of the natives the village was circular in form

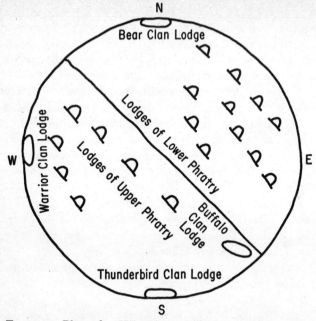

FIGURE 6. Plan of a Winnebago village according to informants of the upper phratry. (After P. Radin, *The Winnebago Tribe*, Fig. 33.)

and was divided into two halves, with the lodges scattered throughout the circle. For the others, there remained a twofold partition of a circular village, but with two important differences: Instead of a diameter cutting the circle, there was a smaller circle within a larger one; and instead of a division of the nucleated village, the inner circle represented the lodges grouped together, as against the outer circle, which represented the cleared ground and which was again differentiated from the virgin forest that surrounded the whole.

Radin did not stress this discrepancy; he merely regretted that insufficient information made it impossible for him to determine which was the true village organization. I should like to show here that the question is not necessarily one of alternatives. These forms, as described, do not necessarily relate to two different organizations. They may also correspond to two different ways of describing one organization too complex to be formalized by means of

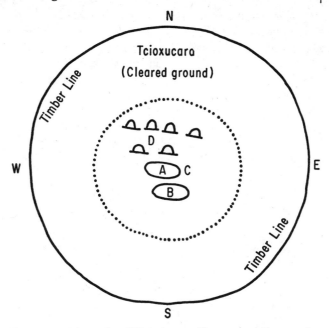

FIGURE 7. Plan of a Winnebago village according to informants of the lower phratry. (After Radin, *op. cit.*, Fig. 34.)

a single model, so that the members of each moiety would tend to conceptualize it one way rather than the other, depending upon their position in the social structure. For even in such an apparently symmetrical type of social structure as dual organization, the relationship between moieties is never as static, or as fully reciprocal, as one might tend to imagine.

The discrepancy among the answers of the Winnebago informants expresses the remarkable fact that both of the forms described correspond to real arrangements. We know of villages which are actually patterned (or which conceive of their patterning) in terms of one or the other of the above models. Hereafter, to simplify, I shall call the arrangement of Figure 6 *diametric structure* and that of Figure 7 *concentric structure.*

Examples of diametric structure abound. We find them first of all in North America, where, in addition to the Winnebago, almost all Sioux camps were set up in this fashion. In South America, the work of Curt Nimuendajú has shown the wide distribution of diametric structure among the Ge tribes, to which we must add, for geographic, cultural, and linguistic reasons, the Bororo of the central Matto Grosso, studied by Fathers Colbacchini and Albisetti and by the present author. This may even have been the type of structure in the towns of Tiahuanaco and Cuzco. Further examples are to be observed in various parts of Melanesia.

As for concentric structure, the village plan of Omarakana in the Trobriand Islands, published by Malinowski, furnishes a striking example (Figure 8). (We shall never find a better occasion to

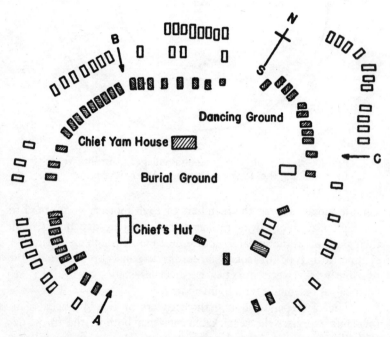

FIGURE 8. Plan of an Omarakana village. (After B. Malinowski, *The Sexual Life of Savages in Northwestern Melanesia*, Fig. 1.)

deplore Malinowski's indifference to structural problems. He sketched all too briefly a highly significant structure, the further analysis of which would have been richly rewarding.) The village of Omarakana is arranged in two concentric rings. At the center lies the plaza, the "scene of public and festive life." [3] Around this are the yam storehouses, sacred in character and the object of many taboos. A circular street runs around the storehouses, with the huts of the married couples built at the outer edge. This Malinowski called the "profane" part of the village. But not only are there oppositions between *central* and *peripheral* and between *sacred* and *profane*. There are other aspects too. In the storehouses of the inner ring *raw* food is *stored* and cooking is not allowed: "The main distinction between the two rings is the taboo on cooking" because ". . . cooking . . . is believed to be inimical to the stored yam." [4] Food can be *cooked* and *consumed* only in or around the family dwellings of the outer ring. The yam-houses are more elaborately constructed and decorated than the dwellings. Only *bachelors* may live in the inner ring, while *married couples* must live on the periphery—which recalls one point cursorily noted by Radin of the Winnebago: "It was customary for a young couple to set up their home at some distance from their village." [5] This is all the more curious because in Omarakana only the chief may establish his residence in the inner ring, and because the Winnebago informants who described concentric structure spoke of a village reduced, for all intents and purposes, to the huts of the principal chiefs. Where, then, did the others live? And, finally, the two concentric rings in Omarakana are opposed with respect to sex: "Without over-labouring the point, the central place might be called the male portion of the village and the street that of the women." [6] Malinowski emphasized several times that the yam-houses and the bachelors' quarters could both be considered as a part, or an extension of, the sacred plaza, with the family huts having a similar relationship to the circular street.

In the Trobriands we see, therefore, a complex system of oppositions between sacred and profane, raw and cooked, celibacy and marriage, male and female, central and peripheral. The roles ascribed to raw and cooked foods in the marriage gifts, which are themselves divided into male and female throughout the Pacific, would confirm (if such confirmation were needed) the social importance and the wide diffusion of the underlying concepts.

Without undertaking an extensive comparison, we shall simply note the parallels between Trobriand village structure and certain Indonesian phenomena. The opposition between central and peripheral, or inner and outer, immediately recalls the organization of the Baduj of western Java. They divide themselves into inner Baduj, considered superior and sacred, and outer Baduj, considered inferior and profane.[7] Perhaps we ought to follow the suggestion of J. M. van der Kroef[8] and relate this opposition to that between "bride-givers" and "bride-takers" in the asymmetric-marriage systems of southeast Asia, where the "bride-givers" are superior to the "bride-takers" both in social prestige and in magical power. This might lead us still further, to the Chinese division of the two descent groups into *t'ang* and *piao*. If we view the Baduj as occupying a transitional position between a ternary system and a binary one, we recall Omarakana, where we have a simultaneous distinction between *two* rings of the village subdivided into *three* sectors. These sectors are attributed, respectively, to the chief's matrilineal clan, to the chief's wives (that is, the representatives of clans allied by marriage), and, finally, to the commoners, who are themselves subdivided into secondary owners of the village lands and foreigners who have no property rights in the village. In any case, we must not forget that the dual structure of the Baduj does not actually function on the village level but, rather, defines the relations between territories, each of which is composed of numerous villages. This fact should inspire great caution. Nevertheless, P. E. de Josselin de Jong has made some legitimate generalizations, on another level, relative to the Baduj. He points out that their type of opposition recalls others in Java and Sumatra, for instance that between "relatives of the bid" and "relatives of the overbid" (this one so "Chinese"), or that between *kampung*, or "built-up village area" and *bukit*, or "outlying hill district," among the Minangkabau.[9] This concentric structure is nonetheless the theme of a mock battle in the village plaza between representatives of the two groups: "sailors" and "soldiers," who are arrayed for the occasion according to a diametric, east-west formation. The same author indirectly raises the question of the relationship between the two types of structure when he notes, "It would be of even more interest to know whether the contrast of *kampung* and *bukit* coincided with that of Koto-Piliang and Bodi-Tjaniago,"[10] that is, with the older division postulated by him of the Minangkabau into two moieties.

From our point of view here, this distinction is even more important. Clearly, the opposition between the center of the village and the periphery corresponds approximately to the Melanesian structure described above. But the analogy with the concentric structure of the Winnebago village is striking, especially because the Winnebago informants spontaneously introduced into their descriptions ecological characteristics which serve, just as in Indonesia, to conceptualize this opposition. Here the built-up village area is opposed to the peripheral ring, or cleared ground, which is in turn opposed to the encircling forest (see Figure 7). We note with great interest that P. E. de Josselin de Jong finds the same type of structure among the Negri-Sembilan of the Malay peninsula. He describes the opposition between Coast (upper) and Inland (lower) reinforced by an opposition, quite common both on the mainland and in the islands, between rice fields and palm trees, on the one hand, and mountains and plains, on the other—that is, between cultivated and uncultivated land.[11] This type of division is also found in Indochina.

All the Dutch writers have striven to emphasize the curious contrasts brought to light by these complex types of social organization, for the study of which Indonesia undoubtedly constitutes an excellent field. Let us try to outline these contrasts in our own terms.

First of all, we find dual forms, from which some scholars have attempted to deduce the vestiges of an earlier moiety system. It is useless to join this debate. The important point, for us, is that the dualism is itself twofold. It seems in some cases to be conceived as the result of a balanced and symmetrical dichotomy between social groups, between aspects of the physical world, or between moral or metaphysical attributes; that is, it seems to be—to generalize somewhat the concept proposed above—a diametric type of structure. And according to a concentric perspective it is also conceived in terms of opposition, with the one difference that the opposition is, with regard to social and/or religious prestige, necessarily unequal.

We are of course aware that the elements of a diametric structure may also be unequal. Indeed, this is probably the more frequent occurrence, since we find words such as *superior* and *inferior*, *elder* and *younger*, *noble* and *commoner*, *strong* and *weak*, etc., used to describe them. But this inequality does not always exist in diametric structures, and at any rate it does not stem from their basic nature, which is steeped in reciprocity. As I noted some time ago,[12] this inequality is a mysterious phenomenon, the interpretation of which is one of the aims of the present study.

How can moieties involved in reciprocal obligations and exercising symmetrical rights be at the same time hierarchically related? In the case of concentric structures, the inequality may be taken for granted, since the two elements are, so to speak, arranged with respect to the same point of reference—the center—to which one of the circles is closer than the other. From this first point of view we encounter three problems: the nature of diametric structures; the nature of concentric structures; and why it is that most diametric structures, in apparent contradiction to their nature, present an asymmetrical character, one which places them midway between those rare diametric forms that are absolutely symmetrical and the concentric forms, which are always asymmetrical.

In the second place, whatever their form, diametric or concentric, the dual structures of Indonesia seem to co-exist with structures containing an odd number of elements—most frequently three, but also five, seven, or nine. What relationships, if any, exist between these apparently distinct forms? This problem arises especially in relation to the marriage rules, for there is an incompatibility between bilateral marriage, which normally accompanies systems with exogamous moieties, and unilateral marriage, the frequent occurrence of which in Indonesia has been verified many times over since the work of Van Wouden.

Actually the distinction between female cross-cousins (father's sister's daughter and mother's brother's daughter) implies at least three distinct groups, and is radically impossible with two. Nevertheless, at Ambon there seem to have been moieties associated with a system of asymmetrical exchange. In Java, Bali, and elsewhere, we find vestiges of the dual type of opposition associated with other types of opposition and giving rise to five, seven, or nine categories. Furthermore, while it is impossible to reduce the latter to the former as conceived in terms of diametric structure, the problem holds a theoretical solution if we conceive the dualism in concentric terms, in which case the additional element falls in the center, while the others are symmetrically arranged at the periphery. As J. P. B. de Josselin de Jong has clearly perceived, any odd-numbered system can be reduced to an even-numbered one by treating it as a form of "opposition between the center and the adjacent sides." Thus the first group of problems is related to the second, at least in a formal sense.

In the preceding paragraphs I raised the problem of the typology of dual structures and their underlying dialectic, using a North American example. This first phase of the discussion used Melanesian and Indonesian illustrations. Now I should like to show that the problem may at least be brought closer to a solution by the consideration of a new example, this time borrowed from a South American people, the Bororo.

Let us briefly recall the structure of the Bororo village (Figure 9). At the center is the men's house, which serves as a home

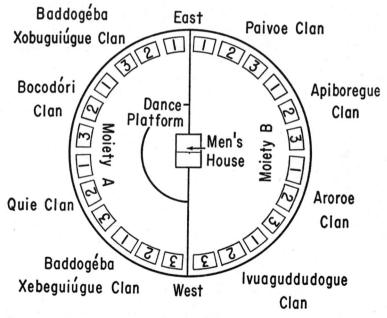

FIGURE 9. Plan of a Bororo village. (After C. Albisetti, *Contribuções missionárias*, Fig. 1.)

for bachelors and a meeting place for the married men, and which is strictly forbidden to women. Around this is a vast circle of uncultivated scrub-land. At the center, adjacent to the men's house, is a dancing place of beaten earth, bare of vegetation and marked off by pickets. Paths lead through the scrub-covered area to the family huts, which form a circle at the forest edge. In these huts live the married couples and their children. Descent is matrilineal, and residence matrilocal. Thus the opposition between the center and the periphery is also an opposition between men (owners of the men's house) and women (owners of the encircling family huts).

We are dealing here with a concentric structure of which the natives are fully aware, where the relationship between center and periphery expresses two kinds of opposition, that which we have just noted between *male* and *female,* and another between *sacred* and *profane.* The central area containing the men's house and the dancing place serves as a stage for the ceremonial life, while the periphery is reserved for the domestic activities of the women, who are by definition excluded from the mysteries of the religion. Thus the making and use of bull-roarers take place in the men's house, and women are forbidden under pain of death to watch them.

However, this concentric structure co-exists with several other structures of diametric type. The Bororo village is, first of all, separated into two moieties by an east-west axis which divides the eight clans into two groups of four ostensibly exogamous units. This axis is cross-cut by another, perpendicular to the first and running north-south. The north-south axis splits up the eight clans into two other groups of four, called respectively "upper" and "lower," or—when a village is located on a watercourse—"upstream" and "downstream." [13]

This complex arrangement is found not only in the permanent villages but also in encampments set up for a single night. In the latter case, the women and children settle in a circle around the periphery in order of clan position, while the young men clear an area in the center which stands for the men's house and the dancing place.[14]

The natives of Rio Vermelho explained to me in 1936 that formerly, when the villages were more densely populated, the huts were arranged in the same way, but in several concentric circles instead of a single one.

As I write these lines, I have just learned of the archaeological discoveries at Poverty Point, Louisiana, in the Lower Mississippi Valley.[15] Let me insert a parenthetical remark, for this Hopewellian town, dating from the first millennium before the beginning of the Christian era, offers an interesting resemblance to the Bororo village as it may have existed in the past. The plan is octagonal (recalling the eight Bororo clans), and the dwellings are arranged six deep, forming six concentric octagonal figures. Two perpendicular axes cross-cut the village, one running east-west, the other north-south. The ends of these axes were marked by bird-shaped mounds,[16] two of which have been recovered (those at the northern and western ends). The other two were probably erased by a shift in the course of the Arkansas River. When we note that remains of cremation have been discovered in the vicinity of one of the mounds (the western one), we recall the two Bororo "villages of the dead," situated at the eastern and western ends of the moiety axis.

We are therefore dealing with a type of structure which in America extends far back into antiquity, and whose later analogues were to be found in pre-Conquest Peru and Bolivia and, more recently, in the social structure of the Sioux in North America and of the Ge and related tribes in South America. These are facts worthy of consideration.

Finally, the Bororo village reveals a third form of dualism, this one implicit, which has remained unnoticed until now and whose analysis requires that we first explore another aspect of the social structure.

In the village, we have already singled out a concentric structure and two diametric structures. These varied manifestations of dualism exist side by side with a triadic structure. Actually, each of the eight clans is divided into three classes, which I shall call Upper, Middle, and Lower. On the basis of observations made by Father Albisetti,[17] I have shown earlier (Chapter VII) that the rule which requires an Upper of one moiety to marry an Upper of the other moiety, a Middle a Middle, and a Lower a Lower, converts the apparently dual exogamous system of Bororo society into what is in reality a triadic endogamous system, since we are dealing with three sub-societies, each made up of individuals who have no kinship ties with the members of the other two. Furthermore, in the same analysis, a brief comparison of Bororo society with that of the central and eastern Ge tribes (Apinayé, Sherente, and Timbira) led me to postulate a social organization of the same type for all these tribes.

If the exogamy of the Bororo seems to be of an epiphenomenal nature, it will not come as a surprise that the Salesian Fathers report an exception to the rule of moiety exogamy that permits two pairs of clans of one of the moieties to marry among themselves. But at the same time, it becomes possible to distinguish a third form of dualism. Let 1, 2, 3, and 4 represent the clans of one moiety and 5, 6, 7, and 8 the clans of the other moiety, taken in sequence according to their spatial distribution around the village circle. The rule of exogamy is suspended for clans 1 and 2 on the one hand, and 3 and 4 on the other. We must therefore distinguish eight territorial relationships, such that four imply marriage and four exclude it, and this new dualist formulation of the law of exogamy will express reality just as faithfully as does the more obvious division into moieties:

PAIRS OF CLANS IN TERRITORIAL RELATIONSHIP	MARRIAGE POSSIBLE ($+$) OR IMPOSSIBLE ($-$)
1, 2	$+$
2, 3	$-$
3, 4	$+$
4, 5	$+$
5, 6	$-$
6, 7	$-$
7, 8	$-$
8, 1	$+$

This gives a total of $4+$ and $4-$.

We note that the structure of the Bororo village presents two remarkable anomalies. The first has to do with the disposition of the U, M, and L classes in the two pseudo-exogamous moieties. This arrangement is regular only within each moiety, where we find (according to the Salesians) a succession of huts, three to each clan, in the order U, M, L; U, M, L; etc. But the order of succession of the U's, M's, and L's in one moiety is reversed in the other. In other words, the classes are symmetrically arranged in a mirror image in relation to moieties, the two semicircles being joined at one end by two U's and at the other by two L's. Disregarding for the moment the circular form of the village, we have, thus:

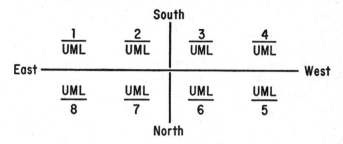

In the above diagram, the numbers 1 through 8 represent the clans, and the letters U, M, and L represent the classes of which each clan is composed. The horizontal east-west line corresponds to the axis of the pseudo-exogamous moieties and the vertical north-south line to the axis of the upper and lower moieties.

From this remarkable arrangement it appears to follow that despite its circular form the natives do not conceive of the village as a single entity susceptible of analysis into two parts, but rather as two distinct entities joined together.

Let us turn now to the second anomaly. In each moiety, 1 through 4 and 5 through 8, two clans occupy a privileged position in the sense that they represent, on the social level, the two great culture heroes and deities of the Bororo pantheon, Bakororo and Itubori, guardians of the West and East. In the above diagram, clans 1 and 7 represent Itubori, while clans 4 and 6 represent Bakororo. For clans 1 and 4, situated at the eastern and western ends respectively, there is no problem. But why clan 7 rather than 8? And why clan 6 and not 5? The first answer that comes to mind is that the clans to which these functions are delegated must also be contiguous with one of the two axes, east-west or north-south. Clans 1 and 4 are contiguous with the east-west axis: They stand at the *two ends* and on the *same side*, while 6 and 7 are contiguous with the north-south axis, standing at the *same end* but on *either side* of the axis. Since clans 1 and 7 are east and clans 4 and 6 are west (by definition), there is no other way to fulfill the condition of contiguity.

We should here point out—with all the caution necessary in such a theoretical treatment of an empirical problem—that a single hypothesis does account for both anomalies. We need only postulate that the Bororo, like the Winnebago, consider their social structure in both diametric and concentric terms. If one moiety, or both, conceive of themselves, regularly or occasionally, as being one central and the other peripheral, then the mental operation required to shift from such an ideal arrangement to the concrete arrangement of the village would be as follows: first, to open the inside circle at the south and shift it northward; second, to open the outside circle at the north and shift it southward (Figure 10). By reversing the directions, each moiety can at will regard itself

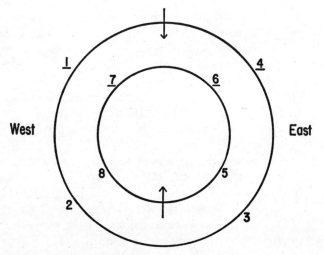

FIGURE 10. Transition from a concentric to a diametric structure.

and the other moiety as either central or peripheral. This freedom is not unimportant, since the Chera moiety is now superior to the Tugare moiety, while the myths imply the reverse situation. Furthermore, while it would perhaps be incorrect to say that the Chera are more sacred than the Tugare, each moiety seems at least to maintain a privileged relationship with a certain type of the sacred that one might call, as a simplification, religious for the Chera and magical for the Tugare.

Let us summarize the major features of Bororo society. We have distinguished three, namely, (1) several manifestations of the diametric type of dualism: (a) a pseudo-exogamous east-west axis, (b) an apparently non-functional north-south axis, and (c) an exogamous dichotomy of the relationships of contiguity between clans; (2) several manifestations of the concentric type of dualism (oppositions between male and female, celibacy and marriage, sacred and profane; finally, the diametric structures may be conceived in a concentric form and the concentric structures in a diametric form, a phenomenon which has only been implied thus far, but whose empirical expression will be described below for the eastern Timbira); (3) a triadic structure which brings about a rearrangement of all the clans into three endogamous classes (each class divided into two exogamous moieties, resulting in a total of six classes, just as we shall find six male classes among the Timbira).

We are dealing with a complexity inherent to dual organizations, as we have shown above with examples derived from North America, Indonesia, and Melanesia, and as is made clearer by an additional observation. Among the Bororo the sacred center of the village contains three parts: the men's house, half of which belongs to the Chera and half to the Tugare, since it is cross-cut by the east-west axis (this is evidenced by the names given to the two doors facing each other); and the *boróro* or dancing place lying east of the men's house, where the entire village comes together as a unit. This might well be, almost word for word, a description of the Balinese temple, with its two inner yards and an outer courtyard. The former two symbolize a general dichotomy of the cosmos and the third stands for a reconciliation of the antithetical divisions.[18]

The social organization of the Eastern Timbira includes the following structures:

1. Two matrilineal exogamous moieties, called respectively East and West, neither of which has priority over the other (however, the marriage rules transcend a simple exogamy based on moieties, since all first cousins are forbidden to marry).

2. Patronymic classes, 2 in number for the women and

3 × 2 = 6 for the men. The bearing of a name leads, for both sexes, to an allocation into one of two groups, called *kamakrã*, "people of the plaza," and *atukmakrã*, "people from without."

3. For the men the patronymic classes have an additional function, which consists in dividing them into 6 groups "of the plaza," associated 3 by 3 in two non-exogamous moieties which are called East and West and which differ in composition from the moieties described under number 1, above.

4. Four age classes, distributed at ten-year intervals, which form four sections arranged in consecutive pairs into another system of moieties (the fourth), different from the preceding ones but also called East and West.

This complex organization calls for a few remarks. There are two rules of descent. The first is matrilineal for the exogamous moieties, at least in principle, since the secondary rule which prohibits first-cousin marriage may be interpreted (from the point of view of a formal analysis, since nothing insures that such is actually the case) as the result of the cross-cutting of the explicit matrilineal descent by an implicit patrilineal form of descent, resulting in a double moiety system. The second rule of descent applies to the patronymic classes. Women's names are transmitted from father's sister to brother's daughter, and men's names from mother's brother to sister's son.

Of the four moiety systems outlined, three are diametric (east and west) and one concentric in type (central plaza and periphery). This last serves as a model for a more general dichotomy:

kamakrã	*atukmakrã*
East	West
Sun	Moon
Day	Night
Dry season	Rainy season
Fire	Firewood
Earth	Water
Red color	Black color

From a functional point of view, System number 3 plays a role only in the initiation ceremonies. System 1 regulates exogamy in the broadest sense of the term. Systems 2 and 4 define two recreational and work groups, which operate one in the rainy season and the other in the dry season.

To complete this description we must add one last group of male moieties, whose function is purely ceremonial and restricted to certain festivals.

Although gaps in the work of Nimuendajú (from which all the preceding observations have been drawn)[19] prevent our making a complete formalization of the system, it is evident that this labyrinth of institutions contains the essential features which we should like to emphasize in this study.

In the first place, there is the juxtaposition of diametric structures with a concentric structure, including even an attempt to express one type in terms of the other. Actually, the East is at the same time east and center, and the West is at the same time west and periphery. While it is true that the women as well as the men are divided between center and periphery, the six groups of the plaza are composed only of men. In striking analogy with Melanesia, the hearths of the groups of the plaza may not be used to cook food, and the kitchens must be installed behind (or in certain ceremonies, in front of) the huts of the periphery, which are indisputably female[20] (see Figure 11).

Nimuendajú even pointed out that during the dry season the ceremonial activity takes place on the "boulevard" (that is, the circular alley in front of the peripheral huts), while during the rainy season it is strictly confined to the central plaza.[21]

Secondly, all these binary forms are combined with ternary forms, in two different ways. The moieties fulfill three functions. System 1 regulates marriage. Systems 2 and 4 regulate collective work and recreation, according to the seasonal cycle:

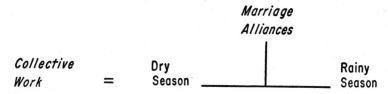

Furthermore, the triad reappears in the men's groups "of the plaza," which are six in number—three from the East and three from the West.

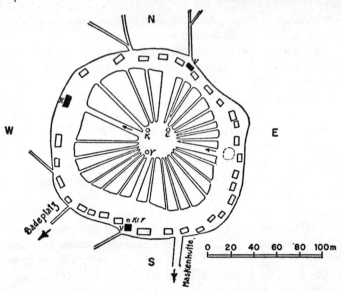

FIGURE 11. Plan of a Timbira village. (After C. Nimuendajú, *The Eastern Timbira*, Fig. 1.)

We now come to the core of the problem. What is the relationship among these three types of representations—diametric dualism, concentric dualism, and triad? And how is it that what we generally call "dual organization" is in many instances (and perhaps in all) actually an inextricable mixture of the three types? For convenience we shall examine separately the relationship between dualism and triadism and the relationship between the two forms of dualism proper.

I do not intend to deal here with the first question in the preceding paragraph, because it would carry us too far afield. It will be enough to indicate along what lines the solution should be sought. The fundamental principle of my book *Les Structures élémentaires de la parenté* [22] was a distinction between two types of reciprocity, to which I gave the names *restricted exchange* and *generalized exchange*, restricted exchange being possible only in an even number of groups, generalized exchange being compatible with any number of groups. Today this distinction appears to me naïve, because it is still too close to the natives' classifications. From a logical point of view, it is more reasonable and more efficient to treat restricted exchange as a special case of generalized exchange. If the observations presented in this study are confirmed by other examples, we shall perhaps reach the conclusion that even this particular case is never found empirically other than in the form of an imperfect rationalization of systems which remain irreducible to a dualism, in which guise they vainly try to masquerade.

If we concede this point—if only as a working hypothesis—it follows that triadism and dualism are inseparable, since dualism is never conceived of as such, but only as a "borderline" form of the triadic type. We may then examine another aspect of the problem, which concerns the co-existence of the two forms of dualism—diametric and concentric. The answer is immediately apparent: Concentric dualism is a mediator between diametric dualism and triadism, since it is through the agency of the former that the transition takes place between the other two.

Let us try to formulate the simplest possible geometric representation of diametric dualism as it exists empirically in village structures such as those we have considered. We may draw a diagram of the village on a straight line. Diametric dualism will be represented by two segments of a straight line placed along the same axis with one extremity in common.

But when we try to proceed in the same fashion with concentric dualism, the situation changes. Though it is possible to spread out the peripheral circle on a straight line (this time a continuous line, not two segments), the center will be outside the straight line, represented by a point. Thus instead of two segments of a straight line, we have one straight line and one point. And since the significant elements of this straight line are the two points of origin, the diagram may be analyzed in terms of three poles (Figure 12).

There is thus a profound difference between diametric and concentric dualism. Diametric dualism is static, that is, it cannot transcend its own limitations; its transformations merely give rise to the same sort of dualism as that from which they arose. But concentric dualism is dynamic and contains an implicit triadism. Or, strictly speaking, any attempt to move from an asymmetric triad to a symmetric dyad presupposes concentric dualism, which is dyadic like the latter but asymmetric like the former.

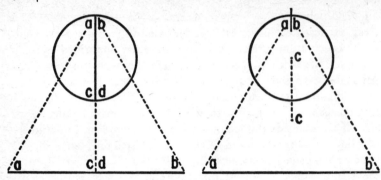

FIGURE 12. Representation on a straight line of a diametric structure (*left*) and a concentric structure (*right*).

The ternary nature of concentric dualism also derives from another source. The system is not self-sufficient, and its frame of reference is always the environment. The opposition between cleared ground (central circle) and waste land (peripheral circle) demands a third element, brush or forest—that is, virgin land—which circumscribes the binary whole while at the same time extending it, since cleared land is to waste land as waste land is to virgin land. In a diametric system, on the other hand, virgin land constitutes an irrelevant element; the moieties are defined by their opposition to each other, and the apparent symmetry of their structure creates the illusion of a closed system.

In support of the above demonstration, which some readers will undoubtedly consider too theoretical, we can offer a number of observations.

In the first place, among the Bororo it seems that each of the two moieties unconsciously uses a different type of projection in relation to the north-south axis. The two Chera clans, which represent the gods of West and East, are actually located at the west and the east of the village. But if the Tugare thought in terms of concentric structure, then the projection of the village circle in a straight line, made from the north-south axis, would result in a straight line parallel to the east-west axis, whose two points of origin would therefore correspond to the location of clans 7 and 6, which are respectively guardians of the east and the west (points *a* and *b* on the right-hand side of Figure 12).

In the second place, the representation of a concentric system in the form of an opposition between a point and a straight line[23] is an excellent example of a peculiarity of dualism (both concentric and diametric) which may be observed in a great many cases—namely, the heterogeneous nature of certain symbols used to express the antithesis of the moieties. Undoubtedly these symbols can also be homogeneous, as in the opposition between summer and winter, land and water, earth and sky, upper and lower, left and right, red and black (or other colors), noble and commoner, strong and weak, elder and younger, etc. But sometimes we find a different symbolism, in which the opposition is drawn between terms which are logically heterogeneous, such as: stability and change, state (or act) and process, being and becoming, synchronic and diachronic, simple and ambiguous, unequivocal and equivocal. All these forms of opposition can be subsumed under a single category—the opposition between continuous and discontinuous.

An admittedly simple example (simple to the point of not meeting the preceding definition) will serve as an initial approximation. The Winnebago have an apparently diametric dualism of "upper" and "lower," which masks imperfectly a system with three poles. The upper might be represented by one pole—the sky—while the lower must have two poles—earth and water.

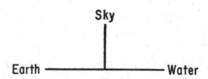

Frequently, too, the opposition between moieties expresses a more subtle dialectic; thus, among the Winnebago, the roles ascribed to the two moieties—warfare and policing for those who are below, and the arts of peace and arbitration for those who are above. More explicitly, the latter have a consistent function, while the former have an ambivalent one, consisting of both protection and coercion.[24] In another realm, one moiety is responsible for the creation of the cosmos and the other for its preservation. These functions are quite distinct, since creation is carried out at a given moment and preservation extends in time. The opposition which we have noted in Melanesia and South America between cooked food and raw food (like the concomitant opposition between marriage and celibacy) implies the same type of asymmetry between state and process, stability and change, identity and transformation. We thus see that the antitheses which serve to express dualism belong to two different categories, the first truly, the others only apparently, symmetrical. The latter are none other than triads, disguised as dyads through the logical subterfuge of treating as two homologous terms a whole that actually consists of a pole and an axis, which are not entities of the same nature.

This leads us to the last stage of our demonstration. If we treat in terms of ternary systems those forms of social organization which are usually described as binary, their anomalies vanish, and it becomes possible to reduce them all to the same type of formalization. We shall consider only three of the several examples discussed in this chapter. Actually, our information about the marriage rules of the Timbira and the way in which those rules are integrated into an unusually complex social structure are too fragmentary and ambiguous to permit formalization. The data for the Winnebago and the Bororo are clearer; to these we shall add an Indonesian model. Yet we should note that the Indonesian social structures have often been reconstructed rather than actually observed, owing to their having disintegrated by the time it became possible to study them. The association of an asymmetrical marriage system (preferential marriage with the mother's brother's daughter) with dual organization seems to have been very widespread in Indonesia. We shall schematize it here in the form of a simplified model containing two moieties and three marriage classes. It should be understood that the number 3 does not necessarily correspond to an empirical datum but stands for any number except 2—because in that case marriage would become symmetrical and we should then be working outside the premises of our hypothesis.

Given the above assumptions, we present our three models, Winnebago, Indonesian, and Bororo, in the three diagrams shown below. They are all of the same type and each illustrates all the properties of the corresponding system. The three diagrams have an identical structure, namely: (1) a group of three small circles;

(2) a triskelion; (3) a large circle. But the functions of these three elements are not the same in each instance. Let us examine them each in turn.

The Winnebago village consists of twelve clans divided into three groups. The lower moiety contains two groups of four clans each ("earth" and "water"). The upper moiety contains one group of four clans ("sky"). The triskelion represents the possibilities of marriage according to the exogamy rule of the moieties. The large circle, which coincides with the perimeter of the village, encompasses the whole, making it a residential unit. (See Figure 13.)

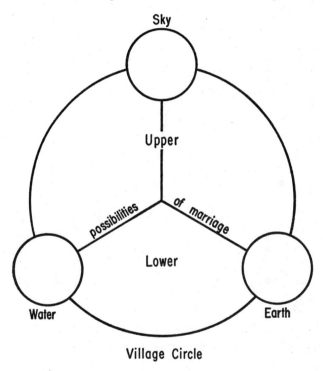

FIGURE 13. Diagram of the Winnebago social structure.

The Indonesian model is more complex. We are no longer dealing with grouped clans, but with non-residential marriage classes, whose members may be scattered among several villages.

The asymmetric-marriage rule between these classes is of the following type: A man *A* marries a woman *B*; a man *B* marries a woman *C*; a man *C* marries a woman *A*. This implies: (1) a dichotomy between the sexes operating within these classes (a brother and a sister each have a different matrimonial destiny); this dichotomy of function is expressed in the diagram by the triskelion, which divides each class into two groups, men on the one hand, women on the other; (2) in such a system, the place of residence is unimportant, and another function is attributed, therefore, to the large circle, which represents the possibilities of

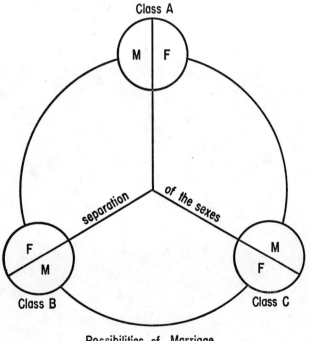

FIGURE 14. Diagram of an Indonesian-type social structure.

marriage between the men of one class and the women of another, as we can easily ascertain by inspection of the diagram (Figure 14).

Let us pause for a moment to examine this point. Our formalization of the Indonesian model brings to light a remarkable property of asymmetric marriage. Once the conditions are met—that is, a minimum of three classes—the principle of a dualist dichotomy appears, based upon the opposition between male and female. That this opposition, inherent to the system, has provided Indonesia with the model upon which it has built its dual organizations, stems, in our opinion, from the fact that the Indonesian moieties are always conceived of as being one male, the other female. The Indonesians do not seem to have been troubled by the presence of moieties which, theoretically, may be either male or female, although each one comprises an approximately equal number of male and female members. But in a society of the same type (asymmetrical marriage associated with a dual organization), namely, the Miwok of California, the natives were faced with this problem and found it somewhat difficult to resolve.

The Miwok moieties, like those of Indonesia, express a general dual classification of objects and phenomena. The moieties are called *kikua* (of water) and *tunuka* (of land). Although all animals, plants, physical geographical features, and meteorological and astronomical phenomena are divided between the two moieties, the male and female principles are excluded from this universal dichotomy, as though the native dialectic were unable to overcome the objective consideration that men and women exist in both moieties. But—and this fact is significant—this situation is not considered self-evident. A rather complicated myth is invoked to explain it:

> Coyote-girl and her husband told each other they would have four children, two girls and two boys. . . . Coyote named one of the male children Tunuka and one of the female children Kikua. The other male child he named Kikua and the other female Tunuka. Coyote thus made the moieties and gave people their first names.[25]

The original couple is not enough, and by a true mythological sleight-of-hand it is necessary to postulate four original classes (in other words, an implicit division of each moiety into male and female) so that the moieties will not reflect (among other things) a sexual dichotomy, as in Indonesia, where this is accepted although it contradicts the empirical situation.

Let us turn now to the third diagram (Figure 15), in which we have formalized Bororo social structure in terms of the same

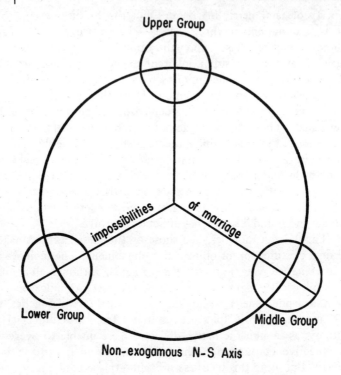

FIGURE 15. Diagram of the Bororo social structure.

type of model as the other two. Here the small circles represent neither the groups of clans (as among the Winnebago) nor the marriage classes (as in Indonesia), but rather *groups of classes*. And, contrary to the first two cases, these units are endogamous. It will be remembered, of course, that the pseudo-exogamous Bororo moieties were each composed of four clans divided into three classes. In the diagram we have regrouped all the Uppers, Middles, and Lowers. The exogamous division thus becomes internal to each group of classes, according to the rule whereby the Uppers of one moiety marry the Uppers of the other moiety, the Middles marry Middles, and so forth. The triskelion then functions as an expression of the impossibilities of marriage for each class.

What is the function here of the large circle? Its relation to the three small circles (groups of classes) and to the triskelion (impossible marriages) leaves no doubt that it corresponds to the non-exogamous north-south axis which at least in some Bororo villages divides the clans, perpendicularly to the axis of the pseudo-exogamous moieties, into two groups, called respectively "Upper" and "Lower," or "Upstream" and "Downstream." I have often noted that the role of this second division is obscure.[26] And for good reason, for if the present analysis is correct, the conclusion will emerge—at first sight surprising—that the north-south axis has no function except that of permitting Bororo society to exist. Let us consider the diagram. The three small circles represent the endogamous groups, sub-societies which exist indefinitely side by side without ever establishing any kinship ties between their members. Nor does the triskelion correspond to any unifying principle, since in representing the impossibilities of marriage it expresses only a negative element of the system. The sole available unifying element is thus provided by the north-south axis, and even this is subject to qualification, for although this axis is functionally significant with respect to residence, its significance remains ambiguous; though it relates to the village, it splits the village into two distinct areas.

This hypothesis must certainly be tested in the field. But it would not be the first time that research would lead us to institutional forms which one might characterize by a *zero value*.[27] These institutions have no intrinsic property other than that of establishing the necessary preconditions for the existence of the social system to which they belong; their presence—in itself devoid of significance—enables the social system to exist as a whole. Anthropology here encounters an essential problem, one which it shares with linguistics, but with which it does not seem to have come to grips in its own field. This is the problem posed by the existence of institutions having no function other than that of giving meaning to the society in which they are found.

Without further discussion of this point, which is beyond the scope of the present study, we shall return to our three systems, whose properties may be summarized in terms of five binary oppositions.

We are dealing with classes or clans; these elements are either grouped (groups of clans, groups of classes) or isolated (classes); the marriage rules are expressed in either positive or negative terms; the sexes are either distinguished (as in asymmetrical marriage) or merged (as in symmetrical marriage, where brother and sister have the same matrimonial destiny); and, finally, residence is either a significant or a non-significant factor, depending upon the system under consideration. We may thus construct the following table, where the sign + is arbitrarily given to the first term of each opposition and the sign — to the second.

		WINNEBAGO	INDONESIA	BORORO
1	Class/Clan	—	+	+
2	Group/Unit	+	—	+
3	Marriage prescribed/ Marriage prohibited	+	+ —	—
4	Sexes distinguished/ Sexes merged	—	+	—
5	Residence significant/ Residence non-significant	+	—	+ —

Opposition 3 (marriage) is ambivalent in Indonesia because of the asymmetric character of marriage: For any two classes, the marriage rule between the men of x and the women of y is symmetrical and opposite to the rule of marriage between the men of y and the women of x. Opposition 5 (residence) is ambivalent among the Bororo for the reason indicated above: The north-south axis implies common residence while at the same time splitting residence in terms of the axis.

An examination of the diagrams shows that our model includes the binary and ternary characteristics of the social structures considered. There also seems to be a relationship between the diametric or concentric elements of the binary oppositions, according to the nature of the symbols to which the latter are ascribed. In Indonesia, the diametric aspect expresses a male/female opposition, and the concentric aspect is thus dedicated to the complementary opposition between high and low (which provides a triad: high/middle/low). Conversely, among the Bororo (and undoubtedly among the Winnebago as well), a triad—high/middle/low, or sky/water/earth—ascribes the role of expressing the male/female opposition to the concentric aspect. It would be interesting to find out, with the aid of other examples, whether this correlation is to be found elsewhere—that is, to see if attributing concentric dualism to the opposition between high and low always results in attributing diametric dualism to the opposition between male and female, and conversely.

From the preceding, it becomes clear that the most widespread opposition (that between binary and ternary structure) leads to symmetrical and inverse applications in South America and Indonesia. In the Indonesian case, we have a system of moieties associated with generalized exchange, that is, an asymmetric form of exogamy. Ternary structure is thus used to define groups of affinal relatives, while binary structure expresses the two directions in which men and women, respectively, circulate. In other words, ternary structure refers to *classes*, binary structure to *relationships* between those classes. In South America, on the other hand (and apparently among all the Ge tribes), binary structure is used to define the groups, while ternary structure defines the two directions, not of the circulation of men and women this time, but the directions in which marriage is permitted or prohibited, to both sexes indiscriminately (since exchange is restricted according to a symmetric form of endogamy). In this case, then, binary structure refers to *classes* and ternary structure to *relationships*.

In this essay I have tried to show that the study of so-called dual organizations discloses so many anomalies and contradictions in relation to extant theory that we should be well advised to reject the theory and to treat the apparent manifestations of dualism as superficial distortions of structures whose real nature is quite different and vastly more complex. Yet these anomalies in no way escaped the attention of Rivers and his school—the originators of the dualist theory. They were not perturbed by them because they saw dual organizations (on the basis of the anomalies) as the historical result of the fusion of two populations differing in race, in culture, or simply in power. In such a formulation, the social structures considered could be both dual and asymmetrical at the same time—and indeed they had to be.

First Marcel Mauss, then Radcliffe-Brown and Malinowski, revolutionized anthropological theory by substituting a sociopsychological interpretation, based on the concept of reciprocity, for the historical interpretation.[28] But as schools grew up around these masters, asymmetrical phenomena faded into the background, since they were not easily integrated into the new perspective. The inequality of the moieties came to be treated as an irregularity of the system. And—much more serious—the striking anomalies that were discovered later were completely neglected. As has often happened in the history of science, an essential property of an object was first taken by researchers to be a special case; later on, scientists were afraid to jeopardize their conclusions by submitting them to more rigorous proof.

It is not the theory of reciprocity which is in doubt. In anthropology this theory continues to stand, as soundly based as the gravity theory in astronomy. There is another lesson in this comparison: Anthropology found its Galileo in Rivers, its Newton in Mauss. We can only hope that in the world of men, often as indifferent as the infinite universe whose silence terrified Pascal, the rare so-called dual organizations still functioning may find their Einstein before they—less enduring than the planets—disintegrate.

NOTES

1. P. Radin, *The Winnebago Tribe*, 37th Annual Report, Bureau of American Ethnology, 1915-1916 (Washington, D. C.: 1923).
2. *Ibid.*, p. 188.
3. B. Malinowski, *The Sexual Life of Savages in Northwestern Melanesia* (New York-London: 1929), I, 10.
4. *Ibid.*, p. 71.
5. P. Radin, "The Culture of the Winnebago as Described by Themselves," *Special Publications of the Bollingen Foundation*, No. 1 (1949), p. 38, *n* 13.
6. Malinowski, *op. cit.*, I, 10. See also *Coral Gardens and Their Magic* (London: 1935), I, 32.
7. N. J. C. Geise, *Baduys en Moslims* (Leiden: 1952).
8. J. M. van der Kroef, "Dualism and Symbolic Antithesis in Indonesian Society," *American Anthropologist*, n.s., LVI, No. 5 (1954), pp. 847-62.
9. P. E. de Josselin de Jong, *Minangkabau and Negri-Sembilan Sociopolitical Structure in Indonesia* (Leiden: 1951), pp. 79-80 and 83-4.
10. *Ibid.*, pp. 80-1.
11. *Ibid.*, pp. 139, 165, 167.
12. C. Lévi-Strauss, "Reciprocity and Hierarchy," *American Anthropologist*, n.s., XLVI, No. 2 (1944).
13. This moot point has led to a discussion between Dr. D. Maybury-Lewis and myself in *Bijdragen tot de taal-, land-, en Volkenkunde*, Deel 116, 1e Aflevering (1960).

14. Fr. A. Colbacchini and Fr. C. Albisetti, *Os Bororos orientais* (São Paulo: 1942), p. 35.

15. James A. Ford, "The Puzzle of Poverty Point," *Natural History*, LXIV, No. 9 (November, 1955), pp. 466-72.

16. The Bororo believe in a cycle of transmigrations whose ultimate stage takes the form of a bird.

17. Fr. C. Albisetti, "Contribuções missionárias," *Publicações da Sociedade Brasileira de Antropologia e Etnologia*, No. 2 (Rio de Janeiro: 1948), p. 8.

18. Van der Kroef, "Dualism and Symbolic Antithesis . . . ," *op. cit.*, p. 856, citing Swellengrebel, *Kerk en Tempel op Bali* (The Hague: 1948).

19. C. Nimuendajú, "The Eastern Timbira," *University of California Publications in American Archaeology and Ethnology*, XLI (1946).

20. *Ibid.*, pp. 42-3.

21. *Ibid.*, p. 92.

22. Paris: 1949.

23. The objection has been voiced that the "concentric" type of structure should be represented by two straight lines rather than by a straight line and a point. I thought it would be better to adopt the second diagram at the outset, for it is a simplification of the first. As I have already shown, the arrangement in concentric circles is the empirical expression of a more profound opposition between the center and the periphery. But even if we adhere to the more complex diagram, the binary or ternary character of each system is immediately apparent.

24. This opposition between two terms, one of them unambiguous and the other ambiguous, recurs constantly in Pawnee ritual. See C. Lévi-Strauss, "Le Symbolisme cosmique dans la structure sociale et l'organisation cérémonielle de plusieurs populations nord et sud-américaines," in *Le Symbolisme cosmique des monuments religieux*, Serie Orientale Roma (Rome: 1957).

25. E. W. Gifford, "Miwok Moieties," *University of California Publications in American Archaeology and Ethnology*, XII, No. 4 (1916), pp. 143-4.

26. C. Lévi-Strauss, *Tristes Tropiques* (Paris: 1955), p. 231. See also Note 13, above.

27. This is the way in which I defined the concept of *mana* some time ago. See C. Lévi-Strauss, "Introduction à l'oeuvre de Marcel Mauss," in Marcel Mauss, *Sociologie et Anthropologie* (Paris: 1950), pp. xli-lii.

28. Actually, Rivers, whose genius is largely ignored today, employed both types of interpretation simultaneously; since his time, no one has said anything not already anticipated by that great theoretician. What I am suggesting here still stands, however, to the extent that Rivers' contemporaries and successors have chiefly acknowledged his historical and geographical interpretations, while the psychological and logical aspects of his theory were quietly assimilated by Mauss, Radcliffe-Brown, and Malinowski, who developed them further with great brilliance.

PART THREE

Magic and
Religion

CHAPTER IX

The Sorcerer
and His Magic

Since the pioneering work of Cannon, we understand more clearly the psycho-physiological mechanisms underlying the instances reported from many parts of the world of death by exorcism and the casting of spells.[1] An individual who is aware that he is the object of sorcery is thoroughly convinced that he is doomed according to the most solemn traditions of his group. His friends and relatives share this certainty. From then on the community withdraws. Standing aloof from the accursed, it treats him not only as though he were already dead but as though he were a source of danger to the entire group. On every occasion and by every action, the social body suggests death to the unfortunate victim, who no longer hopes to escape what he considers to be his ineluctable fate. Shortly thereafter, sacred rites are held to dispatch him to the realm of shadows. First brutally torn from all of his family and social ties and excluded from all functions and activities through which he experienced self-awareness, then banished by the same forces from the world of the living, the victim yields to the combined effect of intense terror, the sudden total withdrawal of the multiple reference systems provided by the support of the group, and, finally, to the group's decisive reversal in proclaiming him—once a living man, with rights and obligations—dead and an object of fear, ritual, and taboo. Physical integrity cannot withstand the dissolution of the social personality.[2]

How are these complex phenomena expressed on the physiological level? Cannon showed that fear, like rage, is associated with a particularly intense activity of the sympathetic nervous system. This activity is ordinarily useful, involving organic modifications which enable the individual to adapt himself to a new situation. But if the individual cannot avail himself of any instinctive or acquired response to an extraordinary situation (or to one which he conceives of as such), the activity of the sympathetic nervous system becomes intensified and disorganized; it may, sometimes within a few hours, lead to a decrease in the volume of blood and a concomitant drop in blood pressure, which result in irreparable damage to the circulatory organs. The rejection of food and drink, frequent among patients in the throes of intense anxiety, precipitates this process; dehydration acts as a stimulus to the sympathetic nervous system, and the decrease in blood volume is accentuated by the growing permeability of the capillary vessels. These hypotheses were confirmed by the study of several cases of trauma resulting from bombings, battle shock, and even surgical operations; death results, yet the autopsy reveals no lesions.

There is, therefore, no reason to doubt the efficacy of certain magical practices. But at the same time we see that the efficacy of magic implies a belief in magic. The latter has three complementary aspects: first, the sorcerer's belief in the effectiveness of his techniques; second, the patient's or victim's belief in the sorcerer's power; and, finally, the faith and expectations of the group, which constantly act as a sort of gravitational field within which the relationship between sorcerer and bewitched is located and defined.[3] Obviously, none of the three parties is capable of forming a clear picture of the sympathetic nervous system's activity or of the disturbances which Cannon called homeostatic. When the sorcerer claims to suck out of the patient's body a foreign object whose presence would explain the illness and produces a stone which he had previously hidden in his mouth, how does he justify this procedure in his own eyes? How can an innocent person accused of sorcery prove his innocence if the accusation is unanimous—since the magical situation is a consensual phenomenon? And, finally, how much credulity and how much skepticism are involved in the attitude of the group toward those in whom it recognizes extraordinary powers, to whom it accords corresponding privileges, but from whom it also requires adequate satisfaction? Let us begin by examining this last point.

It was in September, 1938. For several weeks we had been camping with a small band of Nambicuara Indians near the headwaters of the Tapajoz, in those desolate savannas of central Brazil where the natives wander during the greater part of the year, collecting seeds and wild fruits, hunting small mammals, insects, and reptiles, and whatever else might prevent them from dying of starvation. Thirty of them were camped together there, quite by chance. They were grouped in families under frail lean-tos of branches, which give scant protection from the scorching sun, nocturnal chill, rain, and wind. Like most bands, this one had both a secular chief and a sorcerer; the latter's daily activities—hunting, fishing, and handicrafts—were in no way different from those of the other men of the group. He was a robust man, about forty-five years old, and a *bon vivant*.

One evening, however, he did not return to camp at the usual time. Night fell and fires were lit; the natives were visibly worried. Countless perils lurk in the bush: torrential rivers, the somewhat improbable danger of encountering a large wild beast—jaguar or anteater—or, more readily pictured by the Nambicuara, an apparently harmless animal which is the incarnation of an evil spirit of the waters or forest. And above all, each night for the past week we had seen mysterious campfires, which sometimes approached and sometimes receded from our own. Any unknown band is always potentially hostile. After a two-hour wait, the natives were convinced that their companion had been killed in ambush and, while his two young wives and his son wept noisily in mourning for their dead husband and father, the other natives discussed the tragic consequences foreshadowed by the disappearance of their sorcerer.

Toward ten that evening, the anguished anticipation of imminent disaster, the lamentations in which the other women began to join, and the agitation of the men had created an intolerable atmosphere, and we decided to reconnoiter with several natives who had remained relatively calm. We had not gone two hundred yards when we stumbled upon a motionless figure. It was our man, crouching silently, shivering in the chilly night air, disheveled and without his belt, necklaces, and arm-bands (the Nambicuara wear nothing else). He allowed us to lead him back to the camp site without resistance, but only after long exhortations by his group and pleading by his family was he persuaded to talk. Finally, bit by bit, we extracted the details of his story. A thunderstorm, the first of the season, had burst during the afternoon, and the thunder had carried him off to a site several miles distant, which he named, and then, after stripping him completely, had brought him back to the spot where we found him. Everyone went off to sleep commenting on the event. The next day the thunder victim had recovered his joviality and, what is more, all his ornaments. This last detail did not appear to surprise anyone, and life resumed its normal course.

A few days later, however, another version of these prodigious events began to be circulated by certain natives. We must note that this band was actually composed of individuals of different origins and had been fused into a new social entity as a result of unknown circumstances. One of the groups had been decimated by an epidemic several years before and was no longer sufficiently large to lead an independent life; the other had seceded from its original tribe and found itself in the same straits. When and under what circumstances the two groups met and decided to unite their efforts, we could not discover. The secular leader of the new band came from one group and the sorcerer, or religious leader, from the other. The fusion was obviously recent, for no marriage had yet taken place between the two groups when we met them, although the children of one were usually betrothed to the children of the other; each group had retained its own dialect, and their members could communicate only through two or three bilingual natives.

This is the rumor that was spread. There was good reason to suppose that the unknown bands crossing the savanna belonged to the tribe of the seceded group of which the sorcerer was a member.

The sorcerer, impinging on the functions of his colleague the political chief, had doubtless wanted to contact his former tribesmen, perhaps to ask to return to the fold, or to provoke an attack upon his new companions, or perhaps even to reassure them of the friendly intentions of the latter. In any case, the sorcerer had needed a pretext for his absence, and his kidnapping by thunder and its subsequent staging were invented toward this end. It was, of course, the natives of the other group who spread this interpretation, which they secretly believed and which filled them with apprehension. But the official version was never publicly disputed, and until we left, shortly after the incident, it remained ostensibly accepted by all.[4]

Although the skeptics had analyzed the sorcerer's motives with great psychological finesse and political acumen, they would have been greatly astonished had someone suggested (quite plausibly) that the incident was a hoax which cast doubt upon the sorcerer's good faith and competence. He had probably not flown on the wings of thunder to the Rio Ananaz and had only staged an act. But these things might have happened, they had certainly happened in other circumstances, and they belonged to the realm of real experience. Certainly the sorcerer maintains an intimate relationship with the forces of the supernatural. The idea that in a particular case he had used his power to conceal a secular activity belongs to the realm of conjecture and provides an opportunity for critical judgment. The important point is that these two possibilities were not mutually exclusive; no more than are, for us, the alternate interpretations of war as the dying gasp of national independence or as the result of the schemes of munitions manufacturers. The two explanations are logically incompatible, but we admit that one or the other may be true; since they are equally plausible, we easily make the transition from one to the other, depending on the occasion and the moment. Many people have both explanations in the back of their minds.

Whatever their true origin, these divergent interpretations come from individual consciousness not as the result of objective analysis but rather as complementary ideas resulting from hazy and unelaborated attitudes which have an experiential character for each of us. These experiences, however, remain intellectually diffuse and emotionally intolerable unless they incorporate one or another of the patterns present in the group's culture. The assimilation of such patterns is the only means of objectivizing subjective states, of formulating inexpressible feelings, and of integrating inarticulated experiences into a system.

These mechanisms become clearer in the light of some observations made many years ago among the Zuni of New Mexico by an admirable field-worker, M. C. Stevenson.[5] A twelve-year-old girl was stricken with a nervous seizure directly after an adolescent boy had seized her hands. The youth was accused of sorcery and dragged before the court of the Bow priesthood. For an hour he denied having any knowledge of occult power, but this defense proved futile. Because the crime of sorcery was at that time still punished by death among the Zuni, the accused changed his tactics. He improvised a tale explaining the circumstances by which he had been initiated into sorcery. He said he had received two substances from his teachers, one which drove girls insane and another which cured them. This point constituted an ingenious precaution against later developments. Having been ordered to produce his medicines, he went home under guard and came back with two roots, which he proceeded to use in a complicated ritual. He simulated a trance after taking one of the drugs, and after taking the other he pretended to return to his normal state. Then he administered the remedy to the sick girl and declared her cured. The session was adjourned until the following day, but during the night the alleged sorcerer escaped. He was soon captured, and the girl's family set itself up as a court and continued the trial. Faced with the reluctance of his new judges to accept his first story, the boy then invented a new one. He told them that all his relatives and ancestors had been witches and that he had received marvellous powers from them. He claimed that he could assume the form of a cat, fill his mouth with cactus needles, and kill his victims—two infants, three girls, and two boys—by shooting the needles into them. These feats, he claimed, were due to the magical powers of certain plumes which were used to change him and his family into shapes other than human. This last detail was a tactical error, for the judges called upon him to produce the plumes as proof of his new story. He gave various excuses which were rejected one after another, and he was forced to take his judges to his house. He began by declaring that the plumes were secreted in a wall that he could not destroy. He was commanded to go to work. After breaking down a section of the wall and carefully examining the plaster, he tried to excuse himself by declaring that the plumes had been hidden two years before and that he could not remember their exact location. Forced to search again, he tried another wall, and after another hour's work, an old plume appeared in the plaster. He grabbed it eagerly and presented it to his persecutors as the magic device of which he had spoken. He was then made to explain the details of its use. Finally, dragged into the public plaza, he had to repeat his entire story (to which he added a wealth of new detail). He finished it with a pathetic speech in which he lamented the loss of his supernatural power. Thus reassured, his listeners agreed to free him.

This narrative, which we unfortunately had to abridge and strip of all its psychological nuances, is still instructive in many respects. First of all, we see that the boy tried for witchcraft, for which he risks the death penalty, wins his acquittal not by denying but by admitting his alleged crime. Moreover, he furthers his cause by presenting successive versions, each richer in detail (and thus, in theory, more persuasive of guilt) than the preceding one. The debate does not proceed, as do debates among us, by accusations and denials, but rather by allegations and specifications. The judges do not expect the accused to challenge their theory, much less to refute the facts. Rather, they require him to validate a system of which they possess only a fragment; he must reconstruct it as a whole in an appropriate way. As the field-worker noted in relation to a phase of the trial, "The warriors had become so absorbed by their interest in the narrative of the boy that they seemed entirely to have forgotten the cause of his appearance before them." [6] And when the magic plume was finally uncovered, the author remarks with great insight, "There was consternation among the warriors, who exclaimed in one voice: 'What does this mean?' Now they felt assured that the youth had spoken the truth." [7] Consternation, and not triumph at finding a tangible proof of the crime—for the judges had sought to bear witness to the reality of the system which had made the crime possible (by validating its objective basis through an appropriate emotional expression), rather than simply to punish a crime. By his confession, the defendant is transformed into a witness for the prosecution, with the participation (and even the complicity) of his judges. Through the defendant, witchcraft and the ideas associated with it cease to exist as a diffuse complex of poorly formulated sentiments and representations and become embodied in real experience. The defendant, who serves as a witness, gives the group the satisfaction of truth, which is infinitely greater and richer than the satisfaction of justice that would have been achieved by his execution. And finally, by his ingenious defense which makes his hearers progressively aware of the vitality offered by his corroboration of their system (especially since the choice is not between this system and another, but between the magical system and no system at all—that is, chaos), the youth, who at first was a threat to the physical security of his group, became the guardian of its spiritual coherence.

But is his defense merely ingenious? Everything leads us to believe that after groping for a subterfuge, the defendant participates with sincerity and—the word is not too strong—fervor in the drama enacted between him and his judges. He is proclaimed a sorcerer; since sorcerers do exist, he might well be one. And how would he know beforehand the signs which might reveal his calling to him? Perhaps the signs are there, present in this ordeal and in the convulsions of the little girl brought before the court. For the boy, too, the coherence of the system and the role assigned to him in preserving it are values no less essential than the personal security which he risks in the venture. Thus we see him, with a mixture of cunning and good faith, progressively construct the impersonation which is thrust upon him—chiefly by drawing on his knowledge and his memories, improvising somewhat, but above all living his role and seeking, through his manipulations and the ritual he builds from bits and pieces, the experience of a calling which is, at least theoretically, open to all. At the end of the adventure, what remains of his earlier hoaxes? To what extent has the hero become the dupe of his own impersonation? What is more, has he not truly become a sorcerer? We are told that in his final confession, "The longer the boy talked the more absorbed he became in his subject. . . . At times his face became radiant with satisfaction at his power over his listeners." [8] The girl recovers after he performs his curing ritual. The boy's experiences during the extraordinary ordeal become elaborated and structured. Little more is needed than for the innocent boy finally to confess to the possession of supernatural powers that are already recognized by the group.

We must consider at greater length another especially valuable document, which until now seems to have been valued solely for its linguistic interest. I refer to a fragment of the autobiography of a Kwakiutl Indian from the Vancouver region of Canada, obtained by Franz Boas.[9]

Quesalid (for this was the name he received when he became a sorcerer) did not believe in the power of the sorcerers—or, more accurately, shamans, since this is a better term for their specific type of activity in certain regions of the world. Driven by curiosity about their tricks and by the desire to expose them, he began to associate with the shamans until one of them offered to make him a member of their group. Quesalid did not wait to be asked twice, and his narrative recounts the details of his first lessons, a curious mixture of pantomime, prestidigitation, and empirical knowledge, including the art of simulating fainting and nervous fits, the learning of sacred songs, the technique for inducing vomiting, rather precise notions of auscultation and obstetrics, and the use of "dreamers," that is, spies who listen to private conversations and secretly convey to the shaman bits of information concerning the origins and symptoms of the ills suffered by different people. Above all, he learned the *ars magna* of one of the shamanistic schools of the Northwest Coast: The shaman hides a little tuft of down in a corner of his mouth, and he throws it up, covered with blood, at the proper moment—after having bitten his tongue or made his gums bleed—and solemnly presents it to his patient and the onlookers as the pathological foreign body extracted as a result of his sucking and manipulations.

His worst suspicions confirmed, Quesalid wanted to continue his inquiry. But he was no longer free. His apprenticeship among the shamans began to be noised about, and one day he was summoned by the family of a sick person who had dreamed of Quesalid as his healer. This first treatment (for which he received no payment, any more than he did for those which followed, since he had not completed the required four years of apprenticeship) was an outstanding success. Although Quesalid came to be known from that moment on as a "great shaman," he did not lose his critical faculties. He interpreted his success in psychological terms—it was successful "because he [the sick person] believed strongly in his dream about me." [10] A more complex adventure made him, in his own words, "hesitant and thinking about many things." [11] Here he encountered several varieties of a "false supernatural," and was led to conclude that some forms were less false than others—those, of course, in which he had a personal stake and whose system he was, at the same time, surreptitiously building up in his mind. A summary of the adventure follows.

While visiting the neighboring Koskimo Indians, Quesalid attends a curing ceremony of his illustrious colleagues of the other tribe. To his great astonishment he observes a difference in their technique. Instead of spitting out the illness in the form of a "bloody worm" (the concealed down), the Koskimo shamans merely spit a little saliva into their hands, and they dare to claim that this is "the sickness." What is the value of this method? What is the theory behind it? In order to find out "the strength of the shamans, whether it was real or whether they only pretended to be shamans" like his fellow tribesmen,[12] Quesalid requests and obtains permission to try his method in an instance where the Koskimo method has failed. The sick woman then declares herself cured.

And here our hero vacillates for the first time. Though he had few illusions about his own technique, he has now found one which is more false, more mystifying, and more dishonest than his own. For he at least gives his clients something. He presents them with their sickness in a visible and tangible form, while his foreign colleagues show nothing at all and only claim to have captured the sickness. Moreover, Quesalid's method gets results, while the other is futile. Thus our hero grapples with a problem which perhaps has its parallel in the development of modern science. Two systems which we know to be inadequate present (with respect to each other) a differential validity, from both a logical and an empirical perspective. From which frame of reference shall we judge them? On the level of fact, where they merge, or on their own level, where they take on different values, both theoretically and empirically?

Meanwhile, the Koskimo shamans, "ashamed" and discredited before their tribesmen, are also plunged into doubt. Their colleague has produced, in the form of a material object, the illness which they had always considered as spiritual in nature and had thus never dreamed of rendering visible. They send Quesalid an emissary to invite him to a secret meeting in a cave. Quesalid goes and his foreign colleagues expound their system to him: "Every sickness is a man: boils and swellings, and itch and scabs, and pimples and coughs and consumption and scrofula; and also this, stricture of the bladder and stomach aches. . . . As soon as we get the soul of the sickness which is a man, then dies the sickness which is a man. Its body just disappears in our insides." [13] If this theory is correct, what is there to show? And why, when Quesalid operates, does "the sickness stick to his hand"? But Quesalid takes refuge behind professional rules which forbid him to teach before completing four years of apprenticeship, and refuses to speak. He maintains his silence even when the Koskimo shamans send him their allegedly virgin daughters to try to seduce him and discover his secret.

Thereupon Quesalid returns to his village at Fort Rupert. He learns that the most reputed shaman of a neighboring clan, worried about Quesalid's growing renown, has challenged all his colleagues, inviting them to compete with him in curing several patients. Quesalid comes to the contest and observes the cures of his elder. Like the Koskimo, this shaman does not show the illness. He simply incorporates an invisible object, "what he called the sickness" into his head-ring, made of bark, or into his bird-shaped ritual rattle.[14] These objects can hang suspended in mid-air, owing to the power of the illness which "bites" the house-posts or the shaman's hand. The usual drama unfolds. Quesalid is asked to intervene in cases judged hopeless by his predecessor, and he triumphs with his technique of the bloody worm.

Here we come to the truly pathetic part of the story. The old shaman, ashamed and despairing because of the ill-repute into which he has fallen and by the collapse of his therapeutic technique, sends his daughter to Quesalid to beg him for an interview. The latter finds his colleague sitting under a tree and the old shaman begins thus: "It won't be bad what we say to each other, friend, but only I wish you to try and save my life for me, so that I may not die of shame, for I am a plaything of our people on account of what you did last night. I pray you to have mercy and tell me what stuck on the palm of your hand last night. Was it the true sickness or was it only made up? For I beg you have mercy and tell me about the way you did it so that I can imitate you. Pity me, friend." [15]

Silent at first, Quesalid begins by calling for explanations about the feats of the head-ring and the rattle. His colleague shows him the nail hidden in the head-ring which he can press at right angles into the post, and the way in which he tucks the head of his rattle between his finger joints to make it look as if the bird were hanging by its beak from his hand. He himself probably does nothing but lie and fake, simulating shamanism for material gain, for he admits to being "covetous for the property of the sick men." He knows that shamans cannot catch souls, "for . . . we all own a soul"; so he resorts to using tallow and pretends that "it is a soul . . . that white thing . . . sitting on my hand." The daughter then adds her entreaties to those of her father: "Do have mercy that he may live." But Quesalid remains silent. That very night, following this tragic conversation, the shaman disappears with his entire family, heartsick and feared by the community, who think that he may be tempted to take revenge. Needless fears: He returned a year later, but both he and his daughter had gone mad. Three years later, he died.

And Quesalid, rich in secrets, pursued his career, exposing the impostors and full of contempt for the profession. "Only one shaman was seen by me, who sucked at a sick man and I never found out whether he was a real shaman or only made up. Only for this reason I believe that he is a shaman; he does not allow those who are made well to pay him. I truly never once saw him laugh." [16] Thus his original attitude has changed considerably. The radical negativism of the free thinker has given way to more moderate feelings. Real shamans do exist. And what about him? At the end of the narrative we cannot tell, but it is evident that he carries on his craft conscientiously, takes pride in his achievements, and warmly defends the technique of the bloody down against all rival schools. He seems to have completely lost sight of the fallaciousness of the technique which he had so disparaged at the beginning.

We see that the psychology of the sorcerer is not simple. In order to analyze it, we shall first examine the case of the old shaman who begs his young rival to tell him the truth—whether the illness glued in the palm of his hand like a sticky red worm is real or made up—and who goes mad when he receives no answer. Before the tragedy, he was fully convinced of two things—first, that pathological conditions have a cause which may be discovered and second, that a system of interpretation in which personal inventiveness is important structures the phases of the illness, from the diagnosis to the cure. This fabulation of a reality unknown in itself —a fabulation consisting of procedures and representations—is founded on a threefold experience: first, that of the shaman himself, who, if his calling is a true one (and even if it is not, simply by virtue of his practicing it), undergoes specific states of a psychosomatic nature; second, that of the sick person, who may or may not experience an improvement of his condition; and, finally, that of the public, who also participate in the cure, experiencing an enthusiasm and an intellectual and emotional satisfaction which produce collective support, which in turn inaugurates a new cycle.

These three elements of what we might call the "shamanistic complex" cannot be separated. But they are clustered around two poles, one formed by the intimate experience of the shaman and the other by group consensus. There is no reason to doubt that sorcerers, or at least the more sincere among them, believe in their calling and that this belief is founded on the experiencing of specific states. The hardships and privations which they undergo would often be sufficient in themselves to provoke these states, even if we refuse to admit them as proof of a serious and fervent calling. But there is also linguistic evidence which, because it is indirect, is more convincing. In the Wintu dialect of California, there are five verbal classes which correspond to knowledge by sight, by bodily experience, by inference, by reasoning, and by hearsay. All five make up the category of knowledge as opposed to conjecture, which is differently expressed. Curiously enough, relationships with the supernatural world are expressed by means of the modes of knowledge—by bodily impression (that is, the most intuitive kind of experience), by inference, and by reasoning. Thus the native who becomes a shaman after a spiritual crisis conceives of his state grammatically, as a consequence to be inferred from the fact—formulated as real experience—that he has received divine guidance. From the latter he concludes deductively that he must have been on a journey to the beyond, at the end of which he found himself—again, an immediate experience—once more among his people.[17]

The experiences of the sick person represent the least important aspect of the system, except for the fact that a patient successfully treated by a shaman is in an especially good position to become a shaman in his own right, as we see today in the case of psychoanalysis. In any event, we must remember that the shaman does not completely lack empirical knowledge and experimental techniques, which may in part explain his success. Furthermore, disorders of the type currently termed psychosomatic, which constitute a large part of the illnesses prevalent in societies with a low degree of security, probably often yield to psychotherapy. At any rate, it seems probable that medicine men, like their civilized colleagues, cure at least some of the cases they treat and that without this relative success magical practices could not have been so widely diffused in time and space. But this point is not fundamental; it is subordinate to the other two. Quesalid did not become a great shaman because he cured his patients; he cured his patients because he had become a great shaman. Thus we have reached the other— that is, the collective—pole of our system.

The true reason for the defeat of Quesalid's rivals must then be sought in the attitude of the group rather than in the pattern of the rivals' successes and failures. The rivals themselves emphasize this when they confess their shame at having become the laughingstock of the group; this is a social sentiment *par excellence*. Failure is secondary, and we see in all their statements that they consider it a function of another phenomenon, which is the disappearance of the *social consensus,* re-created at their expense around another practitioner and another system of curing. Consequently, the fundamental problem revolves around the relationship between the individual and the group, or, more accurately, the relationship between a specific category of individuals and specific expectations of the group.

In treating his patient the shaman also offers his audience a performance. What is this performance? Risking a rash generalization on the basis of a few observations, we shall say that it always involves the shaman's enactment of the "call," or the initial crisis which brought him the revelation of his condition. But we must not be deceived by the word *performance*. The shaman does not limit himself to reproducing or miming certain events. He actually relives them in all their vividness, originality, and violence. And since he returns to his normal state at the end of the séance, we may say, borrowing a key term from psychoanalysis, that he *abreacts*. In psychoanalysis, abreaction refers to the decisive moment in the treatment when the patient intensively relives the initial situation from which his disturbance stems, before he ultimately overcomes it. In this sense, the shaman is a professional abreactor.

We have set forth elsewhere the theoretical hypotheses that might be formulated in order for us to accept the idea that the type of abreaction specific to each shaman—or, at any rate, to each shamanistic school—might symbolically induce an abreaction of his own disturbance in each patient.[18] In any case, if the essential relationship is that between the shaman and the group, we must also state the question from another point of view—that of the relationship between normal and pathological thinking. From any non-scientific perspective (and here we can exclude no society), pathological and normal thought processes are complementary rather than opposed. In a universe which it strives to understand but whose dynamics it cannot fully control, normal thought continually seeks the meaning of things which refuse to reveal their significance. So-called pathological thought, on the other hand, overflows with emotional interpretations and overtones, in order to supplement an otherwise deficient reality. For normal thinking there exists something which cannot be empirically verified and is, therefore, "claimable." For pathological thinking there exist experiences without object, or something "available." We might borrow from linguistics and say that so-called normal thought always suffers from a deficit of meaning, whereas so-called pathological thought (in at least some of its manifestations) disposes of a plethora of meaning. Through collective participation in shamanistic curing, a balance is established between these two complementary situations. Normal thought cannot fathom the problem of illness, and so the group calls upon the neurotic to furnish a wealth of emotion heretofore lacking a focus.

An equilibrium is reached between what might be called supply and demand on the psychic level—but only on two conditions. First, a structure must be elaborated and continually modified through the interaction of group tradition and individual invention. This structure is a system of oppositions and correlations, integrating all the elements of a total situation, in which sorcerer, patient, and audience, as well as representations and procedures, all play their parts. Furthermore, the public must participate in the abreaction, to a certain extent at least, along with the patient and the sorcerer. It is this vital experience of a universe of symbolic effusions which the patient, because he is ill, and the sorcerer, because he is neurotic—in other words, both having types of experience which cannot otherwise be integrated—allow the public to glimpse as "fireworks" from a safe distance. In the absence of any experimental control, which is indeed unnecessary, it is this experience alone, and its relative richness in each case, which makes possible a choice between several systems and elicits adherence to a particular school or practitioner.[19]

In contrast with scientific explanation, the problem here is not to attribute confused and disorganized states, emotions, or representations to an objective cause, but rather to articulate them into a whole or system. The system is valid precisely to the extent that it allows the coalescence or precipitation of these diffuse states, whose discontinuity also makes them painful. To the conscious mind, this last phenomenon constitutes an original experience which cannot be grasped from without. Because of their complementary disorders, the sorcerer-patient dyad incarnates for the group, in vivid and concrete fashion, an antagonism that is inherent in all thought but that normally remains vague and imprecise. The patient is all passivity and self-alienation, just as inexpressibility is the disease of the mind. The sorcerer is activity and self-projection, just as affectivity is the source of symbolism. The cure interrelates these opposite poles, facilitating the transition from one to the other, and demonstrates, within a total experience, the coherence of the psychic universe, itself a projection of the social universe.

Thus it is necessary to extend the notion of abreaction by examining the meanings it acquires in psychotherapies other than psychoanalysis, although the latter deserves the credit for rediscovering and insisting upon its fundamental validity. It may be objected that in psychoanalysis there is only one abreaction, the patient's, rather than three. We are not so sure of this. It is true that in the shamanistic cure the sorcerer speaks and abreacts *for* the silent patient, while in psychoanalysis it is the patient who talks and abreacts *against* the listening therapist. But the therapist's abreaction, while not concomitant with the patient's, is nonetheless required, since he must be analyzed before he himself can become an analyst. It is more difficult to define the role ascribed to the group by each technique. Magic readapts the group to predefined problems through the patient, while psychoanalysis readapts the patient to the group by means of the solutions reached. But the distressing trend which, for several years, has tended to transform the psychoanalytic system from a body of scientific hypotheses that are experimentally verifiable in certain specific and limited cases into a kind of diffuse mythology interpenetrating the consciousness of the group, could rapidly bring about a parallelism. (This group consciousness is an objective phenomenon, which the psychologist expresses through a subjective tendency to extend to normal thought a system of interpretations conceived for pathological thought and to apply to facts of collective psychology a method adapted solely to the study of individual psychology.) When this happens—and perhaps it already has in certain countries—the value of the system will no longer be based upon real cures from which certain individuals can benefit, but on the sense of security that the group receives from the myth underlying the cure and from the popular system upon which the group's universe is reconstructed.

Even at the present time, the comparison between psychoanalysis and older and more widespread psychological therapies can encourage the former to re-examine its principles and methods. By continuously expanding the recruitment of its patients, who begin as clearly characterized abnormal individuals and gradually become representative of the group, psychoanalysis transforms its treatments into conversions. For only a patient can emerge cured; an unstable or maladjusted individual can only be persuaded. A considerable danger thus arises: The treatment (unbeknown to the therapist, naturally), far from leading to the resolution of a specific disturbance within its own context, is reduced to the reorganization of the patient's universe in terms of psychoanalytic interpretations. This means that we would finally arrive at precisely that situation which furnishes the point of departure as well as the theoretical validity of the magico-social system that we have analyzed.

If this analysis is correct, we must see magical behavior as the response to a situation which is revealed to the mind through emotional manifestations, but whose essence is intellectual. For only the history of the symbolic function can allow us to understand the intellectual condition of man, in which the universe is never charged with sufficient meaning and in which the mind always has more meanings available than there are objects to which to relate them. Torn between these two systems of reference—the signifying and the signified—man asks magical thinking to provide him with a new system of reference, within which the thus-far contradictory elements can be integrated. But we know that this system is built at the expense of the progress of knowledge, which would have required us to retain only one of the two previous systems and to refine it to the point where it absorbed the other. This point is still far off. We must not permit the individual, whether normal or neurotic, to repeat this collective misadventure. The study of the mentally sick individual has shown us that all persons are more or less oriented toward contradictory systems and suffer from the resulting conflict; but the fact that a certain form of integration is possible and effective practically is not enough to make it true, or to make us certain that the adaptation thus achieved does not constitute an absolute regression in relation to the previous conflict situation.

The reabsorption of a deviant specific synthesis, through its integration with the normal syntheses, into a general but arbitrary synthesis (aside from critical cases where action is required) would represent a loss on all fronts. A body of elementary hypotheses can have a certain instrumental value for the practitioner without necessarily being recognized, in theoretical analysis, as the final image of reality and without necessarily linking the patient and the therapist in a kind of mystical communion which does not have the same meaning for both parties and which only ends by reducing the treatment to a fabulation.

In the final analysis we could only expect this fabulation to be a language, whose function is to provide a socially authorized translation of phenomena whose deeper nature would become once again equally impenetrable to the group, the patient, and the healer.

NOTES

1. W. B. Cannon, " 'Voodoo' Death," *American Anthropologist*, n.s., XLIV (1942).
2. An Australian aborigine was brought to the Darwin hospital in April 1956, apparently dying of this type of sorcery. He was placed in an oxygen tent and fed intravenously. He gradually recovered, convinced that the white man's magic was the stronger. See Arthur Morley in the *London Sunday Times*, April 22, 1956, p. 11.
3. In this study, whose aim is more psychological than sociological, we feel justified in neglecting the finer distinctions between the several modes of magical operations and different types of sorcerers when these are not absolutely necessary.
4. C. Lévi-Strauss, *Tristes Tropiques* (Paris: 1955), Chapter XXIX.
5. M. C. Stevenson, *The Zuni Indians*, 23rd Annual Report of the Bureau of American Ethnology (Washington, D.C.: Smithsonian Institution, 1905).
6. *Ibid.*, p. 401.
7. *Ibid.*, p. 404.
8. *Ibid.*, p. 406.
9. Franz Boas, *The Religion of the Kwakiutl*, Columbia University Contributions to Anthropology, Vol. X (New York: 1930), Part II, pp. 1-41.
10. *Ibid.*, p. 13.
11. *Ibid.*, p. 19.
12. *Ibid.*, p. 17.
13. *Ibid.*, pp. 20-21.
14. *Ibid.*, p. 27.
15. *Ibid.*, p. 31.
16. *Ibid.*, pp. 40-41.
17. D. D. Lee, "Some Indian Texts Dealing with the Supernatural," *The Review of Religion* (May, 1941).
18. See "The Effectiveness of Symbols," Chapter X of the present volume.
19. This oversimplified equation of sorcerer and neurotic was justly criticized by Michel Leiris. I subsequently refined this concept in my "Introduction à l'oeuvre de Marcel Mauss," in M. Mauss, *Sociologie et Anthropologie* (Paris: 1950), pp. xviii-xxiii.

CHAPTER X

The Effectiveness
of Symbols

THE FIRST IMPORTANT South American magico-religious text to be known, published by Wassén and Holmer,[1] throws new light on certain aspects of shamanistic curing and raises problems of theoretical interpretation by no means exhaustively treated in the editors' excellent commentary. We will re-examine this text for its more general implications, rather than from the linguistic or Americanist perspective primarily employed by the authors.

The text is a long incantation, covering eighteen pages in the native version, divided into 535 sections. It was obtained by the Cuna Indian Guillermo Haya from an elderly informant of his tribe. The Cuna, who live within the Panama Republic, received special attention from the late Erland Nordenskiöld, who even succeeded in training collaborators among the natives. After Nordenskiöld's death, Haya forwarded the text to Nordenskiöld's successor, Dr. Wassén. The text was taken down in the original language and accompanied by a Spanish translation, which Holmer revised with great care.

The purpose of the song is to facilitate difficult childbirth. Its use is somewhat exceptional, since native women of Central and South America have easier deliveries than women of Western societies. The intervention of the shaman is thus rare and occurs in case of failure, at the request of the midwife. The song begins with a picture of the midwife's confusion and describes her visit to the shaman, the latter's departure for the hut of the woman in labor, his arrival, and his preparations—consisting of fumigations of burnt cocoa-nibs, invocations, and the making of sacred figures, or *nuchu*. These images, carved from prescribed kinds of wood which lend them their effectiveness, represent tutelary spirits whom the shaman makes his assistants and whom he leads to the abode of Muu, the power responsible for the formation of the fetus. A difficult childbirth results when Muu has exceeded her functions and captured the *purba*, or "soul," of the mother-to-be. Thus the song expresses a quest: the quest for the lost *purba*, which will be restored after many vicissitudes, such as the overcoming of obstacles, a victory over wild beasts, and, finally, a great contest waged by the shaman and his tutelary spirits against Muu and her daughters, with the help of magical hats whose weight the latter are not able to bear. Muu, once she has been defeated, allows the *purba* of the ailing woman to be discovered and freed. The delivery takes place, and the song ends with a statement of the precautions taken so that Muu will not escape and pursue her visitors. The fight is not waged against Muu herself, who is indispensable to procreation, but only against her abuses of power. Once these have been corrected, relations become friendly, and Muu's parting words to the shaman almost correspond to an invitation: "Friend *nele*, when do you think to visit me again?" (413)[2]

Thus far we have rendered the term *nele* as shaman, which might seem incorrect, since the cure does not appear to require the officiant to experience ecstasy or a transition to another psychic state. Yet the smoke of the cocoa beans aims primarily at "strengthening his garments" and "strengthening" the *nele* himself, "making him brave in front of Muu" (65-66). And above all, the Cuna classification, which distinguishes between several types of medicine men, shows that the power of the *nele* has supernatural sources. The native medicine men are divided into *nele, inatuledi,* and *absogedi.* The functions of the *inatuledi* and *absogedi* are based on knowledge of songs and cures, acquired through study and validated by examinations, while the talent of the *nele,* considered innate, consists of supernatural sight, which instantly discovers the cause of the illness—that is, the whereabouts of the vital forces, whether particular or generalized, that have been carried off by evil spirits. For the *nele* can recruit these spirits, making them his protectors or assistants.[3] There is no doubt, therefore, that he is actually a shaman, even if his intervention in childbirth does not present all the traits which ordinarily accompany this function. And the *nuchu,* protective spirits who at the shaman's bidding become embodied in the figurines he has carved, receive from him—along with invisibility and clairvoyance—*niga. Niga* is "vitality" and "resistance," [4] which make these spirits *nelegan* (plural of *nele*) "in the service of men" or in the "likeness of human beings" (235-237), although endowed with exceptional powers.

From our brief synopsis, the song appears to be rather commonplace. The sick woman suffers because she has lost her spiritual double or, more correctly, one of the specific doubles which together constitute her vital strength. (We shall return to this point.) The shaman, assisted by his tutelary spirits, undertakes a journey to the supernatural world in order to snatch the double from the malevolent spirit who has captured it; by restoring it to its owner, he achieves the cure. The exceptional interest of this text does not lie in this formal framework, but, rather, in the discovery—stemming no doubt from a reading of the text, but for which Holmer and Wassén deserve, nonetheless, full credit—that *Mu-Igala,* that is, "Muu's way," and the abode of Muu are not, to the native mind, simply a mythical itinerary and dwelling-place. They represent, literally, the vagina and uterus of the pregnant woman, which are explored by the shaman and *nuchu* and in whose depths they wage their victorious combat.

This interpretation is based first of all on an analysis of the concept of *purba.* The *purba* is a different spiritual principle from the *niga,* which we defined above. Unlike the *purba* the *niga* cannot be stolen from its possessor, and only human beings and animals own one. A plant or a stone has a *purba* but not a *niga.* The same is true of a corpse; and in a child, the *niga* only develops with age. It seems, therefore, that one could, without too much inaccuracy, interpret *niga* as "vital strength," and *purba* as "double" or "soul," with the understanding that these words do not imply a distinction between animate and inanimate (since everything is animate for the Cuna) but correspond rather to the Platonic notion of "idea" or "archetype" of which every being or object is the material expression.

The sick woman of the song has lost more than her *purba:* the native text attributes fever to her—"the hot garments of the disease" (1 and *passim*)—and the loss or impairment of her sight— "straying . . . asleep on Muu Puklip's path" (97). Above all, as she declares to the shaman who questions her, "It is Muu Puklip who has come to me. She wants to take my *niga purbalele* for good" (98). Holmer proposes translating *niga* as physical strength and *purba* (*lele*) as soul or essence, whence "the soul of her life." [5] It would perhaps be bold to suggest that the *niga,* an attribute of the living being, results from the existence of not one but several *purba,* which are functionally interrelated. Yet each part of the body has its own *purba,* and the *niga* seems to constitute, on the spiritual level, the equivalent of the concept of organism. Just as life results from the cooperation of the organs, so "vital strength" would be none other than the harmonious concurrence of all the *purba,* each of which governs the functions of a specific organ.

As a matter of fact, not only does the shaman retrieve the *niga purbalele;* his discovery is followed immediately by the recapture of other *purba,* those of the heart, bones, teeth, hair, nails, and feet (401-408, 435-442). The omission here of the *purba* governing the most affected organs—the generative organs—might come as a surprise. As the editors of the text emphasize, this is because the *purba* of the uterus is not considered as a victim but as responsible for the pathological disorder. Muu and her daughters, the *muugan,* are, as Nordenskiöld pointed out, the forces that preside over the development of the fetus and that give it its *kurgin,* or natural capacities.[6] The text does not refer to these positive attributes. In it Muu appears as an instigator of disorder, a special "soul" that has captured and paralyzed the other special "souls," thus destroying the cooperation which insures the integrity of the "chief body" (*cuerpo jefe* in Spanish, 430, 435) from which it draws its *niga*. But at the same time, Muu must stay put, for the expedition undertaken to liberate the *purba* might provoke Muu's escape by the road which temporarily remains open; hence the precautions whose details fill the last part of the song. The shaman mobilizes the Lords of the wild animals to guard the way, the road is entangled, golden and silver nets are fastened, and, for four days, the *nelegan* stand watch and beat their sticks (505-535). Muu, therefore, is not a fundamentally evil force: she is a force gone awry. In a difficult delivery the "soul" of the uterus has led astray all the "souls" belonging to other parts of the body. Once these souls are liberated, the soul of the uterus can and must resume its cooperation. Let us emphasize right here the clarity with which the native ideology delineates the emotional content of the physiological disturbance, as it might appear, in an implicit way, to the mind of the sick woman.

To reach Muu, the shaman and his assistants must follow a road, "Muu's way," which may be identified from the many allusions in the text. When the shaman, crouching beneath the sick woman's hammock, has finished carving the *nuchu*, the latter rise up "at the extremity of the road" (72, 83) and the shaman exhorts them in these terms:

> The (sick) woman lies in the hammock in front of you.
> Her white tissue lies in her lap, her white tissues move softly.
> The (sick) woman's body lies weak.
> When they light up (along) Muu's way, it runs over with exudations and like blood.
> Her exudations drip down below the hammock all like blood, all red.
> The inner white tissue extends to the bosom of the earth.
> Into the middle of the woman's white tissue a human being descends. (84-90)

The translators are doubtful as to the meaning of the last two sentences, yet they refer to another native text, published by Nordenskiöld, which leaves no doubt as to the identification of the "white inner tissue" with the vulva:

> *sibugua molul arkaali*
> blanca tela abriendo
> *sibugua molul akinnali*
> blanca tela extendiendo

. . . .
sibugua molul abalase tulapurua ekuanali
blanca tela centro feto caer haciendo[7]

"Muu's way," darkened and completely covered with blood owing to the difficult labor, and which the *nuchu* have to find by the white sheen of their clothes and magical hats, is thus unquestionably the vagina of the sick woman. And "Muu's abode," the "dark whirlpool" where she dwells, corresponds to the uterus, since the native informant comments on the name of this abode, *Amukkapiryawila,* in terms of *omegan purba amurrequedi,* that is, "woman's turbid menstruation," also called "the dark deep whirlpool" (250-251) and "the dark inner place" (32).[8]

The original character of this text gives it a special place among the shamanistic cures ordinarily described. These cures are of three types, which are not, however, mutually exclusive. The sick organ or member may be physically involved, through a manipulation or suction which aims at extracting the cause of the illness—usually a thorn, crystal, or feather made to appear at the opportune moment, as in tropical America, Australia, and Alaska. Curing may also revolve, as among the Araucanians, around a sham battle, waged in the hut and then outdoors, against harmful spirits. Or, as among the Navaho, the officiant may recite incantations and prescribe actions (such as placing the sick person on different parts of a painting traced on the ground with colored sands and pollens) which bear no direct relationship to the specific disturbance to be cured. In all these cases, the therapeutic method (which as we know is often effective) is difficult to interpret. When it deals directly with the unhealthy organ, it is too grossly concrete (generally, pure deceit) to be granted intrinsic value. And when it consists in the repetition of often highly abstract ritual, it is difficult for us to understand its direct bearing on the illness. It would be convenient to dismiss these difficulties by declaring that we are dealing with psychological cures. But this term will remain meaningless unless we can explain how specific psychological representations are invoked to combat equally specific physiological disturbances. The text that we have analyzed offers a striking contribution to the solution of this problem. The song constitutes a purely psychological treatment, for the shaman does not touch the body of the sick woman and administers no remedy.

Nevertheless it involves, directly and explicitly, the pathological condition and its locus. In our view, the song constitutes a *psychological manipulation* of the sick organ, and it is precisely from this manipulation that a cure is expected.

To begin, let us demonstrate the existence and the characteristics of this manipulation. Then we shall ask what its purpose and its effectiveness are. First, we are surprised to find that the song, whose subject is a dramatic struggle between helpful and malevolent spirits for the reconquest of a "soul," devotes very little attention to action proper. In eighteen pages of text the contest occupies less than one page and the meeting with Muu Puklip scarcely two pages. The preliminaries, on the other hand, are highly developed and the preparations, the outfitting of the *nuchu*, the itinerary, and the sites are described with a great wealth of detail. Such is the case, at the beginning, for the midwife's visit to the shaman. The conversation between the sick woman and the midwife, followed by that between the midwife and the shaman, recurs twice, for each speaker repeats exactly the utterance of the other before answering him:

> The (sick) woman speaks to the midwife: "I am indeed being dressed in the hot garment of the disease."
> The midwife answers her (sick woman): "You are indeed being dressed in the hot garment of the disease, I also hear you say."
> (1-2)

It might be argued [9] that this stylistic device is common among the Cuna and stems from the necessity, among peoples bound to oral tradition, of memorizing exactly what has been said. And yet here this device is applied not only to speech but to actions:

> The midwife turns about in the hut.
> The midwife looks for some beads.
> The midwife turns about (in order to leave).
> The midwife puts one foot in front of the other.
> The midwife touches the ground with her foot.
> The midwife puts her other foot forward.
> The midwife pushes open the door of her hut; the door of her hut creaks.
> The midwife goes out . . . (7-14).

This minute description of her departure is repeated when she arrives at the shaman's, when she returns to the sick woman, when the shaman departs, and when he arrives. Sometimes the same description is repeated twice in the same terms (37-39 and 45-47 reproduce 33-35). The cure thus begins with a historical account of the events that preceded it, and some elements which might appear secondary ("arrivals" and "departures") are treated with luxuriant detail as if they were, so to speak, filmed in slow-motion. We encounter this technique throughout the text, but it is nowhere applied as systematically as at the beginning and to describe incidents of retrospective interest.

Everything occurs as though the shaman were trying to induce the sick woman—whose contact with reality is no doubt impaired and whose sensitivity is exacerbated—to relive the initial situation through pain, in a very precise and intense way, and to become psychologically aware of its smallest details. Actually this situation sets off a series of events of which the body and internal organs of the sick woman will be the assumed setting. A transition will thus be made from the most prosaic reality to myth, from the physical universe to the physiological universe, from the external world to the internal body. And the myth being enacted in the internal body must retain throughout the vividness and the character of lived experience prescribed by the shaman in the light of the pathological state and through an appropriate obsessing technique.

The next ten pages offer, in breathless rhythm, a more and more rapid oscillation between mythical and physiological themes, as if to abolish in the mind of the sick woman the distinction which separates them, and to make it impossible to differentiate their respective attributes. First there is a description of the woman lying in her hammock or in the native obstetrical position, facing eastward, knees parted, groaning, losing her blood, the vulva dilated and moving (84-92, 123-124, 134-135, 152, 158, 173, 177-178, 202-204). Then the shaman calls by name the spirits of intoxicating drinks; of the winds, waters, and woods; and even—precious testimony to the plasticity of the myth—the spirit of the "silver steamer of the white man" (187). The themes converge: like the sick woman, the *nuchu* are dripping with blood; and the pains of the sick woman assume cosmic proportions: "The inner white tissue extends to the bosom of the earth. . . . Into the bosom of the earth her exudations gather into a pool, all like blood, all red" (84-92). At the same time, each spirit, when it appears, is carefully described, and the magical equipment which he receives from the shaman is enumerated at great length: black beads, flame-colored beads, dark beads, ring-shaped beads, tiger bones, rounded bones, throat bones, and many other bones, silver necklaces, armadillo bones, bones of the bird *kerkettoli,* woodpecker bones, bones for flutes, silver beads (104-118). Then general recruitment begins anew, as if these guarantees were still inadequate and all forces, known or unknown to the sick woman, were to be rallied for the invasion (119-229).

Yet we are released to such a small extent into the realm of myth that the penetration of the vagina, mythical though it be, is proposed to the sick woman in concrete and familiar terms. On two occasions, moreover, "muu" designates the uterus directly, and not the spiritual principle which governs its activity ("the sick woman's muu," 204, 453).[10] Here the *nelegan*, in order to enter Muu's way, take on the appearance and the motions of the erect penis:

The *nelegan*'s hats are shining white, the *nelegan*'s hats are whitish.
The *nelegan* are becoming flat and low (?), all like bits, all straight.
The *nelegan* are beginning to become terrifying (?), the *nelegan*
    are becoming all terrifying (?), for the sake of the (sick)
    woman's *niga purbalele* (230-232).

And further, below:

The *nelegan* go balancing up on top of the hammock, they go
    moving upward like *nusupane* (239).[11]

The technique of the narrative thus aims at recreating a real experience in which the myth merely shifts the protagonists. The *nelegan* enter the natural orifice, and we can imagine that after all this psychological preparation the sick woman actually feels them entering. Not only does she feel them, but they "light up" the route they are preparing to follow—for their own sake, no doubt, and to find the way, but also to make the center of inexpressible and painful sensations "clear" for her and accessible to her consciousness. "The *nelegan* put good sight into the sick woman, the *nelegan* light good eyes in the (sick) woman . . ." (238).

And this "illuminating sight," to paraphrase an expression in the text, enables them to relate in detail a complicated itinerary that is a true mythical anatomy, corresponding less to the real structure of the genital organs than to a kind of emotional geography, identifying each point of resistance and each thrust:

> The *nelegan* set out, the *nelegan* march in a single file along Muu's road, as far as the Low Mountain,
> The *nelegan* set out, etc., as far as the Short Mountain,
> The *nelegan*, etc., as far as the Long Mountain,
> The *nelegan*, etc., (to) Yala Pokuna Yala, (not translated)
> The *nelegan*, etc., (to) Yala Akkwatallekun Yala, (not translated)
> The *nelegan*, etc., (to) Yala Ilamalisuikun Yala, (not translated)
> The *nelegan*, etc., into the center of the Flat Mountain.
> The *nelegan* set out, the *nelegan* march in a single file along Muu's road (241-248).

The picture of the uterine world, peopled with fantastic monsters and dangerous animals, is amenable to the same interpretation —which is, moreover, confirmed by the native informant: "It is the animals," he says, "who increase the diseases of the laboring woman"; that is, the pains themselves are personified. And here again, the song seems to have as its principal aim the description of these pains to the sick woman and the naming of them, that is, their presentation to her in a form accessible to conscious or unconscious thought: Uncle Alligator, who moves about with his bulging eyes, his striped and variegated body, crouching and wriggling his tail; Uncle Alligator Tiikwalele, with glistening body, who moves his glistening flippers, whose flippers conquer the place, push everything aside, drag everything; Nele Ki(k)kirpanalele, the Octopus, whose sticky tentacles are alternately opening and closing; and many others besides: He-who-has-a-hat-that-is-soft, He-who-has-a-red-colored-hat, He-who-has-a-variegated-hat, etc.; and the guardian animals: the black tiger, the red animal, the two-colored animal, the dust-colored animal; each is tied with an iron chain, the tongue hanging down, the tongue hanging out, saliva dripping, saliva foaming, with flourishing tail, the claws coming out and tearing things "all like blood, all red" (253-298).

To enter into this hell à la Hieronymus Bosch and reach its owner, the *nelegan* have to overcome other obstacles, this time material: fibers, loose threads, fastened threads, successive curtains—rainbow-colored, golden, silvery, red, black, maroon, blue, white, wormlike, "like neckties," yellow, twisted, thick (305-330); and for this purpose, the shaman calls reinforcements: Lords of the wood-boring insects, who are to "cut, gather, wind and reduce" the threads, which Holmer and Wassén identify as the internal tissues of the uterus.[12]

The *nelegan*'s invasion follows the downfall of these last obstacles, and here the tournament of the hats takes place. A discussion of this would lead us too far from the immediate purpose of this study. After the liberation of the *niga purbalele* comes the descent, which is just as dangerous as the ascent, since the purpose of the whole undertaking is to induce childbirth—precisely, a difficult descent. The shaman counts his helpers and encourages his troops; still he must summon other reinforcements: the "clearers of the way," Lords-of-the-burrowing animals, such as the armadillo. The *niga* is exhorted to make its way toward the orifice:

> Your body lies in front of you in the hammock,
> (Her) white tissue lies in her lap,
> The white inner tissue moves softly,
> Your (sick) woman lies in your midst . . .
> . . . thinking she cannot see.
> Into her body they put again (her) *niga purbalele* . . . (430-435).

The episode that follows is obscure. It would seem that the sick woman is not yet cured. The shaman leaves for the mountains with people of the village to gather medicinal plants, and he returns to the attack in a different way. This time it is he who, by imitating the penis, penetrates the "opening of muu" and moves in it "like *nusupane* . . . completely drying the inner place" (453-454). Yet the use of astringents suggests that the delivery has taken place. Finally, before the account of the precautions taken to impede Muu's escape, which we have already described, we find the shaman calling for help from a people of Bowmen. Since their task consists in raising a cloud of dust "to obscure . . . Muu's way" (464), and to defend all of Muu's crossroads and byroads (468), their intervention probably also pertains to the conclusion.

The previous episode perhaps refers to a second curing technique, with organ manipulation and the administration of remedies.

Or it may perhaps match, in equally metaphorical terms, the first journey, which is more highly elaborated in the text. Two lines of attack would thus have been developed for the assistance to the sick woman, one of which is supported by a psychophysiological mythology and the other by a psychosocial mythology—indicated by the shaman's call on the inhabitants of the village—which, however, remains undeveloped. At any rate, it should be observed that the song ends after the delivery, just as it had begun before the cure. Both antecedent and subsequent events are carefully related. But it is not only against Muu's elusive stray impulses that the cure must, through careful procedures, be effected; the efficacy of the cure would be jeopardized if, even before any results were to be expected, it failed to offer the sick woman a resolution, that is, a situation wherein all the protagonists have resumed their places and returned to an order which is no longer threatened.

The cure would consist, therefore, in making explicit a situation originally existing on the emotional level and in rendering acceptable to the mind pains which the body refuses to tolerate. That the mythology of the shaman does not correspond to an objective reality does not matter. The sick woman believes in the myth and belongs to a society which believes in it. The tutelary spirits and malevolent spirits, the supernatural monsters and magical animals, are all part of a coherent system on which the native conception of the universe is founded. The sick woman accepts these mythical beings or, more accurately, she has never questioned their existence. What she does not accept are the incoherent and arbitrary pains, which are an alien element in her system but which the shaman, calling upon myth, will re-integrate within a whole where everything is meaningful.

Once the sick woman understands, however, she does more than resign herself; she gets well. But no such thing happens to our sick when the causes of their diseases have been explained to them in terms of secretions, germs, or viruses. We shall perhaps be accused of paradox if we answer that the reason lies in the fact that microbes exist and monsters do not. And yet, the relationship between germ and disease is external to the mind of the patient, for it is a cause-and-effect relationship; whereas the relationship between monster and disease is internal to his mind, whether conscious or unconscious: It is a relationship between symbol and thing symbolized, or, to use the terminology of linguists, between sign and meaning. The shaman provides the sick woman with a *language*, by means of which unexpressed, and otherwise inexpressible, psychic states can be immediately expressed. And it is the transition to this verbal expression—at the same time making it possible to undergo in an ordered and intelligible form a real experience that would otherwise be chaotic and inexpressible—which induces the release of the physiological process, that is, the reorganization, in a favorable direction, of the process to which the sick woman is subjected.

In this respect, the shamanistic cure lies on the borderline between our contemporary physical medicine and such psychological therapies as psychoanalysis. Its originality stems from the application to an organic condition of a method related to psychotherapy. How is this possible? A closer comparison between shamanism and psychoanalysis—which in our view implies no slight to psychoanalysis—will enable us to clarify this point.

In both cases the purpose is to bring to a conscious level conflicts and resistances which have remained unconscious, owing either to their repression by other psychological forces or—in the case of childbirth—to their own specific nature, which is not psychic but organic or even simply mechanical. In both cases also, the conflicts and resistances are resolved, not because of the knowledge, real or alleged, which the sick woman progressively acquires of them, but because this knowledge makes possible a specific experience, in the course of which conflicts materialize in an order and on a level permitting their free development and leading to their resolution. This vital experience is called *abreaction* in psychoanalysis. We know that its precondition is the unprovoked intervention of the analyst, who appears in the conflicts of the patient through a double transference mechanism, as a flesh-and-blood protagonist and in relation to whom the patient can restore and clarify an initial situation which has remained unexpressed or unformulated.

All these characteristics can be found in the shamanistic cure. Here, too, it is a matter of provoking an experience; as this experience becomes structured, regulatory mechanisms beyond the subject's control are spontaneously set in motion and lead to an orderly functioning. The shaman plays the same dual role as the psychoanalyst. A prerequisite role—that of listener for the psycho-analyst and of orator for the shaman—establishes a direct relation-ship with the patient's conscious and an indirect relationship with his unconscious. This is the function of the incantation proper. But the shaman does more than utter the incantation; he is its hero, for it is he who, at the head of a supernatural battalion of spirits, pene-trates the endangered organs and frees the captive soul. In this way he, like the psychoanalyst, becomes the object of transference and, through the representations induced in the patient's mind, the real protagonist of the conflict which the latter experiences on the border between the physical world and the psychic world. The pa-tient suffering from neurosis eliminates an individual myth by fac-ing a "real" psychoanalyst; the native woman in childbed over-comes a true organic disorder by identifying with a "mythically transmuted" shaman.

This parallelism does not exclude certain differences, which are not surprising if we note the character—psychological in the one case and organic in the other—of the ailment to be cured. Actually the shamanistic cure seems to be the exact counterpart to the psychoanalytic cure, but with an inversion of all the elements. Both cures aim at inducing an experience, and both succeed by re-creating a myth which the patient has to live or relive. But in one case, the patient constructs an individual myth with elements drawn from his past; in the other case, the patient receives from the outside a social myth which does not correspond to a former personal state. To prepare for the abreaction, which then becomes an "adreaction," the psychoanalyst listens, whereas the shaman speaks. Better still: When a transference is established, the patient puts words into the mouth of the psychoanalyst by attributing to him alleged feelings and intentions; in the incantation, on the con-trary, the shaman speaks for his patient. He questions her and puts into her mouth answers that correspond to the interpretation of her condition, with which she must become imbued:

> My eyesight is straying, it is asleep on Muu Puklip's path.
> It is Muu Puklip who has come to me. She wants to take my *niga purbalele* for good.
> Muu Nauryaiti has come to me. She wants to possess my *niga purbalele* for good.
> etc. (97-101).

Furthermore, the resemblance becomes even more striking when we compare the shaman's method with certain recent therapeutic techniques of psychoanalysis. R. Desoille, in his research on daydreaming,[13] emphasized that psychopathological disturbances are accessible only through the language of symbols. Thus he speaks to his patients by means of symbols, which remain, nonetheless, verbal metaphors. In a more recent work, with which we were not acquainted when we began this study, M. A. Sechehaye goes much further.[14] It seems to us that the results which she obtained while treating a case of schizophrenia considered incurable fully confirm our preceding views on the similarities between psychoanalysis and shamanism. For Sechehaye became aware that speech, no matter how symbolic it might be, still could not penetrate beyond the conscious and that she could reach deeply buried complexes only through acts. Thus to resolve a weaning complex, the analyst must assume a maternal role, carried out not by a literal reproduction of the appropriate behavior but by means of actions which are, as it were, discontinuous, each symbolizing a fundamental element of the situation—for instance, putting the cheek of the patient in contact with the breast of the analyst. The symbolic load of such acts qualifies them as a language. Actually, the therapist holds a dialogue with the patient, not through the spoken word, but by concrete actions, that is, genuine rites which penetrate the screen of consciousness to carry their message directly to the unconscious.

Here we again encounter the concept of manipulation, which appeared so essential to an understanding of the shamanistic cure but whose traditional definition we must broaden considerably. For it may at one time involve a manipulation of ideas and, at another time, a manipulation of organs. But the basic condition remains that the manipulation must be carried out through symbols, that is, through meaningful equivalents of things meant which belong to another order of reality. The *gestures* of Sechehaye reverberate in the unconscious *mind* of the schizophrenic just as the *representations* evoked by the shaman bring about a modification in the organic *functions* of the woman in childbirth. Labor is impeded at the beginning of the song, the delivery takes place at the end, and the progress of childbirth is reflected in successive stages of the myth. The first penetration of the vagina by the *nelegan* is carried out in Indian file (241) and, since it is an ascent, with the help of magical hats which clear and light up the way. The return corresponds to the second phase of the myth, but to the first phase of the physiological process, since the child must be made to come down. Attention turns toward the *nelegan's* feet. We are told that they have shoes (494-496). When they invade Muu's abode, they no longer march in single file but in "rows of four" (388); and, to come out again in the open air, they go "in a row" (248). No doubt the purpose of such an alteration in the details of the myth is to elicit the corresponding organic reaction, but the sick woman could not integrate it as experience if it were not associated with a true increase in dilatation. It is the effectiveness of symbols which guarantees the harmonious parallel development of myth and action. And myth and action form a pair always associated with the duality of patient and healer. In the schizophrenic cure the healer performs the actions and the patient produces his myth; in the shamanistic cure the healer supplies the myth and the patient performs the actions.

The analogy between these two methods would be even more complete if we could admit, as Freud seems to have suggested on two different occasions,[15] that the description in psychological terms of the structure of psychoses and neuroses must one day be replaced by physiological, or even biochemical, concepts. This possibility may be at hand, since recent Swedish research[16] has demonstrated chemical differences resulting from the amounts of polynucleids in the nerve cells of the normal individual and those of the psychotic. Given this hypothesis or any other of the same type, the shamanistic cure and the psychoanalytic cure would become strictly parallel. It would be a matter, either way, of stimulating an organic transformation which would consist essentially in a structural reorganization, by inducing the patient intensively to live out a myth—either received or created by him—whose structure would be, at the unconscious level, analogous to the structure whose genesis is sought on the organic level. The effectiveness of symbols would consist precisely in this "inductive property," by which formally homologous structures, built out of different materials at different levels of life—organic processes, unconscious mind, rational thought—are related to one another. Poetic metaphor provides a familiar example of this inductive process, but as a rule it does not transcend the unconscious level. Thus we note the significance of Rimbaud's intuition that metaphor can change the world.

The comparison with psychoanalysis has allowed us to shed light on some aspects of shamanistic curing. Conversely, it is not improbable that the study of shamanism may one day serve to elucidate obscure points of Freudian theory. We are thinking specifically of the concepts of myth and the unconscious.

We saw that the only difference between the two methods that would outlive the discovery of a physiological substratum of neurosis concerns the origin of the myth, which in the one case is recovered as an individual possession and in the other case is received from collective tradition. Actually, many psychoanalysts would refuse to admit that the psychic constellations which reappear in the patient's conscious could constitute a myth. These represent, they say, real events which it is sometimes possible to date and whose authenticity can be verified by checking with relatives or servants.[17] We do not question these facts. But we should ask ourselves whether the therapeutic value of the cure depends on the actual character of remembered situations, or whether the traumatizing power of those situations stems from the fact that at the moment when they appear, the subject experiences them immediately as living myth. By this we mean that the traumatizing power of any situation cannot result from its intrinsic features but must, rather, result from the capacity of certain events, appearing within an appropriate psychological, historical, and social context, to induce an emotional crystallization which is molded by a preexisting structure. In relation to the event or anecdote, these structures—or, more accurately, these structural laws—are truly atemporal. For the neurotic, all psychic life and all subsequent experiences are organized in terms of an exclusive or predominant structure, under the catalytic action of the initial myth. But this structure, as well as other structures which the neurotic relegates to a subordinate position, are to be found also in the normal human being, whether primitive or civilized. These structures as an aggregate form what we call the unconscious. The last difference between the theory of shamanism and psychoanalytic theory would, then, vanish. The unconscious ceases to be the ultimate haven of individual peculiarities—the repository of a unique history which makes each of us an irreplaceable being. It is reducible to a function—the symbolic function, which no doubt is specifically human, and which is carried out according to the same laws among all men, and actually corresponds to the aggregate of these laws.

If this view is correct, it will probably be necessary to re-establish a more marked distinction between the unconscious and the preconscious than has been customary in psychology. For the preconscious, as a reservoir of recollections and images amassed in the course of a lifetime,[18] is merely an aspect of memory. While perennial in character, the preconscious also has limitations, since the term refers to the fact that even though memories are preserved they are not always available to the individual. The unconscious, on the other hand, is always empty—or, more accurately, it is as alien to mental images as is the stomach to the foods which pass through it. As the organ of a specific function, the unconscious merely imposes structural laws upon inarticulated elements which originate elsewhere—impulses, emotions, representations, and memories. We might say, therefore, that the preconscious is the individual lexicon where each of us accumulates the vocabulary of his personal history, but that this vocabulary becomes significant, for us and for others, only to the extent that the unconscious structures it according to its laws and thus transforms it into language. Since these laws are the same for all individuals and in all instances where the unconscious pursues its activity, the problem which arose in the preceding paragraph can easily be resolved. The vocabulary matters less than the structure. Whether the myth is re-created by the individual or borrowed from tradition, it derives from its sources—individual or collective (between which inter-penetrations and exchanges constantly occur)—only the stock of representations with which it operates. But the structure remains the same, and through it the symbolic function is fulfilled.

If we add that these structures are not only the same for everyone and for all areas to which the function applies, but that they are few in number, we shall understand why the world of symbolism is infinitely varied in content, but always limited in its laws. There are many languages, but very few structural laws which are valid for all languages. A compilation of known tales and myths would fill an imposing number of volumes. But they can be reduced to a small number of simple types if we abstract, from among the diversity of characters, a few elementary functions. As for the complexes—those individual myths—they also correspond to a few simple types, which mold the fluid multiplicity of cases.

Since the shaman does not psychoanalyze his patient, we may conclude that remembrance of things past, considered by some the key to psychoanalytic therapy, is only one expression (whose value and results are hardly negligible) of a more fundamental method, which must be defined without considering the individual or collective genesis of the myth. For the myth *form* takes precedence over the *content* of the narrative. This is, at any rate, what the analysis of a native text seems to have taught us. But also, from another perspective, we know that any myth represents a quest for the remembrance of things past. The modern version of shamanistic technique called psychoanalysis thus derives its specific characteristics from the fact that in industrial civilization there is no longer any room for mythical time, except within man himself. From this observation, psychoanalysis can draw confirmation of its validity, as well as hope of strengthening its theoretical foundations and understanding better the reasons for its effectiveness, by comparing its methods and goals with those of its precursors, the shamans and sorcerers.

NOTES

1. Nils M. Holmer and Henry Wassén, *Mu-Igala or the Way of Muu, a Medicine Song from the Cunas of Panama* (Göteborg: 1947).
2. The numbers in parentheses refer to the numbered sections in the song.
3. E. Nordenskiöld, *An Historical and Ethnological Survey of the Cuna Indians*, ed. Henry Wassén, Vol. X of *Comparative Ethnographical Studies* (Göteborg: 1938), pp. 80 ff.
4. *Ibid.*, pp. 360 ff.; Holmer and Wassén, *op. cit.*, pp. 78-9.
5. Holmer and Wassén, *op. cit.*, p. 38, *n* 44.
6. Nordenskiöld, *op. cit.*, p. 364 ff.
7. *Ibid.*, pp. 607-8; Holmer and Wassén, *op. cit.*, p. 38, *nn* 35-9.
8. The translation of *ti ipya* as "whirlpool" seems to be strained. For certain South American natives, as also in the languages of the Iberian peninsula (cf. the Portuguese *olho d'agua*), a "water eye" is a spring.
9. Holmer and Wassén, *op. cit.*, pp. 65-6.
10. *Ibid.*, p. 45, *n* 219; p. 57, *n* 539.
11. The question marks are Holmer and Wassén's; *nusupane* derives from

nusu, "worm," and is commonly used for "penis" (see Holmer and Wassén, p. 47, *n* 280; p. 57, *n* 540; and p. 82).

12. *Ibid.,* p. 85.

13. R. Desoille, *Le Rêve éveillé en psychothérapie* (Paris: 1945).

14. M. A. Sechehaye, *La Réalisation symbolique,* Supplement No. 12 to *Revue suisse de psychologie et de psychologie appliquée* (Bern: 1947).

15. In *Beyond the Pleasure Principle,* p. 79, and *New Conferences on Psychoanalysis,* p. 198, cited by E. Kris, "The Nature of Psychoanalytic Propositions and their Validation," in *Freedom and Experience, Essays presented to H. M. Kallen* (Ithaca, N. Y.: 1947), p. 244.

16. Caspersson and Hyden, at the Karolinska Institute in Stockholm.

17. Marie Bonaparte, "Notes on the Analytical Discovery of a Primal Scene," in *The Psychoanalytic Study of the Child,* Vol. I (New York: 1945).

18. This definition, which was subjected to considerable criticism, acquires a new meaning through the radical distinction between preconscious and unconscious.

CHAPTER XI

The Structural Study of Myth

"It would seem that mythological worlds have been built up only to be shattered again, and that new worlds were built from the fragments."

—Franz Boas[1]

DESPITE some recent attempts to renew them, it seems that during the past twenty years anthropology has increasingly turned from studies in the field of religion. At the same time, and precisely because the interest of professional anthropologists has withdrawn from primitive religion, all kinds of amateurs who claim to belong to other disciplines have seized this opportunity to move in, thereby turning into their private playground what we had left as a wasteland. The prospects for the scientific study of religion have thus been undermined in two ways.

The explanation for this situation lies to some extent in the fact that the anthropological study of religion was started by men like Tylor, Frazer, and Durkheim, who were psychologically oriented although not in a position to keep up with the progress of psychological research and theory. Their interpretations, therefore, soon became vitiated by the outmoded psychological approach which they used as their basis. Although they were undoubtedly right in giving their attention to intellectual processes, the way they handled these remained so crude that it discredited them altogether. This is much to be regretted, since, as Hocart so profoundly noted in his introduction to a posthumous book recently published,[2] psychological interpretations were withdrawn from the intellectual field only to be introduced again in the field of affectivity, thus adding to "the inherent defects of the psychological school . . . the mistake of deriving clear-cut ideas . . . from vague emotions." Instead of trying to enlarge the framework of our logic to include processes which, whatever their apparent differences, belong to the same kind of intellectual operation, a naïve attempt was made to reduce them to inarticulate emotional drives, which resulted only in hampering our studies.

Of all the chapters of religious anthropology probably none has tarried to the same extent as studies in the field of mythology. From a theoretical point of view the situation remains very much the same as it was fifty years ago, namely, chaotic. Myths are still widely interpreted in conflicting ways: as collective dreams, as the outcome of a kind of esthetic play, or as the basis of ritual. Mythological figures are considered as personified abstractions, divinized heroes, or fallen gods. Whatever the hypothesis, the choice amounts to reducing mythology either to idle play or to a crude kind of philosophic speculation.

In order to understand what a myth really is, must we choose between platitude and sophism? Some claim that human societies merely express, through their mythology, fundamental feelings common to the whole of mankind, such as love, hate, or revenge or that they try to provide some kind of explanations for phenomena which they cannot otherwise understand—astronomical, meteorological, and the like. But why should these societies do it in such elaborate and devious ways, when all of them are also acquainted with empirical explanations? On the other hand, psychoanalysts and many anthropologists have shifted the problems away from the natural or cosmological toward the sociological and psychological fields. But then the interpretation becomes too easy: If a given mythology confers prominence on a certain figure, let us say an evil grandmother, it will be claimed that in such a society grandmothers are actually evil and that mythology reflects the social structure and the social relations; but should the actual data be conflicting, it would be as readily claimed that the purpose of mythology is to provide an outlet for repressed feelings. Whatever the situation, a clever dialectic will always find a way to pretend that a meaning has been found.

Mythology confronts the student with a situation which at first sight appears contradictory. On the one hand it would seem that in the course of a myth anything is likely to happen. There is no logic, no continuity. Any characteristic can be attributed to any subject; every conceivable relation can be found. With myth, everything becomes possible. But on the other hand, this apparent arbitrariness is belied by the astounding similarity between myths collected in widely different regions. Therefore the problem: If the content of a myth is contingent, how are we going to explain the fact that myths throughout the world are so similar?

It is precisely this awareness of a basic antinomy pertaining to the nature of myth that may lead us toward its solution. For the contradiction which we face is very similar to that which in earlier times brought considerable worry to the first philosophers concerned with linguistic problems; linguistics could only begin to evolve as a science after this contradiction had been overcome. Ancient philosophers reasoned about language the way we do about mythology. On the one hand, they did notice that in a given language certain sequences of sounds were associated with definite meanings, and they earnestly aimed at discovering a reason for the linkage between those *sounds* and that *meaning*. Their attempt, however, was thwarted from the very beginning by the fact that the same sounds were equally present in other languages although the meaning they conveyed was entirely different. The contradiction was surmounted only by the discovery that it is the combination of sounds, not the sounds themselves, which provides the significant data.

It is easy to see, moreover, that some of the more recent interpretations of mythological thought originated from the same kind of misconception under which those early linguists were laboring. Let us consider, for instance, Jung's idea that a given mythological pattern—the so-called archetype—possesses a certain meaning. This is comparable to the long-supported error that a sound may possess a certain affinity with a meaning: for instance, the "liquid" semi-vowels with water, the open vowels with things that are big, large, loud, or heavy, etc., a theory which still has its supporters.[3] Whatever emendations the original formulation may now call for,[4] everybody will agree that the Saussurean principle of the *arbitrary character of linguistic signs* was a prerequisite for the accession of linguistics to the scientific level.

To invite the mythologist to compare his precarious situation with that of the linguist in the prescientific stage is not enough. As a matter of fact we may thus be led only from one difficulty to another. There is a very good reason why myth cannot simply be treated as language if its specific problems are to be solved; myth *is* language: to be known, myth has to be told; it is a part of human speech. In order to preserve its specificity we must be able to show that it is both the same thing as language, and also something different from it. Here, too, the past experience of linguists may help us. For language itself can be analyzed into things which are at the same time similar and yet different. This is precisely what is expressed in Saussure's distinction between *langue* and *parole*, one being the structural side of language, the other the statistical aspect of it, *langue* belonging to a reversible time, *parole* being non-reversible. If those two levels already exist in language, then a third one can conceivably be isolated.

We have distinguished *langue* and *parole* by the different time referents which they use. Keeping this in mind, we may notice that myth uses a third referent which combines the properties of the first two. On the one hand, a myth always refers to events alleged to have taken place long ago. But what gives the myth an operational value is that the specific pattern described is timeless; it explains the present and the past as well as the future. This can be made clear through a comparison between myth and what appears to have largely replaced it in modern societies, namely, politics. When the historian refers to the French Revolution, it is always as a sequence of past happenings, a non-reversible series of events the remote consequences of which may still be felt at present. But to the French politician, as well as to his followers, the French Revolution is both a sequence belonging to the past—as to the historian—and a timeless pattern which can be detected in the contemporary French social structure and which provides a clue for its interpretation, a lead from which to infer future developments. Michelet, for instance, was a politically minded historian. He describes the French Revolution thus: "That day . . . everything was possible. . . . Future became present . . . that is, no more time, a glimpse of eternity." [5] It is that double structure, altogether historical and ahistorical, which explains how myth, while pertaining to the realm of *parole* and calling for an explanation as such, as well as to that of *langue* in which it is expressed, can also be an absolute entity on a third level which, though it remains linguistic by nature, is nevertheless distinct from the other two.

A remark can be introduced at this point which will help to show the originality of myth in relation to other linguistic phenomena. Myth is the part of language where the formula *traduttore, tradittore* reaches its lowest truth value. From that point of view it should be placed in the gamut of linguistic expressions at the end opposite to that of poetry, in spite of all the claims which have been made to prove the contrary. Poetry is a kind of speech which cannot be translated except at the cost of serious distortions; whereas the mythical value of the myth is preserved even through the worst translation. Whatever our ignorance of the language and the culture of the people where it originated, a myth is still felt as a myth by any reader anywhere in the world. Its substance does not lie in its style, its original music, or its syntax, but in the *story* which it tells. Myth is language, functioning on an especially high level where meaning succeeds practically at "taking off" from the linguistic ground on which it keeps on rolling.

To sum up the discussion at this point, we have so far made the following claims: (1) If there is a meaning to be found in mythology, it cannot reside in the isolated elements which enter into the composition of a myth, but only in the way those elements are combined. (2) Although myth belongs to the same category as language, being, as a matter of fact, only part of it, language in myth exhibits specific properties. (3) Those properties are only to be found *above* the ordinary linguistic level, that is, they exhibit more complex features than those which are to be found in any other kind of linguistic expression.

If the above three points are granted, at least as a working hypothesis, two consequences will follow: (1) Myth, like the rest of language, is made up of constituent units. (2) These constituent units presuppose the constituent units present in language when analyzed on other levels—namely, phonemes, morphemes, and sememes—but they, nevertheless, differ from the latter in the same way as the latter differ among themselves; they belong to a higher and more complex order. For this reason, we shall call them *gross constituent units*.

How shall we proceed in order to identify and isolate these gross constituent units or mythemes? We know that they cannot be found among phonemes, morphemes, or sememes, but only on a higher level; otherwise myth would become confused with any other kind of speech. Therefore, we should look for them on the sentence level. The only method we can suggest at this stage is to proceed tentatively, by trial and error, using as a check the principles which serve as a basis for any kind of structural analysis: economy of explanation; unity of solution; and ability to reconstruct the whole from a fragment, as well as later stages from previous ones.

The technique which has been applied so far by this writer consists in analyzing each myth individually, breaking down its story into the shortest possible sentences, and writing each sentence on an index card bearing a number corresponding to the unfolding of the story.

Practically each card will thus show that a certain function is, at a given time, linked to a given subject. Or, to put it otherwise, each gross constituent unit will consist of a *relation*.

However, the above definition remains highly unsatisfactory for two different reasons. First, it is well known to structural linguists that constituent units on all levels are made up of relations, and the true difference between our *gross* units and the others remains unexplained; second, we still find ourselves in the realm of a non-reversible time, since the numbers of the cards correspond to the unfolding of the narrative. Thus the specific character of mythological time, which as we have seen is both reversible and non-reversible, synchronic and diachronic, remains unaccounted for. From this springs a new hypothesis, which constitutes the very core of our argument: The true constituent units of a myth are not the isolated relations but *bundles of such relations*, and it is only as bundles that these relations can be put to use and combined so as to produce a meaning. Relations pertaining to the same bundle may appear diachronically at remote intervals, but when we have succeeded in grouping them together we have reorganized our myth according to a time referent of a new nature, corresponding to the prerequisite of the initial hypothesis, namely a two-dimensional time referent which is simultaneously diachronic and synchronic, and which accordingly integrates the characteristics of *langue* on the one hand, and those of *parole* on the other. To put it in even more linguistic terms, it is as though a phoneme were always made up of all its variants.

Two comparisons may help to explain what we have in mind.

Let us first suppose that archaeologists of the future coming from another planet would one day, when all human life had disappeared from the earth, excavate one of our libraries. Even if they were at first ignorant of our writing, they might succeed in deciphering it—an undertaking which would require, at some early stage, the discovery that the alphabet, as we are in the habit of printing it, should be read from left to right and from top to bottom. However, they would soon discover that a whole category of books did not fit the usual pattern—these would be the orchestra scores on the shelves of the music division. But after trying, without success, to decipher staffs one after the other, from the upper down to the lower, they would probably notice that the same patterns of notes recurred at intervals, either in full or in part, or that some patterns were strongly reminiscent of earlier ones. Hence the hypothesis: What if patterns showing affinity, instead of being considered in succession, were to be treated as one complex pattern and read as a whole? By getting at what we call *harmony*, they would then see that an orchestra score, to be meaningful, must be read diachronically along one axis—that is, page after page, and from left to right—and synchronically along the other axis, all the notes written vertically making up one gross constituent unit, that is, one bundle of relations.

The other comparison is somewhat different. Let us take an observer ignorant of our playing cards, sitting for a long time with a fortune-teller. He would know something of the visitors: sex, age, physical appearance, social situation, etc., in the same way as we know something of the different cultures whose myths we try to study. He would also listen to the séances and record them so as to be able to go over them and make comparisons—as we do when we listen to myth-telling and record it. Mathematicians to whom I have put the problem agree that if the man is bright and if the material available to him is sufficient, he may be able to reconstruct the nature of the deck of cards being used, that is, fifty-two or thirty-two cards according to the case, made up of four homologous sets consisting of the same units (the individual cards) with only one varying feature, the suit.

Now for a concrete example of the method we propose. We shall use the Oedipus myth, which is well known to everyone. I am well aware that the Oedipus myth has only reached us under late forms and through literary transmutations concerned more with esthetic and moral preoccupations than with religious or ritual ones, whatever these may have been. But we shall not interpret the Oedipus myth in literal terms, much less offer an explanation acceptable to the specialist. We simply wish to illustrate—and without reaching any conclusions with respect to it—a certain technique, whose use is probably not legitimate in this particular instance, owing to the problematic elements indicated above. The "demonstration" should therefore be conceived, not in terms of what the scientist means by this term, but at best in terms of what is meant by the street peddler, whose aim is not to achieve a concrete result, but to explain, as succinctly as possible, the functioning of the mechanical toy which he is trying to sell to the onlookers.

The myth will be treated as an orchestra score would be if it were unwittingly considered as a unilinear series; our task is to re-establish the correct arrangement. Say, for instance, we were confronted with a sequence of the type: 1,2,4,7,8,2,3,4,6,8,1,4,5,7,8,1, 2,5,7,3,4,5,6,8 . . . , the assignment being to put all the 1's together, all the 2's, the 3's, etc.; the result is a chart:

1	2		4			7	8
	2	3	4		6		8
1			4	5		7	8
1	2			5		7	
		3	4	5	6		8

We shall attempt to perform the same kind of operation on the Oedipus myth, trying out several arrangements of the mythemes until we find one which is in harmony with the principles enumerated above. Let us suppose, for the sake of argument, that the best arrangement is the following (although it might certainly be improved with the help of a specialist in Greek mythology):

Cadmos seeks his sister Europa, ravished by Zeus			
		Cadmos kills the dragon	
	The Spartoi kill one another		
			Labdacos (Laios' father) = *lame* (?)
	Oedipus kills his father, Laios		Laios (Oedipus' father) = *left-sided* (?)
		Oedipus kills the Sphinx	
			Oedipus = *swollen-foot* (?)
Oedipus marries his mother, Jocasta			
	Eteocles kills his brother, Polynices		
Antigone buries her brother, Polynices, despite prohibition			

We thus find ourselves confronted with four vertical columns, each of which includes several relations belonging to the same bundle. Were we to *tell* the myth, we would disregard the columns and read the rows from left to right and from top to bottom. But if we want to *understand* the myth, then we will have to disregard one half of the diachronic dimension (top to bottom) and read from left to right, column after column, each one being considered as a unit.

All the relations belonging to the same column exhibit one common feature which it is our task to discover. For instance, all the events grouped in the first column on the left have something to do with blood relations which are overemphasized, that is, are more intimate than they should be. Let us say, then, that the first column has as its common feature the *overrating of blood relations*. It is obvious that the second column expresses the same thing, but inverted: *underrating of blood relations*. The third column refers to monsters being slain. As to the fourth, a few words of clarification are needed. The remarkable connotation of the surnames in Oedipus' father-line has often been noticed. However, linguists usually disregard it, since to them the only way to define the meaning of a term is to investigate all the contexts in which it appears, and personal names, precisely because they are used as such, are not accompanied by any context. With the method we propose to follow the objection disappears, since the myth itself provides its own context. The significance is no longer to be sought in the eventual meaning of each name, but in the fact that all the names have a common feature: All the hypothetical meanings (which may well remain hypothetical) refer to *difficulties in walking straight and standing upright*.

What then is the relationship between the two columns on the right? Column three refers to monsters. The dragon is a chthonian being which has to be killed in order that mankind be born from the Earth; the Sphinx is a monster unwilling to permit men to live. The last unit reproduces the first one, which has to do with the *autochthonous origin* of mankind. Since the monsters are overcome by men, we may thus say that the common feature of the third column is *denial of the autochthonous origin of man*.[6]

This immediately helps us to understand the meaning of the fourth column. In mythology it is a universal characteristic of men born from the Earth that at the moment they emerge from the depth they either cannot walk or they walk clumsily. This is the case of the chthonian beings in the mythology of the Pueblo: Muyingwu, who leads the emergence, and the chthonian Shumaikoli are lame ("bleeding-foot," "sore-foot"). The same happens to the Koskimo of the Kwakiutl after they have been swallowed by the chthonian monster, Tsiakish: When they returned to the surface of the earth "they limped forward or tripped sideways." Thus the common feature of the fourth column is *the persistence of the autochthonous origin of man.* It follows that column four is to column three as column one is to column two. The inability to connect two kinds of relationships is overcome (or rather replaced) by the assertion that contradictory relationships are identical inasmuch as they are both self-contradictory in a similar way. Although this is still a provisional formulation of the structure of mythical thought, it is sufficient at this stage.

Turning back to the Oedipus myth, we may now see what it means. The myth has to do with the inability, for a culture which holds the belief that mankind is autochthonous (see, for instance, Pausanias, VIII, xxix, 4: plants provide a *model* for humans), to find a satisfactory transition between this theory and the knowledge that human beings are actually born from the union of man and woman. Although the problem obviously cannot be solved, the Oedipus myth provides a kind of logical tool which relates the original problem—born from one or born from two?—to the derivative problem: born from different or born from same? By a correlation of this type, the overrating of blood relations is to the underrating of blood relations as the attempt to escape autochthony is to the impossibility to succeed in it. Although experience contradicts theory, social life validates cosmology by its similarity of structure. Hence cosmology is true.

Two remarks should be made at this stage.

In order to interpret the myth, we left aside a point which has worried the specialists until now, namely, that in the earlier (Homeric) versions of the Oedipus myth, some basic elements are lacking, such as Jocasta killing herself and Oedipus piercing his own eyes. These events do not alter the substance of the myth although they can easily be integrated, the first one as a new case of autodestruction (column three) and the second as another case of crippledness (column four). At the same time there is something significant in these additions, since the shift from foot to head is to be correlated with the shift from autochthonous origin to self-destruction.

Our method thus eliminates a problem which has, so far, been one of the main obstacles to the progress of mythological studies, namely, the quest for the *true* version, or the *earlier* one. On the contrary, we define the myth as consisting of all its versions; or to put it otherwise, a myth remains the same as long as it is felt as such. A striking example is offered by the fact that our interpretation may take into account the Freudian use of the Oedipus myth and is certainly applicable to it. Although the Freudian problem has ceased to be that of autochthony *versus* bisexual reproduction, it is still the problem of understanding how *one* can be born from *two:* How is it that we do not have only one procreator, but a mother plus a father? Therefore, not only Sophocles, but Freud himself, should be included among the recorded versions of the Oedipus myth on a par with earlier or seemingly more "authentic" versions.

An important consequence follows. If a myth is made up of all its variants, structural analysis should take all of them into account. After analyzing all the known variants of the Theban version, we should thus treat the others in the same way: first, the tales about Labdacos' collateral line including Agave, Pentheus, and Jocasta herself; the Theban variant about Lycos with Amphion and Zetos as the city founders; more remote variants concerning Dionysus (Oedipus' matrilateral cousin); and Athenian legends where Cecrops takes the place of Cadmos, etc. For each of them a similar chart should be drawn and then compared and reorganized according to the findings: Cecrops killing the serpent with the parallel episode of Cadmos; abandonment of Dionysus with abandonment of Oedipus; "Swollen Foot" with Dionysus' *loxias*, that is, walking obliquely; Europa's quest with Antiope's; the founding of Thebes by the Spartoi or by the brothers Amphion and Zetos; Zeus kidnapping Europa and Antiope and the same with Semele; the Theban Oedipus and the Argian Perseus, etc. We shall then have several two-dimensional charts, each dealing with a variant, to be organized in a three-dimensional order, as shown in Figure 16, so that three different readings become possible: left to right, top to bottom, front to back (or vice versa). All of these charts cannot be expected to be identical; but experience shows that any difference to be observed may be correlated with other differences, so that a logical treatment of the whole will allow simplifications, the final outcome being the structural law of the myth.

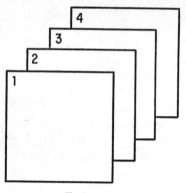

At this point the objection may be raised that the task is impossible to perform, since we can only work with known versions. Is it not possible that a new version might alter the picture? This is true enough if only one or two versions are available, but the objection becomes theoretical as soon as a reasonably large number have been recorded. Let us make this point clear by a comparison. If the furniture of a room and its arrangement were known to us only through its reflection in two mirrors placed on opposite walls, we should theoretically dispose of an almost infinite number of mirror images which would provide us with a complete knowledge. However, should the two mirrors be obliquely set, the number of mirror images would become very small; nevertheless, four or five such images would very likely give us, if not complete information, at least a sufficient coverage so that we would feel sure that no large piece of furniture is missing in our description.

On the other hand, it cannot be too strongly emphasized that all available variants should be taken into account. If Freudian comments on the Oedipus complex are a part of the Oedipus myth, then questions such as whether Cushing's version of the Zuni origin myth should be retained or discarded become irrelevant. There is no single "true" version of which all the others are but copies or distortions. Every version belongs to the myth.

The reason for the discouraging results in works on general mythology can finally be understood. They stem from two causes. First, comparative mythologists have selected preferred versions instead of using them all. Second, we have seen that the structural analysis of *one* variant of *one* myth belonging to *one* tribe (in some cases, even *one* village) already requires two dimensions. When we use several variants of the same myth for the same tribe or village, the frame of reference becomes three-dimensional, and as soon as we try to enlarge the comparison, the number of dimensions required increases until it appears quite impossible to handle them intuitively. The confusions and platitudes which are the outcome of comparative mythology can be explained by the fact that multi-dimensional frames of reference are often ignored or are naïvely replaced by two- or three-dimensional ones. Indeed, progress in comparative mythology depends largely on the cooperation of mathematicians who would undertake to express in symbols multi-dimensional relations which cannot be handled otherwise.

To check this theory,[7] an attempt was made from 1952 to 1954 toward an exhaustive analysis of all the known versions of the Zuni origin and emergence myth: Cushing, 1883 and 1896; Stevenson, 1904; Parsons, 1923; Bunzel, 1932; Benedict, 1934. Furthermore, a preliminary attempt was made at a comparison of the results with similar myths in other Pueblo tribes, Western and Eastern. Finally, a test was undertaken with Plains mythology. In all cases, it was found that the theory was sound; light was thrown, not only on North American mythology, but also on a previously unnoticed kind of logical operation, or one known so far only in a wholly different context. The bulk of material which needs to be handled practically at the outset of the work makes it impossible to enter into details, and we shall have to limit ourselves here to a few illustrations.

A simplified chart of the Zuni emergence myth would read:

CHANGE			DEATH
mechanical value of plants (used as ladders to emerge from lower world)	emergence led by Beloved Twins	sibling incest (origin of water)	gods kill children of men (by drowning)
food value of wild plants	migration led by the two Newekwe		magical contest with People of the Dew (col-
DEATH			PERMANENCE

CHANGE

DEATH

(ceremonial
clowns)

lecting wild
food *versus* cul-
tivation)

brother and
sister sacrificed
(to gain vic-
tory)

food value of
cultivated plants

brother and
sister adopted
(in exchange
for corn)

periodical char-
acter of agri-
cultural work

war against the
Kyanakwe (gar-
deners *versus*
hunters)

food value of
game (hunting)

war led by the
two War-
Gods

inevitability of
warfare

salvation of the
tribe (center of
the World
found)

brother and
sister sacrificed
(to avoid the
Flood)

DEATH

PERMANENCE

As the chart indicates, the problem is the discovery of a life-death mediation. For the Pueblo, this is especially difficult; they understand the origin of human life in terms of the model of plant life (emergence from the earth). They share that belief with the ancient Greeks, and it is not without reason that we chose the Oedipus myth as our first example. But in the American Indian case, the highest form of plant life is to be found in agriculture which is periodical in nature, that is, which consists in an alternation between life and death. If this is disregarded, the contradiction appears elsewhere: Agriculture provides food, therefore life; but hunting provides food and is similar to warfare which means death. Hence there are three different ways of handling the problem. In the Cushing version, the difficulty revolves around an opposition between activities yielding an immediate result (collecting wild food) and activities yielding a delayed result—death has to become integrated so that agriculture can exist. Parsons' version shifts from hunting to agriculture, while Stevenson's version operates the other way around. It can be shown that all the differences between these versions can be rigorously correlated with these basic structures.

Thus the three versions describe the great war waged by the ancestors of the Zuni against a mythical population, the Kyanakwe, by introducing into the narrative significant variations which consist (1) in the friendship or hostility of the gods; (2) in the granting of final victory to one camp or the other; (3) in the attribution of the symbolic function to the Kyanakwe, described sometimes as hunters (whose bows are strung with animal sinews) and sometimes as gardeners (whose bows are strung with plant fibers).

	CUSHING	PARSONS	STEVENSON
Gods, Kyanakwe	allied, use fiber string on their bows (garden-ers)	Kyanakwe, alone, use fiber string	Gods, Men ⎱ allied, use fiber string
	VICTORIOUS OVER	VICTORIOUS OVER	VICTORIOUS OVER
	Men, alone, use sinew (until they shift to fiber)	Gods, Men ⎱ allied, use sinew string	Kyanakwe, alone, use sinew string

Since fiber string (agriculture) is always superior to sinew string (hunting), and since (to a lesser extent) the gods' alliance is preferable to their antagonism, it follows that in Cushing's version, men are seen as doubly underprivileged (hostile gods, sinew string);

in the Stevenson version, doubly privileged (friendly gods, fiber string); while Parsons' version confronts us with an intermediary situation (friendly gods, but sinew strings, since men begin by being hunters). Hence:

OPPOSITIONS	CUSHING	PARSONS	STEVENSON
gods/men	—	+	+
fiber/sinew	—	—	+

Bunzel's version is of the same type as Cushing's from a structural point of view. However, it differs from both Cushing's and Stevenson's, inasmuch as the latter two explain the emergence as the result of man's need to evade his pitiful condition, while Bunzel's version makes it the consequence of a call from the higher powers—hence the inverted sequences of the means resorted to for the emergence: In both Cushing and Stevenson, they go from plants to animals; in Bunzel, from mammals to insects, and from insects to plants.

Among the Western Pueblo the logical approach always remains the same; the starting point and the point of arrival are simplest, whereas the intermediate stage is characterized by ambiguity:

LIFE (= INCREASE)		
(Mechanical) value of the plant kingdom, taking growth alone into account		ORIGINS
Food value of the plant kingdom, limited to wild plants		FOOD-GATHERING
Food value of the plant kingdom, including wild and cultivated plants		AGRICULTURE
Food value of the animal kingdom, limited to animals	*(but there is a contradiction here, owing to the negation of life = destruction, hence:)*	
Destruction of the animal kingdom, extended to human beings		HUNTING
		WARFARE
DEATH (= DECREASE)		

The fact that contradiction appears in the middle of the dialectical process results in a double set of dioscuric pairs, the purpose of which is to mediate between conflicting terms:

1. 2 divine messengers	2 ceremonial clowns		2 war-gods
2. homogeneous pair: dioscuri (2 brothers)	siblings (brother and sister)	couple (husband and wife)	heterogeneous pair: (grandmother and grandchild)

We have here combinational variants of the same function in different contexts (hence the war attribute of the clowns, which has given rise to so many queries).

The problem, often regarded as insoluble, vanishes when it is shown that the clowns—gluttons who may with impunity make excessive use of agricultural products—have the same function in relation to food production as the war-gods. (This function appears, in the dialectical process, as *overstepping the boundaries* of hunting, that is, hunting for men instead of for animals for human consumption.)

Some Central and Eastern Pueblos proceed the other way around. They begin by stating the identity of hunting and cultivation (first corn obtained by Game-Father sowing deer-dewclaws), and they try to derive both life and death from that central notion. Then, instead of extreme terms being simple and intermediary ones duplicated as among the Western groups, the extreme terms become duplicated (i.e., the two sisters of the Eastern Pueblo) while a simple mediating term comes to the foreground (for instance, the Poshaiyanne of the Zia), but endowed with equivocal attributes. Hence the attributes of this "messiah" can be deduced from the place it occupies in the time sequence: good when at the beginning (Zuni, Cushing), equivocal in the middle (Central Pueblo), bad at the end (Zia), except in Bunzel's version, where the sequence is reversed as has been shown.

By systematically using this kind of structural analysis it becomes possible to organize all the known variants of a myth into a set forming a kind of permutation group, the two variants placed at the far ends being in a symmetrical, though inverted, relationship to each other.

Our method not only has the advantage of bringing some kind of order to what was previously chaos; it also enables us to perceive some basic logical processes which are at the root of mythical thought.[8] Three main processes should be distinguished.

The trickster of American mythology has remained so far a problematic figure. Why is it that throughout North America his role is assigned practically everywhere to either coyote or raven? If we keep in mind that mythical thought always progresses from the awareness of oppositions toward their resolution, the reason for these choices becomes clearer. We need only assume that two opposite terms with no intermediary always tend to be replaced by two equivalent terms which admit of a third one as a mediator; then one of the polar terms and the mediator become replaced by a new triad, and so on. Thus we have a mediating structure of the following type:

INITIAL PAIR	FIRST TRIAD	SECOND TRIAD
Life		
	Agriculture	
		Herbivorous animals
		Carrion-eating animals (raven; coyote)
	Hunting	
		Beasts of prey
	Warfare	
Death		

The unformulated argument is as follows: carrion-eating animals are like beasts of prey (they eat animal food), but they are also like food-plant producers (they do not kill what they eat). Or to put it otherwise, Pueblo style (for Pueblo agriculture is more "meaningful" than hunting): ravens are to gardens as beasts of prey are to herbivorous animals. But it is also clear that herbivorous animals may be called first to act as mediators on the assumption that they are like collectors and gatherers (plant-food eaters), while they can be used as animal food though they are not themselves hunters. Thus we may have mediators of the first order, of the second order, and so on, where each term generates the next by a double process of opposition and correlation.

This kind of process can be followed in the mythology of the Plains, where we may order the data according to the set:

> Unsuccessful mediator between Earth and Sky
> (Star-Husband's wife)
>
> Heterogeneous pair of mediators
> (grandmother and grandchild)
>
> Semi-homogeneous pair of mediators
> (Lodge-Boy and Thrown-away)

While among the Pueblo (Zuni) we have the corresponding set:

> Successful mediator between Earth and Sky
> (Poshaiyanki)
>
> Semi-homogeneous pair of mediators
> (Uyuyewi and Matsailema)
>
> Homogeneous pair of mediators
> (the two Ahaiyuta)

On the other hand, correlations may appear on a horizontal axis (this is true even on the linguistic level; see the manifold connotation of the root *pose* in Tewa according to Parsons: coyote, mist, scalp, etc.). Coyote (a carrion-eater) is intermediary between herbivorous and carnivorous just as mist between Sky and Earth; as scalp between war and agriculture (scalp is a war crop); as corn smut between wild and cultivated plants; as garments between "nature" and "culture"; as refuse between village and outside; and as ashes (or soot) between roof (sky vault) and hearth (in the ground). This chain of mediators, if one may call them so, not only throws light on entire parts of North American mythology—why the Dew-God may be at the same time the Game-Master and the giver of raiments and be personified as an "Ash-Boy"; or why scalps are mist-producing; or why the Game-Mother is associated with corn smut; etc.—but it also probably corresponds to a universal way of organizing daily experience. See, for instance, the French for plant smut (*nielle*, from Latin *nebula*); the luck-bringing power attributed in Europe to refuse (old shoe) and ashes (kissing chimney sweeps); and compare the

American Ash-Boy cycle with the Indo-European Cinderella: Both are phallic figures (mediators between male and female); masters of the dew and the game; owners of fine raiments; and social mediators (low class marrying into high class); but they are impossible to interpret through recent diffusion, as has been contended, since Ash-Boy and Cinderella are symmetrical but inverted in every detail (while the borrowed Cinderella tale in America—Zuni Turkey-Girl—is parallel to the prototype). Hence the chart:

	EUROPE	AMERICA
Sex	female	male
Family Status	double family (remarried father)	no family (orphan)
Appearance	pretty girl	ugly boy
Sentimental status	nobody likes her	unrequited love for girl
Transformation	luxuriously clothed with supernatural help	stripped of ugliness with supernatural help

Thus, like Ash-Boy and Cinderella, the trickster is a mediator. Since his mediating function occupies a position halfway between two polar terms, he must retain something of that duality—namely an ambiguous and equivocal character. But the trickster figure is not the only conceivable form of mediation; some myths seem to be entirely devoted to the task of exhausting all the possible solutions to the problem of bridging the gap between *two* and *one*. For instance, a comparison between all the variants of the Zuni emergence myth provides us with a series of mediating devices, each of which generates the next one by a process of opposition and correlation:

messiah > dioscuri > trickster > bisexual being > sibling pair > married couple > grandmother-grandchild > four-term group > triad

In Cushing's version, this dialectic is associated with a change from a spatial dimension (mediation between Sky and Earth) to a temporal dimension (mediation between summer and winter, that is, between birth and death). But while the shift is being made from space to time, the final solution (triad) re-introduces space, since a triad consists of a dioscuric pair *plus* a messiah, present simultaneously; and while the point of departure was ostensibly formulated in terms of a space referent (Sky and Earth), this was nevertheless implicitly conceived in terms of a time referent (first the messiah calls, *then* the dioscuri descend). Therefore the logic of myth confronts us with a double, reciprocal exchange of functions to which we shall return shortly.

Not only can we account for the ambiguous character of the trickster, but we can also understand another property of mythical figures the world over, namely, that the same god is endowed with contradictory attributes—for instance, he may be *good* and *bad* at the same time. If we compare the variants of the Hopi myth of the origin of Shalako, we may order them in terms of the following structure:

$$(\text{Masauwu: } x) \simeq (\text{Muyingwu: Masauwu}) \simeq (\text{Shalako: Muyingwu})$$
$$\simeq (y: \text{Masauwu})$$

where x and y represent arbitrary values corresponding to the fact that in the two "extreme" variants the god Masauwu, while appearing alone rather than associated with another god, as in variant two, or being absent, as in variant three, still retains intrinsically a relative value. In variant one, Masauwu (alone) is depicted as helpful to mankind (though not as helpful as he could be), and in version four, harmful to mankind (though not as harmful as he could be). His role is thus defined—at least implicitly—in contrast with another role which is possible but not specified and which is represented here by the values x and y. In version 2, on the other hand, Muyingwu is relatively more helpful than Masauwu, and in version three, Shalako more helpful than Muyingwu. We find an identical series when ordering the Keresan variants:

$$(\text{Poshaiyanki: } x) \simeq (\text{Lea: Poshaiyanki}) \simeq (\text{Poshaiyanki: Tiamoni})$$
$$\simeq (y: \text{Poshaiyanki})$$

This logical framework is particularly interesting, since anthropologists are already acquainted with it on two other levels—

first, in regard to the problem of the pecking order among hens, and second, to what this writer has called *generalized exchange* in the field of kinship. By recognizing it also on the level of mythical thought, we may find ourselves in a better position to appraise its basic importance in anthropological studies and to give it a more inclusive theoretical interpretation.

Finally, when we have succeeded in organizing a whole series of variants into a kind of permutation group, we are in a position to formulate the law of that group. Although it is not possible at the present stage to come closer than an approximate formulation which will certainly need to be refined in the future, it seems that every myth (considered as the aggregate of all its variants) corresponds to a formula of the following type:

$$F_x(a): F_y(b) \simeq F_x(b): F_{a\text{-}1}(y)$$

Here, with two terms, *a* and *b*, being given as well as two functions, *x* and *y*, of these terms, it is assumed that a relation of equivalence exists between two situations defined respectively by an inversion of *terms* and *relations*, under two conditions: (1) that one term be replaced by its opposite (in the above formula, *a* and *a-1*); (2) that an inversion be made between the *function value* and the *term value* of two elements (above, *y* and *a*).

This formula becomes highly significant when we recall that Freud considered that *two traumas* (and not one, as is so commonly said) are necessary in order to generate the individual myth in which a neurosis consists. By trying to apply the formula to the analysis of these traumas (and assuming that they correspond to conditions 1 and 2 respectively) we should not only be able to provide a more precise and rigorous formulation of the genetic law of the myth, but we would find ourselves in the much desired position of developing side by side the anthropological and the psychological aspects of the theory; we might also take it to the laboratory and subject it to experimental verification.

At this point it seems unfortunate that with the limited means at the disposal of French anthropological research no further advance can be made. It should be emphasized that the task of analyzing mythological literature, which is extremely bulky, and of breaking it down into its constituent units, requires team work and technical help. A variant of average length requires several hundred cards to be properly analyzed. To discover a suitable pattern of rows and columns for those cards, special devices are needed, consisting of vertical boards about six feet long and four and a half feet high, where cards can be pigeon-holed and moved at will. In order to build up three-dimensional models enabling one to compare the variants, several such boards are necessary, and this in turn requires a spacious workshop, a commodity particularly unavailable in Western Europe nowadays. Furthermore, as soon as the frame of reference becomes multi-dimensional (which occurs at an early stage, as has been shown above) the board system has to be replaced by perforated cards, which in turn require IBM equipment, etc.

Three final remarks may serve as conclusion.

First, the question has often been raised why myths, and more generally oral literature, are so much addicted to duplication, triplication, or quadruplication of the same sequence. If our hypotheses are accepted, the answer is obvious: The function of repetition is to render the structure of the myth apparent. For we have seen that the synchronic-diachronic structure of the myth permits us to organize it into diachronic sequences (the rows in our tables) which should be read synchronically (the columns). Thus, a myth exhibits a "slated" structure, which comes to the surface, so to speak, through the process of repetition.

However, the slates are not absolutely identical. And since the purpose of myth is to provide a logical model capable of overcoming a contradiction (an impossible achievement if, as it happens, the contradiction is real), a theoretically infinite number of slates will be generated, each one slightly different from the others. Thus, myth grows spiral-wise until the intellectual impulse which has produced it is exhausted. Its *growth* is a continuous process, whereas its *structure* remains discontinuous. If this is the case, we should assume that it closely corresponds, in the realm of the spoken word, to a crystal in the realm of physical matter. This analogy may help us to better understand the relationship of myth to both *langue* on the one hand and *parole* on the other. Myth is an intermediary entity between a statistical aggregate of molecules and the molecular structure itself.

Prevalent attempts to explain alleged differences between the so-called primitive mind and scientific thought have resorted to qualitative differences between the working processes of the mind in both cases, while assuming that the entities which they were studying remained very much the same. If our interpretation is correct, we are led toward a completely different view—namely, that the kind of logic in mythical thought is as rigorous as that of modern science, and that the difference lies, not in the quality of the intellectual process, but in the nature of the things to which it is applied. This is well in agreement with the situation known to prevail in the field of technology: What makes a steel ax superior to a stone ax is not that the first one is better made than the second. They are equally well made, but steel is quite different from stone. In the same way we may be able to show that the same logical processes operate in myth as in science, and that man has always been thinking equally well; the improvement lies, not in an alleged progress of man's mind, but in the discovery of new areas to which it may apply its unchanged and unchanging powers.

NOTES

1. In Boas' Introduction to James Teit, "Traditions of the Thompson River Indians of British Columbia," *Memoirs of the American Folklore Society*, VI (1898), p. 18.
2. A. M. Hocart, *Social Origins* (London: 1954), p. 7.
3. See, for instance, Sir R. A. Paget, "The Origin of Language," *Journal of World History*, I, No. 2 (UNESCO, 1953).
4. See Émile Benveniste, "Nature du signe linguistique," *Acta Linguistica*, I, No. 1 (1939); and Chapter V in the present volume.
5. Jules Michelet, *Histoire de la Révolution française*, IV, 1. I took this quotation from M. Merleau-Ponty, *Les Aventures de la dialectique* (Paris: 1955), p. 273.
6. We are not trying to become involved with specialists in an argument; this would be presumptuous and even meaningless on our part. Since the Oedipus myth is taken here merely as an example treated in arbitrary fashion, the chthonian nature ascribed to the Sphinx might seem surprising; we shall refer to the testimony of Marie Delcourt: "In the archaic legends, [she is] certainly born of the Earth itself" (*Oedipe ou la légende du conquérant* [Liège: 1944], p. 108). No matter how remote from Delcourt's our method may be (and our conclusions would be, no doubt, if we were competent to deal with the problem in depth), it seems to us that she has convincingly established the nature of the Sphinx in the archaic tradition, namely, that of a female monster who attacks and rapes

young men; in other words, the personification of a female being with an inversion of the sign. This explains why, in the handsome iconography compiled by Delcourt at the end of her work, men and women are always found in an inverted "sky/earth" relationship.

As we shall point out below, we selected the Oedipus myth as our first example because of the striking analogies that seem to exist between certain aspects of archaic Greek thought and that of the Pueblo Indians, from whom we have borrowed the examples that follow. In this respect it should be noted that the figure of the Sphinx, as reconstructed by Delcourt, coincides with two figures of North American mythology (who probably merge into one). We are referring, on the one hand, to "the old hag," a repulsive witch whose physical appearance presents a "problem" to the young hero. If he "solves" this problem—that is, if he responds to the advances of the abject creature—he will find in his bed, upon awakening, a beautiful young woman who will confer power upon him (this is also a Celtic theme). The Sphinx, on the other hand, recalls even more "the child-protruding woman" of the Hopi Indians, that is, a phallic mother par excellence. This young woman was abandoned by her group in the course of a difficult migration, just as she was about to give birth. Henceforth she wanders in the desert as the "Mother of Animals," which she withholds from hunters. He who meets her in her bloody clothes "is so frightened that he has an erection," of which she takes advantage to rape him, after which she rewards him with unfailing success in hunting. See H. R. Voth, "The Oraibi Summer Snake Ceremony," *Field Columbian Museum*, Publication No. 83, Anthropological Series, Vol. III, No. 4 (Chicago: 1903), pp. 352-3 and p. 353, *n* 1.

7. See *Annuaire de l'École pratique des Hautes Études,* Section des Sciences religieuses, 1952-1953, pp. 19-21, and 1953-1954, pp. 27-9. Thanks are due here to an unrequested but deeply appreciated grant from the Ford Foundation.

8. For another application of this method, see our study "Four Winnebago Myths: A Structural Sketch," in Stanley Diamond (ed.), *Culture in History: Essays in Honor of Paul Radin* (New York: 1960), pp. 351-62.

CHAPTER XII

Structure
and Dialectics

F ROM Lang to Malinowski, through Durkheim, Lévy-Bruhl, and van der Leeuw, sociologists and anthropologists who were interested in the interrelations between myth and ritual have considered them as mutually redundant. Some of these thinkers see in each myth the ideological projection of a rite, the purpose of the myth being to provide a foundation for the rite. Others reverse the relationship and regard ritual as a kind of dramatized illustration of the myth. Regardless of whether the myth or the ritual is the original, they replicate each other; the myth exists on the conceptual level and the ritual on the level of action. In both cases, one assumes an orderly correspondence between the two—in other words, a homology. Curiously enough, this homology is demonstrable in only a small number of cases. It remains to be seen why all myths do not correspond to rites and vice versa, and most important, why there should be such a curious replication in the first place.

I intend to show by means of a concrete example that this

homology does not always exist; or, more specifically, that when we do find such a homology, it might very well constitute a particular illustration of a more generalized relationship between myth and ritual and between the rites themselves. Such a generalized relationship would imply a one-to-one correspondence between the elements of rites which seem to differ, or between the elements of any one rite and any one myth. Such a correspondence could not, however, be considered a homology. In the example to be discussed here, the reconstruction of the correspondence requires a series of preliminary operations—that is, permutations or transformations which may furnish the key to the correspondence. If this hypothesis is correct, we shall have to give up mechanical causality as an explanation and, instead, conceive of the relationship between myth and ritual as dialectical, accessible only if both have first been reduced to their structural elements.

The demonstration of such a hypothesis seems to me to constitute an appropriate tribute to the work and method of Roman Jakobson. He himself was concerned on several occasions with mythology and folklore; let us merely recall his article on Slavic mythology in the *Standard Dictionary of Folklore, Mythology and Legend*, and his valuable commentaries on *Russian Fairy Tales*.[1] Secondly, it is clear that the method I am employing is simply the extension to another field of structural linguistics, which is associated with the name of Jakobson. And finally, he was always concerned with the intimate relationship between structural analysis and dialectical method. He concluded his well-known work, *Prinzipien der historischen Phonologie*, by saying: "The relationship between statics and dynamics is one of the most fundamental dialectical antinomies which determine the idea of language." In attempting to clarify the mutual implications of the concept of structure and dialectical thought, I am merely following one of the paths which he himself charted.

In the work of G. A. Dorsey devoted to the mythology of the Pawnee Indians of the North American Plains,[2] we find a series of myths (numbered 77 through 116) which give an account of the origin of shamanistic powers. One theme recurs several times (see numbers 77, 86, 89, and *passim*); I shall call it, for purposes of simplification, the theme of the *pregnant boy*. Let us examine, for example, myth number 77.

An ignorant young boy becomes aware that he possesses magical powers that enable him to cure the sick. Jealous of the boy's increasing reputation, an old medicine man of established position visits him on several different occasions, accompanied by his wife. Enraged because he obtains no secret in exchange for his own teachings, the medicine man offers the boy a pipe filled with magical herbs. Thus bewitched, the boy discovers that he is pregnant. Full of shame, he leaves his village and seeks death among wild animals. The animals, moved to pity by his misfortune, decide to cure him. They extract the fetus from his body. They teach him their magical powers, by means of which the boy, on returning to his home, kills the evil medicine man and becomes himself a famous and respected healer.

A careful analysis of the text of this myth, which in one version alone takes up thirteen pages of Dorsey's work, discloses that it is built on a long series of oppositions: (1) *initiated shaman* versus *non-initiated shaman*, that is, the opposition between acquired power and innate power; (2) *child* versus *old man*, since the myth insists on the youth of one protagonist and the old age of the other; (3) *confusion of sexes* versus *differentiation of sexes*; all of Pawnee metaphysical thought is actually based on the idea that at the time of the creation of the world antagonistic elements were intermingled and that the first work of the gods consisted in sorting them out. The young child is asexual or, more accurately, the male and female principles co-exist in him. Conversely, in the old man the distinction is irrevocable—an idea clearly expressed in the myth by the fact that his wife is always with him—in contrast with the boy, who is alone but who harbors in himself both masculinity and femininity (he becomes pregnant); (4) *fertility of the child* (despite his virginity) versus *sterility of the old man* (notwithstanding his constantly mentioned marriage); (5) the irreversible relationship of the fertilization of the "son" by the "father" versus an equally irreversible relationship, namely the revenge of the "father" because the "son" does not reveal any secrets to him (he possesses none) in exchange for his own secrets; (6) the threefold opposition between, on the one hand, *plant* magic, which is *real*, that is, a drug by means of which the old man fertilizes the child (this magic, however, is *curable*) and, on the other hand, magic of *animal* origin, which is *symbolic* (manipulation of a skull), by means of which the child kills the old man *without any possibility of resurrection;* (7) magic which proceeds by *introduction* versus magic which proceeds by *extraction.*

The construction of the myth by oppositions also characterizes details of the text. The animals are moved to pity at the sight of the boy for two reasons, which are well defined in the text: He compounds the characteristics of man and woman, a combination expressed by the opposition between the leanness of his own body (he has been fasting for days) and the swelling of his abdomen (due to his condition). To induce a miscarriage, the *herbivorous* animals *vomit* the *bones,* while the *carnivorous* animals *extract* the *flesh* (threefold opposition). And finally, while the boy risks death from a swollen stomach (in myth number 89 the fetus is replaced by a ball of clay, which continues to grow until its bearer bursts), the medicine man actually dies of an abdominal constriction.

The version given in myth number 86 both retains and elaborates some of these oppositions. The murderer lowers his victim at the end of a rope down into the subterranean world (the abode of mammals, which are magical mammals) to pick up some eagle and woodpecker feathers, that is, feathers of sky-dwelling birds, the former specifically associated with the empyreal heavens and the latter with thunderstorms. This inversion of the system of the world is accompanied by a concomitant "rectification" of the inverted opposition (found in the "right-side-up" system of myth number 77) between carnivorous and herbivorous animals. As seems to be "normal," the former are now concerned with the bones of the fetus, the latter with its blood. We see, then, what a structural analysis of the myth content can achieve in itself: It furnishes rules of transformation which enable us to shift from one variant to another by means of operations similar to those of algebra.

At this point, however, I wish to consider another aspect of the problem. To what Pawnee ritual does the myth of the pregnant boy correspond? On first inspection, none. Whereas the myth emphasizes the opposition between generations, the Pawnee have no shamanistic societies based on age-grades. Membership in these societies is not subjected to trials or payments. According to Murie, "the usual way to become a medicine-man was to succeed one's teacher at his death."[3] The myth, on the contrary, is based upon a twofold concept of innate power, which, because it is *innate*, is denied the boy by the master; because the boy's power is not taught him by the master, the master refuses to acknowledge him as his successor.

Shall we say, therefore, that the Pawnee myth reflects a system which is correlated with and yet the reverse of the system which prevails in Pawnee ritual? This would be only partly correct, because the opposition would not be pertinent; that is, the concept of opposition is not heuristic here: It accounts for certain differences between the myth and the rite but leaves others unexplained. It especially neglects the theme of the pregnant boy, to which we nevertheless attributed a central position in the group of myths under consideration.

On the other hand, all the elements of the myth fall into place when we compare it, not with the corresponding Pawnee ritual, but rather with the symmetrical and inverse ritual that prevails among those tribes of the American Plains which conceive their shamanistic societies and the rules for membership in the reverse manner from that of the Pawnee themselves. As Lowie expresses it, "The Pawnee have the distinction of having developed the most elaborate system of societies outside the age-series." [4] In this respect they contrast with the Blackfoot and with such sedentary tribes as the Mandan and Hidatsa, which exemplify most elaborately the other type and to which they are related, not only culturally, but also geographically and historically through the Arikara, whose separation from the Skidi Pawnee (precisely those whose myths Dorsey collected) dates only from the first half of the eighteenth century.

Among these tribes, societies are based on age-grades. The transition from one to another is achieved by purchase, and the relationship between seller and buyer is conceived as a relationship between "father" and "son." Finally, the candidate always appears in the company of his wife, and the central motif of the transaction is the handing over of the "son's" wife to the "father," who carries out with her an act of real or symbolic coitus, which is, however, always represented as a fertility act.

We thus rediscover all the oppositions already analyzed on the level of myth, but there is a reversal of the values attributed to each pair: initiated and non-initiated, youth and old age, confusion and differentiation of sexes, and so on. In fact, in the Mandan, Hidatsa, and Blackfoot rites, the "son" is accompanied by his wife, just as in the Pawnee myth the wife accompanied the "father." But whereas in the latter case she was a mere supernumerary, here it is she who plays the principal role: Fertilized by the "father" and conceiving the "son," she thus represents the bisexuality which the Pawnee myth ascribed to the "son." In other words, the semantic values are the same; they are merely permuted in relation to the symbols which express them. It is interesting to compare, in this respect, the objects which are considered to be fertilizing agents in the two systems. In the Pawnee myth, a pipe is transferred by the father and his wife to the son. In the Blackfoot rite, a wild turnip is first transferred by the father to the son's wife, then by the latter to the son. The pipe, a hollow tube, is the intermediary between the sky and the middle world; hence its role is symmetrical to, and the reverse of, the role ascribed to the wild turnip in Plains mythology —as is evident in the innumerable variants of the cycle called "Star-Husband," where the turnip is a plug, functioning as a circuit-breaker between the two worlds. The elements are expressed by different symbols when their order is reversed.

The extraordinary Hidatsa rite (whose archaic Chinese parallels were never, to my knowledge, pointed out), concerning the prestation of women in an arbor roofed over with dried meat, also corresponds to the Pawnee myth. A payment of meat is made, sometimes to the fertilizing fathers who own the magic, sometimes to the magical animals playing the role of non-fathers (that is, abortionists). But in the first case, meat is offered in the form of a container (hut covered with meat), whereas in the other it is specified that meat should be presented as content (satchels stuffed with meat). We could further pursue these comparisons, which would all lead to the same conclusion, namely, that the Pawnee myth reveals a ritual system which is the reverse, not of that prevailing among the Pawnee, but of a system which they do not employ and which exists among related tribes whose ritual organization is exactly the opposite of that of the Pawnee. Moreover, the relationship between the two systems has a contrapuntal character: If one system is considered as a progression, the other appears as a retrogression.

We have thus defined a Pawnee myth in terms of both its correlation with and its opposition to an alien ritual. It is remarkable that a relationship of the same type, but of a still more complex order, may be detected between this very myth and a ritual which, while not characteristic of the Pawnee alone, was the subject of a particularly elaborate study—namely, the Hako.[5]

The Hako is a ritual of alliance between two groups. In contrast to the Pawnee societies, whose position in the social structure is fixed, these groups may freely choose one another. By operating in this fashion, however, they place themselves in a father-son relationship that also defines the stable relationship between consecutive age-grades in the sedentary tribes. As Hocart once demonstrated, the father-son relationship upon which the Hako is based may be considered a permutation of an affinal relationship between paternal and maternal kin.[6] In other words, the myth of the pregnant boy, the Mandan and Hidatsa ritual of accession to the highest rank of a series of age-grades, and the Hako represent so many groups of permutations whose formula is an equivalence between the opposition *father/son* and the opposition *man/woman*. I, for one, am prepared to hold that this equation is based on the distinctive characteristics of the kinship system known as Crow-Omaha, in which the relationships between affinal groups are specifically formalized in terms of relationships between ascendants and descendants. But this aspect of the problem will have to be developed elsewhere.

I shall limit myself to examining briefly the last phases of the Hako ritual (16 to 19 in Fletcher's breakdown). These phases are invested with the most sacred character and offer a series of remarkable analogies with the myth of the pregnant boy. The father's group arrives in the village of the son. It symbolically captures a young child. The child's sex is immaterial, or, more accurately, he is of unidentified sex.[7] The group consecrates him by means of a series of anointings, in order to identify him with Tirawa, the supreme deity of the celestial world. Then the child is raised in a robe with his legs projecting forward, and in this position he is handled in the fashion of a phallus for a symbolic coitus with the world, represented by a circle outlined on the ground, into which he is to drop, like an egg, an oriole's nest: "The putting

of the child's feet in the circle means the giving of new life . . . ,"
comments the native informer unambiguously.[8] Finally, the circle is
erased and the anointments are removed from the child, who is sent
away to join his playmates.

All these operations may be considered clearly as a permutation of the elements of the myth of the pregnant child. In the myth
as well as the ritual, we have three protagonists:

Myth: son	father (or husband)	wife of father
Ritual: son (permu- tation of wife)	father (permutation of husband)	child (permuta- tion of son)

In both myth and ritual, two protagonists are identified with respect to sex, and one is left unidentified (son or child).

In the myth, the lack of identification of the son enables
him to be half-man and half-woman; in the ritual, he becomes
fully a man (an agent of coitus) and fully a woman (he actually
gives birth to a nest, which symbolizes an egg, in a circle, which
symbolizes a nest).

The entire symbolism of the Hako implies that the father
fertilizes the son by means of the ambivalent function of the child;
just as in the myth, the ambivalent function of the couple (the
medicine man and his wife) fertilizes the child and, similarly, in
the ritual of the sedentary tribes, the father fertilizes the son
through the ambivalent function of the son's wife. This ambiguity as
to the sex of one of the protagonists is constantly emphasized regardless of context. Compare, in this respect, the sack from which
the legs of the child emerge (Hako); the male child with protuberant abdomen (Pawnee myth); the woman holding in her
mouth a protuberant turnip (Blackfoot myth constituting the basis
of the rite of access to the society of *Kit-foxes* by prestation of the
wife).

In another study [9] I attempted to show that the genetic model
of the myth—that is, the model which generates it and simultaneously gives it its structure—consists of the application of *four*
functions to *three* symbols. Here, the four functions are defined
by the twofold opposition *elder/younger* and *male/female*, from
which stem the father, mother, son, and daughter functions. In the
myth of the pregnant boy, the father and mother each use a different symbol, and the functions of son and daughter are merged under

the third available symbol, the child. In the Mandan-Hidatsa ritual, it is the father and son who are distinguished, while the wife of the son embodies the functions of mother and daughter. The Hako appears to be more complex, since here the symbols, always three in number, require that besides the father and son a new figure play a role—namely, the child (boy or girl) of the son. The reason for this is that the allocation of functions to symbols requires here an ideal dichotomization of the latter. As we noted before, the father is both father and mother; the son, both son and daughter; and the child borrows from each of the other two symbols one of their half-functions: fertilizing agent (father) and fertilized object (daughter). It is remarkable that this more complex distribution of the functions among the symbols characterizes the only one of the three systems which is based on reciprocity. Although the purpose of each system is to establish an alliance, this alliance is rejected in the first case, solicited in the second, and negotiated only in the third.

The dialectical relationship between myth and ritual is based on considerations of structure which we cannot take up here, and we must refer the reader to the study already cited. But we hope to have shown that in order to understand this relationship it is indispensable to compare myth and ritual, not only within the confines of one and the same society, but also with the beliefs and practices of neighboring societies. If a certain group of Pawnee myths represents a permutation of certain rituals, not only of the same tribe, but also of other peoples, one cannot rest content with a purely formal analysis. Such an analysis constitutes a preliminary stage of research, which is fruitful to the extent that it permits the formulation of geographical and historical problems in more rigorous terms than is customary. Structural dialectics does not contradict historical determinism, but rather promotes it by giving it a new tool. Along with Meillet and Troubetzkoy, Jakobson proved, moreover, on several occasions that the phenomena of reciprocal influence between geographically related linguistic areas cannot remain outside of structural analysis; this constitutes the well-known theory of linguistic affinities. I have attempted to bring a modest contribution to this theory, which I applied in another field, by emphasizing that the affinity can be seen not only in the diffusion of certain structural properties outside their area of origin or in their rejection, which impedes this propagation. The affinity may also be demonstrated by antithesis, which generates structures presenting the character of answers, cures, excuses, or even remorse. In mythology, as in linguistics, formal analysis immediately raises the question of *meaning*.

NOTES

1. *Standard Dictionary of Folklore, Mythology and Legend,* Vol. I (New York: 1949); *Russian Fairy Tales* (New York: 1945).
2. *The Pawnee: Mythology,* Part I (Washington: 1906).
3. J. R. Murie, "Pawnee Societies," *Anthropological Papers of the American Museum of Natural History,* Vol. XI (1916), pp. vii, 603.
4. R. H. Lowie, "Plains-Indian Age-Societies: Historical and Comparative Summary," *Anthropological Papers of the American Museum of Natural History,* Vol. XI (1916), pp. xiii, 890.
5. A. C. Fletcher and J. R. Murie, *The Hako: A Pawnee Ceremony,* Bureau of American Ethnology, 22nd Annual Report, Part II (Washington: 1900-1901 [1904]).
6. A. M. Hocart, "Covenants," in *The Life Giving Myth* (London: 1952).
7. Fletcher and Murie, *op. cit.,* p. 201.
8. *Ibid.,* p. 245.
9. "The Structural Study of Myth," Chapter XI of the present volume.

PART FOUR

Art

CHAPTER XIII

Split Representation in the Art of Asia and America

Contemporary anthropologists seem to be somewhat reluctant to undertake comparative studies of primitive art. We can easily understand their reasons. Until now, studies of this nature have tended almost exclusively to demonstrate cultural contacts, diffusion phenomena, and borrowings. The discovery of a decorative detail or an unusual pattern in two different parts of the world, regardless of the geographical distance between them and an often considerable historical gap, brought enthusiastic proclamations about common origin and the unquestionable existence of prehistoric relationships between cultures which could not be compared in other respects. Leaving aside some fruitful discoveries, we know to what abuses this hurried search for analogies "at any cost" has led. To save us from these errors, experts in material culture even now need to define the specific characteristics which distinguish a trait, trait complex, or style that may be subject to multiple independent recurrences from one whose nature and characteristics exclude the possibility of repetition without borrowing.

It is, therefore, with some hesitation that I propose to contribute several documents to a hotly and legitimately debated body of materials. This voluminous collection involves the Northwest Coast of America, China, Siberia, New Zealand, and perhaps even India and Persia. What is more, the documents belong to entirely different periods: the eighteenth and nineteenth centuries for Alaska; the first to second millennia B.C. for China; the prehistoric era for the Amur region; and a period stretching from the fourteenth to the eighteenth century for New Zealand. A more difficult case could hardly be conceived. I have mentioned elsewhere[1] the almost insuperable obstacles generated by the hypothesis of pre-Columbian contacts between Alaska and New Zealand. The problem is perhaps simpler when one compares Siberia and China with North America: Distances are more reasonable and one need overcome only the obstacle of one or two millenia. Even in this case, however, and whatever the intuitive convictions which irresistibly sway the mind, what an immense marshalling of facts becomes necessary! For his ingenious and brilliant work, C. Hentze can be called the "scrap-collector" of Americanism, pulling his evidence together from fragments gathered from the most diverse cultures and often mounting insignificant details[2] for exhibition. Instead of justifying the intuitive feeling of connectedness, his analysis dissolves it; nothing among these *membra disjecta poetae* appears to justify the deep sense of affinity which familiarity with both arts had so strongly elicited.

And yet, it is impossible not to be struck by the analogies presented by Northwest Coast and ancient Chinese art. These analogies derive not so much from the external aspect of the objects as from the fundamental principles which an analysis of both arts yields. This work was undertaken by Leonhard Adam, whose conclusions I shall summarize here.[3] The two arts proceed by means of: (1) intense stylization; (2) schematization or symbolism, expressed by emphasizing characteristic features or adding significant attributes (thus, in Northwest Coast art, the beaver is portrayed by the small log which it holds between its paws); (3) depiction of the body by "split representation"; (4) dislocation of details, which are arbitrarily isolated from the whole; (5) representation of *one* individual shown in front view with *two* profiles; (6) highly elaborate symmetry, which often involves asymmetric details; (7) illogical transformation of details into new elements (thus, a paw becomes a beak, an eye motif is used to represent a joint, or vice-versa); (8) finally, intellectual rather than intuitive representation, where the skeleton or internal organs take precedence over the representation of the body (a technique which is equally striking in northern Australia).[4] These techniques are not characteristic solely of Northwest Coast art. As Leonhard Adam writes, "The various technological and artistic principles displayed in both China and North West America are almost entirely identical." [5]

Once these similarities have been noted, it is curious to observe that, for entirely different reasons, ancient Chinese and Northwest Coast art have been independently compared with Maori art in New Zealand.[6] This fact is the more remarkable when we note that Neolithic art of the Amur—some of whose themes (such as the bird, with wings unfolded, whose abdomen is formed by a solar face) are almost identical with themes of the Northwest Coast—exhibits, according to some scholars, "an unexpectedly rich, curvilinear ornamentation related to that of the Ainu and Maori on one side and to the Neolithic cultures of China (Yangshao) and Japan (Jomon) on the other; consisting particularly of that type of ribbon ornamentation characterized by complex motifs such as the weave, spiral and meander in contradistinction to the rectangular geometric decoration of the Baikalian culture." [7] Thus art forms from very different regions and periods which exhibit obvious analogies suggest, each of them and for independent reasons, relationships which are, however, incompatible with geographical and historical requirements.

Do we rest, then, on the horns of a dilemma which condemns us either to deny history or to remain blind to similarities so often confirmed? Anthropologists of the diffusionist school did not hesitate to force the hand of historical criticism. I do not intend to defend their adventurous hypotheses, but it must be admitted that the negative attitude of their cautious opponents is no more satisfactory than the fabulous pretensions which the latter merely reject. Comparative studies of primitive art have probably been jeopardized by the zeal of investigators of cultural contacts and borrowings. But let us state in no uncertain terms that these studies have been jeopardized even more by intellectual pharisees who prefer to deny obvious relationships because science does not yet provide an adequate method for their interpretation. The rejection of facts because they appear to be unintelligible is surely more sterile from the viewpoint of scientific progress than the formulation of hypotheses. Even if these should prove to be unacceptable, they will elicit, precisely because of their inadequacy, the criticism and research that will one day enable us to progress beyond them.[8]

We reserve, therefore, the right to compare American Indian art with that of China or New Zealand, even if it has been proved a thousand times over that the Maori could not have brought their weapons and ornaments to the Pacific Coast. Cultural contact doubtless constitutes the one hypothesis which most easily accounts for complex similarities that chance cannot explain. But if historians maintain that contact is impossible, this does not prove that the similarities are illusory, but only that one must look elsewhere for the explanation. The fruitfulness of the diffusionist approach derives precisely from its systematic exploration of the possibilities of history. If history, when it is called upon unremittingly (and it must be called upon *first*), cannot yield an answer, then let us appeal to psychology, or the structural analysis of forms; let us ask ourselves if internal connections, whether of a psychological or logical nature, will allow us to understand parallel recurrences whose frequency and cohesion cannot possibly be the result of chance. It is in this spirit that I shall now present my contribution to the debate.

Split representation in Northwest Coast art has been described by Franz Boas as follows: "The animal is imagined cut in two from head to tail . . . there is a deep depression between the eyes, extending down the nose. This shows that the head itself must not have been considered a front view, but as consisting of two profiles which adjoin at mouth and nose, while they are not in contact with each other on a level with the eyes and forehead . . . either the animals are represented as split in two so that the profiles are joined in the middle, or a front view of the head is shown with two adjoining profiles of the body." [9] Boas analyzes the two paintings reproduced here (Figures 17 and 18, which correspond respectively to Figures 222 and 223 in the text cited) in the following terms:

FIGURE 17. Haida. Painting representing a bear. (After F. Boas, *Primitive Art*, Fig. 222.)

FIGURE 18. Tsimshian. Painting representing a bear; from the front of a house. (After Boas, *op. cit.*, Fig. 223.)

Figure 222 (a Haida painting) shows a design which has been obtained in this manner. It represents a bear. The enormous breadth of mouth observed in these cases is brought about by the junction of the two profiles of which the head consists. This cutting of the head is brought out most clearly in the painting Figure 223, which also represents the bear. It is the painting on the front of a Tsimshian house, the circular hole in the middle of the design being the door of the house. The animal is cut from back to front, so that only the front part of the head coheres. The two halves of the lower jaw do not touch each other. The back is represented by the black outlines on which the hair is indicated by fine lines. The Tsimshian call such a design "bears meeting," as though two bears had been represented.[10]

Let us now compare this analysis with that given by H. G. Creel of a similar technique in the art of ancient China: "One of the most distinctive characteristics of Shang decorative art is a peculiar method by which animals were represented in flat or in rounded surfaces. It is as if one took the animal and split it

FIGURE 19. Bronze discovered near An-Yang (China). In the middle
panel, a split *t'ao t'ieh* mask without a lower jaw. The ears make up a
second mask above the first. The eyes in the second mask may also be
seen as belonging to two small dragons represented by the ears of the
first mask. The two small dragons are shown in profile and face to face,
like those in the upper panel. The latter may in turn be seen as a ram
mask shown in front view, the horns being represented by the bodies
of the dragons. The design on the lid can be similarly interpreted.
(After W. P. Yetts, *An-Yang. A Retrospect.*)

PLATE II. Storage box representing a frog, Northwest Coast, nineteenth century. (Collection of Dr. J. Lacan.)

PLATE I. Shang bronze, China, 1766–1122 B.C. (After W. P. Yetts, *The George Eumorphopoulos Collection Catalogue*.)

PLATE III. Haida. Painting representing a shark. The head is shown in front view to bring out the features characteristic of the shark, but the body is split lengthwise, with the two halves laid out flat on the surface to the right and left of the head. (After Bureau of American Ethnology, *Tenth Annual Report*, Plate XXV.)

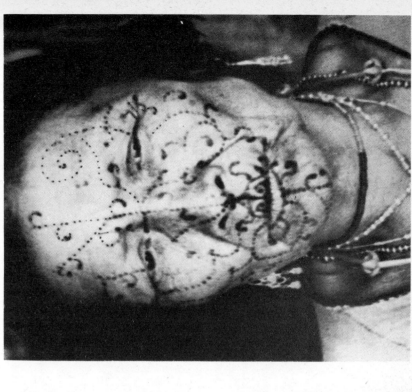

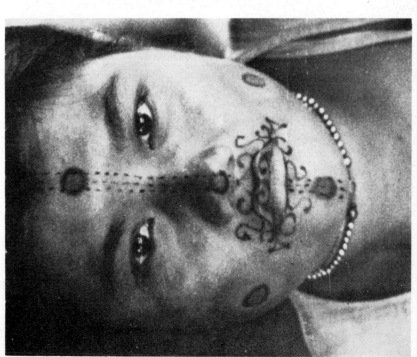

PLATES IV and V. Two Caduveo women with painted faces. (Photographed by the author, 1935.)

PLATE VII. Maori chief's drawing representing his own tattooed face. (After H. G. Robley, *Moko, or Maori Tattooing.*)

PLATE VI. Caduveo woman with painted face. Drawing by Boggiani, an Italian painter who visited the Caduveo in 1892. (After G. Boggiani, *Viaggi d'un artista nell' America Meridionale.*)

PLATE IX. Jade figure (tiki), New Zealand, characterized by the three-lobed division of the face. (Courtesy of the American Museum of Natural History.)

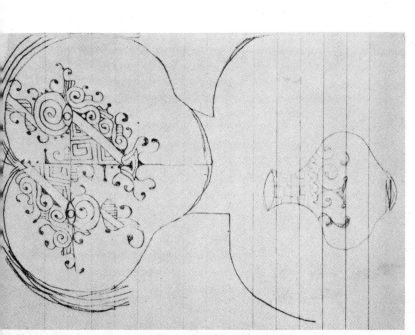

PLATE VIII. Caduveo woman's drawing representing a figure with painted face. (Author's collection.)

PLATE X. Maori wood carving, New Zealand, eighteenth century (?). (After A. Hamilton, *The Art Workmanship of the Maori in New Zealand*.)

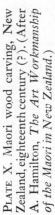

PLATE XI. Head ornament, carved wood, Northwest Coast, nineteenth century. Note the two small human heads which adorn the solar plexus and the abdomen as well as the cleft end of the sternum. (Formerly in the author's collection.)

PLATE XII. Three Maori tattooing designs carved in wood, late nineteenth century. (*Top row:*) Men's faces. (*Bottom row:*) Woman's face. (After Hamilton, *op. cit.*)

PLATE XIII. Three Maori wood carvings, eighteenth or nineteenth century. (After Hamilton, *op. cit.*)

lengthwise, starting at the tip of the tail and carrying the operation almost, not quite, to the tip of the nose, then the two halves are pulled apart and the bisected animal is laid out flat on the surface, the two halves joined only at the tip of the nose." [11] The same author, who apparently does not know Boas' work, after having employed almost exactly the same terminology as the latter, adds: "In studying Shang design I have constantly been aware of the feeling that this art has great resemblance, certainly in spirit and possibly in detail, to that of . . . the Northwest Coast Indians." [12]

This distinctive technique, which is found in ancient Chinese art, among the Siberian primitives, and in New Zealand, also appears at the other extremity of the American continent, among the Caduveo Indians. A drawing, which we reproduce here in Figure 20, represents a face painted according to the traditional custom of the women of this small tribe of southern Brazil, one of the last remnants of the once flourishing Guaicuru nation. I have described elsewhere how these paintings are executed and what their function is in the native culture.[13] For present purposes it is, therefore, sufficient to recall that these paintings have been known since the first contacts with the Guaicuru in the seventeenth century and that they do not seem to have evolved since that time. They are not tattooings, but cosmetic facial paintings, which must be renewed after a few days and which are executed with a wooden spatula dipped in the juices of wild fruit and leaves. The women, who paint one another's faces (and who formerly also painted men), do not work from a model but improvise within the limits of a complex, traditionally defined range of themes. Among four hundred original drawings gathered in the field in 1935, I did not find two alike. The differences, however, stem more from the ever-varied arrangement of fundamental elements than from a renewal of these elements—whether simple and double spirals, hatching, volutes, frets, tendrils, or crosses and whorls. The possibility of Spanish influence should be excluded, given the remote date when this refined art was described for the first time. At present, only a few old women possess the ancient skill, and it is not difficult to foresee the time when it will have disappeared altogether.

Plate VIII (after p. 250) presents a good example of these

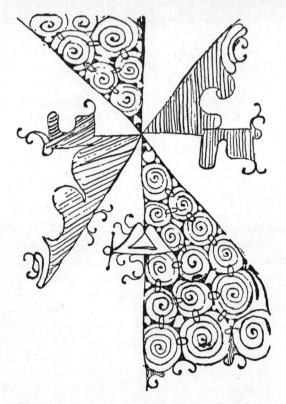

FIGURE 20. Caduveo. Facial design reproduced by a native woman on a sheet of paper. (Author's collection.)

paintings. The design is built symmetrically in relation to two linear axes, one of them vertical, following the median plane of the face, the other horizontal, dividing the face at eye level. The eyes are schematically represented on a reduced scale. They are used as starting points for two inverted spirals, one of which covers the right cheek and the other the left side of the forehead. A motif in the shape of a compound bow, which is located in the lower part of the painting, represents the upper lip and is applied on it. We find this motif, more or less elaborated and more or less transformed, in all the facial paintings, where it seems to constitute a constant element. It is not easy to analyze the design, because of its apparent asymmetry—which, nonetheless masks a real, though complex, symmetry. The two axes intersect at the root of the nose, thus dividing the face into four triangular sections: left side of the forehead, right side of the forehead, right wing of the nose and right cheek, and left wing of the nose and left cheek. Opposite triangles have a symmetrical design, but the design within each triangle itself is a double design, which is repeated in inverted form in the opposite triangle. Thus, the right side of the forehead and the left cheek are covered, first by a triangle of frets, and, after a separation in the form of an empty oblique strip, by two double spirals in alignment, which are decorated with tendrils. The left side of the forehead and the right cheek are decorated with a simple large spiral adorned with tendrils; it is topped by another motif in the shape of a bird or flame, which contains an element reminiscent of the empty oblique stripe in the opposite design. We thus have two pairs of themes, each of which is repeated twice in symmetrical fashion. But this symmetry is expressed either in relation to one of the two horizontal and vertical axes, or in relation to the triangles defined by the bisection of these axes. While far more complex, this pattern recalls that of playing cards. Plates IV, V, and VI are other examples which illustrate variations on what is fundamentally the same pattern.

In Plate VIII, however, it is not only the painted design which draws the attention. The artist, a woman approximately thirty years old, intended also to represent the face and even the hair. Now she obviously accomplished this by split representation: The face is not really seen in a frontal view; it consists of two joined profiles. This explains its extraordinary width and its heart-shaped outline. The depression dividing the forehead into two halves is a part of the representation of the profiles, which merge only from the root of the nose down to the chin. A comparison of Figures 17 and 18 and Plate VIII shows that this technique is identical with that used by artists of the Northwest Coast of America.

Other important traits are also characteristic of both North and South American art. We have already stressed the dislocation of the subject into elements which are recombined according to conventional rules having nothing to do with nature. Dislocation is just as striking in Caduveo art, where it takes, however, an indirect form. Boas minutely described the dislocation of bodies and faces in Northwest Coast art: The organs and limbs themselves are split and used to reconstitute an arbitrary individual. Thus, in a Haida totem pole, "the figure must be . . . explained in such a way that the animal is twisted twice, the tail being turned up over the back, and the head being first turned down under the stomach, then split and extended outward." [14] In a Kwakiutl representation of a killer whale (*Orca sp.*), "the animal has been split along its whole back towards the front. The two profiles of the head have been joined. . . . The dorsal fin, which according to the methods described heretofore [split representation] would appear on both sides of the body, has been cut off from the back before the animal was split, and appears now placed over the junction of the two profiles of the head. The flippers are laid along the two sides of the body, with which they cohere only at one point each. The two halves of the tail have been twisted outward so that the lower part of the figure forms a straight line." [15] See Figure 21. These examples could easily be multiplied.

FIGURE 21. Kwakiutl. Painting for the front of a house, the design representing a killer whale. (After F. Boas, *op. cit.*, Fig. 247.)

Caduveo art carries the dislocation process both further than, yet not as far as, Northwest Coast art. It does not carry it as far, because the face or body on which the artist works is a flesh-and-bone face and body, which cannot be taken apart and put together again. The integrity of the real face is thus respected, but it is dislocated just the same by the systematic asymmetry by means of which its natural harmony is denied on behalf of the artificial harmony of the painting. But since this painting, instead of representing the image of a deformed face, actually deforms a real face, the dislocation goes further than in the case previously described. The dislocation here involves, besides the decorative value, a subtle element of sadism, which at least partly explains why the erotic appeal of Caduveo women (expressed in the paintings) formerly attracted outlaws and adventurers toward the shores of the Paraguay River. Several of these now aging men, who intermarried with the natives, described to me with quivering emotion the nude bodies of adolescent girls completely covered with interlacings and arabesques of a perverse subtlety. The tattooings and body paintings of the Northwest Coast, where this sexual element was probably lacking and whose symbolism, often abstract, presents a less decorative character, also disregarded symmetry in the human face.[16]

In addition, we observe that the arrangement of Caduveo paintings around a double axis, horizontal and vertical, divides the face according to a process of double splitting, so to speak—that is, the painting recombines the face not into two profiles but into four quarters (see Figure 20). Asymmetry serves the formal function of insuring the distinction between quarters, which would merge into two profiles if the fields were to be symmetrically repeated to the right and left instead of being joined by their tips. Dislocation and splitting are thus functionally related.

If we pursue this comparison between Northwest Coast and Caduveo art, several other points are worthy of consideration. In each case, sculpture and drawing provide the two fundamental means of expression; in each case, sculpture presents a realistic character, while drawing is more symbolic and decorative. Caduveo sculpture is probably limited, at least during the historical period, to fetishes and representations of gods, which are always of small size, in contrast to the monumental art of Canada and

Alaska. But the realistic character and the tendency toward both portrait and stylization are the same, as well as the essentially symbolic meaning of drawn or painted motifs. In both cases, masculine art, centered on sculpture, expresses its representational intention, while feminine art—limited to weaving and plaiting on the Northwest Coast, but also including drawing among these natives of southern Brazil and Paraguay—is a non-representational art. This is true, in both cases, for textile motifs; as regards the Guaicuru facial paintings, we know nothing about their archaic character. It is possible that the themes of these paintings, whose import has become lost today, formerly had a realistic or at any rate symbolical meaning. Northwest Coast and Caduveo art both carry out decoration by means of stencils, and create ever-new combinations through the varied arrangement of basic motifs. Finally, in both cases, art is intimately related to social organization: Motifs and themes express rank differences, nobility privileges, and degrees of prestige. The two societies were organized along similar hierarchical lines and their decorative art functioned to interpret and validate the ranks in the hierarchy.[17]

I should now like to make a brief comparison between Caduveo art and another art which also used split representation—that of the Maori of New Zealand. Let us first recall that Northwest Coast art has been frequently compared, for other reasons, to the art of New Zealand. Some of these reasons turned out to be specious—for instance, the apparently identical character of woven blankets used in the two areas. Others seem more valid—for example, those deriving from the similarity between Alaskan clubs and the Maori *patu mere*. I have mentioned this enigma elsewhere.[18]

The comparison of Maori with Guaicuru art is based on other convergences. In no other region of the world has facial and corporal decoration attained such high levels of development and refinement. Maori tattooings are well known. I reproduce four of them (Plates VII and XII), which may be fruitfully compared with the photographs of Caduveo faces.

The analogies between them are striking: complexity of design, involving hatching, meanders, and spirals (the spirals are often replaced in Caduveo art by frets, which suggest Andean influences); the same tendency to fill the entire surface of the face; and the same localization of the design around the lips in the simpler types. The differences between the two arts must also be considered. The difference due to the fact that Maori design is tattooed whereas Caduveo design is painted may be dismissed, since there is hardly any doubt that in South America, too, tattooing was the primitive technique. Tattooing explains why the Abipone women of Paraguay, as late as the eighteenth century, had "their face, breast, and arms covered with black figures of various shapes, so that they present the appearance of a Turkish carpet." [19] This made them, according to their own words as recorded by the old missionary "more beautiful than beauty itself." [20] On the other hand, one is struck by the rigorous symmetry of Maori tattooings, in contrast with the almost licentious asymmetry of some Caduveo paintings. But this asymmetry does not always exist; and I have shown that it resulted from a logical development of the splitting principle. It is thus more apparent than real. It is clear, nevertheless, that as regards typological classification, Caduveo facial designs occupy an intermediary position between those of the Maori and those of the Northwest Coast. Like the latter, they have an asymmetrical appearance, while they present the essentially decorative character of the former.

This continuity is also apparent when one considers the psychological and social implications. Among the Maori, as among the natives of the Paraguayan border, facial and corporal decoration is executed in a semi-religious atmosphere. Tattooings are not only ornaments. As we already noted with respect to the Northwest Coast (and the same thing may be said of New Zealand), they are not only emblems of nobility and symbols of rank in the social hierarchy; they are also messages fraught with spiritual and moral significance. The purpose of Maori tattooings is not only to imprint a drawing onto the flesh but also to stamp onto the mind all the traditions and philosophy of the group. Similarly, the Jesuit missionary Sanchez Labrador has described the passionate seriousness with which the natives devoted whole days to letting themselves be painted. He who is not painted, they said, is "dumb." [21] And, like the Caduveo, the Maori use split representation. In Plates VII, IX, X, and XIII, we note the same division of the forehead into two lobes; the same representation of the mouth where the two halves meet; the same representation of the body, as though it had been split in the back from top to bottom and the two halves brought forward on the same plane. We note, in other words, all the techniques which are now familiar to us.

How shall we explain the recurrence of a far from natural method of representation among cultures so widely separated in time and space? The simplest hypothesis is that of historical contact or independent development from a common civilization. But even if this hypothesis is refuted by facts, or if, as seems more likely, it should lack adequate evidence, attempts at interpretation are not necessarily doomed to failure. I shall go further: Even if the most ambitious reconstructions of the diffusionist school were to be confirmed, we should still be faced with an essential problem which has nothing to do with history. Why should a cultural trait that has been borrowed or diffused through a long historical period remain intact? Stability is no less mysterious than change. The discovery of a unique origin for split representation would leave unanswered the question of why this means of expression was preserved by cultures which, in other respects, evolved along very different lines. External connections can explain transmission, but only internal connections can account for persistence. Two entirely different kinds of problems are involved here, and the attempt to explain one in no way prejudges the solution that must be given to the other.

One observation immediately follows from the comparison between Maori and Guaicuru art. In both cases, split representation appears as a consequence of the importance that both cultures ascribe to tattooing. Let us consider Plate VIII again and ask ourselves why the outline of the face is represented by two joined profiles. It is clear that the artist intended to draw, not a face, but a facial painting; it is upon doing the latter that she concentrated all her attention. Even the eyes, which are sketchily indicated, exist only as points of reference for starting the two great inverted spirals into whose structure they merge. The artist drew the facial design in a realistic manner; she respected its true proportions as if she had painted on a face and not on a flat surface. She painted on a sheet of paper exactly as she was accustomed to paint on a face. And because the paper *is* for her a face, she finds it impossible to *represent* a face on paper, at any rate without distortion. It was necessary either to draw the face exactly and distort the design in accordance with the laws of perspective, or to respect the integrity of the design and for this reason represent the face as split in two. It cannot even be said that the artist *chose* the second solution, since the alternative never occurred to her. In native thought, as we saw, the design *is* the face, or rather it creates it. It is the design which confers upon the face its social existence, its human dignity, its spiritual significance. Split representation of the face, considered as a graphic device, thus expresses a deeper and more fundamental splitting, namely that between the "dumb" biological individual and the social person whom he must embody. We already foresee that split representation can be explained as a function of a sociological theory of the splitting of the personality.

The same relationship between split image and tattooing may be observed in Maori art. If we compare Plates VII, IX, X, and XIII, we will see that the splitting of the forehead into two lobes is only the projection, on a plastic level, of the symmetrical design tattooed on the skin.

In the light of these observations, the interpretation of split representation proposed by Boas in his study of Northwest Coast art should be elaborated and refined. For Boas, split representation in painting or drawing would consist only in the extension to flat surfaces of a technique which is naturally appropriate in the case of three-dimensional objects. When an animal is going to be represented on a square box, for instance, one must necessarily distort the shape of the animal so that it can be adapted to the angular contours of the box. According to Boas,

> In the decoration of silver bracelets a similar principle is followed but the problem differs somewhat from that offered in the decoration of square boxes. While in the latter case the four edges make a natural division between the four views of the animal,—front and right profile, back and left profile,—there is no such sharp line of division in the round bracelet, and there would be great difficulty in joining the four aspects artistically, while two profiles offer no such difficulty. . . . The animal is imagined cut in two from head to tail, so that the two halves cohere only at the tip of the nose and at the tip of the tail. The hand is put through this hole and the animal now surrounds the wrist. In this position it is represented on the bracelet. . . . The transition from the bracelet to the painting or carving of animals on a flat surface is not a difficult one. The same principle is adhered to. . . .[22]

Thus the principle of split representation would gradually emerge in the process of transition from angular to rounded objects and from rounded objects to flat surfaces. In the first case, there is occasional dislocation and splitting; in the second case, splitting is systematically applied, but the animal still remains intact at the level of the head and the tail; finally, in the third case, dislocation goes to the extreme of splitting the caudal tie, and the two halves of the body, now free, are folded forward to the right and left on the same plane as the face.

This treatment of the problem by the great master of modern anthropology is remarkable for its elegance and simplicity. However, this elegance and simplicity are mainly theoretical. If we consider the decoration of flat and rounded surfaces as special cases of the decoration of angular surfaces, then nothing has been demonstrated with respect to the latter. And, above all, no necessary relationship exists a priori, which implies that the artist must remain faithful to the same principle in moving from angular to rounded surfaces, and from rounded to flat surfaces. Many cultures have decorated boxes with human and animal figures without splitting or dislocating them. A bracelet may be adorned with friezes or in a hundred other ways. There must, then, be some fundamental element of Northwest Coast art (and of Guaicuru art, and Maori art, and the art of ancient China) which accounts for the continuity and rigidity with which the technique of split representation is applied in them.

We are tempted to perceive this fundamental element in the very special relationship which, in the four arts considered here, links the plastic and graphic components. These two elements are not independent; they have an ambivalent relationship, which is simultaneously one of opposition and one which is functional. It is a relationship of opposition because the requirements of decoration are imposed upon the structure and change it, hence the splitting and dislocation; but it is also a functional relationship, since the object is always conceived in both its plastic and graphic aspects. A vase, a box, a wall, are not independent, pre-existing objects which are subsequently decorated. They acquire their definitive existence only through the integration of the decoration with the utilitarian function. Thus, the chests of Northwest Coast art are not merely containers embellished with a painted or carved animal.

They are the animal itself, keeping an active watch over the ceremonial ornaments which have been entrusted to its care. Structure modifies decoration, but decoration is the final cause of structure, which must also adapt itself to the requirements of the former. The final product is a whole: utensil-ornament, object-animal, box-that-speaks. The "living boats" of the Northwest Coast have their exact counterparts in the New Zealand correspondences between boat and woman, woman and spoon, utensils and organs.[23]

We have thus pushed to its most abstract expression the study of dualism, which has been commanding our attention with increasing persistence. We saw in the course of our analysis that the dualism between representational and non-representational art became transformed into other kinds of dualism: carving and drawing, face and decoration, person and impersonation, individual existence and social function, community and hierarchy. We are thus led to acknowledge a dualism, which is also a correlation, between plastic and graphic expression, which provides us with a true "common denominator" of the diverse manifestations of the principle of split representation.

In the end, our problem may be formulated as follows: Under what conditions are the plastic and graphic components necessarily correlated? Under what conditions are they inevitably functionally related, so that the modes of expression of the one always transform those of the other, and vice versa? The comparison between Maori and Guaicuru art already provided us with the answer to the latter question. We saw, indeed, that the relationship had to be functional when the plastic component consisted of the face or human body and the graphic component of the facial or corporal decoration (painting or tattooing), which is applied to them. Decoration is actually *created* for the face; but in another sense the face is predestined to be decorated, since it is only by means of decoration that the face receives its social dignity and mystical significance. Decoration is conceived for the face, but the face itself exists only through decoration. In the final analysis, the dualism is that of the actor and his role, and the concept of *mask* gives us the key to its interpretation.

All the cultures considered here are, in fact, mask cultures, whether the masking is achieved predominantly by tattooing (as is the case for the Guaicuru and Maori) or whether the stress is placed literally on the mask, as the Northwest Coast has done in a fashion unsurpassed elsewhere. In archaic China, there are many references to the ancient role of masks, which is reminiscent of their role in Alaskan societies. Thus, the "Impersonation of the Bear" described in the *Chou Li*, with its "four eyes of yellow metal," [24] recalls the multiple masks of the Eskimo and Kwakiutl.

Those masks with louvers, which present alternately several aspects of the totemic ancestor—sometimes peaceful, sometimes angry, at one time human, at another time animal—strikingly illustrate the relationship between split representation and masquerade. Their function is to offer a series of intermediate forms which insure the transition from symbol to meaning, from magical to normal, from supernatural to social. They hold at the same time the function of masking and unmasking. But when it comes to unmasking, it is the mask which, by a kind of reverse splitting, opens up into two halves, while the actor himself is dissociated in the split representation, which aims, as we saw, at flattening out as well as displaying the mask at the expense of the individual wearing it.

Our analysis thus converges with that of Boas, once we have explored its substructure. It is true that split representation on a flat surface is a special case of its appearance on a rounded surface, just as the latter is itself a special case on three-dimensional surfaces. But not on *any* three-dimensional surface; only on the three-dimensional surface *par excellence*, where the decoration and form cannot be dissociated either physically or socially, namely, the *human face*. At the same time, other curious analogies between the various art forms considered here are illuminated in a similar way.

In the four arts, we discover not one but two decorative styles. One of these styles tends toward a representational, or at least symbolic, expression, and its most common feature is the predominance of motifs. This is Karlgren's Style A for archaic China,[25] painting and low relief for the Northwest Coast and New Zealand, and facial painting for the Guaicuru. But another style exists, of a more strictly formal and decorative character, with geometric tendencies. It consists of Karlgren's Style B, the rafter decoration of New Zealand, the woven or plaited designs of New Zealand and the Northwest Coast, and, for the Guaicuru, a style easily identifiable, ordinarily found in decorated pottery, corporal paintings (different from facial paintings), and painted leatherwork. How can we explain this dualism, and especially its recurrence? The first style is decorative only in appearance; it does not have a plastic function in any of the four arts. On the contrary, its function is social, magical, and religious. The decoration is the graphic or plastic projection of a reality of another order, in the same way that split representation results from the projection of a three-dimensional mask onto a two-dimensional surface (or onto a three-dimensional one which nevertheless does not conform to the human archetype) and in the same way that, finally, the biological individual himself is also projected onto the social scene by his dress. There is thus room for the birth and development of a true decorative art, although one would actually expect its contamination by the symbolism which permeates all social life.

Another characteristic, shared at least by New Zealand and the Northwest Coast, appears in the treatment of tree trunks, which are carved in the form of superimposed figures, each of which occupies a whole section of the trunk. The last vestiges of Caduveo carving are so sparse that we can hardly formulate hypotheses about the archaic manifestations of it; and we are still poorly informed about the treatment of wood by Shang carvers, several examples of which came to light in the excavations at An-Yang.[26]

I would like to draw attention, nevertheless, to a bronze of the Loo collection reproduced by Hentze.[27] It looks as though it could be the reduction of a carved pole, comparable to the slate reductions of totem poles in Alaska and British Columbia. In any case, the cylindrical section of the trunk plays the same role of archetype or "absolute limit" which we ascribed to the human face and body; but it plays this role only because the trunk is interpreted as a living being, a kind of "speaking pole." Here again, the plastic and stylistic expression serves only as a concrete embodiment of *impersonations*.

However, our analysis would be inadequate if it permitted us only to define split representation as a trait common to mask cultures. From a purely formal point of view there has never been any hesitation in considering the *t'ao t'ieh* of archaic Chinese bronzes as a mask. On his part, Boas interpreted the split representation of the shark in Northwest Coast art as a consequence of the fact that the characteristic symbols of this animal are better perceived in a front view[28] (see Plate III). But we have gone further: We discovered in the splitting technique, not only the graphic representation of the mask, but the functional expression of a specific type of civilization. Not all mask cultures employ split representation. We do not find it (at least in as developed a form) in the art of the Pueblo of the American Southwest nor in that of New Guinea.[29] In both these cultures, however, masks play a considerable role. Masks also represent ancestors, and by wearing the mask the actor incarnates the ancestor. What, therefore, is the difference? The difference is that, in contrast to the civilizations we have been considering here, there is no chain of privileges, emblems, and degrees of prestige which, by means of masks, validate social hierarchy through the primacy of genealogies. The supernatural does not have as its chief function the creation of castes and classes. The world of masks constitutes a *pantheon* rather than an *ancestrality*. Thus, the actor incarnates the god only on the intermittent occasions of feasts and ceremonies. He does not acquire from the god, by a continuous process of creation at each moment of social life, his titles, his rank, his position in the status hierarchy. The parallelism which we established is thus confirmed, rather than invalidated, by these examples. The mutual independence of the plastic and graphic components corresponds to the more flexible interplay between the social and supernatural orders, in the same way that split representation expresses the strict conformity of the actor to his role and of social rank to myths, ritual, and pedigrees. This conformity is so rigorous that, in order for the individual to be dissociated from his social role, he must be torn asunder.

Even if we knew nothing about archaic Chinese society, an inspection of its art would be sufficient to enable us to recognize prestige struggles, rivalry between hierarchies, and competition between social and economic privileges—showing through the function of masks and the veneration of lineages. Fortunately, however, there are additional data at our disposal. Analyzing the psychological background of bronze art, Perceval Yetts writes: "The impulse seems almost invariably to have been self-glorification, even when show is made of solacing ancestors or of enhancing the family prestige." [30] And elsewhere he remarks: "There is the familiar history of certain *ting* being treasured as emblems of sovereignty down to the end of the feudal period in the third century B.C." [31] In the An-Yang tombs, bronzes were found which commemorate successive members of the same lineage.[32] And the differences in quality between the specimens excavated can be explained, according to Creel, in terms of the fact that "the exquisite and the crude were produced side by side at Anyang, for people of various economic status or prestige." [33] Comparative anthropological analysis, therefore, is in agreement with the conclusions of Sinologists. It also confirms the theories of Karlgren, who, unlike Leroi-Gourhan[34] and others, states, on the basis of a statistical and chronological study of themes, that the representational mask existed before the mask's dissolution into decorative elements and therefore could not have grown out of the experimentation of the artist who discovers resemblances in the fortuitous arrangement of abstract themes.[35] In another work Karlgren showed how the animal decorations of archaic objects became transformed in the later bronzes into flamboyant arabesques, and he related phenomena of stylistic evolution to the collapse of feudal society.[36] We are tempted to perceive in the arabesques of Guaicuru art, which are so strongly suggestive of birds and flames, the final stage of a parallel transformation. The baroque and affected quality of the style would thus represent the formal survival of a decadent or terminated social order. It constitutes, on the esthetic level, its dying echo.

The conclusions of our work do not preclude in any respect the always-possible discovery of hitherto unsuspected historical connections.[37] We are still faced with the question of finding out whether these hierarchical societies based on prestige appeared independently in different parts of the world, or whether some of them do not share a common cradle. With Creel,[38] I think that the similarities between the art of archaic China and that of the Northwest Coast, perhaps even with the arts of other American areas, are too marked for us not to keep this possibility in mind. But even if there were ground for invoking diffusion, it would not be a diffusion of details—that is, independent traits traveling each on its own and disconnected freely from any one culture in order to be linked to another—but a diffusion of organic wholes wherein style, esthetic conventions, social organization, and religion are structurally related. Drawing a particularly striking analogy between archaic Chinese and Northwest Coast art, Creel writes: "The many isolated eyes used by the Northwest Coast designers recall most forcibly their similar use in Shang art and cause me to wonder if there was some magical reason for this which was possessed by both peoples."[39] Perhaps; but magical connections, like optical illusions, exist only in men's minds, and we must resort to scientific investigation to explain their causes.

NOTES

1. "The Art of the North West Coast," *Gazette des Beaux-Arts* (1943).
2. Carl Hentze, *Objets rituels, Croyances et Dieux de la Chine antique et de l'Amérique* (Antwerp: 1936).
3. Leonhard Adam, "Das Problem der asiatisch-altamerikanischen Kulturbeziehungen mit besonderer Berücksichtigung der Kunst," *Wiener Beiträge zur Kunst und Kulturgeschichte Asiens*, V (1931); "Northwest American Indian Art and Its Early Chinese Parallels," *Man* XXXVI, No. 3 (1936).
4. See, for example, F. D. McCarthy, *Australian Aboriginal Decorative Art* (Sydney: 1938), Fig. 21, p. 38.
5. Review of Carl Hentze, *Frühchinesische bronzen und Kultdarstellungen* (Antwerp: 1937), in *Man*, XXXIX, No. 60 (1939).
6. For China and New Zealand, see R. Heine-Geldern in *Zeitschrift für Rassenkunde*, Vol. 2 (Stuttgart: 1935).
7. Henry Field and Eugene Prostov, "Results of Soviet Investigation in Siberia, 1940-1941," *American Anthropologist*, XLIV (1942), p. 396.
8. In his book, *Medieval American Art* (New York: 1943), Pal Kelemen regards the resemblances between American art and some of the arts of the highest civilizations of the Eastern hemisphere as only "optical illusions" (Vol. I, p. 377). He justifies this opinion by writing that "Pre-Columbian art was created and developed by a mentality totally alien to ours" (p. 378). I doubt that in the whole work of the diffusionist school one could find a single statement so completely unwarranted, superficial, and meaningless.
9. Franz Boas, *Primitive Art*, Instituttet for Sammenlignende Kulturforskning, series B, Vol. VIII (Oslo: 1927), pp. 223-24.
10. *Ibid.*, pp. 224-25.
11. H. G. Creel, "On the Origins of the Manufacture and Decoration of Bronze in the Shang Period," *Monumenta Serica*, Vol. I (1935), p. 64.
12. *Loc. cit.*
13. "Indian Cosmetics," *VVV*, no. 1 (New York: 1942). *Tristes Tropiques* (Paris: 1955).
14. Franz Boas, *op. cit.*, p. 238.
15. *Ibid.*, p. 239 and Fig. 247.
16. See, for example, the Tlingit tattooings reproduced by J. R. Swanton in

Bureau of American Ethnology, 26th Annual Report, Plates XLVIII to LVI; and Franz Boas, *op. cit.,* pp. 250-1 (body paintings).

17. I have developed this analysis further in *Tristes Tropiques,* chapter XX (Paris: 1955).

18. "The Art of the North West Coast," *op. cit.*

19. M. Dobrizhoffer, *An Account of the Abipones,* trans. from the Latin, Vol. II (London: 1822), p. 20.

20. *Ibid.,* p. 21.

21. See also H. G. Creel: "The fine Shang pieces are executed with a care, extending to the most minute detail, which is truly religious. And we know, through the study of the oracle bone inscriptions, that almost all the motifs found on Shang bronzes can be linked with the life and religion of the Shang people. They had meaning and the production of the bronzes was probably in some degree a sacred task." "Notes on Shang Bronzes in the Burlington House Exhibition," *Revue des Arts asiatiques,* X (1936), p. 21.

22. Boas, *op. cit.,* pp. 222-24.

23. John R. Swanton, *Tlingit Myths and Texts,* Bureau of American Ethnology, Bulletin 59 (1909), pp. 254-255; E. A. Rout, *Maori Symbolism* (London: 1926), p. 280.

24. Florance Waterbury, *Early Chinese Symbols and Literature: Vestiges and Speculations* (New York: 1942).

25. Bernhard Karlgren, "New Studies on Chinese Bronzes," *The Museum of Far Eastern Antiquities,* Bulletin 9 (Stockholm: 1937).

26. H. G. Creel, *Monumenta Serica,* Vol. I (1935), p. 40.

27. Carl Hentze, *Frühchinesische bronzen und Kultdarstellungen* (Antwerp: 1937), Table 5.

28. Boas, *op. cit.,* p. 229. One should distinguish, however, between two forms of split representation—namely, split representation proper, where a face and sometimes a whole individual are represented by two joined profiles, and split representation as shown in Plate III, where *one* face is shown with *two* bodies. We cannot be certain that the two types derive from the same principle, and in the passage which we summarized at the beginning of this chapter, Leonhard Adam wisely distinguishes between them. The split representation so well illustrated in Plate III reminds us, indeed, of a similar technique well known in European and Oriental archaeology This is the *beast with two bodies,* whose history E. Pottier attempted to reconstruct ("Histoire d'une bête," in *Recueil E. Pottier,* Bibliothèque des Ecoles d'Athènes et de Rome, section 142). Pottier traces the beast with two bodies to the Chaldean representation of an animal whose head appears in a front view and the body in profile. A second body, also seen in profile, is assumed to have been subsequently attached to the head. If this hypothesis is correct, the representation of the shark analyzed by Boas should be considered either as an independent invention or as the easternmost evidence of the diffusion of an Asiatic theme. This last interpretation would be based on evidence which is far from negligible, namely the recurrence of another theme, the "whirl of animals" (see Anna Roes, "Tierwirbel," *Ipek* [1936-37]) in the art of the Eurasian Steppes and in that of certain areas of America (especially in Moundville). It is also possible that the beast

with two bodies derives independently, in Asia and America, from a technique of split representation which has not survived in the archaeological sites of the Near East, but which left traces in China and may still be observed in certain areas of the Pacific and in America.

29. The art of Melanesia presents rudimentary forms of split representation and dislocation. See, for example, the wooden containers of the Admiralty Islands reproduced by Gladys A. Reichard, "Melanesian Design: A Study of Style in Wood and Tortoise Shell Carving," *Columbia University Contributions to Anthropology*, II, no. 18 (1933), and the following comment by the same author: "Among the Tami, joints are represented by an eye motif. In the face of the fact that tattooing is exceedingly important to the Maori and that it is represented on the carvings, it seems to me more than possible that the spiral often used on the human figures may emphasize the joints" (p. 151).

30. W. Perceval Yetts, *The Cull Chinese Bronzes*, London, 1939, p. 75.

31. W. Perceval Yetts, *The George Eumorphopoulos Collection Catalogue*, Vol. I (London: 1929), p. 43.

32. W. Perceval Yetts, "An-Yang: A Retrospect," *China Society Occasional Papers*, n.s., No. 2 (1942).

33. H. C. Creel, *op. cit.*, p. 46.

34. A. Leroi-Gourhan, "L'Art animalier dans les Bronzes chinois," *Revue des Arts asiatiques* (Paris: 1935).

35. B. Karlgren, *op. cit.*, pp. 76-78.

36. B. Karlgren, "Huai and Han," *The Museum of Far Eastern Antiquities*, Bulletin 13 (Stockholm: 1941).

37. The problem of ancient relations across the Pacific Ocean has recently come to the fore again, owing to the surprising discovery, in a provincial museum of southeastern Formosa, of a low-relief in wood which could be of local origin. It represents three persons standing. Those located at the extremities are in the purest Maori style, while the person in the middle offers a kind of transition between Maori art and that of the Northwest Coast. See Ling Shun Sheng, "Human Figures with Protruding Tongue," *Bulletin of the Institute of Ethnology, Academia Sinica*, No. 2 (September 1956), Nankang, Taipei, Taiwan.

38. H. C. Creel, *op. cit.*, pp. 65-66.

39. *Ibid.*, p. 65.

CHAPTER **XIV**

The Serpent with Fish
inside His Body

In a study devoted to the oral traditions of the Toba and Pilagá Indians,[1] Alfred Métraux points out certain parallels between the great mythological themes which are still to be found in the modern Chaco and the myths of the Andean regions reported by ancient authors. Thus, the Toba, the Vilela, and the Mataco know the myth of "The Long Night," which Avila obtained in the province of Huarochiri; and the Chiriguano relate the tale of the rebellion of the utensils against their masters, a story which is also to be found in the Popol-Vuh and in the work of Montesinos. Métraux adds that the latter episode "is also portrayed on a Chimu vase."

Another myth collected by Métraux strikingly illuminates a curious motif which we know from at least two pre-Columbian illustrations. (A careful study of the Peruvian collections in the principal museums would doubtless yield other examples.) This myth is the legend of the serpent Lik, "as large as a table." A kindly native, at first afraid of its appearance, carried the serpent to the river from which it had unwisely strayed:

> The serpent asked, "Won't you carry me?" "How can I? You are very heavy." "No, I am light." "But you are so large," countered the man. "Yes, I am large, but light." "But you are full of fish." (It is true, Lik is full of fish. The fish are under his tail and when he moves he carries them with him.) The serpent went on, "If you carry me I shall give you all the fish I have inside me." Later on, the man tells his adventure and describes the fabulous animal: "He is loaded with fish, which are in his tail." [2]

In his excellent commentary following this tale, Métraux adds:

> I obtained the following information about the mythical Lik. Lik is a supernatural animal, a huge serpent who carries fish within his tail. Some particularly lucky people may meet Lik stranded on high ground in winter, when water disappears from many lagoons and cañadas. Lik asks them to take him back to a lagoon which contains water. Those who are not frightened by the very sight of the serpent generally object that he is too heavy to be carried, but in each case Lik uses his magic and makes himself light. When he is once more swimming in deep water, he promises those who have helped him to give them as many fish as they want whenever they ask for them, but on one condition—that they never reveal to anyone how the fish were obtained. . . . [3]

It is interesting to recall this myth in connection with the two vases illustrated here. The first one (Figure 22) is a vase from

FIGURE 22. *Design on a vase from Nazca.* (*Collection of Dr. J. Lacan.*)

Nazca with a rounded base; the body, roughly cylindrical, nar-rows gradually toward the opening, which is 3½ inches in diam-eter. The total height of the vase is 7 inches. The decoration is in five colors on a white background: black, deep purple, dark ocher, light ocher, and grayish beige. A mythical animal is represented with a human body. Its head is armed with tentacles, and it has a jaw with huge teeth. Toward the rear of its body there is a caudal appendix, at first straight, then curved, and ending in a hind ex-tremity with a second head, which is smaller. This sinuous tail bristles with spikes, among which fish are circulating; and the whole serpentine part, represented as though in cross-section, is also filled with fish. The monster is devouring a man, whose bent body is held between its teeth, while a protuberant limb in the shape of an arm and hand is ready to stab the victim with a spear. Two small fish look on, apparently waiting for their share of the feast. The whole scene seems to illustrate an episode obtained by Métraux from his informants: "Lik sometimes swallows people. If they have their knife when they are inside the snake, they can cut his heart and make their way out, and at the same time secure all the fish in his tail." [4] In the old Nazca vase, however, it is the ser-pent who seems to be more effectively armed.

The second vase (Figure 23), the illustration of which we borrow from Bässler, derives from Pacasmayo. We see here the same monster, half serpent, half human, whose curved body is also filled with fish. A stripe ornamented with stylized waves sug-gests that the animal is in a river, on whose surface a man is sail-ing a boat. In this case, too, the archaeological object presents a surprisingly faithful illustration of the modern narrative: "*Kidos'k*'s uncle told me that he had actually seen Lik. Once when he was fishing in a boat he suddenly heard a big noise which he recognized as being produced by Lik. He immediately made for the river bank, paddling with all his strength." [5]

These parallels, which survive in areas that are far apart and separated by several centuries in time, lead us to hope for a coun-terdemonstration, that is, pictorial representations of these legends made by contemporary natives, so that we could compare them with the two objects reproduced here. This does not seem to be impossible, since Métraux points out that a Toba artist drew him a picture of Lik with fish inside his body.

FIGURE 23. Vase from Pacasmayo. (After A. Bäss-ler, *Alte peruanische Kunst,* Vol. II, Fig. 271.)

Above all, it appears certain that in those areas of South America where high and low cultures have been in regular or intermittent contact for a long period of time, ethnographers and archaeologists can collaborate in elucidating common problems. The "serpent with fish inside his body" is only one theme among the hundreds which are illustrated almost *ad infinitum* in Peruvian ceramics. We can no longer doubt that the key to so many heretofore incomprehensible motifs is directly accessible in myths and tales which are still current. One would be mistaken to neglect these means which enable us to gain access to the past. Only the myths can guide us into the labyrinth of monsters and gods when, in the absence of writing, the plastic documentation cannot lead us any further. By reconstructing the connections between distant areas, various historical periods, and cultures at different stages of development, this kind of research documents, illuminates—and, perhaps, one day will explain—the vast syncretism that has persistently frustrated Americanists in their search for the historical antecedents of specific phenomena.[6]

NOTES

1. Alfred Métraux, *Myths of the Toba and Pilagá Indians of the Gran Chaco*, Memoirs of the American Folklore Society, Vol. XL (Philadelphia: 1946).
2. *Ibid.*, p. 57.
3. *Ibid.*, p. 59.
4. *Loc. cit.*
5. *Ibid.*, p. 69.
6. In an article entitled "La Deidad primitiva de los Nasca," published in 1932 in the *Revista del Museo Nacional* (Lima, Peru), II, No. 2, E. Yacovleff approached the same problem and formulated the hypothesis that the animal that is represented on the vase might be a terrible hunter of the seas, a fish 13 to 30 feet long, the *Orca gladiator*. If this is correct, the Pilagá legend collected by Métraux is an echo among inland peoples of a maritime theme. At any rate, the similarity between the modern document and archaeological finds would remain a striking one. (See especially Figure 9, *h, m*, p. 132 of Yacovleff's article.)

   We should also keep in mind the fact that the same myth, with its characteristic leitmotif—"You are heavy." "No, I am light!"—recurs as far away as North America, particularly among the Sioux, except that among these hunters the aquatic monster is not a Mother of Fish, but a Mother of Bisons. Curiously enough, the Mother of Fish appears among the Iroquois (who are not fishermen), with an additional specification: "My mane is heavy with fish." We cannot fail to be reminded of the Maya frescoes of Bonampak in which some figures wear a headdress (or hair) laden with fish, as well as of certain myths, especially of the southeastern United States, in which the hero multiplies fish by washing his hair in a river.

PART FIVE

Problems of Method
and Teaching

CHAPTER XV

Social Structure

> The investigations we may enter into, in treating this subject, must not be considered as historical truths, but only as mere conditional and hypothetical reasonings, rather calculated to explain the nature of things, than to ascertain their actual origin; just like the hypotheses which our physicists daily form respecting the formation of the world.
>
> J.-J. Rousseau, *On the Origin of Inequality*

THE TERM "social structure" refers to a group of problems the scope of which appears so wide and the definition so imprecise that it is hardly possible for a paper strictly limited in size to meet them fully. This is reflected in the program of this symposium, in which problems closely related to social structure have been allotted to several papers, such as those on "Style," "Universal Categories of Culture," and "Structural Linguistics." These should be read in connection with the present paper.

On the other hand, studies in social structure have to do with the formal aspects of social phenomena; they are therefore difficult to define, and still more difficult to discuss, without overlapping other fields pertaining to the exact and natural sciences, where problems are similarly set in formal terms or, rather, where the formal expression of different problems admits of the same kind of treatment. As a matter of fact, the main interest of social-structure studies seems to be that they give the anthropologist hope that, thanks to the formalization of his problems, he may borrow methods and types of solutions from disciplines which have gone far ahead of his own in that direction.

Such being the case, it is obvious that the term "social structure" needs first to be defined and that some explanation should be given of the difference which helps to distinguish studies in social structure from the unlimited field of descriptions, analyses, and theories dealing with social relations at large, which merge with the whole scope of social anthropology. This is all the more necessary, since some of those who have contributed toward setting apart social structure as a special field of anthropological studies conceived the former in many different manners and even sometimes, so it seems, came to nurture grave doubts as to the validity of their enterprise. For instance, Kroeber writes in the second edition of his *Anthropology*:

> "Structure" appears to be just a yielding to a word that has a perfectly good meaning but suddenly becomes fashionably attractive for a decade or so—like "streamlining"—and during its vogue tends to be applied indiscriminately because of the pleasurable connotations of its sound. Of course a typical personality can be viewed as having a structure. But so can a physiology, any organism, all societies and all cultures, crystals, machines—in fact everything that is not wholly amorphous has a structure. So what "structure" adds to the meaning of our phrase seems to be nothing, except to provoke a degree of pleasant puzzlement.[1]

Although this passage concerns more particularly the notion of "basic personality structure," it has devastating implications as regards the generalized use of the notion of structure in anthropology.

Another reason makes a definition of social structure compulsory: From the structuralist point of view which one has to adopt if only to give the problem its meaning, it would be hopeless to try to reach a valid definition of social structure on an inductive basis, by abstracting common elements from the uses and definitions current among all the scholars who claim to have made "social structure" the object of their studies. If these concepts have a meaning at all, they mean, first, that the notion of structure has a structure. This we shall try to outline from the beginning as a precaution against letting ourselves be submerged by a tedious inventory of books and papers dealing with social relations, the mere listing of which would more than exhaust the limited space at our disposal. At a further stage we will have to see how far and in what directions the term "social structure," as used by the different authors, departs from our definition. This will be done in the section devoted to kinship, since the notion of structure has found its chief application in that field and since anthropologists have generally chosen to express their theoretical views also in that connection.

DEFINITION AND PROBLEMS OF METHOD

Passing now to the task of defining "social structure," there is a point which should be cleared up immediately. The term "social structure" has nothing to do with empirical reality but with models which are built up after it. This should help one to clarify the difference between two concepts which are so close to each other that they have often been confused, namely, those of *social structure* and of *social relations*. It will be enough to state at this time that social relations consist of the raw materials out of which the models making up the social structure are built, while social structure can, by no means, be reduced to the ensemble of the social relations to be described in a given society.[2] Therefore, social structure cannot claim a field of its own among others in the social studies. It is rather a method to be applied to any kind of social studies, similar to the structural analysis current in other disciplines.

The question then becomes that of ascertaining what kind of model deserves the name "structure." This is not an anthropological question, but one which belongs to the methodology of science in general. Keeping this in mind, we can say that a structure consists of a model meeting with several requirements.

First, the structure exhibits the characteristics of a system. It is made up of several elements, none of which can undergo a change without effecting changes in all the other elements.

Second, for any given model there should be a possibility of ordering a series of transformations resulting in a group of models of the same type.

Third, the above properties make it possible to predict how the model will react if one or more of its elements are submitted to certain modifications.

Finally, the model should be constituted so as to make immediately intelligible all the observed facts.[3]

These being the requirements for any model with structural value, several consequences follow. These, however, do not pertain to the definition of structure, but have to do with the chief properties exhibited and problems raised by structural analysis when contemplated in the social and other fields.

Observation and Experimentation. Great care should be taken to distinguish between the observational and the experimental levels. To observe facts and elaborate methodological devices which permit the construction of models out of these facts is not at all the same thing as to experiment on the models. By "experimenting on models," we mean the set of procedures aiming at ascertaining how a given model will react when subjected to change and at comparing models of the same or different types. This distinction is all the more necessary, since many discussions on social structure revolve around the apparent contradiction between the concreteness and individuality of ethnological data and the abstract and formal character generally exhibited by structural studies. This contradiction disappears as one comes to realize that these features belong to two entirely different levels, or rather to two stages of the same process. On the observational level, the main— one could almost say the only—rule is that all the facts should be carefully observed and described, without allowing any theoretical preconception to decide whether some are more important than others. This rule implies, in turn, that facts should be studied in relation to themselves (by what kind of concrete process did they come into being?) and in relation to the whole (always aiming to relate each modification which can be observed in a sector to the global situation in which it first appeared).

This rule together with its corollaries has been explicitly formulated by K. Goldstein[4] in relation to psychophysiological studies, and it may be considered valid for any kind of structural analysis. Its immediate consequence is that, far from being contradictory, there is a direct relationship between the detail and concreteness of ethnographical description and the validity and generality of the model which is constructed after it. For, though many models may be used as convenient devices to describe and explain the phenomena, it is obvious that the best model will always be that which is *true,* that is, the simplest possible model which, while being derived exclusively from the facts under consideration, also makes it possible to account for all of them. Therefore, the first task is to ascertain what those facts are.

Consciousness and Unconsciousness. A second distinction has to do with the conscious or unconscious character of the models. In the history of structural thought, Boas may be credited with having introduced this distinction. He made clear that a category of facts can more easily yield to structural analysis when the social group in which it is manifested has not elaborated a conscious model to interpret or justify it.[5] Some readers may be surprised to find Boas' name quoted in connection with structural theory, since he has often been described as one of the main obstacles in its path. But this writer has tried to demonstrate that Boas' shortcomings in matters of structural studies did not lie in his failure to understand their importance and significance, which he did, as a matter of fact, in the most prophetic way. They rather resulted from the fact that he imposed on structural studies conditions of validity, some of which will remain forever part of their methodology, while some others are so exacting and impossible to meet that they would have withered scientific development in any field.[6]

A structural model may be conscious or unconscious without this difference affecting its nature. It can only be said that when the structure of a certain type of phenomena does not lie at a great depth, it is more likely that some kind of model, standing as a screen to hide it, will exist in the collective consciousness. For conscious models, which are usually known as "norms," are by definition very poor ones, since they are not intended to explain the phenomena but to perpetuate them. Therefore, structural analysis is confronted with a strange paradox well known to the linguist, that is: the more obvious structural organization is, the more difficult it becomes to reach it because of the inaccurate conscious models lying across the path which leads to it.

From the point of view of the degree of consciousness, the anthropologist is confronted with two kinds of situations. He may have to construct a model from phenomena the systematic character of which has evoked no awareness on the part of the culture; this is the kind of simpler situation referred to by Boas as providing the easiest ground for anthropological research. Or else the anthropologist will be dealing on the one hand with raw phenomena and on the other with the models already constructed by the culture to interpret the former. Though it is likely that, for the reasons stated above, these models will prove unsatisfactory, it is by no means necessary that this should always be the case. As a matter of fact, many "primitive" cultures have built models of their marriage regulations which are much more to the point than models built by professional anthropologists.[7] Thus one cannot dispense with studying a culture's "home-made" models for two reasons. First, these models might prove to be accurate or, at least, to provide some insight into the structure of the phenomena; after all, each culture has its own theoreticians whose contributions deserve the same attention as that which the anthropologist gives to colleagues. And, second, even if the models are biased or erroneous, the very bias and type of error are a part of the facts under study and probably rank among the most significant ones. But even when taking into consideration these culturally produced models, the anthropologist does not forget—as he has sometimes been accused of doing[8]—that the cultural norms are not of themselves structures. Rather, they furnish an important contribution to an understanding of the structures, either as factual documents or as theoretical contributions similar to those of the anthropologist himself.

This point has been given great attention by the French sociological school. Durkheim and Mauss, for instance, have always taken care to substitute, as a starting point for the survey of native categories of thought, the conscious representations prevailing among the natives themselves for those stemming from the anthropologist's own culture. This was undoubtedly an important step, which, nevertheless, fell short of its goal because these authors were not sufficiently aware that native conscious representations, important as they are, may be just as remote from the unconscious reality as any other.[9]

Structure and Measure. It is often believed that one of the main interests of the notion of structure is to permit the introduction of measurement in social anthropology. This view has been favored by the frequent appearance of mathematical or semimathematical aids in books or articles dealing with social structure. It is true that in some cases structural analysis has made it possible to attach numerical values to invariants. This was, for instance, the result of Kroeber's study of women's dress fashions, a landmark in structural research,[10] as well as of a few other studies which will be discussed below.

However, one should keep in mind that there is no necessary connection between *measure* and *structure*. Structural studies are, in the social sciences, the indirect outcome of modern developments in mathematics which have given increasing importance to the qualitative point of view in contradistinction to the quantitative point of view of traditional mathematics. It has become possible, therefore, in fields such as mathematical logic, set theory, group theory, and topology, to develop a rigorous approach to problems which do not admit of a metrical solution. The outstanding achievements in this connection—which offer themselves as springboards not yet utilized by social scientists—are to be found in J. von Neumann and O. Morgenstern, *Theory of Games and Economic Behavior*;[11] N. Wiener, *Cybernetics*;[12] and C. Shannon and W. Weaver, *The Mathematical Theory of Communication*.[13]

Mechanical Models and Statistical Models. A last distinction refers to the relation between the scale of the model and that of the phenomena. According to the nature of these phenomena, it becomes possible or impossible to build a model, the elements of which are on the same scale as the phenomena themselves. A model the elements of which are on the same scale as the phenomena will be called a "mechanical model"; when the elements of the model are on a different scale, we shall be dealing with a "statistical model." The laws of marriage provide the best illustration of this difference. In primitive societies these laws can be expressed in models calling for actual grouping of the individuals according to kin or clan; these are mechanical models. No such distribution exists in our own society, where types of marriage are determined by the size of the primary and secondary groups to which prospective mates belong, social fluidity, amount of information, and the like. A satisfactory (though yet untried) attempt to formulate the invariants of our marriage system would therefore have to determine average values—thresholds; it would be a statistical model. There may be intermediate forms between these two. Such is the case in societies which (as even our own) have a mechanical model to determine prohibited marriages and rely on a statistical model for those which are permissible. It should also be kept in mind that the same phenomena may admit of different models, some mechanical and some statistical, according to the way in which they are grouped together and with other phenomena. A society which recommends cross-cousin marriage but where this ideal marriage type occurs only with limited frequency needs, in order that the system may be properly explained, both a mechanical and a statistical model, as was well understood by Forde and Elwin.[14]

It should also be kept in mind that what makes social-structure studies valuable is that structures are models, the formal properties of which can be compared independently of their elements. The structuralist's task is thus to recognize and isolate levels of reality which have strategic value from his point of view, namely, which admit of representation as models, whatever their type. It often happens that the same data may be considered from different perspectives embodying equally strategic values, though the resulting models will be in some cases mechanical and in others statistical. This situation is well known in the exact and natural sciences; for instance, the theory of a small number of physical bodies belongs to classical mechanics, but if the number of bodies becomes greater, then one should rely on the laws of thermodynamics, that is, use a statistical model instead of a mechanical one, though the nature of the data remains the same in both cases.

The same situation prevails in the human and the social sciences. If one takes a phenomenon such as suicide, for instance, it can be studied on two different levels. First, it is possible by studying individual situations to establish what may be called mechanical models of suicide, taking into account in each case the personality of the victim, his or her life history, the characteristics of the primary and secondary groups in which he or she developed, and the like; or else one can build models of a statistical nature, by recording suicide frequency over a certain period of time in one or more societies and in different types of primary and secondary groups, etc. These would be levels at which the structural study of suicide carries a strategic value, that is, where it becomes possible to build models which may be compared (1) for different types of suicides, (2) for different societies, and (3) for different types of social phenomena. Scientific progress consists not only in discovering new invariants belonging to those levels but also in discovering new levels where the study of the same phenomena offers the same strategic value. Such a result was achieved, for instance, by psychoanalysis, which discovered the means to set up models in a new field, that of the psychological life of the patient considered as a whole.

The foregoing should help to make clear the dual (and at first sight almost contradictory) nature of structural studies. On the one hand, they aim at isolating strategic levels, and this can be achieved only by "carving out" a certain constellation of phenomena. From that point of view, each type of structural study appears autonomous, entirely independent of all the others and even of different methodological approaches to the same field. On the other hand, the essential value of these studies is to construct models the formal properties of which can be compared with, and explained by, the same properties as in models corresponding to other strategic levels. Thus it may be said that their ultimate end is to override traditional boundaries between different disciplines and to promote a true interdisciplinary approach.

An example may be given. A great deal of discussion has taken place lately about the difference between history and anthropology, and Kroeber and others have made clear that the time dimension is of minor significance in this connection.[15] From what has been stated above, one can see exactly where the difference lies, not only between these two disciplines but also between them and others. Ethnography and history differ from social anthropology and sociology, inasmuch as the former two aim at gathering data, while the latter two deal with models constructed from these data. Similarly, ethnography and social anthropology correspond to two different stages in the same research, the ultimate result of which is to construct mechanical models, while history (together with its so-called "auxiliary" disciplines) and sociology end ultimately in statistical models. The relations between these four disciplines may thus be reduced to two oppositions, one between empirical observation and model building, which characterizes the initial stage of research, and the other between the statistical and the mechanical nature of models, which constitutes the products of research. By arbitrarily assigning the sign + to the first term of each opposition and the sign — to the second, we obtain the following chart:

	HISTORY	SOCIOLOGY	ETHNOG- RAPHY	SOCIAL ANTHRO- POLOGY
empirical observation/ model building	+	—	+	—
mechanical models/ statistical models	—	—	+	+

This is the reason why the social sciences, though they all have to do with the time dimension, nevertheless deal with two different categories of time. Anthropology uses a "mechanical" time, reversible and non-cumulative. For instance, the model of, let us say, a patrilineal kinship system does not in itself show whether or not the system has always remained patrilineal, or has been preceded by a matrilineal form, or by any number of shifts from patrilineal to matrilineal and vice versa. On the contrary, historical time is "statistical"; it always appears as an oriented and non-reversible process. An evolution which would take contemporary Italian society back to that of the Roman Republic is as impossible to conceive of as is the reversibility of the processes belonging to the second law of thermodynamics.

This discussion helps to clarify Firth's distinction between social structure, which he conceives as outside the time dimension, and social organization, where time re-enters.[16] Also in this connection, the debate which has been going on for the past few years between followers of the Boasian anti-evolutionist tradition and of Professor Leslie White[17] may become better understood. The Boasian school has been mainly concerned with models of a mechanical type, and from this point of view the concept of evolution has no operational value. On the other hand, it is certainly legitimate to speak of evolution in a historical and sociological sense, but the elements to be organized into an evolutionary process cannot be borrowed from the level of a cultural typology which consists of mechanical models. They should be sought at a sufficiently deep level to insure that these elements will remain unaffected by different cultural contexts (as, let us say, genes are identical elements combined into different patterns corresponding to the different racial [statistical] models) and can accordingly permit the drawing of long statistical runs. Boas and his followers are therefore right in rejecting the concept of evolution, since it is not relevant on the level of the mechanical models which they employ exclusively. As for Leslie White, he is mistaken in his attempts to reintroduce the concept of evolution, since he persists in utilizing models of the same type as those of his opponents. The evolutionists would find it easier to regain their position if they consented to substitute statistical for mechanical models, that is, models whose elements are independent of their combinations and which remain identical through a sufficiently long period of time.[18]

The distinction between mechanical and statistical models has also become fundamental in another respect; it makes it possible to clarify the role of the comparative method in structural studies. This method was greatly emphasized by both Radcliffe-Brown and Lowie. The former writes:

> Theoretical sociology is commonly regarded as an inductive science, induction being the logical method of inference by which we arrive at general propositions from the consideration of particular instances. Although Professor Evans-Pritchard . . . seems to imply in some of his statements that the logical method of induction, using comparison, classification and generalization, is not applicable to the phenomena of human social life . . . I hold that social anthropology must depend on systematic comparative studies of many societies.[19]

Writing about religion, he states:

> The experimental method of social religion . . . means that we must study in the light of our hypothesis a sufficient number of diverse particular religions or religious cults in relation to the particular societies in which they are found. This is a task not for one person but for a number.[20]

Similarly, Lowie, after pointing out that "the literature of anthropology is full of alleged correlations which lack empirical support," [21] insists on the need for a "broad inductive basis" for generalization.[22] It is interesting to note that by this claim for inductive support these authors dissent not only from Durkheim—"When a law has been proved by a well performed experiment, this law is valid universally," [23]—but also from Goldstein, who, as already mentioned, has lucidly expressed what may be called "the rules of structuralist method" in a way general enough to make them valid outside the more limited field in which they were first applied by their author. Goldstein remarks that the need to make a thorough study of each case implies that the amount of cases to be studied should be small; and he proceeds by raising the question whether or not the risk exists that the cases under consideration may be special ones, allowing no general conclusions about the others. His answer is as follows:

> This objection completely misunderstands the real situation . . . an accumulation of facts even numerous is of no help if these facts were imperfectly established; it does not lead to the knowledge of things as they really happen. . . . We must choose only those cases which permit of formulating final judgments. And then, what is true for one case will also be true for any other.[24]

Probably very few anthropologists would be ready to support these bold statements. However, no structuralist study may be undertaken without a clear awareness of Goldstein's dilemma: either to study many cases in a superficial and in the end ineffective way; or to limit oneself to a thorough study of a small number of cases, thus proving that in the last analysis one well done experiment is sufficient to make a demonstration.

Now the reason for so many anthropologists' faithfulness to the comparative method may be sought in some sort of confusion between the procedures used to establish mechanical and statistical models. While Durkheim and Goldstein's position undoubtedly holds true for the former, it is obvious that no statistical model can be achieved without statistics, that is, without gathering a large amount of data. But in this case the method is no more comparative than in the other, since the data to be collected will be acceptable only insofar as they are all of the same kind. We remain, therefore, confronted with only one alternative, namely, to make a thorough study of one case. The real difference lies in the selection of the "case," which will be patterned so as to include elements which are either on the same scale as the model to be constructed or on a different scale.

Having thus clarified these basic questions revolving around the nature of studies in social structure, it becomes possible to make an inventory of the main fields of inquiry and to discuss some of the results achieved so far.

SOCIAL MORPHOLOGY OR GROUP STRUCTURE

In this section, "group" is not intended to mean the social group but, in a more general sense, the manner in which the phenomena under study are grouped together.

The object of social-structure studies is to understand social relations with the aid of models. Now it is impossible to conceive of social relations outside a common framework. Space and time are the two frames of reference we use to situate social relations, either alone or together. These space and time dimensions are not the same as the analogous ones used by other disciplines but consist of a "social" space and of a "social" time, meaning that they have no properties outside those which derive from the properties of the social phenomena which "furnish" them. According to their social structure, human societies have elaborated many types of such "continuums," and there should be no undue concern on the part of the anthropologist that, in the course of his studies, he might temporarily have to borrow types widely different from the existing patterns and eventually to evolve new ones.

We have already noticed that the time continuum may be reversible or oriented in accordance with the level of reality embodying strategic value from the point of view of the research at hand. Many other possibilities may arise: The time dimension may be conceived of as independent from the observer and unlimited or as a function of the observer's own (biological) time and limited; it may be considered as consisting of parts which are, or are not, homologous with one another, etc. Evans-Pritchard has shown how such formal properties underlie the qualitative distinctions between the observer's life span and history, legend, and myth.[25] His basic distinctions have been found, furthermore, to be valid for contemporary societies.[26]

What is true of the time dimension applies equally well to space. It has been Durkheim's and Mauss's great merit to call attention for the first time to the variable properties of space which should be considered in order to understand properly the structure of several primitive societies.[27] In this undertaking they received their inspiration from the work of Cushing, which it has become fashionable in recent years to belittle. However, Frank Hamilton Cushing's insight and sociological imagination entitle him to a seat on Morgan's right, as one of the great forerunners of social-structure studies. The gaps and inaccuracies in his descriptions, less serious than the indictment of having "over-interpreted" some of his material, will be viewed in their true proportions when it is realized that, albeit in an unconscious fashion, Cushing was aiming less at giving an actual description of Zuni society than at elaborating a model (his famous sevenfold division) which would explain most of its processes and structure.

Social time and space should also be characterized according to scale. There is in social studies a "macro-time" and a "micro-time"; the same distinction applies also to space. This explains why social structure may have to deal with prehistory, archaeology, and diffusion processes as well as with psychological topology, such as that initiated by Lewin or Moreno's sociometry. As a matter of fact, structures of the same type may exist on quite different time and space levels, and it is far from inconceivable that, for instance, a statistical model resulting from sociometric studies might be of greater help in building a similar model in the field of the history of cultures than an apparently more direct approach would permit.

Therefore, historico-geographical concerns should not be excluded from the field of structural studies, as was generally implied by the widely accepted opposition between "diffusionism" and "functionalism."[28] A functionalist may be far from a structuralist, as is clearly shown by the example of Malinowski. On the other hand, undertakings such as those of G. Dumézil,[29] as well as A. L. Kroeber's personal case of a highly structure-minded scholar devoting most of his time to distribution studies, are proofs that even history can be approached in a structural way.

Since synchronic studies raise fewer problems than diachronic ones (the data being more homogeneous in the first case), the simplest morphological studies are those having to do with the qualitative, non-measurable properties of social space, that is, the manner in which social phenomena can be situated on a map and the regularities exhibited in their configurations. Much might have been expected from the researches of the so-called "Chicago school" dealing with urban ecology, and the reasons for the gradual loss of interest in this line of research are not altogether clear. It has to do mostly with ecology, which was made the subject of another paper in this symposium.[30] However, it is not inappropriate to state at this point what kind of relationship prevails between ecology on the one hand and social structure on the other. Both have to do with the spatial distribution of phenomena. But social structure deals exclusively with those "spaces" the properties of which are of a purely sociological nature, that is, not affected by such natural determinants as geology, climatology, physiography, and the like. This is the reason why so-called urban ecology should hold great interest for the social anthropologist; the urban space is small enough and homogeneous enough (from every point of view except the social one) for all its differential qualitative aspects to be ascribed mostly to the action of internal forces accessible to structural sociology.

It would perhaps have been wiser, instead of starting with complex communities hard to isolate from external influences, to approach first—as suggested by Marcel Mauss[31]—those small and relatively isolated communities with which the anthropologist usually deals. A few such studies may be found,[32] but they rarely and then reluctantly go beyond the descriptive stage. There have been practically no attempts to correlate the spatial configurations with the formal properties of the other aspects of social life.

This is much to be regretted, since in many parts of the world there is an obvious relationship between the social structure and the spatial structure of settlements, villages, or camps. To limit ourselves to America, the camp shapes of the Plains Indians have long demanded attention by virtue of regular variations connected with the social organization of each tribe; and the same holds true for the circular disposition of huts in Ge villages of eastern and central Brazil. In both cases we are dealing with relatively homogeneous cultural areas where important series of concomitant variations may be observed. Another kind of problem results from the comparison of areas where different types of village structures may be compared to different types of social relations, for example, the circular-village structure of the Ge and the parallel-layers structure of the Pueblo. The latter could even be studied diachronically with the archaeologist's help, which would raise questions such as the possible linkage of the transition from semi-circular structures to parallel ones, with the shift of village sites from valley to mesa top, of the structural distribution of clan houses suggested by many myths to the present-day statistical one, etc.

These few examples are not intended to prove that spatial configuration is the mirror image of social organization but to call attention to the fact that, while among numerous peoples it would be extremely difficult to discover any such relation, among others (who must accordingly have something in common) the existence of a relation is evident, though unclear, and in a third group spatial configuration seems to be almost a projective representation of the social structure. But even the most striking cases call for a critical study; for example, this writer has attempted to demonstrate that, among the Bororo, spatial configuration reflects not the true, unconscious social organization but a model existing consciously in the native mind, though its nature is entirely illusory and even contradictory to reality.[33] Problems of this kind (which are raised not only by the consideration of relatively durable spatial configurations but also in regard to recurrent temporary ones, such as those shown in dance, ritual, etc.[34]) offer an opportunity to study social and mental processes through objective and crystallized external projections of them.

Another approach which may lead more directly to a mathematical expression of social phenomena starts with the numerical properties of human groups. This has traditionally been the field of demography, but it is only recently that a few scholars coming from different fields—demography, sociology, anthropology—have begun to elaborate a kind of qualitative demography, that is, dealing no longer with continuous variations within human groups selected for empirical reasons but with significant discontinuities

evidenced in the behavior of groups considered as wholes and chosen on the basis of these discontinuities. This "socio-demography,"
as it was called by one of its proponents,[35] is "on a level" with
social anthropology, and it is not difficult to foresee that in the
very near future it will be called upon to provide firm grounds for
any kind of anthropological research. Therefore, it is surprising
that so little attention was paid in anthropological circles to the
study by a demographer, L. Livi, of the formal properties characteristic of the smallest possible size of a group compatible with its
existence as a group.[36] His researches, closely connected with
G. Dahlberg's, are all the more important for anthropologists, in
that the latter usually deal with populations very close to Livi's
minimum. There is an obvious relation between the functioning and
even the durability of the social structure and the actual size of the
population.[37] It is thus becoming increasingly evident that formal
properties exist which are immediately and directly related to the
absolute size of the population, whatever the group under consideration. These should be the first to be assessed and taken into account in an interpretation of other properties.

Next come numerical properties expressing, not the group
size taken globally, but the size and interaction of subsets of the
group which can be defined by significant discontinuities. Two lines
of inquiry should be mentioned in this connection.

There is, first, the vast body of research deriving from the
famous "rank-size law" for cities, which makes it possible to establish a correlation between the absolute size of cities (calculated on
the basis of population size) and the position of each city within a
rank order, and even, it appears, to infer one of the elements from
the other.[38]

Of a much more direct bearing on current anthropological
research is the recent work of two French demographers, who, by
using Dahlberg's demonstration that the size of an isolate (that is,
a group of intermarrying people) can be computed from the frequency of marriage between cross-cousins,[39] have succeeded in
computing the average size of isolates in all French *départements*,
thus throwing open to anthropological investigation the marriage
system of a complex modern society.[40] The average size of the
French isolate varies from less than 1,000 to over 2,800 individuals.
This numerical evaluation shows that even in a modern society the

network of people united by kinship ties is much smaller than might be expected—about the same size as in primitive groups. The inference is that, while the absolute size of the intermarrying group remains approximately on the same scale in all human societies (the ratio of the French types in relation to the average primitive types being about 10 to 1), a complex society becomes such not so much because of an expansion of the isolate itself as on account of an expansion of other types of social links (economic, political, intellectual); and these are used to connect a great number of isolates which, by themselves, remain relatively static.

But the most striking result of this research is the discovery that the smallest isolates are found not only in mountain areas, as was expected, but also (and even more) in areas including a large urban center; the following *départements:* Rhône (Lyon), Gironde (Bordeaux), and Seine (Paris) are at the bottom of the list, with the size of their isolates respectively 740, 910, and 930. In the Seine *département,* which is practically limited to Paris and its suburbs, the frequency of consanguineous marriages is higher than in any of the fifteen rural *départements* which surround it.

It is not necessary to emphasize the bearing of such studies on social structure; the main fact, from the point of view of this paper, is that they, at the same time, make possible and call for an immediate extension on the anthropological level. An approach has been found which enables us to break down a modern complex society into smaller units which are of the same nature as those commonly studied by anthropologists; on the other hand, this approach remains incomplete, since the absolute size of the isolate is only a part of the phenomenon, the other one, equally important, being the length of the marriage cycles. For a small isolate may admit of long marriage cycles (that is, tending to be of the same size as the isolate itself), while a relatively large isolate can be made up of shorter cycles.[41] This problem, which could be solved only with the help of genealogies, points the way toward close cooperation between the structural demographer and the social anthropologist.

Another contribution, this time on a theoretical level, may be expected from this cooperation. The concept of isolate may help to solve a problem in social structure which has given rise to a controversy between Radcliffe-Brown and Lowie. The former has labeled as "a fantastic reification of abstraction" the suggestion made by some anthropologists, mostly in America, that anthropology should be defined as the study not of society but of culture. To him, "European culture is an abstraction and so is the culture of an African tribe." All that exists are human beings connected by an unlimited series of social relations.[42] This, Lowie says, is "a factitious quarrel." [43] However, the misunderstandings which lie at its root appear to be very real, since they arose all over again on the occasion of the publication of a book by White[44] and its criticism by Bidney.[45]

It seems that both the reality and the autonomy of the concept of culture could better be validated if culture were treated, from an operational point of view, in the same way as the geneticist and demographer treat the closely allied concept of "isolate." What is called a "culture" is a fragment of humanity which, from the point of view of the research at hand and of the scale on which the latter is carried out, presents significant discontinuities in relation to the rest of humanity. If our aim is to ascertain significant discontinuities between, let us say, North America and Europe, then we are dealing with two different cultures; but should we become concerned with significant discontinuities between New York and Chicago, we would be allowed to speak of these two groups as different cultural "units." Since these discontinuities can be reduced to *invariants*, which is the goal of structural analysis, we see that culture may, at the same time, correspond to an objective reality and be a function of the kind of research undertaken. Accordingly, the same set of individuals may be considered to be parts of many different cultural contexts: universal, continental, national, regional, local, etc., as well as familial, occupational, religious, political, etc. This is true as a limit; however, anthropologists usually reserve the term "culture" to designate a *group* of discontinuities which is significant on several of these levels at the same time. That it can never be valid for all levels does not prevent the concept of "culture" from being as fundamental for the anthropologist as that of "isolate" for the demographer. Both belong to the same epistemological family. On a question such as that of the positivistic character of a concept, the anthropologist can rely on a physicist's judgment; it is Niels Bohr who states that "the traditional differences of [human cultures] in many ways resemble the different equivalent modes in which physical experience can be described." [46]

SOCIAL STATICS OR COMMUNICATION STRUCTURES

A society consists of individuals and groups which communicate with one another. The existence of, or lack of, communication can never be defined in an absolute manner. Communication does not cease at society's borders. These borders, rather, constitute thresholds where the rate and forms of communication, without waning altogether, reach a much lower level. This condition is usually meaningful enough for the population, both inside and outside the borders, to become aware of it. This awareness is not, however, a prerequisite for the definition of a given society. It only accompanies the more precise and stable forms.

In any society, communication operates on three different levels: communication of women, communication of goods and services, communication of messages. Therefore, kinship studies, economics, and linguistics approach the same kinds of problems on different strategic levels and really pertain to the same field. Theoretically at least, it might be said that kinship and marriage rules regulate a fourth type of communication, that of genes between phenotypes. Therefore, it should be kept in mind that culture does not consist exclusively of forms of communication of its own, like language, but also (and perhaps mostly) of *rules* stating how the "games of communication" should be played both on the natural and on the cultural levels.

The above comparison between the fields of kinship, economics, and linguistics cannot hide the fact that they refer to forms of communication which are on a different scale. Should one try to compute the communication rate involved, on the one hand, in the intermarriages and, on the other, in the exchange of messages occurring in a given society, one would probably discover the difference to be of about the same magnitude as, let us say, that between the exchange of heavy molecules of two viscous liquids through a not very permeable film and radio communication. Thus, from marriage to language one passes from low- to high-speed communication; this arises from the fact that what is communicated in marriage is almost of the same nature as those who communicate (women, on the one hand, men, on the other), while speakers of language are not of the same nature as their utterances. The opposition is thus one of *person* to *symbol*, or of *value* to *sign*. This helps to clarify the somewhat intermediate position of economics between these two extremes—goods and services are not persons, but they still are values. And, though neither symbols nor signs, they require symbols or signs in order to be successfully exchanged when the exchange system reaches a certain degree of complexity.

From this outline of the structure of social communication three important sets of considerations follow.

First, the position of economics in social structure can be precisely defined. Economics in the past has been suspect among anthropologists. Even in this symposium, no paper was explicitly assigned to economic problems. Yet, whenever this highly important topic has been broached, a close relationship has been shown to prevail between economic pattern and social structure. Since Mauss's pioneer papers[47] and Malinowski's book on the *kula*[48]—by far his masterpiece—every attempt in this direction has shown that the economic system provides sociological formulations with some of their more fundamental invariants.[49]

The anthropologist's reluctance originated in the condition of economic studies themselves; these were ridden with conflicts between bitterly opposed schools and at the same time bathed in an aura of mystery and conceit. Thus the anthropologist labored under the impression that economics dealt mostly with abstractions and that there was little connection between the actual life of actual groups of people and such notions as value, utility, profit, and the like.

The complete upheaval of economic studies resulting from the publication of Von Neumann and Morgenstern's book[50] ushers in an era of closer cooperation between the economist and the anthropologist, and for two reasons. First—though economics achieves here a rigorous approach—this book deals not with abstractions such as those just mentioned but with concrete individuals and groups which are represented in their actual and empirical relations of cooperation and competition. Surprising though the parallel may seem, this formalism converges with certain aspects of Marxian thought.[51]

Next—and as a consequence—it introduces for the first time mechanical models which are of the same type as, and intermediate between, those used in mathematical physics and in social anthropology—especially in the field of kinship. In this connection it is striking that Von Neumann's models are borrowed from the theory of games, a line of thought which was initiated independently by Kroeber when he compared social institutions "to the play of earnest children." [52] There is, true enough, an important difference between games of entertainment and marriage rules: The former are constructed in such a way as to permit each player to extract from statistical regularities maximal differential values, while marriage rules, acting in the opposite direction, aim at establishing statistical regularities in spite of the differential values existing between individuals and generations. In this sense they constitute a special kind of "upturned game." Nevertheless, they can be treated with the same methods. Besides, such being the rules, each individual and group tries to play it in the "normal" way, that is, by maximizing his own advantage at the expense of the others (i.e., to get more wives, or better ones, whether from the esthetic, erotic, or economic point of view). The theory of courtship is thus a part of formal sociology. To those who are afraid that sociology might in this way get hopelessly involved in individual psychology, it will be enough to recall that Von Neumann has succeeded in giving a mathematical demonstration of the nature and strategy of a psychological technique as sophisticated as bluffing at the game of poker.[53]

The next advantage of this increasing consolidation of social anthropology, economics, and linguistics into one great field, that of communication, is to make clear that they consist exclusively of the study of *rules* and have little concern with the nature of the partners (either individuals or groups) whose play is being patterned after these rules. As Von Neumann puts it, "The game is simply the totality of the rules which describe it." [54] Besides that of game, other operational notions are those of play, move, choice, and strategy.[55] But the nature of the players need not be considered. What is important is to find out when a given player can make a choice and when he cannot.

This outlook should open the study of kinship and marriage to approaches directly derived from the theory of communication. In the terminology of this theory it is possible to speak of the information of a marriage system by the number of choices at the observer's disposal to define the marriage status of an individual. Thus the information is unity for a dual exogamous system, and, in an Australian kind of kinship typology, it would increase with the logarithm of the number of matrimonial classes. A theoretical system where everybody could marry everybody would be a system with no redundancy, since each marriage choice would not be determined by previous choices, while the positive content of marriage rules constitutes the redundancy of the system under consideration. By studying the percentage of "free" choices in a matrimonial population (not absolutely free, but in relation to certain postulated conditions), it would thus become possible to offer numerical estimates of its entropy, both absolute and relative.

As a consequence, it would become possible to translate statistical models into mechanical ones and vice versa, thus bridging the gap still existing between population studies on the one hand and anthropological ones on the other, thereby laying a foundation for prediction and control. To give an example: In our own society the organization of marriage choices does not go beyond (1) the prohibition of close kin, (2) the size of the isolate, and (3) the accepted standard of behavior, which limits the frequency of certain choices within the isolate. With these data at hand, one could compute the information of the system, that is, translate our loosely organized and highly statistical marriage system into a mechanical model, thus making possible its comparison with the large series of marriage systems of a "mechanical" type available from simpler societies.

Similarly, a great deal of discussion has been carried on recently about the Murngin kinship system, which has been treated by different authors as a seven-class system, or less than seven, or four, or thirty-two, or three,[56] before recent research resolved the question in favor of the last number.[57]

In the preceding pages an attempt has been made to assess the bearing of some recent lines of mathematical research upon anthropological studies. We have seen that their main contribution was to provide anthropology with a unifying concept—communication—enabling it to consolidate widely different types of inquiry into one, and at the same time providing the theoretical and methodological tools to further knowledge in that direction. The question which should now be raised is: To what extent is social anthropology ready to make use of these tools?

The main feature of the development of social anthropology in the past years has been the increased attention to kinship. This is, indeed, not a new phenomenon, since it can be said that, with his *Systems of Consanguinity and Affinity of the Human Family*, Lewis Morgan's genius at one and the same time founded social anthropology and kinship studies and brought to the fore the basic reasons for attaching such importance to the latter: permanency, systematic character, continuity of changes.[58] The views outlined in the preceding pages may help to explain this fundamental interest in kinship, since we have considered it as the anthropologist's special and privileged share in the science of communication.

Unfortunately, despite the enormous development of kinship studies in recent years, the amount of usable material in relation to that actually collected remains small. This is clearly reflected in the fact that, in order to undertake his survey, Murdock found it possible to retain information concerning no more than about 250 societies (from our point of view, a still overindulgent estimate) out of the 3,000 to 4,000 distinct societies still in existence.[59] It is somewhat disheartening that the enormous work devoted in the last fifty years to the gathering of ethnographic material has yielded so little, although kinship has been one of the main concerns of those undertaking this work.

However, it should be kept in mind that what has brought about this unhappy result is not a lack of coverage—on the contrary. If the workable material is small, it is rather on account of the inductive illusion; it was believed that as many cultures as possible should be covered, albeit lightly, rather than a few thoroughly enough to yield significant results. Accordingly, there is no lack of consistency in the fact that, following their individual temperaments, anthropologists have preferred one or the other of the alternatives imposed by the situation. While Radcliffe-Brown, Eggan, Spoehr, Fortes, and this writer have tried to consider limited areas where dense information was available, Murdock has followed the complementary (but not contradictory) path of widening the field even at the expense of the reliability of the data, and Lowie[60] has tried to pursue a kind of middle road between the two approaches.

The case of the Pueblo area is especially striking, since for probably no other area in the world is there available such an amount of data of such controversial quality. It is almost with despair that one comes to realize that the voluminous material accumulated by Voth, Fewkes, Dorsey, Parsons, and, to some extent, Stevenson is practically unworkable, since these authors have been feverishly piling up information without any clear idea of what it meant or, above all, of the hypotheses which it should have helped to test. The situation changed when Lowie and Kroeber entered the field, but the lack of statistical data on marriage choices and types of intermarriages, which might have been gathered for more than fifty years, will probably be impossible to overcome. This is to be regretted, since Eggan's book[61] presents an outstanding example of what can be expected from intensive and thorough study of a limited area. Here we observe closely connected forms, each of which preserves a structural consistency, although they present, in relation to one another, discontinuities which become significant when compared to homologous discontinuities in other fields, such as clan organization, marriage rules, ritual, religious beliefs, etc.

It is by means of such studies, which exhibit a truly "Galilean" outlook,[62] that one may hope to reach a depth where social structure is put on a level with other types of mental structures, particularly the linguistic one. To give an example: It follows from Eggan's survey that the Hopi kinship system requires no less than three different models for the time dimension. There is, first, an "empty" time, stable and reversible, illustrated by the father's mother's and mother's father's lineages, where the same terms are consistently applied throughout the generations; second, there is a progressive, non-reversible time, as shown in (female) Ego's lineage with the sequence:

$$\text{grandmother} > \text{mother} > \text{sister} > \text{child} > \text{grandchild};$$

and, third, there is an undulating, cyclical, reversible time, as in (male) Ego's lineage with the continuous alternation between sister and sister's child. On the other hand, these three linear structures are clearly distinct from the circular structure of the Zuni (female) Ego's lineage, where three terms, mother's mother (or daughter's daughter), mother, and daughter, are disposed in a kind of ringlike arrangement, this conceptual grouping being accompanied, as regards the other lineages, by a greater poverty both of terms inside the acknowledged kin and of kin acknowledgment. Since time aspects also belong to linguistic analysis, the question can be raised whether or not there is a correlation between their manifestations in language and kinship and, if so, at what level.[63]

Progress in this and other directions would undoubtedly have been more substantial if general agreement had existed among social anthropologists on the definition of social structure, the goals which may be achieved by its study, and the methodological principles to be applied at the different stages of research. Unfortunately, this is not the case, but it may be welcomed as a promising sign that some kind of understanding can be reached, at least on the nature and scope of these differences. This seems an appropriate place to offer a rapid sketch of the attitude of the main contributors to social-structure research in relation to the working assumptions which were made at the beginning of this paper.

The term "social structure" is in many ways linked with the name of A. R. Radcliffe-Brown. Though his contribution is not limited to the study of kinship systems, he has stated the goal of these studies in terms which every scholar in the same field would probably be ready to underwrite. The aim of kinship studies, he says, is (1) to make a systematic classification; (2) to understand particular features of particular systems (a) by revealing the particular feature as a part of an organized whole, and (b) by showing that it is a special example of a recognizable class of phenomena; (3) to arrive at valid generalizations about the nature of human societies. And he concludes: "To reduce this diversity (of 2 or 300 kinship systems) to some sort of order is the task of analysis. . . . We can . . . find . . . beneath the diversities, a limited number of general principles applied and combined in various ways." [64] There is nothing to add to this lucid program besides pointing out that this is precisely what Radcliffe-Brown has done in his study of Australian kinship systems. He brought forth a tremendous amount of material; he introduced some kind of order where there was only chaos; he defined the basic operational terms, such as "cycle," "pair," and "couple." Finally, his discovery of the Kariera system in the region, with the characteristics inferred from the study of the available data previous to visiting Australia, will forever remain one of the great results of socio-structural studies.[65] His masterly introduction to *African Systems of Kinship and Marriage* may be considered a true treatise on kinship; at the same time it takes a step toward integrating kinship systems of the Western world (which are considered in their early forms) into a world-wide theoretical interpretation. Another capital contribution by the same scholar, about the homologous structure of kinship terminology and behavior, will be dealt with later on.

However, it is obvious that, in many respects, Radcliffe-Brown's conception of social structure differs from the postulates which were set up at the outset of the present paper. In the first place, the notion of structure appears to him as a means to link social anthropology to the biological sciences: "There is a real and significant analogy between organic structure and social structure." [66] Then, instead of "lifting up" kinship studies to put them on the same level as communication theory, as has been suggested by this writer, he has lowered them to the same plane as the phenomena dealt with in descriptive morphology and physiology.[67] In that respect, his approach is in line with the naturalistic trend of the British school. In contradistinction to Kroeber[68] and Lowie,[69] who have emphasized the artificiality of kinship, Radcliffe-Brown agrees with Malinowski that biological ties are, at one and the same time, the origin of and the model for every type of kinship tie.[70]

These principles are responsible for two consequences. In the first place, Radcliffe-Brown's empirical approach makes him very reluctant to distinguish between *social structure* and *social relations*. As a matter of fact, social structure appears in his work to be nothing else than the whole network of social relations. It is true that he has sometimes outlined a distinction between *structure* and *structural form*. The latter concept, however, seems to be limited to the diachronic perspective, and its functional role in Radcliffe-Brown's theoretical thought appears quite reduced.[71] This distinction was thoroughly discussed by Fortes, who has contributed a great deal to the distinction, quite foreign to Radcliffe-Brown's outlook (and to which I myself attribute considerable importance), between "model" and "reality": "Structure is not immediately visible in the 'concrete reality.' . . . When we describe structure . . . we are, as it were, in the realm of grammar and syntax, not of the spoken word." [72]

In the second place, this merging of social structure and social relations induces him to break down the former into the simplest forms of the latter, that is, relations between two persons: "The kinship structure of any society consists of a number of . . . dyadic relations. . . . In an Australian tribe, the whole social structure is based on a network of such relations of person to person. . . ." [73] It may be questioned whether such dyadic relations are the materials out of which social structure is built, or whether they do not themselves result from a pre-existing structure which should be defined in more complex terms. Structural linguistics has a lot to teach in this respect. Examples of the kind of analysis commended by Radcliffe-Brown may be found in the works of Bateson and Mead. However, in *Naven*,[74] Bateson has gone a step further than Radcliffe-Brown's classification[75] of dyadic relations according to order. He has attempted to place them in specific categories, an undertaking which implies that there is something more to social structure than the dyadic relations, that is, the structure itself.

Since it is possible to extend almost indefinitely the string of dyadic relations, Radcliffe-Brown has shown some reluctance toward the isolation of social structures conceived as self-sufficient wholes (in this respect he disagrees with Malinowski). His is a philosophy of continuity, not of discontinuity; this accounts for his hostility toward the notion of culture, already alluded to, and his avoidance of the teachings of structural linguistics and of modern mathematics.

All these considerations may explain why Radcliffe-Brown, though an incomparable observer, analyst, and classifier, has sometimes proved to be disappointing when he turned to interpretations. These, in his work, often appear vague or circular. Have marriage prohibitions really no other function than to help perpetuate the kinship system?[76] Are all the peculiar features of the Crow-Omaha system satisfactorily accounted for when it has been said that they emphasize the lineage principle? [77] These doubts, as well as many others, some of which will be mentioned later on in this chapter, explain why the work of Radcliffe-Brown, to which no one can deny a central place in social-structure studies, has often given rise to bitter arguments.

For instance, Murdock has called the kind of interpretation to which Radcliffe-Brown seems to be addicted "mere verbalizations reified into causal forces," [78] and Lowie expressed himself in similar terms.[79] As regards Murdock, the lively controversy which was carried on between him and W. E. Lawrence,[80] on the one hand, and Radcliffe-Brown,[81] on the other, may help to clarify the basic differences in their respective positions. This was about the so-called Murngin type of kinship system, a focal point in social-structure studies not only because of its many intricacies but because, thanks to Lloyd Warner's book and articles,[82] we possess a thorough and extensive study of this system.[83] However, Warner's study leaves some basic problems unanswered, especially the way in which marriage takes place on the lateral borders of the system.

For Radcliffe-Brown, however, there is no problem involved, since he considers any kind of social organization as a mere conglomerate of simple person-to-person relations and since, in any society, there is always somebody who may be regarded as one's mother's brother's daughter (the preferred spouse among the Murngin) or as standing in an equivalent relation. But the problem is elsewhere: It lies in the fact that the natives have chosen to express these person-to-person relations in a class system, and Warner's description of this system (as acknowledged by himself) makes it impossible in some cases for the same individual to belong simultaneously to the right kind of class and to the right kind of relation.

Under these circumstances, Lawrence and Murdock have tried to invent some system which would fit the requirements of both the marriage rules and a system of the same kind as the one described by Warner. They invented it, however, as a sort of abstract game, the result being that, while their system meets some of the difficulties involved in Warner's account, it also raises many others. One of the main difficulties implied in Warner's system is that it would require, on the part of the natives, an awareness of relationships too remote to make it believable. Since the new system adds a new line to the seven already assumed by Warner, it goes still further in that direction. Therefore, it seems a good hunch that the "hidden" or "unknown" system underlying the clumsy model which the Murngin borrowed recently from tribes with completely different marriage rules is simpler than the latter and not more complicated.[84]

One sees, then, that Murdock favors a systematic and formal approach, different from Radcliffe-Brown's empirical and naturalistic one. But he remains, at the same time, psychologically and even biologically minded, and he can comply with the resulting requirements only by calling upon other disciplines, such as psychoanalysis and behavioristic psychology. Thus he succeeds in unloading from his interpretations of kinship problems the empiricism which still burdens Radcliffe-Brown's work, though, perhaps, at the risk of leaving them incomplete or having to be completed on grounds alien to anthropology, if not contradictory to its goals. Instead of seeing in kinship systems a sociological means to achieve a sociological result, he rather treats them as sociological results deriving from biological and psychological premises.[85]

Two parts should be distinguished in Murdock's contribution to the study of social structure. There is, first, a rejuvenation of a statistical method to test assumed correlations between social traits and to establish new ones, a method already tried by Tylor but which Murdock, thanks to the painstaking efforts of his Yale Cross-Cultural Survey and the use of a more complex and exacting technique, was able to carry much further than had his predecessor.

Everything has been said on the manifold difficulties with which this kind of inquiry is fraught,[86] and since no one is better aware of them than its author, it is unnecessary to dwell upon this theme. Let it only be recalled that while the uncertainty involved in the process of "carving out" the data will always make any alleged correlation dubious, the method is quite efficient in a negative way, that is, in exploding false correlations. In this respect Murdock has achieved many results which no social anthropologist can permit himself to ignore.

The second aspect of Murdock's contribution is a scheme of the historical evolution of kinship systems. This suggests a startling conclusion, namely, that the so-called "Hawaiian type" of social organization should be placed at the origin of a much greater number of systems than has generally been admitted since Lowie's criticism of Morgan's similar hypothesis.[87] However, it should be kept in mind that Murdock's scheme is not based upon the consideration of individual societies taken as historico-geographical units or as coordinated wholes, but on abstractions and even, if one may say so, on abstractions "twice removed": In the first place, social organization is isolated from the other aspects of culture (and sometimes even kinship systems from social organization); next, social organization itself is broken up into disconnected elements which are the product of the traditional categories of ethnological theory rather than of the concrete analysis of each group. This being understood, the method for establishing a historical scheme can only be ideological; it proceeds by extracting common elements pertaining to each stage, in order to define a previous stage, and so on. Therefore, it is obvious that systems placed at the beginning can be only those which exhibit the more general features, while systems with special features must occupy a more recent rank. It is as though the origin of the modern horse were ascribed to the order of vertebrates instead of to *Hipparion*.

Regardless of the difficulties raised by his approach, Murdock's book should be credited with presenting new material and raising fascinating problems, many of which are new to anthropological thought. It is not doing him an injustice, then, to state that his contribution consists more in perfecting a method of discovering new problems than in solving them. Though this method remains "Aristotelian," it is perhaps unavoidable in the development of any science. Murdock has at least been faithful to the best part of the Aristotelian outlook by demonstrating convincingly that "cultural forms in the field of social organization reveal a degree of regularity and of conformity to scientific law not significantly inferior to that found in the so-called natural sciences." [88]

In relation to the distinctions made in the first section of this paper, it can be said that Radcliffe-Brown's work expresses a disregard for the difference between *observation* and *experimentation*, while Murdock shows a similar disregard for the difference between *mechanical* and *statistical* models (since he tries to construct mechanical models with the help of a statistical method). Conversely, Lowie's work seems to consist entirely in an exacting endeavor to meet the question (which was acknowledged as a prerequisite for any study in social structure): *What are the facts?* When he became active in research as well as in theoretical ethnology, the latter field was fraught with philosophical prejudices and an aura of sociological mysticism; therefore, his paramount contribution toward assessing the subject matter of social anthropology has sometimes been misunderstood and thought of as wholly negative.[89] But, although this situation made it imperative at that time to state, in the first place, what the facts were *not*, the creative energy liberated by his merciless destruction of arbitrary systems and alleged correlations has furnished, to a very large extent, the power used by his followers. His own positive contributions are not always easy to outline on account of the extreme modesty of his thought and his aversion to any kind of wide-scope theoretical claim. He himself used the words "active skepticism" to define his position. However, it is Lowie who, as early as 1915, stated in modern terms the role of kinship studies in relation to social behavior and organization: "Sometimes the very essence of social fabric may be demonstrably connected with the mode of classifying kin." [90] In the same paper he was able to reverse the narrow historical trend which, at that time, was blinding anthropological thinking to the universal action of structural forces: Exogamy was shown to be a scheme defined by truly genetic characteristics and, whenever present, determining identical features of social organization, without calling for historico-geographical relations.

When, a few years later, he exploded the "matrilineal complex," [91] he achieved two results which are the fundamentals of social-structure studies. First, by dismissing the notion that every so-called matrilineal feature was to be understood as an expression or as a vestige of the complex, he made it possible to break it up into several variables. Second, the elements thus liberated could be used for a permutative treatment of the differential features of kinship systems.[92] Thus he was laying the foundations for a structural analysis of kinship on two different levels: that of the terminological system, on the one hand, and, on the other, that of the correlation between the system of attitudes and terminology, thus revealing which later on was to be followed by others.[93]

Lowie should be credited with many other theoretical contributions. He was probably the first to demonstrate the true bilateral nature of most of the so-called "unilineal" systems.[94] He made clear the impact of residence on descent.[95] He convincingly dissociated avoidance customs from incest prohibitions.[96] His care to interpret social organization not only as a set of institutionalized rules but also as the outcome of individual psychological reactions, which sometimes contradicted or inflected the rules, led to the strange result that the same scholar who was so abused for his famous "shreds and patches" statement on culture was able to offer some of the most thorough and well-balanced pictures we have of cultures treated as wholes.[97] Finally, Lowie's role as a promoter and exponent of South American social anthropology is well known; either directly or indirectly, through guidance and encouragement, he has contributed toward breaking new ground.

SOCIAL DYNAMICS: SUBORDINATION STRUCTURES

Order of Elements (*Individuals or Groups*) *in the Social Structure.* According to this writer's interpretation, which does not need to be expounded systematically since (in spite of efforts toward objectivity) it probably permeates this paper, kinship systems, marriage rules, and descent groups constitute a coordinated whole, the function of which is to insure the permanency of the social group by means of intertwining consanguineous and affinal ties. They may be considered as the blueprint of a mechanism which "pumps" women out of their consanguineous families to redistribute them in affinal groups, the result of this process being to create new consanguineous groups, and so on.[98]

If no external factor were affecting this mechanism, it would work indefinitely, and the social structure would remain static. This is not the case, however; hence the need to introduce into the theoretical model new elements to account for the diachronic changes of the structure, on the one hand, and, on the other, for the fact that kinship structure does not exhaust social structure. This can be done in three different ways.

As always, the first step consists in ascertaining the facts. Since the time when Lowie expressed regret that so little had been done by anthropologists in the field of political organization,[99] some progress has been made; in the first place, Lowie himself has clarified the issue by devoting most of his recent book to problems of that sort and by regrouping the facts concerning the North American area.[100] A recent work has brought together significant data concerning Africa.[101] To this day, the best way to organize the still-confused material remains Lowie's basic distinctions among social strata, sodalities, and the state.[102]

The second type of approach would be an attempt to correlate the phenomena belonging to the order first studied, that is, kinship, with phenomena belonging to the new order but showing a direct connection with the former. This approach raises, in turn, two different problems: (1) Can the kinship structure by itself result in structures of a new type (that is, dynamically oriented)? (2) How do *communication structures* and *subordination structures* interact with one another?

The first problem should be related to education, i.e., to the fact that each generation plays alternately a submissive and a dominant part in relation to the preceding and to the following generation. This aspect has been dealt with chiefly by Margaret Mead.[103]

Another side of the question lies in the important attempt to correlate static positions in the kinship structure (as defined by terminology) with dynamic attitudes expressed, on the one hand, in rights, duties, obligations and, on the other, in privileges, avoidance, etc. It is impossible to go into the discussion of these problems, to which many writers have contributed. Especially significant is a protracted controversy between Radcliffe-Brown and others about the kind of correlation, if any, which exists between the *system of terminology* and the *system of attitudes.*[104]

According to Radcliffe-Brown's well-known position, such a correlation exhibits a high degree of accuracy, while his opponents have generally tried to demonstrate that it is neither absolute nor detailed. In contrast to both opinions, this writer has tried to establish that the relation between terminology and attitudes is of a dialectical nature. The modalities of behavior between relatives express to some extent the terminological classification, and they provide at the same time a means of overcoming difficulties and contradictions resulting from this classification. Thus the rules of behavior result from an attempt to overcome contradictions in the field of terminology and marriage rules; the functional unwedging

—if one may call it that—which is bound to exist between the two orders causes changes in terminology; and these, in turn, call for new behavior patterns, and so on indefinitely.[105]

The second problem confronts us with the kind of situation arising when the kinship system regulates marriage exchanges not between equals but between members of a hierarchy (either economic or political). Under that heading comes the problem of polygamy which, in some cases at least, may be shown to provide a bridge between two different types of guarantees, one collective and political, the other individual and economic,[106] and that of hypergamy (or hypogamy). This deserves much more attention than it has received thus far, since it is the doorway to the study of the caste system[107] and hence to that of social structures based on race and class distinctions.

The third and last approach to our problem is purely formal. It consists in an a priori deduction of the types of structures likely to result from relations of dominance or dependency as they might appear at random. Of a very promising nature for the study of social structure are Rapoport's attempts to formulate a mathematical theory of the pecking order among hens.[108] It is true that there seems to be a complete opposition between, let us say, the pecking order of hens, which is intransitive and cyclical, and the social order (for instance, the circle of *kava* in Polynesia), which is transitive and non-cyclical (since those who are seated at the far end can never sit at the top).[109] But the study of kinship systems shows precisely that, under given circumstances, a transitive and non-cyclical order can result in an intransitive and cyclical one. This happens, for instance, in a hypergamous society, where a circular marriage system with mother's brother's daughter leaves at one end a girl unable to find a husband (since her status is the highest) and at the other end a boy without a wife (since no girl, except his sister, has a status lower than his own). Therefore, either the society under consideration will succumb to its contradictions, or its transitive and non-cyclical order will be transformed into an intransitive and cyclical one, temporarily or locally.[110]

Thus, with the help of such notions as transitivity, order, and cycle, which admit of mathematical treatment, it becomes possible to study, on a purely formal level, generalized types of social structure where both the communication and the subordination aspects are fully integrated. It is also possible to enlarge the field of inquiry and to integrate, for a given society, actual and potential types of order. For instance, in human societies the actual forms of social order are practically always of a transitive and non-cyclical type: If A is above B and B above C, then A is above C; and C cannot be above A. But most of the human "potential" or "ideological" forms of social order, as illustrated in politics, myth, and religion, are conceived as intransitive and cyclical; for instance, in tales about kings marrying lasses and in Stendhal's indictment of American democracy as a system where a gentleman takes his orders from his grocer.

Order of Orders. Thus anthropology considers the whole social fabric as a network of different types of orders. The kinship system provides a way to order individuals according to certain rules; social organization is another way of ordering individuals and groups; social stratifications, whether economic or political, provide us with a third type; and all these orders can themselves be ordered by showing the kind of relationships which exist among them, how they interact with one another on both the synchronic and the diachronic levels. Meyer Fortes has successfully tried to construct models valid not only for one type of order (kinship, social organization, economic relations, etc.) but where numerous models for all types of orders are themselves ordered inside a total model.[111]

When dealing with these orders, however, anthropologists are confronted with a basic problem which was taken up at the beginning of this paper, that is, to what extent does the manner according to which a society conceives its orders and their ordering correspond to the real situation? It has been shown that this problem can be solved in different ways, depending on the data at hand.

All the models considered so far, however, are "lived-in" orders: they correspond to mechanisms which can be studied from the outside as a part of objective reality. But no systematic studies of these orders can be undertaken without acknowledging the fact that social groups, to achieve their reciprocal ordering, need to call upon orders of different types, corresponding to a field external to objective reality and which we call the "supernatural." These "thought-of" orders cannot be checked against the experience to which they refer, since they are one and the same as this experience. Therefore, we are in the position of studying them only in their relationships with the other types of "lived-in" orders. The "thought-of" orders are those of myth and religion. The question may be raised whether, in our own society, political ideology does not belong to the same category.

After Durkheim, Radcliffe-Brown has contributed greatly to the demonstration that religion is a part of the social structure. The anthropologist's task is to discover correlations between different types of religions and different types of social organization.[112] Radcliffe-Brown failed to achieve significant results, however, for two reasons. In the first place, he tried to link ritual and beliefs directly to sentiments; besides, he was more concerned with giving universal formulation to the kind of correlation prevailing between religion and social structure than in showing the variability of one in relation to the other. It is perhaps as a result of this that the study of religion has fallen into the background, to the extent that the word "religion" does not even appear in the program of this symposium. The field of myth, ritual, and religion seems nevertheless to be one of the more fruitful for the study of social structure; though relatively little has been done in this respect, the results which have been obtained recently are among the most rewarding in our field.

Great strides have been made toward the study of religious systems as coordinated wholes. Documentary material, such as P. Radin's *The Road of Life and Death*[113] and R. M. Berndt's *Kunapipi*,[114] should help in undertaking, with respect to several religious cults, the kind of ordering of data so masterfully achieved by Gladys Reichard for the Navaho.[115] This should be complemented by small-scale comparative studies on the permanent and non-permanent elements in religious thought as exemplified by Lowie.

With the help of such well-organized material it becomes possible, as Nadel puts it, to prepare "small-scale models of a comparative analysis . . . of an analysis of 'concomitant variations' . . . such as any inquiry concerned with the explanation of social facts must employ."[116] The results thus achieved may be small; they are, however, some of the most convincing and rigorous in the entire field of social organization. Nadel himself has demonstrated a correlation between shamanism and some aspects of psychological development;[117] using Indo-European comparative material borrowed from Iceland, Ireland, and the Caucasus, Dumézil has interpreted an enigmatic mythological figure in relation to specific features of social organization;[118] Wittfogel and Goldfrank have shown how significant variations in mythological themes can be related to the socioeconomic background.[119] Monica Hunter has established beyond doubt that the structure of magical beliefs may vary in correlation with the structure of the society itself.[120] These results, together with some others (on which space prevents our commenting), give hope that we may be close to understanding not only what kind of function religious beliefs fulfill in social life (this has been known more or less clearly since Lucretius' time) but how they fulfill this function.

A few words may be added as a conclusion. This chapter was started by working out the notion of "model," and the same notion has reappeared at its end. Social anthropology, in its incipient stage, could only seek, as model for its first models, among those of the simplest kinds provided by more advanced sciences, and it was natural enough to seek them in the field of classical mechanics. However, in doing so, anthropology has been working under some sort of illusion, since, as Von Neumann puts it, "an almost exact theory of a gas, containing about 10^{25} freely moving particles, is incomparably easier than that of the solar system, made up of 9 major bodies." [121] But when it tries to construct its models, anthropology finds itself in a situation which is neither the one nor the other: The objects with which we deal—social roles and human beings—are considerably more numerous than those dealt with in Newtonian mechanics, and at the same time, far less numerous than would be required to allow a satisfactory use of the laws of statistics and probability. Thus we find ourselves in an intermediate zone: too complicated for one treatment and not complicated enough for the other.

The tremendous change brought about by the theory of communication consists precisely in the discovery of methods to deal with objects—signs—which can be subjected to a rigorous study despite the fact that they are altogether much more numerous than those of classical mechanics and much less than those of thermodynamics. Language consists of morphemes, a few thousand in number; significant regularities in phoneme frequencies can be obtained by limited counts. The threshold for the use of statistical laws becomes lower, and that for operating with mechanical models higher, than was the case when operating on other grounds. And, at the same time, the size-order of the phenomena has become significantly closer to that of anthropological data.

Therefore, the present conditions of social-structure studies can be summarized as follows: Phenomena are found to be of the same kind as those which, in strategics and communication theory, were made the subject of a rigorous approach. Anthropological facts are on a scale which is sufficiently close to that of these other phenomena as not to preclude their similar treatment. Surprisingly enough, it is at the very moment when anthropology finds itself closer than ever to the long-awaited goal of becoming a true science that the ground seems to fail where it was expected to be the firmest: The facts themselves are lacking, either not numerous enough or not collected under conditions insuring their comparability.

Though it is not our fault, we have been behaving like amateur botanists, haphazardly picking up heterogeneous specimens, which were further distorted and mutilated by preservation in our herbarium. And we are, all of a sudden, confronted with the need of ordering complete series, ascertaining original shades, and measuring minute parts which have either shrunk or been lost. When we come to realize not only what should be done but also what we should be in a position to do, and when we make at the same time an inventory of our material, we cannot help feeling in a disheartened mood. It looks almost as if cosmic physics were asked to work with Babylonian observations. The celestial bodies are still there, but unfortunately the native cultures from which we used to gather our data are rapidly disappearing and that which they are being replaced by can only furnish data of a very different type. To adjust our techniques of observation to a theoretical framework which is far more advanced is a paradoxical situation, quite opposite to that which has prevailed in the history of sciences. Nevertheless, such is the challenge to modern anthropology.

NOTES

1. A. L. Kroeber, *Anthropology* (New York: 1948), p. 325. Compare with the statement by the same author: ". . . the term 'social structure' which is tending to replace 'social organization' without appearing to add either content or emphasis of meaning." A. L. Kroeber, "Structure, Function and Pattern in Biology and Anthropology," *Scientific Monthly*, LVI (1943), p. 105.
2. The same idea appears to underlie E. R. Leach's remarkable study, "Jinghpaw Kinship Terminology," *Journal of the Royal Anthropological Institute*, LXXV (1945).
3. Compare Von Neumann: "Such models [as games] are theoretical constructs with a precise, exhaustive and not too complicated definition; and they must be similar to reality in those respects which are essential to the investigation at hand. To recapitulate in detail: The definition must be precise and exhaustive in order to make a mathematical treatment possible. The construct must not be unduly complicated so that the mathematical treatment can be brought beyond the mere formalism to the point where it yields complete numerical results. Similarity to reality is needed to make the operation significant. And this similarity must usually be restricted to a few traits deemed 'essential' *pro tempore* —since otherwise the above requirements would conflict with each other." J. Von Neumann and O. Morgenstern, *Theory of Games and Economic Behavior* (Princeton: 1944).
4. K. Goldstein, *Der Aufbau des Organismus*. French translation (Paris: 1951), pp. 18-25. [English translation, New York: 1939.]
5. F. Boas (ed.), *Handbook of American Indian Languages*, Bureau of American Ethnology Bulletin 40 (1908), 1911, Part I.
6. See "Introduction: History and Anthropology," Chapter I of the present volume.
7. For examples and detailed discussion, see C. Lévi-Strauss, *Les Structures élémentaires de la parenté* (Paris: 1949), p. 558 ff.
8. R. Firth, *Elements of Social Organization* (London: 1951), pp. 28-31.
9. On this point, see Chapters VII and VIII of the present volume.
10. J. Richardson and A. L. Kroeber, "Three Centuries of Women's Dress Fashions: A Quantitative Analysis," *Anthropological Records* (Berkeley, Calif.), V, No. 2 (1940).
11. Princeton, 1944.
12. Paris-Cambridge-New York, 1948.
13. Urbana, 1950.
14. D. Forde, "Marriage and the Family among the Yakö in S. E. Nigeria," *Monographs in Social Anthropology*, No. 5, London School of Economics (1941); V. Elwin, *The Muria and Their Ghotul* (Oxford: 1947).
15. Despite the criticism which has been leveled at me, I also maintain that the time dimension is irrelevant to the argument. For these discussions, see Chapter I of the present volume, already cited, and my *Race and History* (Paris: 1952). These studies have elicited criticisms and commentaries from C. Lefort, "L'Echange et la lutte des hommes," *Les Temps Modernes* (February, 1951); "Sociétés sans histoire et histori-

cité," *Cahiers internationaux de Sociologie*, XII (1952); J. Pouillon, "L'Oeuvre de Claude Lévi-Strauss," *Les Temps Modernes* (July, 1956); R. Bastide, "Lévi-Strauss ou l'ethnographe 'à la recherche du temps perdu,'" *Présence africaine* (April-May, 1956); G. Balandier, "Grandeur et servitude de l'ethnologie," *Cahiers du Sud*, No. 337 (1956).

16. R. Firth, *op. cit.*, p. 40.

17. L. A. White, *The Science of Culture* (New York: 1949).

18. This is, indeed, how modern biological evolutionism is being developed in the researches of J. B. S. Haldane, G. G. Simpson, and others

19. A. R. Radcliffe-Brown, "Social Anthropology, Past and Present," *Man*, LII (1952).

20. A. R. Radcliffe-Brown, "Religion and Society," Henry Myers Lecture, *Journal of the Royal Anthropological Institute*, LXXV (1945), p. 1.

21. R. H. Lowie, *op. cit.*, p. 38.

22. *Ibid.*, p. 68.

23. E. Durkheim, *Les Formes élémentaires de la vie religieuse* (Paris: 1912), p. 593.

24. K. Goldstein, *op. cit.*, p. 25.

25. E. E. Evans-Pritchard, "Nuer Time Reckoning," *Africa* (1939), XII, 189-216; *The Nuer* (Oxford: 1940).

26. L. Bernot and R. Blancard, "Nouville, un village français," *Travaux et mémoires de l'Institut d'Ethnologie*, LVII (1953).

27. E. Durkheim and M. Mauss, "De quelques Formes primitives de classification: Contribution à l'étude des représentations collectives," *Année sociologique*, VI (1903), pp. 1-72.

28. This opposition was never accepted by Lowie; see the preface to his *Primitive Society* (New York: 1920).

29. These studies were summarized by their author in *L'Héritage indo-européen à Rome* (Paris: 1949).

30. We refer to the chapter "Human Ecology," by M. Bates in *Anthropology Today*, pp. 700-13.

31. "Division et proportion des divisions de la sociologie," *Année sociologique*, n.s., II (1924-1925), p. 98 ff.

32. See, for example, R. Firth, *We, the Tikopia* (London-New York: 1936); J. Steward, *Basin-Plateau Aboriginal Sociopolitical Groups*, Bureau of American Ethnology, Smithsonian Institution Bulletin 120 (Washington: 1938); S. F. Nadel, *The Nuba* (London-NewYork: 1947); D. Forde, "Double-Descent among the Yakö," in A. R. Radcliffe-Brown and D. Forde (eds.), *African Systems of Kinship and Marriage* (London: 1950).

33. See Chapters VII and VIII of this volume.

34. See, for instance, the "configuration" of a ritual at its various stages, as they were mapped in A. C. Fletcher, *The Hako: A Pawnee Ceremony*, 22nd Annual Report, Bureau of American Ethnology, Vol. II (1904).

35. M. de Lestrange, "Pour une Méthode socio-démographique," *Journal de la Société des Africanistes*, XXI (1951).

36. L. Livi, *Trattato di demografia* (Padua: 1940-1941); "Considérations théoriques et pratiques sur le concept de 'minimum de population,'" *Population*, IV, No. 4 (1949), pp. 754-56.

37. C. Wagley, "The Effects of Depopulation upon Social Organization as Illustrated by the Tapirapé Indians," *Transactions of the New York Academy of Sciences*, Series 2, III, No. 1 (1940), pp. 12-16.

38. See K. Davis, *The Development of the City in Society: Proceedings of the First Conference on Long Term Social Trends* (Washington, D.C.: Social Science Research Council, 1947); J. Q. Stewart, "Empirical Mathematical Rules Concerning the Distribution and Equilibrium of Population," *Geographical Review*, XXXVII, No. 3 (1947), 461-85; G. K. Zipf, *Human Behavior and the Principle of Least Effort* (Cambridge, Mass.: 1949). An expert on the theater told me recently that Louis Jouvet was always surprised that the house was filled approximately to capacity every night—that is to say, that a house with a capacity of 500 should have approximately 500 customers, and that one with a capacity of 2,000 should have about this number, with few people being turned away in the first case and the house never being three-quarters empty in the second case. This built-in balance would indeed be unexplainable, if all seats in each house were similar. But since the bad seats quickly acquire a bad reputation, a compensating effect occurs: If only poor seats remain, connoisseurs prefer to attend another performance or go to another theater. It would be interesting to investigate whether this phenomenon is of the same type as the rank-size law. From a more general perspective, the study of this theater phenomenon, considered from a quantitative viewpoint (relationship among the number of theaters, their respective size, the size of the cities, box office receipts, etc.) would provide a convenient and heretofore neglected method of clarifying—almost as in a laboratory—both diachronically and synchronically, certain fundamental problems of social structure.

39. G. Dahlberg, *Mathematical Methods for Population Genetics* (London-New York: 1948).

40. J. Sutter and L. Tabah, "Les Notions d'isolat et de population minimum," *Population*, VI, No. 3 (1951), pp. 481-89.

41. These two situations correspond respectively to marriages of the matrilateral type (long cycles) and patrilateral type (short cycles). On this topic, see my *Les Structures élémentaires de la parenté*, Chapter XXVII. It is evident from this example that considerations of a purely quantitative nature are not adequate. We must add to them the study of structures, which differ qualitatively.

42. A. R. Radcliffe-Brown, "On Social Structure," *Journal of the Royal Anthropological Institute*, LXX (1940), pp. 10-11.

43. R. H. Lowie, "A Marginal Note to Professor Radcliffe-Brown's Paper on 'Social Structure,'" *American Anthropologist*, XLIV, No. 3 (1942), pp. 520-21.

44. L. A. White, *op. cit.*

45. D. Bidney, review of L. A. White, *The Science of Culture*, in *American Anthropologist*, LII, No. 4, Part I (1950), pp. 518-19. See also A. R. Radcliffe-Brown, "White's View of a Science of Culture," *American Anthropologist*, LI, No. 3 (1949), pp. 503-12.

46. N. Bohr, "Natural Philosophy and Human Culture," *Nature*, CXLIII (1939), p. 9.

47. M. Mauss, "Essai sur les variations saisonnières dans les sociétés eskimos:

Étude de morphologie sociale," *Année Sociologique*, IX, 1904-1905 (1906), pp. 39-132; "Essai sur le don, forme archaïque de l'échange," *op. cit.*, I (1923-1924), pp. 30-186.

48. B. Malinowski, *Argonauts of the Western Pacific* (London: 1922).

49. F. G. Speck, *Family Hunting Territories and Social Life of Various Algonkian Bands of the Ottawa Valley*, Canada Department of Mines, Geological Survey Memoir 70, Anthropological Series, No. 8 (Ottawa: 1915); A. I. Richards, *Hunger and Work in a Savage Tribe* (London: 1932), "A Dietary Study in Northeastern Rhodesia," *Africa*, IX, No. 2 (1936), pp. 166-96, and *Land, Labour and Diet in Northern Rhodesia* (Oxford: 1939); J. H. Steward, *Basin-Plateau Aboriginal Sociopolitical Groups, op. cit.;* E. E. Evans-Pritchard, *The Nuer* (Oxford: 1940); M. J. Herskovits, *The Economic Life of Primitive Peoples* (New York: 1940); K. A. Wittfogel and E. S. Goldfrank, "Some Aspects of Pueblo Mythology and Society," *Journal of American Folklore*, LVI (1943), pp. 17-30.

50. *Op. cit.*

51. This parallel did not appear in the original version of this paper, but it was suggested in the course of the discussion that followed. I subsequently developed it in an article, "The Mathematics of Man," which was the introduction to "Mathematics and the Social Sciences," a special issue of the *International Social Science Bulletin*, VI, No. 4 (UNESCO, Paris: 1954), pp. 581-90.

52. A. L. Kroeber, "The Societies of Primitive Man," *Biological Symposia*, VIII (1942), p. 215.

53. Von Neumann and Morgenstern, *op. cit.*, pp. 186-219.

54. *Ibid.*, p. 49.

55. We attempted to introduce these notions in another work. See *Race and History*, already mentioned.

56. W. L. Warner, "Morphology and Functions of the Australian Murngin Type of Kinship System," *American Anthropologist*, XXXII, No. 2 (1930), pp. 207-56, and XXXIII, No. 2 (1931), pp. 172-98; C. Lévi-Strauss, *Les Structures élémentaires de la parenté;* W. E. Lawrence and G. P. Murdock, "Murngin Social Organization," *American Anthropologist*, LI, No. 1 (1949), pp. 58-65; A. R. Radcliffe-Brown, "Murngin Social Organization," *American Anthropologist*, LIII, No. 1 (1951), pp. 37-55; A. P. Elkin, personal correspondence.

57. See pp. 305-6, *supra*, and notes 83-84.

58. Smithsonian Institution Contributions to Knowledge, XVII, No. 218 (Washington: 1871).

59. C. S. Ford and F. A. Beach, *Patterns of Sexual Behavior* (New York: 1951), p. 5.

60. R. H. Lowie, *Social Organization* (New York: 1948).

61. F. Eggan, *Social Organization of the Western Pueblos* (Chicago: 1950).

62. That is, aiming to uncover the law of variation, in contradistinction to the "Aristotelian" outlook, which is concerned primarily with inductive correlations; for this distinction, fundamental to structural analysis, see K. Lewin, *A Dynamic Theory of Personality* (New York: 1935).

63. See Chapters III and IV of the present volume, where this problem is treated more fully.

64. A. R. Radcliffe-Brown, "The Study of Kinship Systems," *Journal of the Royal Anthropological Institute*, LXXI (1941), p. 17.
65. A. R. Radcliffe-Brown, "The Social Organization of Australian Tribes," *Oceania*, I, No. 1 (1930-1931), pp. 34-63, No. 2, pp. 206-46, No. 3, pp. 322-41, and No. 4, pp. 426-56.
66. A. R. Radcliffe-Brown, "On Social Structure," *Journal of the Royal Anthropological Institute*, LXX (1940), p. 6.
67. *Ibid.*, p. 10.
68. A. L. Kroeber, "Basic and Secondary Patterns of Social Structure," *Journal of the Royal Anthropological Institute*, LXVIII (1938), pp. 299-309, and "The Societies of Primitive Man," *op. cit.*, p. 205 ff.
69. R. H. Lowie, *Social Organization*, Chapter IV.
70. A. R. Radcliffe-Brown, "Father, Mother, and Child," *Man*, XXVI, No. 103 (1926), pp. 159-61.
71. Radcliffe-Brown, "On Social Structure," *op. cit.*, p. 4.
72. M. Fortes (ed.), *Social Structure: Studies Presented to A. R. Radcliffe-Brown* (Oxford: 1949), p. 56.
73. Radcliffe-Brown, "On Social Structure," *op. cit.*, p. 3.
74. G. Bateson, *Naven* (Cambridge: 1936).
75. Radcliffe-Brown, "The Study of Kinship Systems," *op. cit.*
76. A. R. Radcliffe-Brown, "White's View of a Science of Culture," *American Anthropologist*, LI, No. 3 (1949), pp. 503-12.
77. Radcliffe-Brown, "The Study of Kinship Systems," *op. cit.*
78. G. P. Murdock, *op. cit.*, p. 121.
79. R. H. Lowie, *The History of Ethnological Theory* (New York: 1937), pp. 224-5.
80. Lawrence and Murdock, *op. cit.*
81. Radcliffe-Brown, "Murngin Social Organization," *op. cit.*
82. W. L. Warner, "Morphology and Functions of the Australian Murngin Type of Kinship System," *op. cit.*; *A Black Civilization: A Social Study of an Australian Tribe* (New York: 1937).
83. For a further word on this question, which appeared after this chapter was first published, see R. M. Berndt, " 'Murngin,' (Wulamba) Social Organization," *American Anthropologist*, n.s., LVII, No. 1, Part I (1955).
84. Warner postulated a system with seven lines of descent corresponding to seven classes. Lawrence and Murdock substituted for it a system with eight lines of descent and thirty-two classes. At that time (see my *Les Structures élémentaires de la parenté*, Chapter XII) I suggested reducing Warner's scheme to four lines of descent one of which would be ambiguous. In 1951, E. R. Leach, a British anthropologist, adopted my interpretation, which he then undertook to defend against me while attributing to me another interpretation invented by him to further the argument. See E. R. Leach, "The Structural Implications of Matrilateral Cross-Cousin Marriage," *Journal of the Royal Anthropological Institute*, LXXXI (1951). In the article cited in Note 83, above, Berndt set the number of lines of descent at three. Criticized by Leach at the time when he wrote his article, he acknowledged subsequently, in private conversation and correspondence, that I had obtained, on purely deductive grounds, the solution that among all those proposed until then

came closest to the one which he validated himself in the field. My interpretation of the Murngin system was the object of an admirably lucid and penetrating analysis by J. P. B. de Josselin de Jong, *Lévi-Strauss's Theory on Kinship and Marriage* (Leiden: 1952).

85. Murdock, *op. cit.*, pp. 131-2.
86. Lowie, *Social Organization, op. cit.*, Chapter III.
87. Lowie, *Primitive Society, op. cit.*, Chapter III.
88. Murdock, *op. cit.*, p. 259.
89. A. L. Kroeber, review of R. H. Lowie, *Primitive Society*, in *American Anthropologist*, XXII, No. 4 (1920), pp. 377-81.
90. R. H. Lowie, "Exogamy, and the Classificatory Systems of Relationship," *American Anthropologist*, XVII, No. 2 (1915); "Relationship Terms" in *Encyclopaedia Britannica* (1929).
91. R. H. Lowie, "The Matrilineal Complex," *University of California Publications in American Archaeology and Anthropology*, XVI, No. 2 (1919), pp. 29-45.
92. R. H. Lowie, "Notes on Hopi Clans," *American Museum of Natural History, Anthropological Papers*, XXX, Part VI (1929), pp. 303-60.
93. A. R. Radcliffe-Brown, "The Mother's Brother in South Africa," *South African Journal of Science*, XXI (1924), pp. 542-55; C. Lévi-Strauss, "Structural Analysis in Linguistics and in Anthropology," Chapter II of the present volume.
94. Lowie, *Primitive Society;* "Hopi Kinship," *American Museum of Natural History, Anthropological Papers*, XXX, Part VII (1929), pp. 361-88.
95. Lowie, *Primitive Society*.
96. *Ibid.*, pp. 104-5.
97. R. H. Lowie, *The Crow Indians* (New York: 1935), and *Social Organization*, Chapters XV, XVI, XVII.
98. On this point, see C. Lévi-Strauss, "The Family," in H. L. Shapiro (ed.), *Man, Culture and Society* (Oxford: 1956), Chapter XII.
99. Lowie, *Primitive Society*, Chapter XIII.
100. Lowie, *The Origin of the State* (New York: 1927), *Social Organization*, Chapters VI, VII, XII-XIV, "Some Aspects of Political Organization among American Aborigines" (Huxley Memorial Lecture), *Journal of the Royal Anthropological Institute*, LXXVIII (1948), pp. 11-24.
101. M. Fortes and E. E. Evans-Pritchard, *op. cit.*
102. Lowie, *Social Organization*.
103. In connection with the approach of this chapter, see especially M. Mead's "Character Formation and Diachronic Theory" in M. Fortes (ed.), *Social Structure: Studies Presented to A. R. Radcliffe-Brown*, pp. 18-34.
104. A. R. Radcliffe-Brown, "Kinship Terminology in California," *American Anthropologist*, XXXVII, No. 3 (1935), pp. 530-35, "On Joking Relationships," *Africa*, XIII, No. 3 (1940), pp. 195-210, and "A Further Note on Joking Relationships," *Africa*, XIX, No. 2 (1949), pp. 133-40; M. E. Opler, "Apache Data Concerning the Relation of Kinship Terminology to Social Classification," *American Anthropologist*, XXXIX, No. 2 (1937), pp. 201-12, and "Rule and Practice in the Behavior Pattern between Jicarilla Apache Affinal Relatives," *American*

Anthropologist, XLIX, No. 3 (1947), pp. 453-62; C. S. Brand, "On Joking Relationships," *American Anthropologist*, L (1948), pp. 160-1.

105. In a short book devoted to refuting *Les Structures élémentaires de la parenté*, Homans and Schneider attempt to reduce the rules of preferential marriage to systems of attitudes. They attack the principle, postulated in *Les Structures*, that there is no necessary connection between matrilateral or patrilateral marriage on the one hand, and the type of descent—patrilineal or matrilineal—on the other. In support of their own interpretation, according to which matrilateral marriage would be a function of patrilineal descent, they invoke statistical correlations which prove nothing. Actually, societies with patrilineal descent are much more numerous than societies with matrilineal descent. Furthermore, matrilateral marriage is more frequent than patrilateral marriage. Thus, if the distribution occurred at random, we might expect that the incidence of societies characterized by an association between patrilineal descent and matrilateral marriage would be higher, and thus the correlation claimed by my critics would be meaningless. After re-examining this postulated correlation on the basis of a larger sample (564 societies), Murdock concludes: "The worldwide incidence of such preferences . . . is so low as to cast some doubt on the validity of the theoretical interpretation advanced." (G. P. Murdock, "World Ethnographic Sample," *American Anthropologist*, n.s., LIX, No. 4 [1957], p. 687.)

I still maintain, in the same terms that I first employed, that there is no necessary connection between marriage with the unilateral cross-cousin and type of descent; in other words, that none of the conceivable combinations implies a contradiction. It is possible and even probable, however, that empirically the two types of marriage are more frequently associated with one or the other type of descent. If this should be the case, this *statistical correlation* (not to be confused with a *logical connection*) would require an explanation. I would be inclined to find it in the instability characteristic of matrilineal societies (a theme already developed in *Les Structures*), which would make it more difficult for them to adopt long cycles of reciprocity, while the extremely short cycles of patrilateral marriage would be less affected by the conflicts always found in matrilineal societies. Homans and Schneider's theoretical interpretation seems to me completely unacceptable. They explain the preference of patrilineal societies for matrilateral marriage in terms of psychological factors, such as the transference of an adolescent's emotional feelings to his maternal uncle's group. If such were the case, matrilateral marriage would be more frequent; but it would not have to be *prescribed*. With reference to a particular case, Homans and Schneider revert to the psychological theory advocated by Westermarck to explain the incest taboo; we had hoped that anthropology had outgrown its old errors. See G. C. Homans and D. M. Schneider, *Marriage, Authority, and Final Causes: A Study of Unilateral Cross-Cousin Marriage* (Glencoe: 1955).

106. See C. Lévi-Strauss, *Tristes Tropiques* (Paris: 1955), Chapter XXIX, which re-examines the themes of a previous study, "The Social and Psychological Aspects of Chieftainship in a Primitive Tribe," *Transac-*

tions of the New York Academy of Sciences, series 2, VII, No. 1 (1944).

107. A. M. Hocart, "Les Castes," *Annales du Musée Guimet, Bibliothèque de vulgarisation*, LIV (Paris: 1938); K. Davis, "Intermarriage in Caste Societies," *American Anthropologist*, XLIII (1941), pp. 376-95; C. Lévi-Strauss, *Les Structures élémentaires de la parenté*, Chapters XXIV to XXVII.

108. A. Rapoport, "Outline of Probabilistic Approach to Animal Sociology," *Bulletin of Mathematical Biophysics*, XI (1949), pp. 183-96, 273-81.

109. This qualification appears to me today (1957) to be superfluous. There are societies characterized by hierarchical and intransitive cycles and quite comparable to the pecking order—as, for instance, in the Fiji Islands, where the population was organized until the beginning of the twentieth century into fiefs which were interconnected by relations of fealty, so that fief A might be a vassal of fief B, B of C, C of D, and D of A. Hocart described and explained this structure, which at first sight seems unintelligible, by pointing out that in Fiji two forms of vassalage exist—vassalage by right and vassalage by conquest. Fief A might thus be traditionally a vassal of B, B of C, and C of D, whereas fief D might have recently become, as a result of an ill-fated war, a vassal of A. Not only is this structure the same as that of the pecking order, but—and this passed unnoticed—anthropological theory outdistanced mathematical interpretation by several years, since the latter is based on the distinction between two variables which operate with a time-lag between them—and this corresponds exactly to Hocart's (posthumous) description. See A. M. Hocart, *The Northern States of Fiji*, Occasional Publications No. 11, Royal Anthropological Institute (London: 1952).

110. For a striking example of the local transformation from one type into another, see K. Gough, "Female Initiation Rites on the Malabar Coast," *Journal of the Royal Anthropological Institute*, LXXXV (1955), pp. 47-48.

111. M. Fortes, in *Social Structure: Studies Presented to A. R. Radcliffe-Brown*.

112. Radcliffe-Brown, "Religion and Society," *op. cit.*

113. New York, 1945.

114. New York, 1951.

115. G. A. Reichard, *Navaho Religion: A Study in Symbolism*, 2 vols., Bollingen Series, No. XVIII (New York: 1950).

116. S. F. Nadel, "Witchcraft in Four African Societies: An Essay in Comparison," *American Anthropologist*, LIV, Part I (1952), pp. 18-29.

117. S. F. Nadel, "Shamanism in the Nuba Mountains," *Journal of the Royal Anthropological Institute*, LXXVI, Part I (1946), pp. 25-38.

118. G. Dumézil, *Loki* (Paris: 1948).

119. Wittfogel and Goldfrank, *op. cit.*

120. M. Hunter-Wilson, "Witch Beliefs and Social Structure," *American Journal of Sociology*, LVI, No. 4 (1951), pp. 307-13.

121. Von Neumann and Morgenstern, *op. cit.*, p. 14.

CHAPTER **XVI**

Postscript to Chapter XV

Georges Gurvitch, whom I must admit I understand less and less each time I happen to read his works,[1] attacks my analysis of the concept of social structure,[2] but his arguments amount mostly to exclamation marks tacked on to some distorted paraphrases of my text. We shall attempt, however, to get to the bottom of this disagreement.

Gurvitch offers what he believes to be a fresh discovery: "There is . . . a striking affinity between the *Gestalt* approach in psychology and *structuralism* in sociology, and, so far as we know, it has not been emphasized until now."[3] Gurvitch is mistaken. All anthropologists, sociologists, and linguists who are structure-minded are aware of the interrelations between their disciplines and Gestalt psychology. As early as 1934, Ruth Benedict drew the parallel by citing Köhler and Koffka.[4]

I myself was so determined to bring this affinity to light that I concluded the 1947 preface to *Les Structures élémentaires de la parenté* with an acknowledgment to Gestalt psychology:

Having cited Eddington—"Physics is becoming the 'study of organization'—Köhler wrote, almost twenty years ago, that "Along this road . . . it will converge with biology and psychology." My work will have served its purpose if, when the reader has finished it, he feels inclined to add—"and also sociology." [5]

In a similar vein, Kroeber in his *Anthropology* asserts that:

A system or configuration is always, in its nature, more than the mere sum of its parts; there is also the relation of the parts, their total interconnections, which add up to something additionally significant. This is well recognized in "Gestalt" or configurational psychology. The "form" of a culture may therefore be regarded as the pattern of the interrelations among its constituent parts. [6]

On a still deeper level, finally, a Norwegian sociologist, Sverre Holm, having noted also that the science of culture has long drawn its inspiration from the message of Gestalt psychology, attempts to trace structuralism back to one of the remote sources of Gestalt thinking—the natural philosophy of Goethe. [7]

As for the scholars in structural linguistics, Troubetzkoy and Jakobson have often acknowledged their indebtedness to Gestalt theory, notably to the work of K. Bühler.

However remote Gurvitch's thinking may be from mine, we occasionally happen to agree, as the following excerpt from his article indicates:

When our aim is to study types of global societies (which must be distinguished from microsociological types—that is, forms of sociability—and specific types of groups), the construction of such a typology is possible only on the basis of their structures. Actually, in contrast to specific groups (let alone astructural forms of sociability), every global society *without exception* [Gurvitch's italics] possesses a structure, and studying structure is the only means of establishing and re-creating the types of global social phenomena. We went so far as to say in *Déterminisme sociaux et liberté humaine* that global societies and global social structures coincide. This is true with respect to types of global societies, but it demands strict reservations when we speak of a concrete global society, which obviously is incomparably richer than its structure, however complex that structure may be, since it is never more than an aspect, a segment, or a partial expression of the total social phenomenon. To grasp the total social phenomenon in its entirety, we have found no solution other than to begin with a constructed type, which, in this case, can only be a specific type of the global social structure. . . .[8]

If we keep in mind that by global societies Gurvitch means those which the anthropologist makes the object of study and that his "constructed type" bears a remarkable resemblance to what I myself mean by "model," I do not understand his grounds for criticism. For I am the one who is retreating here from his position, since I am anything but inclined to believe, as Gurvitch asserts, that "global societies and social structures coincide." However, I do think that social structures can help us to understand and classify global societies.

Yet Gurvitch objects in the quoted excerpt that what is true for types ceases to be true for a concrete society. By what authority does Gurvitch appoint himself our mentor? And what in fact does he know of concrete societies? The crux of his philosophy would appear to be high regard for the concrete (involving praise of its richness, complexity, fluidity, inexpressible character, and creative spontaneity), and yet this philosopher is imbued with such pious reverence that he has never dared to undertake a description or analysis of any concrete society.

Those anthropologists who have spent many years of their lives steeped in the concrete existence of particular societies may rest at ease, since among them Gurvitch will never discover an indifference to the concrete comparable to that which he displays when he reduces the diversity and specificity of thousands of societies to four (*sic*) types; for he merges all the South American tribes with all the Australian societies, and Melanesia with Polynesia, and as far as he is concerned North America, on the one hand, and Africa, on the other, constitute but two homogeneous blocks.[9]

Because Gurvitch is a pure theoretician, he is interested only in the theoretical aspect of our work. And since he does not care for our theories, because they invalidate his own, he bids us dedicate ourselves to descriptive ethnography. From this division of roles he would derive the twofold advantage of reigning supreme over theory and providing himself with impunity the luxury of invoking pell-mell a large number of descriptive studies in support of his speculations. I might add that the arbitrary interpretation he makes of these studies shows that he does not often trouble to read them.

Without waiting for advice from Gurvitch, the anthropologists whom he attacks have dedicated the greater part of their scientific lives to observing, describing, and analyzing, often with an exhaustive thoroughness, the "forms of sociability," the "groups," and the smallest details of collective life which, together with structures, constitute the individual character, impossible to mistake for any other, of the society among which they have lived. None of us would ever think of substituting a frozen abstract type or structure for that living reality. The search for structures comes at a later stage, when, after observing what exists, we try to isolate those stable—yet always partial—elements that will make possible comparison and classification. In clear contrast to Gurvitch, we do not begin with an a priori definition of what can be structured and what cannot. We are too much aware that it is impossible to know in advance where, and at what level of observation, structural analysis can be applied. Our experience of the concrete has taught us that it is quite often the most fluid and the most transient aspects of a culture which provide access to structure. This is why we pay such intense, almost compulsive attention to details. We bear in mind the example of the natural sciences, whose progress from one structure to another (ever more comprehensive and more adequate as an explanation) always lies in discovering better methods of structuring, by means of the small facts ignored in previous hypotheses as being "astructural." Thus the anomalies in Mercury's perihelion, which were considered "astructural" according to the Newtonian system, became the basis for discovering a better structure through the theory of relativity. Anthropology, a residual science par excellence, since it has been assigned the "residue" of societies which the traditional social sciences did not deign to take into account (precisely because they considered them to be "astructural"), cannot, by definition, use any method other than that of residues.

But we know that a concrete society can never be reduced to its structure, or, rather, structures (since there are so many of them, located at different levels, and these various structures are themselves, at least partially, integrated into a structure). As I wrote in

1949, when criticizing that rudimentary version of structuralism called functionalism: "To say that a society functions is a truism; but to say that everything in a society functions is an absurdity." [10]

Gurvitch's error, like that of most opponents of anthropology —and they exist[11]—stems from the fact that he regards the goal of our discipline as the acquisition of a complete knowledge of the societies we study.[12] The disparity between such an ambition and the resources which are available to us is so great that we might be called charlatans, and with good reason. How would one penetrate the dynamics of an alien society after a stay of a few months, knowing nothing of its history and usually very little of its language? Confidence diminishes even more when some of us are prone to replace with schemes and diagrams those facts which elude us. But actually our ultimate purpose is not so much to discover the unique characteristics of the societies that we study, as it is to discover in what way these societies differ from one another. As in linguistics, it is the *discontinuities* which constitute the true subject matter of anthropology. To those who question the possibility of defining the interrelations between entities whose nature is not completely understood, I shall reply with the following comment by a great naturalist:

> In a very large part of morphology, our essential task lies in the comparison of related forms rather than in the precise definition of each; and the *deformation* of a complicated figure may be a phenomenon easy of comprehension, though the figure itself have to be left unanalyzed and undefined.[13]

But the author adds immediately, thus providing us with an answer to Gurvitch's objections:

> This process of comparison, of recognizing in one form a definite permutation or *deformation* of another, apart altogether from a precise and adequate understanding of the original "type" or standard of comparison, lies within the immediate province of mathematics, and finds its solution in the elementary use of a certain method of the mathematician. This method is the Method of Coordinates, on which is based the Theory of Transformations . . . which is part of the Theory of Groups.[14]

I shall now deal with the specific points of Gurvitch's criticism. The most important of these is directed at the role I attributed to certain mathematical methods in anthropological theory.

Gurvitch declares that I have attempted "to carry out a synthesis of all the interpretations relating social structure and mathematics," [15] and thus I have succeeded in presenting "a real breviary of the major errors committed, or even possible, with respect to the concept under discussion," by drawing "from each of the four sources of deviation or error" which he has just denounced. And Gurvitch continues: "Not only does he [Lévi-Strauss] claim them [the errors] as his own, but he—as it were—sublimates them and becomes their apologist by integrating them into his own theory of structures. . . ." [16]

Gurvitch's claim that the study in question is an attempt at synthesis indicates that he either did not read it or failed to understand what he read. The reader here may easily verify that I take the greatest care to dissociate my conceptions from those of Radcliffe-Brown and Murdock.[17] Therefore, I feel in no way affected by the objections which Gurvitch addresses to them, especially regarding the statistical method, which I have never utilized and whose dangers I have explicitly stressed, at least in connection with the way Murdock sometimes employs it.

Furthermore, and without setting myself up as a "founding father" of structural anthropology, I should like to point out that my views on social structure were already formulated in my book on kinship, which I finished writing at the beginning of 1947—that is, before, or at the same time as, the works of Fortes, Murdock, and others for whom Gurvitch would like to make me merely the commentator and apologist. I think it is worth noting that several anthropologists independently turned toward the concept of structure during the war years, when circumstances condemned some of us to a certain degree of isolation; their simultaneous recognition of structure demonstrated how indispensable the concept is in solving problems that our predecessors found insoluble. It brings to our common inquiry a claim to validity, whatever the differences which separate us in other respects.

Of what deviations and errors have I been guilty, according to Gurvitch?

They all appear to stem from the artificial relationship which I wish to impose "between the application of measurement . . . and the problem of social structure" [18]—in other words, my tendency "to relate the concept of social structure to mathematical measurement." [19] Does Gurvitch read carelessly, or too closely, always finding what he is seeking for purposes of contradiction? Far from ever asserting anything of the kind, I have often said the opposite. Let the reader refer to another section in this book:

> It is often believed that one of the main interests of the notion of structure is to permit the introduction of measurement in social anthropology. . . . However, one should keep in mind that there is no necessary connection between *measure* and *structure*. . . . It has become possible . . . to develop a rigorous approach to problems which do not admit of a metrical solution.[20]

And in another article, to which Gurvitch does not hesitate to refer in support of his allegations, I wrote:

> There are, no doubt, many things in our fields of study which can be . . . measured; but it is by no means certain that they are the most important things. . . . It was found that the quantification of [social] phenomena was not by any means in step with the discovery of their signification. . . .

Had we been concerned exclusively with measurement, we should not have added in that same statement that "the new school of mathematics" introduces "a rigorous treatment [which] no longer means recourse to measurement. . . . This new mathematics . . . teaches us that the domain of necessity is not necessarily the same as that of quantity." [21]

The use Gurvitch makes of the terms *measure, measurement,* and *quantification* (all of which, incidentally, he employs interchangeably) makes us doubt that he has any idea of the problems on which we are working. After all, the use of certain mathematical methods in anthropology is not a topic for academic discussion. With the collaboration of a mathematician, I have applied these methods to a specific problem;[22] with other mathematicians, I am continuing to apply them to other problems. The only question which may justifiably be raised is whether or not problems are brought nearer to their solution by these means.

Although more respectful of structural linguistics than he is of structural anthropology, Gurvitch also endeavors to restrict its theoretical scope. But, contrary to what he believes, mathematical statistics (whose role in linguistic analysis is quite legitimate) is by no means limited to the distributional study of phonemes. It can be applied to grammar and discourse, as the theory of machine translation—now being elaborated—shows, and its importance has already been demonstrated in the field of stylistics and philology. When Gurvitch argues that structuralism has its place only in phonemics and that it loses all meaning at the level of language in general, he is overlooking the structuralist contributions with respect to grammar, syntax, and even vocabulary, in the rich and variegated forms given to them by Benveniste, Hjelmslev, and especially Jakobson, who in a recent work attacks the problem of figures of speech, which is far removed from phonemics.[23] In addition, the theoreticians of machine translation are in the process of laying the foundations of grammatical and lexical analysis, which belongs both to mathematics and to structuralism.[24]

Gurvitch censures me for "regrettable confusion . . . between what is called structure and the externally perceptible and palpable surface of social reality, located in stretches conceptualized as morphological spaces."[25] The reader may not immediately grasp (and he is readily excused) that what is being attacked here are the phenomena of spatial distribution and the qualitative representation of space as exemplified in many societies. This "regrettable confusion," however, far from being a product of the American school, as the author would have it, is one of the principal discoveries of the French sociological school, to which we are indebted for far more than "allusions . . . rapidly superseded."[26] This is the central point of the memorable studies *De quelques Formes primitives de classification*, by Durkheim and Mauss, and *Les Variations saisonnières dans les sociétés eskimos*, by Mauss.[27] In France we need only read Jacques Soustelle's *La Pensée cosmologique des anciens Mexicains*,[28] to be convinced that, almost a half-century later, this method retains its entire validity.

But no one, either in France or in the United States, has ever believed, as Gurvitch says I claim, that this level should be isolated from others and that spatial structure and social structure are identical. Let me make two observations on this:

(1) A large number of native societies have consciously chosen to project into space a schema of their institutions: thus, for instance, the circular distribution of Sioux camping sites and Ge villages in central Brazil; or the layout of towns, the network of

roads, and the location of temples and shrines in ancient Peru. Study of these spatial phenomena permits us to grasp the natives' own conception of their social structure; and, through our examination of the gaps and contradictions, the real structure, which is often very different from the natives' conception, becomes accessible. (Chapter VIII of this book presents an illustration of this method.)

(2) Even when a society is indifferent to space or to a certain type of space (for instance, in our society, urban space when it has not been the object of planning), what happens is that unconscious structures seem to take advantage, as it were, of the indifference in order to invade the vacant area and assert themselves, symbolically or in actual fact, somewhat after the fashion of unconscious preoccupations, which, according to Freud, utilize the "emptiness" of sleep to find expression in the form of dreams. This second observation applies both to those so-called primitive societies which appear to be indifferent to spatial expression and to more complex societies which profess the same attitude: Thus, most modern cities present spatial structures which can be reduced to a few types and which provide certain indexes of the underlying social structure.

By now it should hardly be necessary to comment on Gurvitch's opinion that in my work "there is nothing of a *sui generis* reality, of 'total social phenomena,' of macrosociological collective units." [29] I have spent the best part of my life studying "macrosociological collective units." But in discussing them I see no reason to use such an unwieldy term, which is as unattractive as it is overabstract. For my memory calls them by their names—Caduveo, Bororo, Nambicuara, Mundé, Tupi-Cawahib, Mogh, and Kuki; and each name reminds me of a place on earth and a moment of my history and that of the world. All of these names are associated with men and women of whom I have been fond, whom I have respected, whose faces remain in my memory. They remind me of joys, hardships, weariness, and, sometimes, dangers. These are my witnesses, the living link between my theoretical views and reality.

Finally, as to Gurvitch's censuring me for regressing, "in a thinly veiled fashion, after so much effort, to the traditional conception of the social order," [30] I shall take it up here only because other writers too have seemed confused by the concept of *order of orders* introduced at the end of my article on social structure.[31]

According to my critics, the *order of orders* as I conceive it consists either in a total reconstruction of the concrete society I would first attempt to break down into structures (which would make the breaking-down endeavor useless) or in the assertion that, for a given society, all structures are homologous—which would really be saying that each society constitutes a kind of monad, at the same time perfectly coherent and hermetically sealed. Neither of these interpretations could be more remote from my position.

The *order of orders* is not a mere logical reformulation of phenomena which have been subjected to analysis. It is the most abstract expression of the interrelationships between the levels to which structural analysis can be applied, general enough to account for the fact that the models must sometimes be the same for societies which are historically and geographically disparate. This is a little as though—if I may be allowed this comparison—molecules of different chemical composition, some of them simple, others complex, could nevertheless all be said to have a "right-hand" structure or a "left-hand" structure. By *order of orders*, then, I mean the formal properties of the whole made up of subwholes, each of which corresponds to a given structural level.

Thus, I fully agree with Jean Pouillon's interpretation of my position when he describes it as trying to elaborate "a system of differences which leads neither to their mere juxtaposition nor to their artificial obliteration." [32]

I do not postulate a kind of pre-existent harmony between the different levels of structure. They may be—and often are—completely contradictory, but the modes of contradiction all belong to the same type. Indeed, according to dialectic materialism it should always be possible to proceed, by transformation, from economic or social structure to the structure of law, art, or religion. But Marx never claimed that there was only one type of transformation—for example, that ideology was simply a "mirror image" of social relations. In his view, these transformations were dialectic, and in some cases he went to great lengths to discover the crucial transformation which at first sight seemed to defy analysis. [33]

If we grant, following Marxian thought, that infrastructures and superstructures are made up of multiple levels and that there are various types of transformations from one level to another, it becomes possible—in the final analysis, and on the condition that we disregard content—to characterize different types of societies in terms of the types of transformations which occur within them. These types of transformations amount to formulas showing the number, magnitude, direction, and order of the convolutions that must be unraveled, so to speak, in order to uncover (logically, not normatively) an ideal homologous relationship between the different structural levels.

Now, this reduction to an ideal homologous relationship is at the same time a critique. By replacing a complex model with a simple model that has greater logical value, the anthropologist reveals the detours and maneuvers, conscious and unconscious, that each society uses in an effort to resolve its inherent contradictions —or at any rate to conceal them.

This clarification, already furnished by my previous studies,[34] which Gurvitch should have taken into consideration, may expose me to still another criticism. If every society has the same flaw, manifested by the twofold problem of logical disharmony and social inequality, why should its more thoughtful members endeavor to change it? Change would mean only the replacement of one social form by another; and if one is no better than the other, why bother?

In support of this argument, Rodinson cites a passage from *Tristes Tropiques:* "No human society is fundamentally good, but neither is any of them fundamentally bad; all offer their members certain advantages, though we must bear in mind a residue of iniquity, apparently more or less constant in its importance. . . ."[35] But here Rodinson isolates, in biased fashion, one step in a reasoning process by which I tried to resolve the apparent conflict between thought and action. Actually:

(1) In the passage criticized by Rodinson, the relativistic argument serves only to oppose any attempt at classifying, *in relation to one another*, societies remote from that of the observer—for instance, from our point of view, a Melanesian group and a North American tribe. I hold that we have no conceptual framework available that can be legitimately applied to societies located at opposite poles of the sociological world and considered in their mutual relationships.

(2) On the other hand, I carefully distinguished this first case from a very different one, which would consist in comparing,

not remote societies, but two historically related stages in the development of our own society—or, to generalize, of the observer's society. When the frame of reference is thus "internalized," everything changes. This second phase permits us, without retaining anything from any particular society,

> . . . to make use of one and all of them in order to distinguish those principles of social life which may be applied to the reform of our own customs, and not of those of societies foreign to our own. That is to say, in relation to our own society we stand in a position of privilege which is exactly contrary to that which I have just described; for our own society is the only one that we can transform and yet not destroy, since the changes we should introduce would come from within.[36]

Far from being satisfied, then, with a static relativism—as are certain American anthropologists justly criticized by Rodinson (but with whom he wrongly identifies me)—I denounce it as a danger ever present on the anthropologist's path. My solution is constructive, since it derives from the same principles two apparently contradictory attitudes, namely, respect for societies very different from ours, and active participation in the transformation of our own society.

Is there any reason here, as Rodinson claims, "to reduce Billancourt[37] to desperation"? Billancourt would deserve little consideration if, cannibalistic in its own way (and more seriously so than primitive man-eaters, for its cannibalism would be *spiritual*), it should feel it necessary to its intellectual and moral security that the Papuans become nothing but proletarians. Fortunately, anthropological theory does not play such an important role in trade-union demands. On the other hand, I am surprised that a scientist with advanced ideas should present an argument already formulated by thinkers of an entirely different orientation.

Neither in *Race and History* nor in *Tristes Tropiques* did I intend to disparage the idea of progress; rather, I should like to see progress transferred from the rank of a universal category of human development to that of a particular mode of existence, characteristic of our own society—and perhaps of several others—whenever that society reaches the stage of self-awareness.

To say that this concept of progress—progress considered as

an internal property of a given society and devoid of a transcendent meaning outside it—would lead men to discouragement seems to me to be a transposition in the historical idiom and on the level of collective life, of the familiar argument that all morality would be jeopardized if the individual ceased to believe in the immortality of his soul. For centuries this argument, so much like Rodinson's, was raised to oppose atheism. Atheism would "reduce men to desperation"—most particularly the working classes, who, it was feared, would lose their motivation for work if there were no punishments or rewards promised in the hereafter.

Nevertheless, there are many men (especially in Billancourt) who accept the idea of a personal existence confined to the duration of their earthly life; they have not for this reason abandoned their sense of morality or their willingness to work for the improvement of their lot and that of their descendants.

Is what is true of individuals less true of groups? A society can live, act, and be transformed, and still avoid becoming intoxicated with the conviction that all the societies which preceded it during tens of millenniums did nothing more than prepare the ground for *its* advent, that all its contemporaries—even those at the antipodes—are diligently striving to overtake it, and that the societies which will succeed it until the end of time ought to be mainly concerned with following in its path. This attitude is as naïve as maintaining that the earth occupies the center of the universe and that man is the summit of creation. When it is professed today in support of our particular society, it is odious.

What is more, Rodinson attacks me in the name of Marxism, whereas my conception is infinitely closer to Marx's position than his. I wish to point out, first, that the distinctions developed in *Race and History* among stationary history, fluctuating history, and cumulative history can be derived from Marx himself:

> The simplicity of the organization for production in those self-sufficing communities that constantly reproduce themselves in the same form and, when accidentally destroyed, spring up again on the spot and with the same name—this simplicity supplies the key to the secret of the unchangeableness of Asiatic *societies*, an unchangeableness in such striking contrast with the constant dissolution and refounding of Asiatic *states*, and the never-ceasing changes of dynasty.[38]

Actually, Marx and Engels frequently express the idea that primitive, or allegedly primitive, societies are governed by "blood ties" (which, today, we call kinship systems) and not by economic relationships. If these societies were not destroyed from without, they might endure indefinitely. The temporal category applicable to them has nothing to do with the one we employ to understand the development of our own society.[39]

Nor does this conception contradict in the least the famous dictum of the *Communist Manifesto* that "the history of all hitherto existing society is the history of class struggles." In the light of Hegel's philosophy of the State, this dictum does not mean that the class struggle is co-extensive with humanity, but that the ideas of history and society can be applied, in the full sense which Marx gives them, only from the time when the class struggle first appeared. The letter to Weydemeyer clearly supports this: "What I did that was new," Marx wrote, "was prove . . . that the *existence of classes* is only bound up with *particular historical phases in the development of production. . . .*"[40]

Rodinson should, therefore, ponder the following comment by Marx in his posthumously published introduction to *A Contribution to the Critique of Political Economy*:

> The so-called historical development amounts in the last analysis to this, that the last form considers its predecessors as stages leading up to itself and perceives them always one-sidedly, since it is very seldom and only under certain conditions that it is capable of self-criticism. . . .[41]

This chapter had already been written when Jean-François Revel published his lively, provocative, but often unfair study.[42] Since part of his chapter VIII concerns my work, I shall briefly reply.

Revel criticizes me, but not without misgivings. If he recognized me for what I am—an anthropologist who has conducted field work and who, having presented his findings, has re-examined the theoretical principles of his discipline on the basis of these specific findings and the findings of his colleagues—Revel would, according to his own principles, refrain from discussing my work. But he begins by changing me into a sociologist, after which he insinuates that, because of my philosophical training, my sociology is nothing but disguised philosophy. From then on we are among colleagues, and Revel can freely tread on my reserves, without realizing that he is behaving toward anthropology exactly as, throughout his book, he upbraids philosophers for behaving toward the other empirical sciences.

But I am not a sociologist, and my interest in our own society is only a secondary one. Those societies which I seek first to understand are the so-called primitive societies with which anthropologists are concerned. When, to Revel's great displeasure, I interpret the exchange of wine in the restaurants of southern France in terms of social prestations, my primary aim is not to explain contemporary customs by means of archaic institutions but to help the reader, a member of a contemporary society, to rediscover, in his own experience and on the basis of either vestigial or embryonic practices, institutions that would otherwise remain unintelligible to him. The question, then, is not whether the exchange of wine is a survival of the *potlatch*, but whether, by means of this comparison, we succeed better in grasping the feelings, intentions, and attitudes of the native involved in a cycle of prestations. The ethnographer who has lived among natives and has experienced such ceremonies, as either a spectator or a participant, is entitled to an opinion on this question; Revel is not.

Moreover, by a curious contradiction, Revel refuses to admit that the categories of primitive societies may be applied to our own society, although he insists upon applying our categories to primitive societies. "It is absolutely certain," he says, that prestations "in which the goods of a society are finally used up . . . correspond to the specific conditions of a mode of production and a social structure." And he further declares that "it is even probable —barring an exception unique in history, which would then have to be explained—that prestations mask the economic exploitation of certain members of each society of this type by others." [43]

How can Revel be "absolutely certain"? And how does he know that the exception would be "unique in history"? Has he studied Melanesian and Amerindian institutions in the field? Has he so much as analyzed the numerous works dealing with the *kula* and its evolution from 1910 to 1950, or with the *potlatch* from the beginning of the nineteenth century until the twentieth? If he had, he would know, first of all, that it is absurd to think that all the goods of a society are used up in these exchanges. And he would have more precise ideas of the proportions and the kinds of goods involved in certain cases and in certain periods. Finally, and above all, he would be aware that, from the particular viewpoint that interests him—namely, the economic exploitation of man by man —the two culture areas to which he refers cannot be compared. In one of them, this exploitation presents characteristics which we might at best call pre-capitalistic. Even in Alaska and British Columbia, however, this exploitation is an external factor: It acts only to give greater scope to institutions which can exist without it, and whose general character must be defined in other terms.

Should Revel hasten to protest, let me add that I am only paraphrasing Engels, who by chance expressed his opinion on this problem, and with respect to the same societies which Revel has in mind. Engels wrote:

> In order finally to get clear about the parallel between the Germans of Tacitus and the American Redskins I have made some gentle extractions from the first volume of your Bancroft [*The Native Races of the Pacific States*, etc.]. The similarity is indeed all the more surprising because the method of production is so fundamentally different—here hunters and fishers without cattle-raising or agriculture, there nomadic cattle-raising passing into agriculture. It just proves how at this stage the type of production is less decisive than the degree in which the old blood bonds and the old mutual community of the sexes within the tribe have been dissolved. Otherwise the Tlingit in the former Russian America could not be the exact counterpart of the Germanic tribes. . . .[44]

It remained for Marcel Mauss, in *Essai sur le Don* (which Revel criticizes quite inappropriately) to justify and develop Engels' hypothesis that there is a striking parallelism between certain Germanic and Celtic institutions and those of societies having the *potlatch*.[45] He did this with no concern about uncovering the "specific conditions of a mode of production," which, as Engels had already understood, would be useless. But then Marx and Engels knew incomparably more anthropology almost a hundred years ago than Revel knows today.

I am, on the other hand, in full agreement with Revel when he writes, "Perhaps the most serious defect which philosophy has transmitted to sociology is . . . the obsession with creating in one stroke holistic explanations." [46] He has here laid down his own indictment. He rebukes me because I have not proposed explanations and because I have acted as if I believed "that there is fundamentally no reason why one society adopts one set of institutions and another society other institutions." He requires anthropologists to answer questions such as: "Why are societies structured along different lines? Why does each structure evolve? . . . *Why are there differences* [Revel's italics] between institutions and between societies, and what responses to what conditions do these differences imply . . . ?" [47] These questions are highly pertinent, and we should like to be able to answer them. In our present state of knowledge, however, we are in a position to provide answers only for specific and limited cases, and even here our interpretations remain fragmentary and isolated. Revel can believe that the task is easy, since for him "it is absolutely certain" that ever since the social evolution of man began, approximately 500,000 years ago, economic exploitation can explain everything.

As we noted, this was not the opinion of Marx and Engels. According to their view, in the non- or pre-capitalistic societies kinship ties played a more important role than class relations. I do not believe that I am being unfaithful to their teachings by trying, seventy years after Lewis H. Morgan, whom they admired so greatly, to resume Morgan's endeavor— that is, to work out a new typology of kinship systems in the light of knowledge acquired in the field since then, by myself and others.[48]

I ask to be judged on the basis of this typology, and not on that of the psychological or sociological hypotheses which Revel seizes upon; these hypotheses are only a kind of mental scaffolding, momentarily useful to the anthropologist as a means of organizing his observations, building his classifications, and arranging his types in some sort of order. If one of my colleagues were to come to me and say that my theoretical analysis of Murngin or Gilyak kinship systems was inconsistent with his observations, or that while I was in the field I misinterpreted chieftainship among the Nambicuara, the place of art in Caduveo society, the social structure of the Bororo, or the nature of clans among the Tupi-Cawahib, I should listen to him with deference and attention. But Revel, who could not care less about patrilineal descent, bilateral marriage, dual organization, or dysharmonic systems, attacks me—

without even understanding that I seek only to describe and analyze certain aspects of the objective world—for "flattening out social reality." For him everything is flat that cannot be instantaneously expressed in a language which he may perhaps use correctly in reference to Western civilization, but to which its inventors explicitly denied any other application. Now it is my turn to exclaim: Indeed, "what is the use of philosophers?"

Reasoning in the fashion of Revel and Rodinson would mean surrendering the social sciences to obscurantism. What would we think of building contractors and architects who condemned cosmic physics in the name of the law of gravity and under the argument that a geometry based on curved spaces would render obsolete the traditional techniques for demolishing or building houses? The house-wrecker and the architect are right to believe only in Euclidean geometry, but they do not try to force it upon the astronomer. And if the help of the astronomer is required in remodeling his house, the categories he uses to understand the universe do not automatically prevent him from handling the pick-ax and plumb-line.

NOTES

1. Yet I tried to read his works some years ago, and not without sympathy. See C. Lévi-Strauss, "French Sociology," in G. Gurvitch and W. E. Moore (eds.), *Twentieth Century Sociology* (New York: 1945), Chapter XVII.
2. G. Gurvitch, "Le Concept de structure sociale," *Cahiers internationaux de Sociologie*, XIX, n.s. (1955). It seems that Gurvitch republished the same essay, with some modifications, in the second edition of *Vocation actuelle de la Sociologie* (Paris: 1957). This present chapter, which I wrote in 1956, refers to Gurvitch's initial text.
3. Gurvitch, "Le Concept de structure sociale," *op. cit.*, p. 11.
4. Ruth Benedict, *Patterns of Culture* (Boston: 1934), pp. 51-2 and 279. Gurvitch more recently made another "discovery" which he was "eager to communicate to the readers of the *Cahiers* as an addendum to . . . [his] study on the concept of social structure": namely, that Spencer is "a forgotten source of the concepts of 'social structure,' 'social function,' and 'institution'" (*Cahiers internationaux de Sociologie*, XXIII [1957], pp. 111-21). However, we fail to see who—besides Gurvitch himself—has "forgotten" Spencer and the paternity which must be attributed to him for these concepts; certainly not, in any case, the contemporary exponents of the concept of structure, who have never lacked memory to this extent. See D. Bidney, *Theoretical Anthropology*

(New York: 1953), Chapters II and IV; and, for England, E. E. Evans-Pritchard, *Social Anthropology* (Glencoe, Ill.: 1951), p. 17, and, especially, A. R. Radcliffe-Brown's introduction to his collection of essays, *Structure and Function in Primitive Society* (Glencoe, Ill.: 1952), in which he comments, after referring several times to Spencer: "[My] . . . theory can be stated by means of the three fundamental and connected concepts of 'process,' 'structure,' and 'function.' It is derived from such earlier writers as Montesquieu, Comte, Spencer, Durkheim and thus belongs to a cultural tradition of two hundred years" (p. 14).

5. C. Lévi-Strauss, *Structures élémentaires de la parenté* (Paris: 1949), p. xiv.

6. A. L. Kroeber, *Anthropology* (New York: 1948), p. 293.

7. Sverre Holm, "Studies towards a Theory of Sociological Transformations," *Studia Norvegica*, No. 7 (Oslo: 1951), p. 40 and *passim*.

8. Gurvitch, "Le Concept de structure sociale," *op. cit.*, pp. 11-2.

9. Gurvitch, *Déterminismes sociaux et liberté humaine* (Paris: 1955), pp. 200-22.

10. See page 13, above.

11. See Brice Parain, "Les Sorciers," *Le Monde nouveau* (May, 1956).

12. This I gather from the terminology used by Gurvitch, who also misinterprets the views of Mauss, to whom we are indebted for the expression: "to apprehend the total social phenomenon."

13. D'Arcy Wentworth Thompson, *On Growth and Form* (Cambridge, Mass.: 1942), II, 1032.

14. *Loc. cit.* and footnote.

15. Gurvitch, "Le Concept de Structure sociale," *op. cit.*, pp. 14-5.

16. *Ibid.*, p. 19.

17. See pp. 287-8, 303-7, and 313 of the present volume.

18. Gurvitch, "Le Concept de structure sociale," *op. cit.*, p. 14.

19. *Ibid.*, p. 17; reiterated in the same terms, p. 19.

20. See pp. 282-3 of this book.

21. C. Lévi-Strauss, "The Mathematics of Man," in *International Social Science Bulletin*, VI, No. 4 (Paris: UNESCO, 1954), p. 585.

22. Lévi-Strauss, *Les Structures* . . . , Chapter XIV.

23. R. Jakobson and M. Halle, *Fundamentals of Language* (The Hague: 1956).

24. V. H. Yngve, "Syntax and the Problem of Multiple Meaning," in W. N. Locke and A. D. Booth (eds.), *Machine Translation of Languages* (New York: 1955); "Sentence for Sentence Translation," *Mechanical Translation*, II, No. 2 (Cambridge, Mass.: 1955); "The Translation of Languages by Machine," *Information Theory, Third London Symposium*, n.d.

25. Gurvitch, "Le Concept . . . ," *op. cit.*, p. 17.

26. *Loc. cit.*

27. *Année sociologique*, respectively VI (1901-1902) and IX (1904-1905).

28. Paris, 1940.

29. Gurvitch, "Le Concept . . . ," *op. cit.*, p. 19.

30. *Ibid.*, p. 21.

31. See page 312, above. I am thinking especially of Maxime Rodinson, in his two articles "Racisme et civilisation," *La Nouvelle Critique*, No. 66

(June, 1955), and "Ethnographie et relativisme," *La Nouvelle Critique,* No. 69 (November, 1955). When the editors of *La Nouvelle Critique* published Rodinson's second article, they assured me in several letters that they "would welcome" my comments. I replied, therefore, with the following letter.

November 25, 1955

To the Editor-in-Chief:

For the second time in several months, Maxime Rodinson has published in *La Nouvelle Critique* an article which is in large part dedicated to me. While the author appears to be more concerned with widening the gap between us than with stressing the points of convergence, I shall disappoint him perhaps by saying that his articles seemed to me vigorous and well-thought-out, and that, on the whole, I agree with him. I regret, however, since so much attention was paid to me, that he did not think it profitable to inquire into my endeavors to reintegrate the anthropological knowledge acquired during the last fifty years into the Marxian tradition. Apparently Mr. Rodinson decided to reject this new knowledge *in toto.* But should we not distinguish scientific findings, strictly speaking, from the political and ideological uses to which they are put, all too frequently, in the United States and elsewhere? Mr. Rodinson's attitude certainly corresponds to that of an orthodoxy which has asserted itself boisterously with respect to linguistics, physics, biology, and cybernetics. All this has changed lately, and Mr. Rodinson will doubtless find out shortly that he is behind the times. I wish to point out, furthermore, that in regard to a question which in certain aspects resembles the one which he discusses—namely the present trends of quantum mechanics—*La Nouvelle Critique* exhibits, in its last issue, an infinitely more cautious and moderate attitude, which could be usefully transferred to the theoretical problems of anthropology.

Mr. Rodinson criticizes me for misinterpreting the concept of structure, which I have borrowed, or so I thought, from Marx and Engels, among others, and to which I attribute a primary role—this constituting a more frequent ground for criticism addressed to me. In regard to Mr. Rodinson's critique of the concept of culture, or, rather, of certain of its connotations, I agree with him. The merits of Kroeber, which I have explicitly recognized, reside in other works (especially the admirable *Handbook of the Indians of California*), rather than in that unfortunate attempt at cultural statistics which Mr. Rodinson subjects to a fundamentally just critique—but which is really beside the point. An apparently fruitless undertaking all the same presented a certain amount of interest within the very special and in many respects privileged geographic framework offered by California. The diversity and ethnographic density of California were so accentuated that one was tempted to find out whether, despite a classification of culture traits made in a systematically mechanical and avowedly unintelligent fashion, the significant elements might not emerge spontaneously. This endeavor has been taken up in psychology by L. Guttman since then, with positive results.

Finally, Mr. Rodinson advises me to adopt the concept of society in lieu of the concept of culture. Without rejecting the latter, I have not waited for him to attempt embodying both concepts within a perspective compatible with Marxian principles. If he had read my book, instead of confining himself to the extracts published a few months ago, he would have discovered—in addition to a Marxian hypothesis on the origins of writing—two studies dedicated to Brazilian tribes (the Caduveo and the Bororo), which are efforts to interpret native superstructures based upon dialectic materialism. The novelty of this approach in the Western anthropological literature perhaps deserves more attention and sympathy.

Among contemporary critics Mr. Rodinson is certainly not the only one who finds it natural to refute an author on the basis of a few fragments. The other liberties which he takes are less common, particularly that of using false quotations. This is indeed what Mr. Rodinson does in his second article (page 61), by putting into italics and quotation marks three lines which he attributes to me—the reference to which he gives in a footnote (*Race and History*, page 40). The "quoted" lines do not appear there and I do not recall ever having written them.

Sincerely yours,

La Nouvelle Critique rectified the erroneous quotation in its next issue. As for my letter, it was never published.

32. Jean Pouillon, "L'Oeuvre de Claude Lévi-Strauss," *Les Temps Modernes*, XII, No. 126 (July, 1956), p. 155.

33. For instance, in the famous passage on Greek art in the posthumously published introduction to *A Contribution to the Critique of Political Economy;* and also, from another viewpoint, in the *Eighteenth Brumaire of Louis Bonaparte*.

34. See Chapters I and VII in this book.

35. Claude Lévi-Strauss, *Tristes Tropiques* (Paris: 1955), p. 417 (English trans., New York: 1961, p. 385). Cited by Rodinson, *op. cit.*, pp. 50-2, and *passim*.

36. *Tristes Tropiques*, p. 424 (English trans., pp. 391-92).

[37. *Translator's note:* The author uses the term *Billancourt* to stand for working-class ideology. Billancourt is the name of a Seine district, the largest industrial complex of the Paris region, where the Renault automobile works are located. Its workers are organized into one of the most powerful trade unions in France.]

38. K. Marx, *Capital* (New York: 1906), pp. 393-4. [The italics are the present author's.]

39. These themes recur constantly in *Capital* with respect to India and the ancient Germanic societies, which were at that time the most "primitive" societies Marx knew. Engels generalized these themes in *Anti-Dühring* and *The Origin of the Family, Private Property and the State*.

40. Letter to Weydemeyer, March 5, 1852, in K. Marx and F. Engels, *Selected Correspondence, 1846-1895* (New York: 1942), p. 57.

41. K. Marx, *A Contribution to the Critique of Political Economy*, trans. N. I. Stone (Chicago: 1904), p. 301.
42. J. F. Revel, *Pourquoi des philosophes?* (Paris: 1957).
43. *Ibid.*, p. 138.
44. Letter to Marx, December 8, 1882, in Marx and Engels, *op. cit.*, pp. 405-6.
45. *Année sociologique*, n.s., I (1923-1924). English trans., I. Cunnison, *The Gift* (Glencoe, Ill.: 1954).
46. Revel, *op. cit.*, p. 147.
47. *Ibid.*, p. 141.
48. In the history of Marxism, Revel's deviation, which is also Rodinson's, is not new. It can be traced back to Kautsky, and as early as 1883 Engels was forced to denounce it. Like Revel and Rodinson afterward, Kautsky also wanted to interpret primitive societies in terms of historical materialism, by employing exclusively economic concepts, such as *barbarism,* which was defined by Engels, following Lewis H. Morgan, as "the period during which man learns to breed domestic animals and to practice agriculture, and acquires methods of increasing the supply of natural products by human agency" (*The Origin of the Family, Private Property and the State* [London: 1940], p. 25). Engels replied to Kautsky as follows: "It is not barbarism that establishes the primitive character of a society, but, rather, the degree of integrity of the old blood ties in the tribe. It is these blood ties which must be demonstrated in each particular instance, before drawing conclusions for this and that tribe from isolated phenomena" (letter to Kautsky, February 10, 1883, cited in M. Rubel, *Karl Marx, Essai de biographie intellectuelle* [Paris: 1957], pp. 301-2). What have I done in *Structures élémentaires*, if not to demonstrate, "in each particular instance," the nature of the "blood ties," "for this and that tribe"?

CHAPTER XVII

The Place of Anthropology in the Social Sciences and Problems Raised in Teaching It

THE PURPOSE OF THIS STUDY

THE PRESENT organization of anthropological studies is, in a way, a challenge to the authors of this volume.[1] Logically they ought to have provided a general report on the teaching of social anthropology, since the name of that discipline places it among the social sciences and it appears to have a separate content. But difficulties at once arise; where, save in Great Britain, do we find "social anthropology" taught as a separate, organic discipline in an autonomous department? All the other countries (and certain establishments in Great Britain itself) speak of anthropology pure and simple, or of cultural anthropology, or again of ethnology, ethnography, folklore, etc. These names certainly cover social anthropology (or the subjects grouped under it elsewhere), but they cover many other things at the same time— and is it possible to regard technology, prehistory, archaeology, certain aspects of linguistics, or physical anthropology, as social sciences? We seem to be departing from the problem in the very act of approaching it.

But the position is even more complicated. Social anthropology tends to be present in a vast series of studies which have no evident association with the social sciences; yet, by a singular paradox, these studies are frequently connected with the social sciences in another way: Many universities, particularly in the United States, have departments of "anthropology and sociology," "anthropology and social sciences," or similar titles. Just when we think we have grasped the connection between anthropology and social science, it evades us; and it is scarcely lost before we find it again on a new plane.

It is as though social and cultural anthropology, far from appearing on the scene of scientific development as an independent subject claiming a place among the other disciplines, had taken shape somewhat in the manner of a nebula, gradually incorporating a substance previously diffused or distributed in another way and, by this concentration, bringing about a general redistribution of research subjects among the humanistic and social sciences.

It is important to realize, from the outset, that anthropology is not distinguished from other humanistic and social sciences by any subject of study peculiar to it alone. At first, indeed, it was concerned with so-called savage or primitive societies, and we shall later investigate the reasons for this. But this interest is increasingly shared by other disciplines, especially demography, social psychology, political science, and law. On the other hand, we have the strange phenomenon that anthropology develops as those societies tend to disappear, or at least to lose their distinctive features—it is no longer entirely bound up with stone axes, totemism, and polygamy! This has been well exemplified in the last few years, during which anthropologists have turned to the study of so-called civilized societies. What then, in fact, *is* anthropology? For the time being we shall merely say that it proceeds from a particular conception of the world or from an original way of approaching problems, both discovered *during* the study of social phenomena which are not necessarily simpler (as people often tend to think) than those appearing in the observer's own society, but which are so remote from them that they throw into relief certain *general features* of social life which anthropology makes it its business to study.

This conclusion may be reached in different ways. In some

cases it is the outcome of ethnographical research; in others, of linguistic analysis; in yet others, of attempts to interpret the findings of archaeological excavations. Anthropology is too young a science for its teaching not to reflect the local and historical circumstances that are at the root of each particular development. One university may thus combine cultural anthropology and linguistics in a single department, because linguistic studies there early assumed an anthropological character; another may arrange matters differently, but for the same kind of reason.

In these circumstances, the present authors might well wonder whether it was possible, or even desirable, artificially to "systematize" different situations, each of which justifies a separate explanation. A general report on the teaching of anthropology would be bound either to distort facts by placing them in arbitrary frameworks or to be reduced to historical surveys which would differ for each country and often even for each university. Since anthropology is a growing science whose independence is not yet universally recognized, it has seemed necessary to proceed by another method. A statement of facts must be based on the *de facto* situation; and since social anthropology, in the great majority of cases, is allied to other disciplines, and the social science in whose company it is most frequently found is sociology, both have finally been linked together in the same general report. This however is only a temporary arrangement, resulting not from a considered plan but from chance and improvisation. It is not, therefore, enough to define the general terrain in which the teaching of anthropology is now emerging; we must also try to discover its present trend, and the main lines of an evolution which is unfolding in various places. The general report on the teaching of sociology and anthropology meets the first requirement; the present work meets the second.

A GLANCE AT THE SITUATION TODAY

From the facts contained in the general report, certain conclusions emerge. Irrespective of local variations and idiosyncrasies, three main methods of teaching anthropology can be distinguished. It is taught either by means of isolated chairs (of which there may be only one in the university in question or, alternatively, several attached to various faculties or establishments); or by departments (which may be purely anthropological or may combine anthropology with other disciplines); or, again, by institutes or schools which are of an inter- or extra-faculty nature, i.e., which regroup subjects taught under other titles in the various faculties, or organize instruction in the subjects proper to them (both of these systems may, moreover, be combined).

Isolated Chairs of Anthropology.   This method is very widespread, but never seems to be adopted deliberately. A country or university which decides to start teaching anthropology usually begins by founding a chair and goes no further if developments are hindered by a lack of students or a lack of openings for them (the latter generally explains the former). If the position is more favorable, other chairs are added to the first and the whole tends to form an institute or department. This trend is very apparent in the United States, where a survey of the range of teaching establishments, from the smallest to the largest, reveals all stages of development—from a single anthropology course taught by the teacher of an adjacent discipline to a department of anthropology containing a team of teachers and conferring a Ph.D. Between these two extremes may be found a single chair attached to another department, a mixed department, or, finally, a department of anthropology that does not take the student beyond his B.A. or M.A. But the formation of a complete department is always the object aimed at.

Another type of development can also lead to isolated chairs —as when we have chairs which, originally founded in a discipline far removed from anthropology, are brought back toward it by a process of academic evolution that was unforeseeable at the time of their foundation. France presents two striking examples. The École Nationale des Langues Orientales Vivantes (National School of Modern Oriental Languages) was started at a period when it was thought that the study of all the world's languages would develop along lines similar to those of classical philology; but experience has shown that a knowledge of certain unwritten languages can be acquired only by unorthodox methods, much more dependent on anthropology than on traditional linguistics. Similarly, at the École Pratique des Hautes Études (Practical School of Higher

Studies), the chairs devoted to religions of peoples with little or no written traditions tend to diverge, in trend, from the others and to assume an increasingly anthropological character. In cases of this kind, anthropology, if one may so put it, "contaminates" other disciplines sporadically and faces the administration and the educator with unforeseen problems that are very difficult to solve within the framework of traditional groupings.

Finally, we must cite the case of a mixed department, well illustrated in Great Britain. At the time when oriental studies were becoming increasingly tinged with anthropology, the rapid development of African studies showed the need for introducing philological, historical, and archaeological considerations into this field. An opportunity for regrouping was thus opened up and was sanctioned some years ago by the conversion of the School of Oriental Studies into the School of Oriental and African Studies, where anthropology became closely associated both with the social sciences and with humanistic studies—an arrangement that would not have been possible, for studies bearing on those particular regions of the world, under any conventional academic structure.

Departments. In theory, the departmental system may seem ideal. American universities, as we have just seen, are tending toward it; and in other countries where anthropological studies are in full development—like Great Britain, Australia, and India—departments of anthropology are being founded and are increasing in number. In fact, a department of anthropology meets two requirements—well-coordinated courses suited to the different sections or aspects of research, and gradual preparation for diplomas, from the elementary examinations up to the doctorate. But the system involves certain difficulties. In countries with a rigid academic tradition, which strictly separates sciences from the arts or humanities, the department of anthropology implies a choice between the two types of faculty; so that one is led to envisage two departments, one of social or cultural anthropology and another of physical anthropology. It is of course in the interest of these two branches to specialize; yet an anthropologist, whatever his particular line, cannot dispense with a basic knowledge of physical anthropology, while this latter branch is lost unless it constantly keeps in mind the sociological aspects. We shall return to this point later.

France may be cited as an example of the abnormal situation arising in anthropological work from a rigid separation between the faculties of science and arts. The University of Paris grants three diplomas in anthropology—a diploma in ethnology (with arts optional) awarded by the faculty of arts; the same diploma with sciences optional, awarded by the two faculties combined; and, lastly, a diploma in physical anthropology, awarded by the faculty of science alone. The students are neither sufficiently numerous nor, above all, sufficiently specialized (since these diplomas involve only a year's study) to justify such complexity.

But the inconveniences of the departmental system are felt even in the countries that have most readily adopted it. In England itself, the University of Oxford prefers the system of institutes (with the Institute of Social Anthropology), and in America increasing doubts are arising: The departmental system often entails premature specialization, with inadequate general education as its corollary. The example of the University of Chicago is typical in this respect; to remedy the defects just mentioned, the department of anthropology first became part of a division of social sciences, but this change had hardly been effected before expert minds began to feel the need for similar contacts with humanistic studies. Thus arose the third system, that of schools or institutes.

Schools or Institutes. The best known examples of these are the Escuela Nacional de Antropología (National School of Anthropology) in Mexico City and the Institut d'Ethnologie (Institute of Ethnology) at the University of Paris. The former offers a comprehensive form of professional training which amounts to a specialization and completion of past university studies; the latter aims, rather, at regrouping and supplementing current university studies. The Institut d'Ethnologie stems from three faculties—law, arts, and science. In preparation for a university examination—the ethnology diploma of the arts or science degree—it prescribes for students courses given in the three faculties, adding other courses organized under its own responsibility but sanctioned by the University. The same interfaculty approach is seen in the courses for the Overseas Peoples Studies Degree, which involve certificates awarded by the faculties of law and arts and, sometimes, by the faculty of science.

We shall later explain why this seems to us the most satisfactory system. For the moment we shall merely note that it, too, raises problems; the autonomy of the institute often has to be paid for by a lowering of status, in comparison with teaching conceived on more traditional lines. It is a somewhat irregular system; hence the difficulty of introducing a sufficiently long period of study culminating in diplomas which rank with those awarded by the faculties. At the University of Paris there has been partial success in extending the length of the courses to two years for the most promising students, thanks to the foundation of another establishment, the Centre de Formation aux Recherches Ethnologiques (Ethnological Training Center), devoted to specialized courses and practical work; but this solution too is questionable, as it removes anthropological teaching further from traditional lines instead of bringing it nearer and raises the standard of the work without permitting it to culminate in the usual highest type of award.

These few examples show the difficulty of solving the problems of anthropology teaching on the basis of experience gained. We can, in fact, hardly talk of "experience gained"; the experiments are still in progress, and neither their ultimate trend nor their results can yet be seen. Perhaps we should state the problem in another way. For lack of facts from which to draw conclusions by induction, let us seek the answer in anthropology itself. Let us try to see not only where anthropology stands at present, but where it is heading. A long-term view may—better than any non-forward-looking analysis of the present confused situation, characteristic of an enthusiastic period—enable us to discern the principles that should govern its teaching.

THE QUESTION OF PHYSICAL ANTHROPOLOGY

The first problem is one of classification. Is anthropology, whose appearance has made so marked an impact upon the social sciences, itself a social science? Undoubtedly it is, since it deals with human groups. But being by definition a "science of man," does it not come within the range of the so-called humanistic sciences or studies? And by reason of that branch of it which is known almost everywhere under the name of physical anthropology (though as "anthropology" pure and simple in several European countries), does it not belong to the natural sciences? No one will deny that anthropology has this threefold aspect. And in the United States, where a "tripartite" division of the sciences has been carried fairly far, anthropological societies have secured the right of affiliation with the three great science councils, each of which controls one of the fields we have just differentiated. Let us take a closer look at the nature of this threefold relationship.

First let us deal with physical anthropology. This is concerned with questions such as man's evolution from animal form and the present division into racial groups distinguishable by anatomical or physiological characteristics. Can it therefore be described as a *natural* study of man? To define it thus would be to forget that the last phases, at least, of human evolution—those which have differentiated the races of *Homo sapiens*, and even perhaps the stages which led to him—occurred under conditions very different from those governing the development of other living species. From the time when man acquired the power of speech (the very complex techniques and the marked similarity of form which characterize prehistoric industries imply that he already had a language wherewith to teach them and pass them on), he himself determined, though not necessarily consciously, the processes of his biological evolution. Each human society conditions its own physical perpetuation by a complex body of rules, such as the prohibition of incest, endogamy, exogamy, preferential marriage between certain types of relatives, polygamy, or monogamy—or simply by the more or less systematic application of moral, social, economic, and esthetic standards. By conforming to these rules, a society facilitates certain types of unions or associations and excludes others. An anthropologist who tried to interpret the evolution of human races or subraces as though it were simply the result of natural conditions would enter the same blind alley as a zoologist attempting to explain the present differences among dogs by purely biological or ecological considerations, without taking human intervention into account. Men have *made* themselves to no less an extent than they have made the races of their domestic animals, the only difference being that the process has been less conscious or voluntary. Consequently, physical anthropology, though using knowledge and methods derived from the natural sciences, has particularly close connections with the social sciences. To a very great extent, it amounts to a study of the anatomical and physiological changes resulting, in a given living species, from the emergence of social life, of language, and of a system of values—or, to use a more general term, of *culture*.

ETHNOGRAPHY, ETHNOLOGY, AND ANTHROPOLOGY

We are, then, very far from the period when the various aspects of human civilizations (tools, clothing, institutions, beliefs) were treated as a kind of extension of, or as dependent upon, the somatic qualities characterizing various human groups. The opposite relationship would be nearer the truth. The term *ethnology* with this outmoded meaning survives here and there, notably in India, where the system of castes (endogamous and technically specialized) has given it a measure of tardy and superficial consistency, and in France, where an extremely rigid academic structure tends to perpetuate traditional terminology (cf. the Chair of Ethnology of Living and Fossilized Man in the National Museum of Natural History, as though there were any significant relation between the anatomical structure of fossilized man and his tools and as though the ethnology of present-day man raised the question of his anatomical structure). But once these confusions have been eliminated, we remain puzzled, after reading the general report, by the disturbing diversity of terms that require precise definition. What are the connections and the differences among ethnography, ethnology, and anthropology? What is meant by the distinction (so irksome, apparently, to persons of different nationalities preparing reports) between social anthropology and cultural anthropology? And what is the relationship between anthropology and the disciplines frequently combined with it in a single department—sociology, social science, geography, and, sometimes, even archaeology and linguistics?

The answer to the first question is relatively simple. In all countries, it seems, ethnography is interpreted in the same way: It corresponds to the first stages in research—observation and description, field work. The typical ethnographical study consists of a monograph dealing with a social group small enough for the author to be able to collect most of his material by personal observation. Ethnography also includes the methods and techniques connected with field work, with the classification, description, and analysis of particular cultural phenomena—whether weapons, tools, beliefs, or institutions. In the case of material objects, these operations are generally performed in the museum, which in this respect may be regarded as an extension of field work (an important point, to which we shall return).

In relation to ethnography, ethnology represents a first step toward synthesis. Without excluding direct observation, it leads toward conclusions sufficiently comprehensive to preclude, or almost to preclude, their being based solely on first-hand information. The synthesis may be of three kinds: geographical, if information about neighboring groups is to be collated; historical, if the purpose is to reconstruct the past of one or several peoples; systematic, if one type of technique, custom, or institution is selected for special attention. It is in this sense that the term *ethnology* is applied, for instance, to the Bureau of American Ethnology in the Smithsonian Institute, to the Zeitschrift für Ethnologie (Journal of Ethnology), or to the Institut d'Ethnologie (Institute of Ethnology) at the University of Paris. In all these cases, ethnology includes ethnography as its first step and is an extension of it.

For a considerable time, and in several countries, this "duality" was regarded as sufficient unto itself. This was especially so wherever historical and geographical considerations predominated and where the opinion prevailed that synthesis could not range beyond determination of the origins and centers of cultural diffusion. Other countries—France, for instance—held to the same view, but for different reasons; the final stage of the synthesis was left to other disciplines—sociology (in the French sense of the term), human geography, history, and, sometimes, even philosophy. Thus, apparently, it came about that in several European countries the term *anthropology* was left undefined and was therefore limited in practice to physical anthropology.

On the other hand, wherever we meet with the terms *social anthropology* or *cultural anthropology* they are linked to a second and final stage of the synthesis, based upon ethnographical and ethnological conclusions. In the Anglo-Saxon countries, anthropology aims at a global knowledge of man—embracing the subject in its full historical and geographical extension, seeking knowledge applicable to the whole of human evolution from, let us say, *Hominidae* to the races of today, and leading to conclusions which may be either positive or negative but which are valid for all human societies, from the large modern city to the smallest Melanesian tribe. In this sense it may thus be said that there is the same connection between anthropology and ethnology as that, described above, between ethnology and ethnography. Ethnography, ethnology, and anthropology do not form three different disciplines, or three different conceptions of the same branch of study. They are in fact three stages, or three moments of time, in the same line of investigation, and preference for one or another of these only means that attention is concentrated on one type of research, which can never exclude the other two.

SOCIAL ANTHROPOLOGY AND CULTURAL ANTHROPOLOGY

If the terms *social anthropology* and *cultural anthropology* were intended simply to distinguish certain fields of study from those covered by physical anthropology, there would be no difficulty. But the preference of the United Kingdom for the former and that of the United States for the latter term, and the light thrown on this difference of opinion in the course of a recent controversy between the American G. P. Murdock and the Englishman R. Firth,[2] show that each term, where chosen, has been chosen for definite theoretical reasons. In many instances, no doubt, chance has determined the choice of a particular term (especially for the titles of university chairs). It seems, indeed, that the term *social anthropology* came into use in England because a title had to be found to distinguish a new chair from others for which all the traditional terms had already been used. Nor is any difference to be seen when we simply consider the actual meanings of the words *cultural* and *social*. The concept of culture originated in England, since it was Tylor who first defined it as "that complex whole which includes knowledge, belief, art, morals, law, custom, and any other capabilities and habits acquired by man as a member of society."[3] Culture therefore relates to the specific differences between men and animals, thus leading to what has ever since been the classic antithesis between *nature* and *culture*. Viewed in this light, man appears chiefly as *Homo faber* or "toolmaker." Customs, beliefs, and institutions are then seen as techniques comparable to other techniques, though no doubt more purely intellectual—techniques promoting social life and making social life possible, just as the techniques of agriculture make it possible to satisfy man's need for food, or those of cloth-making to protect him from the rigors of the weather. Social anthropology denotes merely the study of social organization—an extremely important subject, but only one of the many subjects making up cultural anthropology. This way of stating the problem seems typical of American science, or at least of the early stages of its development.

It was probably not pure chance that the term *social anthropology* was first brought into use in the United Kingdom as the title of the first chair held by Sir J. G. Frazer, who was much less interested in techniques than in beliefs, customs, and institutions. It was A. R. Radcliffe-Brown, however, who brought out the underlying meaning of the term when he defined the object of his own research work as *social relations* and the *social structure*. The dominant idea here is no longer that of the tool-maker but that of the group, and the group considered as such—that is to say, the whole complex of forms of communication on which social life is based. There is no contradiction, be it noted, or even any opposition between the two points of view. The best proof of this is to be found in the development of French sociological thought: Only a few years after Durkheim had shown that social phenomena should be studied *as things* (which, expressed in different terms, is the standpoint of cultural anthropology), his nephew and follower, Mauss, simultaneously with Malinowski, put forward the related thesis that things (manufactured articles, weapons, tools, and ritual objects) are themselves *social phenomena* (which represents the view of social anthropology). We may therefore say that cultural anthropology and social anthropology cover exactly the same ground, but that one starts from techniques and material things and proceeds ultimately to the "super-technique" of social and political activity, which makes life in society possible and determines the forms it takes, while the other starts from social life and works down to the things on which social life leaves its mark and the activities through which it manifests itself. Cultural anthropology and social anthropology are like two books which include the same chapters, though the latter may be arranged in different order and the number of pages in each may vary.

Nevertheless, even on this comparison, certain finer distinctions can be drawn. Social anthropology developed out of the discovery that all the aspects of social life—economic, technical, political, legal, esthetic, and religious—make up a significant complex and that no one of these aspects can be understood unless it is considered together with all the others. It therefore tends to work from the whole to the parts, or, at least, to give the former logical precedence over the latter. A technique does not merely have a *use*: It also fulfills a *function*, and a function, if it is to be properly understood, implies sociological and not only historical, geographical, mechanical, or physico-chemical considerations. The complex of functions, in turn, brings in a new notion, that of *structure*, and the importance attributed to the idea of social structure in contemporary anthropological research is well known.

Admittedly, cultural anthropology was to arrive, almost simultaneously, at a similar conception, although by an entirely different path. Instead of the static view of the whole social group as a sort of system or constellation, the question of dynamics—of how culture is handed on from generation to generation—was to lead cultural anthropology to exactly the same conclusion, i.e., that the system of interconnections among all aspects of social life plays a more important part in the transmission of culture than any one of those aspects considered separately. In this way, the "culture and personality" studies (which, in the tradition of cultural anthropology, can be traced back to the teachings of Franz Boas) were, by this unexpected route, to be linked with the "social structure" studies going back to Radcliffe-Brown and, through him, to Durkheim. Whether anthropology is described as "cultural" or "social," its object always is to discover *the whole man*, as revealed in the one case through his *works* and in the other through his *representations*. It is thus understandable that a "cultural" bias brings anthropology closer to geography, technology, and prehistoric studies, while a "sociological" bias gives it more direct associations with archaeology, history, and psychology. In both cases, there is a particularly close link with linguistics, because language is at once the prototype of the *cultural phenomenon* (distinguishing man from the animals) and the phenomenon whereby all the forms of social life are established and perpetuated. It is therefore logical that, in the systems of academic classification analyzed in the general report, the usual tendency is not to treat anthropology separately but to group it with one or more of the following branches of study:

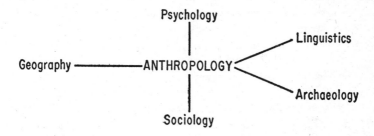

In the above diagram, the horizontals mainly represent the view of cultural anthropology, the verticals that of social anthropology, and the obliques both. But—leaving aside the fact that there is a tendency, among modern research students, for the two standpoints to converge—it must not be forgotten that, even in the extreme cases, the difference is only one of standpoint, not of the subject investigated. The question of the standardization of terms thus becomes much less important. There seems to be almost unanimous agreement today on the use of the term *anthropology*, rather than *ethnography* or *ethnology*, as the best designation for all these three phases of research. A recent international survey shows this clearly.[4] The use of the term *anthropology* can therefore be unhesitatingly recommended for the titles of departments, institutes, or schools in which research or teaching in these subjects is carried on. And it is unnecessary to go further than this: The differences in temperament and interests—which are always productive of good results—between those in charge of teaching and the conduct of research work will determine the choice of the adjective *social* or *cultural* as better reflecting individual particularities.

ANTHROPOLOGY AND FOLKLORE

One brief comment remains to be made on folklore. We shall not attempt to recount the very complicated history of this term;

broadly speaking, it denotes the study of matters which, though relating to the society to which the observer belongs, necessitate the use of methods of investigation and observation techniques, similar to those employed when dealing with far-distant societies. We need not at this time go into the reasons for this state of affairs; but, whether we consider the explanation to lie in the fact that the phenomena studied are very old (and therefore far distant, in time if not in space)[5] or in the unconscious, group character of certain forms of social and mental activity in any society, including our own,[6] the study of folklore is undoubtedly connected, either by its subject or by its methods (and probably by both at once), to anthropology. Certain countries, particularly the Scandinavian ones, seem to prefer to treat folklore as a comparatively distinct branch of study. The reason for this is that they took up the problems of anthropology relatively late, whereas at a very early date they had begun to investigate problems connected with their own particular traditions. They have thus proceeded from the particular to the general, while in France, for instance, the situation has been reversed. In France we started by theorizing on human nature and gradually turned to the study of facts as a basis for speculation or in order to set bounds to it. The best situation is probably that in which both points of view have been adopted and developed simultaneously, as in Germany and the English-speaking countries (in each case, for different reasons), and it is this situation which accounts for the earlier progress made in anthropological studies in those countries.

ANTHROPOLOGY AND THE SOCIAL SCIENCES

From these considerations, which it would be wrong to regard as purely theoretical, an initial conclusion emerges: Under no circumstances can anthropology allow itself to be dissociated from the natural sciences (to which it is linked by physical anthropology) or from the humanistic studies (with which it is closely connected by geography, archaeology, and linguistics). If it had to select a single allegiance, it would declare itself a social science—not in the sense in which this term denotes a single, separate field but, on the contrary, because it underlines a feature that tends to be common to all the disciplines: Today even biologists and physicists are becoming increasingly conscious of the social implications, or rather the *anthropological significance*, of their discoveries. Man is no longer satisfied merely to acquire knowledge; while accumulating more of this, he regards himself as the "knower" and his research is daily brought a little more to bear on the two inseparable factors presented by a humanity that transforms the world and a humanity that, while it acts, is transforming itself.

Thus, when the social sciences demand their own separate place within the university framework, anthropology subscribes to this demand. Not however without certain mental reservations. It realizes that such independence would lead to the development of social psychology, political science, and sociology and to a modification of what are often considered to be overtraditional standpoints on the part of law and economic science. But so far as anthropology itself is concerned, the establishment of faculties of social science, where they do not at present exist, would not resolve its problems; for were anthropology to be included in these faculties, it would feel no less out of place than it would in faculties of science or arts. It stems, in fact, from three different disciplines, for each of which it desires balanced representation in teaching, lest it should itself suffer from lack of balance if unable to give effective proof of its triple allegiance. From its point of view, the only satisfactory solution is the institute or school where the instruction given at the three faculties concerned would be rearranged in an original, comprehensive system, around the syllabuses peculiar to the school or institute itself.

Newly established sciences find difficulty in inserting themselves into traditional structures. It can never be sufficiently emphasized that anthropology is by far the youngest of these young sciences (the social sciences) and that the general solutions appropriate to its elders have what is, for it, an already traditional aspect. It has, as it were, its feet planted on the natural sciences, its back resting against the humanistic studies, and its eyes directed toward the social sciences. And since it is this third relationship which, in this volume entirely devoted to the social sciences, must in particular be studied if we are to draw the necessary practical conclusions, the reader will forgive us for dwelling upon it at greater length.

The uncertainty surrounding the relationship between anthropology and sociology derives first from the ambiguity of sociology's own present position. Sociology should, from its very name, be the science of society par excellence, the science that crowns—or sums up—all the other social sciences. But since the great ambitions of the Durkheim school came to naught, it nowhere now fulfills that function. In some countries, particularly in continental Europe and sometimes also in Latin America, sociology follows the tradition of a social philosophy, in which knowledge (acquired at second or third hand) of concrete research carried out by others serves merely to buttress hypotheses. On the other hand, in the Anglo-Saxon countries (whose standpoint is gradually being accepted by the Latin American and Asian countries), sociology is becoming a special discipline on the same level as the other social sciences; it studies the social relationships within present-day groups and communities on a largely experimental basis, and its methods and subjects do not, in appearance, distinguish it from anthropology, except possibly for the fact that the subjects of sociology (urban centers, agricultural organizations, national states and their component communities, and international society itself) are of quite a different magnitude from, as well as more complex than, the so-called primitive societies. Nevertheless, as anthropology tends to take an ever greater interest in these complex forms of society, it is difficult to perceive the exact difference between the two.

However, sociology is always closely linked with the observer. This is clear from our last example, for urban, rural, religious, occupational, etc.: Sociology is concerned with the observer's society or a society of the same type. But the same applies to the other example—the comprehensive "synthesis" or philosophical sociology. Here, admittedly, the sociologist extends his investigations to much wider ranges of human experience, and he can even seek to interpret human experience as a whole. The subject extends beyond the purview of the observer, but it is always *from the observer's point of view* that the sociologist tries to broaden it. In his attempt to interpret and to assign meanings, he is always first of all concerned with explaining *his own society*; what he applies to the generality are his own logical classifications, his own background perspectives. If a French sociologist of the twentieth century works out a general theory of social life, it will inevitably, and quite legitimately, reveal itself as the work of a twentieth-century French sociologist; whereas the anthropologist undertaking the same task will endeavor, instinctively and deliberately (although it is by no means certain that he will ever succeed), to formulate a theory applicable not only to his own fellow countrymen and contemporaries, but to the most distant native population.

While sociology seeks to advance the social science of the observer, anthropology seeks to advance that of what is observed—either by endeavoring to reproduce, in its description of strange and remote societies, the standpoint of the natives themselves, or by broadening its subject so as to cover the observer's society but at the same time trying to evolve a frame of reference based on ethnographical experience and independent both of the observer and of what he is observing.

We see therefore why sociology can be regarded, and rightly regarded, sometimes as a special form of anthropology (this is the tendency in the United States) and sometimes as the discipline which occupies first place in the hierarchy of the social sciences; for it undoubtedly occupies not merely a particular position but a *position of privilege*, for the reason, with which we are familiar from the history of geometry, that the adoption of the observer's standpoint makes it possible to discover properties which are apparently firmer in outline and certainly easier to employ than those involving an extension of the same perspective to other possible observers. Thus Euclidean geometry can be regarded as a privileged case of a metageometry which would also cover the consideration of spaces with different structures.

THE PARTICULAR TASK OF ANTHROPOLOGY

At this stage of our analysis we must stop once more to examine how we can define what anthropology, as such, has to say—the message which the proper organization of its teaching should enable it to transmit under the best possible conditions.

Objectivity. The first aim of anthropology is to be objective, to inculcate objective habits and to teach objective methods. Not simply an objectivity enabling the observer to place himself above his own personal beliefs, preferences, and prejudices; that kind of objectivity characterizes every social science, or they could not be regarded as sciences at all. The objectivity aimed at by anthropology is on a higher level: The observer must not only place himself above the values accepted by his own society or group, but must adopt certain definite *methods of thought;* he must reason on the basis of concepts which are valid not merely for an honest and objective observer, but for all possible observers. Thus the anthropologist does not simply set aside his own feelings; he creates new mental categories and helps to introduce notions of space and time, opposition and contradiction, which are as foreign to traditional thought as the concepts met with today in certain branches of the natural sciences. This connection between the ways in which the same problems are stated in apparently very different disciplines was admirably perceived by the great physicist Niels Bohr when he wrote: "The traditional differences of [human cultures] . . . in many ways resemble the different equivalent modes in which physical experience can be described." [7]

Yet these unrelenting efforts to achieve complete objectivity can go forward only on a level where phenomena retain a meaning for humanity and can be apprehended, in mind and feeling, by an individual. This is a very important point, for it enables us to distinguish between the type of objectivity to which anthropology aspires and that aimed at by the other social sciences, of which it can be said that it is no less rigorous, although it is on another level. The realities in which economic science and demography are interested are no less objective, but they are not expected to have a meaning so far as the subject's own personal experience is concerned, for in the course of his historical evolution he never encounters such things as value, profitableness, marginal productivity, or maximum population. These are all abstract notions; their use by the social sciences brings the social sciences closer to the natural sciences, but in a quite different way, for in the case of anthropology the connection is more with humanistic studies. Anthropology aims to be a *semeiological* science, and takes as a guiding principle that of "meaning." This is yet another reason (in addition to many others) why anthropology should maintain close contact with linguistics, where, with regard to this social fact of speech, there is the same concern to avoid separating the objective basis of language (*sound*) from its signifying function (*meaning*).[8]

Totality. The second aim of anthropology is *totality*. It regards social life as a system of which all the aspects are organically connected. It readily admits that, in order to acquire a more thorough knowledge of certain types of phenomena, it is essential to subdivide—after the manner of the social psychologist, the jurist, the economist, and the political scientist—and it is too much concerned with the method of models (which it employs itself in certain fields, such as that of kinship) to question the validity of these particular models. But when the anthropologist endeavors to create models, it is always with the underlying motive of discovering a *form that is common* to the various manifestations of social life. This tendency underlies both the notion (introduced by Marcel Mauss) of the *total social phenomenon*, and that of *pattern* (an idea which has loomed large in Anglo-Saxon anthropology during recent years).

Meaningfulness. The third original feature of anthropological research—unquestionably more important than the other two—is not so easy to define. We are so accustomed to attaching negative terms to the types of society that interest the ethnologist that it is difficult for us to realize he is interested in them for positive reasons. Anthropology, we are apt to say—and this is evidenced by the title of the chairs themselves—is concerned with societies that are *non*-civilized, *without* a system of writing, and *pre-* or *non*-industrial in type. Yet behind all these qualifying negative expressions there is a positive reality: These societies are, to a far greater degree than the others, based on personal relationships, on concrete relations between individuals. It would take some time to prove this point, but, without entering into details, it will suffice here to emphasize that the small size of the societies known as "primitive" generally permits of such relationships and that, even where this is impossible because the societies of this type are too extensive or scattered, relations between individuals who are extremely remote from one another are based on the most direct kind of relationship, of which kinship is usually the prototype. Radcliffe-Brown has given us examples in Australia, which have become classic, of this process of projection.

THE CRITERION OF AUTHENTICITY

In this respect it is, rather, modern societies that should be defined in negative terms. Our relations with one another are now only occasionally and fragmentarily based upon global experience, the concrete "apprehension" of one person by another. They are largely the result of a process of indirect reconstruction, through written documents. We are no longer linked to our past by an oral tradition which implies direct contact with others (storytellers, priests, wise men, or elders), but by books amassed in libraries, books from which we endeavor—with extreme difficulty—to form a picture of their authors. And we communicate with the immense majority of our contemporaries by all kinds of intermediaries—written documents or administrative machinery—which undoubtedly vastly extend our contacts but at the same time make those contacts somewhat "unauthentic." This has become typical of the relationship between the citizen and the public authorities.

We should like to avoid describing negatively the tremendous revolution brought about by the invention of writing. But it is essential to realize that writing, while it conferred vast benefits on humanity, did in fact deprive it of something fundamental.[9] The international organizations, and particularly UNESCO, have so far entirely failed to appreciate the loss of personal autonomy that has resulted from the expansion of the indirect forms of communication (books, photographs, press, radio, etc.). But the theorists of the most modern of the social sciences (that of communication) treat this as a major question, as is shown by the following passage from Wiener's *Cybernetics:* "It is no wonder that the larger communities . . . contain far less available information than the smaller communities, to say nothing of the human elements of which all communities are built up."[10] Taking an illustration from a field which is more familiar to the social sciences, there is the dispute—well known to French political scientists—between supporters of the individual constituency poll (*scrutin d'arrondissement*) and supporters of voting for several unknown or little-known members out of a list drawn up by the political parties (*scrutin de liste*). Under the latter system, there is a great loss of information suffered by the community, owing to the substitution of abstract values for personal contacts between the electors and their representatives.

Modern societies are, of course, not completely "unauthentic." On the contrary, if we carefully consider the points on which anthropological investigations have been brought to bear, we note that in its increasingly intensive study of modern societies, anthropology has endeavored to identify *levels of authenticity* within them. When the ethnologist studies a village, an enterprise, or the neighborhood of a large town, his task is facilitated by the fact that almost everyone knows everyone else. Likewise, when demographers identify, in a modern society, "isolates" of the same size as those characterizing primitive societies,[11] they help the anthropologist, who thus discovers a new subject. The community surveys carried out in France under UNESCO's auspices have been very revealing here; those conducting the surveys (some of whom had anthropological training) felt completely at home in a village of 500 inhabitants, the study of which necessitated no change in their classical methods; whereas in an average-sized town they felt they were confronted by an entirely new problem. Why? Because 30,000 persons cannot constitute a society in the same way as 500 persons. In the former case, the main communication is not between persons; the social reality of "senders" and "receivers" (to use two words current in communication terminology) is hidden behind the complex system of "codes and relays." [12]

In the future, it may be recognized that anthropology's most important contribution to social science is to have introduced, if unknowingly, this fundamental distinction between two types of social existence: a way of life recognized at the outset as traditional and archaic and characteristic of "authentic" societies and a more modern form of existence, from which the first-named type is not absent but where groups that are not completely, or are imperfectly, "authentic" are organized within a much larger and specifically "unauthentic" system.

But while this distinction explains and justifies the increasing concern of anthropology with the types of "authentic" relations that persist or appear in modern societies, it shows where the limits of that science's investigations lie. For though it is true that a Melanesian tribe and a French village are, *grosso modo*, social entities of the same type, this ceases to be true if we start to work outward toward larger units. Hence the error which those who favor "national character" studies fall into if they wish to work solely as anthropologists; for by unconsciously confusing forms of social life that cannot in fact be identified, they can achieve only one of two results—to consecrate either the worst forms of prejudice or the most shallow abstractions.

THE ORGANIZATION OF ANTHROPOLOGICAL STUDIES

We perceive the singular crossroads of disciplines at which anthropology stands. In order to resolve the problem of objectivity, which is imposed upon it by the need of a common language wherewith to communicate heterogeneous social experience, anthropology is beginning to seek the help of mathematics and symbolic logic. Our current vocabulary, which is the product of our own social and mental categories, is in fact inadequate to describe markedly different types of sociological experience. We must resort to symbols, like the physicist when he wishes to show what is common between, say, the corpuscular theory and the wave theory of light; here, in the language of the ordinary man, the two notions are contradictory, but, since science regards them as equally "real," it is necessary to employ new symbols in order to be able to proceed from one to the other.[13]

Second, as a "semeiological" science, anthropology turns toward linguistics—first, because only linguistic knowledge provides the key to a system of logical categories and of moral values different from the observer's own; second, because linguistics, more than any other science, can teach him how to pass from the consideration of elements in themselves devoid of meaning to consideration of a semantic system and show him how the latter can be built on the basis of the former. This, perhaps, is primarily the problem of language, but, beyond and through it, the problem of culture in general.

Third, alive to the interrelations of the various types of social phenomena, anthropology aims at simultaneous consideration of their economic, legal, political, moral, esthetic, and religious aspects; consequently, it is careful to note developments in the other social sciences, and especially in such of them—viz., human geography, social and economic history, and sociology—as share with it this total perspective.

Last, being essentially concerned with those forms of social life—of which the so-called primitive societies are merely the most readily identifiable and most developed examples—whose degree of authenticity is estimated according to the scope and variety of the concrete relations between individuals, anthropology maintains, in this respect, the closest contact with psychology (general and social).

There can be no question of overwhelming students with the enormous mass of knowledge which would be necessary in order to do full justice to all these standpoints. The mere realization, however, of this complexity leads to a number of practical consequences.

(1) Anthropology has become too diversified and technical a subject to be taught in one-year courses, generally entitled "Introduction to Anthropology" (or something similar) and usually consisting of vague comments on clan organization, polygamy, and totemism. It would be dangerous to imagine that such superficial ideas can be used to provide effective training for young men who, as missionaries, administrators, diplomats, soldiers, etc., are destined to live in contact with populations very different from their own. An introduction to anthropology no more produces an anthropologist, even an amateur one, than an introduction to physics produces a physicist, or even an assistant physicist.

In this respect, anthropologists bear heavy responsibilities. Having been ignored or disdained for so long, they often feel flattered when asked to provide a smattering of anthropology as a round-off to some form of technical training. They should firmly resist this temptation. There is of course no question of turning everyone into an anthropologist; but if doctors, jurists, and missionaries must acquire certain notions of anthropology, it should be through a process of very thorough technical training in the few branches of anthropological research directly relating to the exercise of their professions and to the particular areas of the world which they propose to serve.

(2) Whatever the number of courses envisaged, it is impossible to train anthropologists in one year. Three years would seem to

be the minimum period within which complete instruction, absorbing the whole of the student's time, can be given; and this minimum should, for the purpose of certain professional qualifications, be increased to four or five years. Consequently it seems essential that in all universities anthropology should cease to be regarded, as it too often is (especially, for example, in France) merely as a complementary subject. Special diplomas should be conferred, up to the highest university levels, on those who have successfully completed full courses devoted exclusively to anthropology.

(3) Even when extended over this period of time, the subject matter of anthropology is too complex not to involve specialized studies. There is, of course, a general form of training which all anthropology students could receive during their first year and which would permit them to choose their subsequent specialized work judiciously. Without wishing to suggest a rigid program, we think that the subjects to be studied would necessarily comprise the basic principles of physical, social, and cultural anthropology; prehistory; the history of ethnological theory; and general linguistics.

Specialization in each subject should begin in the second year: (a) physical anthropology, accompanied by comparative anatomy, biology, and physiology; (b) social anthropology, together with economic and social history, social psychology, and linguistics; (c) cultural anthropology, with technology, geography, and prehistory.

In the third year (and perhaps during the second), this systematic specialization would be accompanied by "regional" specialization, which would include, in addition to regional prehistory, archaeology, and geography, a sound training in one or more of the languages used in the area chosen by the investigator.

(4) The study of anthropology, general or regional, involves extensive reading. We are thinking not so much of textbooks (which can complement but never replace verbal instruction) or of works on theory (which it is not essential to use before the final years of training) as of monographs, i.e., books which enable the student to "relive" experience that has been acquired on the spot and to accumulate a considerable amount of factual knowledge, which alone can guard him against hasty generalizations and simplifications. Throughout the entire training, therefore, the theo-

retical and practical courses would be complemented by compulsory reading, at the rate of some thousands of pages per year; this reading would be checked by various procedures (written summaries, oral précis, etc.) which we cannot describe in detail here. This implies (a) that every institute or school of anthropology must have a library containing copies, in duplicate or triplicate, of a considerable number of works; (b) that, in present circumstances, the student will have to possess, at the outset, adequate knowledge of at least one of the foreign languages which have been most frequently used in recent years by authors of anthropological works.

We hesitate, indeed, to recommend a policy of systematic translations; the technical vocabulary of anthropology is at present in too chaotic a state. Each author tends to use his own terminology, and there is no firm agreement on the meaning of the principal terms. Consequently, it is most unlikely that a country which does not produce, on a large scale, anthropological works in its own national language will possess specialized translators capable of rendering the exact terminological meaning and the subtleties of thought of a foreign author. UNESCO cannot, therefore, be pressed too strongly to carry out its project for the compilation of international scientific vocabularies; this project, once completed, might enable us to be less categorical on the matter of translations.

Last, it is to be desired that use should be made of such media as photographic slides, documentary films, and linguistic or musical recordings. The recent establishment of various institutions—especially that of the International Center for Ethnographic Documentary Films, decided upon by the Fourth World Congress of the Anthropological and Ethnological Sciences (Vienna, 1952)—is an encouraging development.

(5) These three years of theoretical training could be usefully followed by a practical course lasting for one or even two years, at least in the case of those intending to practice anthropology professionally (teaching or research); but this raises some extremely complex problems.

The Training of Teachers. We shall first consider the case of future teachers of anthropology. Whatever the university qualifications required for teaching (in general, the doctoral degree or equivalent accomplishments), no one should be entitled to teach anthropology unless he has carried out considerable field research. It is sheer illusion that anthropology can be taught purely theoretically, with the help of a complete (or usually abridged) edition of *The Golden Bough* and other works, whatever their intrinsic merits may be. Those combating this assertion by referring to the distinguished scholars who have never done field work (Sir James Frazer, in answer to those who raised the question, declared: "Heaven forbid!") should remember that Lévy-Bruhl, for instance, held, not a chair of anthropology or any related chair—in his day, no such chairs existed at the French universities—but a chair of philosophy; in future, nothing will prevent pure theorists from receiving chairs of disciplines bordering on anthropology: history of religions, comparative sociology, etc. Nevertheless, the teaching of anthropology must be reserved for *eyewitnesses*. There is nothing radical in this standpoint; it is adopted *de facto* (if not always *de jure*) in all countries where anthropology has attained some measure of development.

The Training of Research Workers. The problem of training is much less simple with regard to future members of the anthropological profession, i.e., the research workers.[14] Would it not be in the nature of a vicious circle to require them to carry out research before receiving the university training which qualifies them for such research? Here we can usefully refer to what we have already said, by way of clarifying the very special position of anthropology. We pointed out that its fundamental feature and chief merit is that it endeavors to identify, in all forms of social life, what we termed the *level of authenticity*, i.e., either complete societies (most frequently found among the so-called "primitive" societies) or forms of social existence (found even in modern or "civilized" societies) where relations between individuals and the system of social relationships combine to form a whole. These special features have one immediate consequence: Such forms of social existence cannot be apprehended simply from the outside—the investigator must be able to make a personal reconstruction of the synthesis characterizing them; he must not merely analyze their elements, but apprehend them as a whole in the form of a personal experience—his own.

Thus we recognize a profound reason, associated with the very nature of the discipline and the distinctive features of its subject, why the anthropologist needs the experience of field work. It represents for him, not the goal of his profession, or a completion of his schooling, or yet a technical apprenticeship—but a crucial stage of his education, prior to which he may possess miscellaneous knowledge that will never form a whole. After he engages in field work his knowledge will acquire an organic unity and a meaning it did not previously possess. The position is comparable to that in psychoanalysis. The principle is universally recognized today that the professional psychoanalyst must have a specific and irreplaceable practical background, that of analysis itself; hence all the regulations require that every would-be psychoanalyst be psychoanalyzed himself. For the anthropologist, field work represents the equivalent of this unique experience. As in the case of psychoanalysis, this experience may or may not be successful, and no examination, whether competitive or not, can prove conclusively whether it is. Only experienced members of the profession, whose work shows that they have themselves passed the test, can decide if and when a candidate for the anthropological profession has, as a result of field work, accomplished that inner revolution that will really make him into a new man.

From these considerations several consequences flow.

First, the exercise of the anthropological profession—which is full of problems, since it involves a "foreign" person (the investigator) examining an environment whose inner structure and position in the world render it particularly unstable and fragile—demands preliminary qualifications that can be obtained only as a result of field work.

Second, this situation, which theoretically implies a contradiction, is closely akin to two others—that of psychoanalysis, as we have just seen, and that of medical studies in general, where the non-resident and resident systems provide apprenticeship in diagnosis through the practice of diagnosis itself.

Third, these two other cases we have just mentioned show that success can be achieved only through personal contact between the student and an acknowledged practitioner—contact sufficiently close and extensive for the studies to bear the imprint of an inevitably "arbitrary" factor (that is, the evaluation of the "boss" in the case of medical studies and of the "supervisory" analyst in the case of psychoanalysis). This "arbitrary" factor can be reduced in various ways, but it is difficult to see how it can be completely eliminated from the study of anthropology. Here, too, an older member of the profession must personally assist the young research worker in his training. Close contact with someone who has already undergone a change psychologically not only expedites a similar change on the part of the student; it enables the person assisting him to ascertain if, and at what stage, this has occurred.

Let us now consider the practical ways of providing the future research worker with "supervised" field work. It seems that there are three ways:

Practical Work.   This type of work is done under the guidance of teachers in charge of the last years of instruction, or under that of assistants. Its value is relative. Without wishing to advise new institutions, or countries lacking appropriate systems, against it, we would emphasize its provisional nature. Practical work supplementing theoretical training always tends to appear as a form of drudgery, or as spurious experience. A paltry three weeks spent in a village or engaged in some kind of enterprise cannot create that psychological revolution which marks the decisive turning point in the training of the anthropologist or even give the student a faint idea of it. Indeed, these hasty practical courses are sometimes actually harmful; they allow for only the most summary and superficial methods of research; they often amount to a kind of *anti-training*. However useful the Scout movement may be for adolescents, it is impossible to confuse professional training at the higher educational level with forms—even advanced forms—of supervised play.

Outside Practical Training. As an alternative, there might be lengthier practical courses in those institutes, institutions, or other establishments which, without being specifically anthropological, function on the level of those interpersonal relationships and global situations which, as we have already seen, constitute the choicest field for anthropology: municipal administration, social services, vocational guidance centers, etc. This solution, compared with the previous one, would have the immense advantage of dispensing with imitation experimental work. On the other hand, it would have the disadvantage of placing students under the control and responsibility of heads of agencies who may have had no training in anthropology and who therefore may be unable to demonstrate the theoretical bearing of daily experience. This particular solution is, therefore, more or less an idea for the future, to be used once training in anthropology is recognized as having a general value and when a substantial proportion of anthropologists are attached to establishments or agencies of this type.

Anthropological Museums. At the beginning of this discussion we referred to the role of anthropological museums as an extension of the field for research. The museographer enters into close contact with the objects: A spirit of humility is inculcated in him by all the small tasks (unpacking, cleaning, maintenance, etc.) he has to perform. He develops a keen sense of the concrete through the classification, identification, and analysis of the objects in the various collections. He establishes indirect contact with the native environment by means of tools and comes to know this environment and the ways in which to handle it correctly: Texture, form, and, in many cases, smell, repeatedly experienced, make him instinctively familiar with distant forms of life and activities. Finally, he acquires for the various externalizations of human genius that respect which cannot fail to be inspired in him by the constant appeals to his taste, intellect, and knowledge made by apparently insignificant objects.

All this constitutes a wealth and concentration of experience which should not be underestimated. And it explains, not only why the Institut d'Ethnologie of the University of Paris attaches such importance to the hospitality it receives from the Musée de l'Homme, but also why the American report recommends, as a normal situation which is obtaining more and more throughout the United States, that every department of anthropology have attached to it a museum at the university itself.

However, it seems that even more can be done in this direction. Anthropological museums were long regarded in the same light as other establishments of the same type, i.e., as series of galleries for the preservation of objects—inert things fossilized, as it were, inside their showcases and completely detached from the societies that produced them, the only link between them and their originators being the missions periodically dispatched to the field to procure further material for the collections; they were mute witnesses of forms of existence that for the visitor were unknown and inaccessible. The evolution of anthropology as a science and the changes undergone by the modern world make modification of this conception essential. As already shown, anthropology is becoming increasingly aware of its true subject, which consists of certain forms of man's social existence—which, though possibly more easily recognizable in societies differing markedly from the observer's, exist just as much in his own. As anthropology deepens its reflections on its subject and improves its methods, it feels more and more that it is "going back home." Although it assumes very different forms, which may not be easily identifiable, it would be wrong to imagine that this tendency is peculiar to American anthropology. In France and in India, community studies carried out with UNESCO's assistance have been directed by the Musée de l'Homme (Paris) and the Anthropological Museum of Calcutta. The Laboratoire d'Ethnographie Française is attached to the Musée des Arts et Traditions Populaires. The Laboratoire d'Ethnographie Sociale is housed in the Musée de l'Homme, and, despite its name, it is devoted not to the sociology of Melanesia or Africa but to that of the Paris region. In all these cases the purpose should be, not merely to collect objects, but to understand men; not so much to classify dried remains—as in herbariums—as to describe and analyze forms of existence with which the observer is closely and actively in touch.

The same tendency is found in physical anthropology, which is no longer satisfied, as in the past, to assemble measurements and pieces of bone. It studies racial phenomena as revealed in living persons; it studies the softer parts of the body as well as the skeleton and gives no less attention to physiological activity than to simple anatomical structure. Consequently, it is mainly interested in the actual processes of differentiation in all representatives of the human species and is not content merely to obtain "ossified" results (literally as well as figuratively) among the types most easily distinguishable from that of the observer.

Moreover, the expansion of Western civilization, the development of communications, and the frequency of travel that characterizes the modern world have all helped to make the human species "fluid." Today there are practically no such things as isolated cultures; to study a given culture, as a rule it is no longer necessary to travel half-way around the world and "explore." The population of a great city like New York, London, Paris, Calcutta, or Melbourne includes representatives of highly differing cultures; this is well known to linguists, who are astonished to encounter, in these circumstances, persons qualified to inform them about rare and remote languages, some of which had been thought to be practically extinct.

Formerly, anthropological museums sent men traveling in one direction to obtain objects that seemed to be drifting in the opposite direction. Today, however, men travel in all directions; and, as this increase in contacts leads to the "homogenization" of material culture (which for primitive societies usually means extinction), it can be said that, at least in some respects, men tend to replace objects. Anthropological museums must note this vast change. Their task of preserving objects is likely to continue—though not to be expanded. But while it is becoming increasingly difficult to collect bows and arrows, drums and necklaces, baskets and statues of divinities, it is becoming easier to make a systematic study of languages, beliefs, attitudes, and personalities. How many communities of Southeast Asia, North and sub-Saharan Africa, the Near East, etc., do we not find represented in Paris by visitors or residents (whether families or small groups)?

THEORETICAL AND APPLIED ANTHROPOLOGY

From this standpoint, anthropological museums are offered not merely possibilities for research (thus becoming, to a large extent, laboratories),[15] but also new tasks of practical importance. For these representatives of peripheral cultures, unintegrated or ill-integrated, have much to give the ethnographer—language, oral traditions, beliefs, a conception of the world, an attitude toward persons and things. They are, however, also often at grips with real and distressing problems—isolation, separation from their customary environment, unemployment, incomprehension of the milieu in which they have temporarily or permanently been planted, nearly always against their will or at least without knowing what awaited them. No one is better qualified than the ethnologist to help them overcome these difficulties. First, the ethnologist knows their original environment; he has studied their language and culture at first hand, and has a sympathetic feeling for them. Second, the method peculiar to anthropology is marked by that "distantiation" which characterizes the contacts between representatives of very different cultures. *The anthropologist is the astronomer of the social sciences:* His task is to discover a meaning for configurations which, owing to their size and remoteness, are very different from those within the observer's immediate purview. Consequently, there is no reason to limit the anthropologist's role to the analysis and reduction of these external distances; he can also be called upon to take part, together with specialists of other disciplines, in the study of phenomena which exist within his own society but which are also characterized by "distantiation," either because they concern only one section of the group and not the whole of it, or because, even though they are of an over-all nature, they are deeply rooted in the unconscious. Instances of the former case are prostitution and juvenile delinquency and, of the latter, resistance to food or health changes.

Thus, if anthropology's rightful place in the social sciences were more generally recognized and its practical function more clearly identified than it is at present, a number of fundamental problems would be well on the way to solution:

(1) From the practical standpoint, a social function would be performed which is today much neglected. As an example—the problems raised by the immigration of Puerto Ricans to New York or of North Africans to Paris; no general policy is followed in these matters, and various administrative agencies (often poorly qualified to deal with them) fruitlessly refer them to and fro.

(2) New prospects would be opened up for anthropology. We have not yet considered this problem, but its solution is obviously implied in all that we have said above. If it is to be solved rightly, it is not enough to re-emphasize that every person—colonial administrator, soldier, missionary, diplomat, etc.—called upon to live in contact with a society very different from his own must receive general or at least specialized training in anthropology. It must also be remembered that certain essential functions of modern societies, made more involved by the increasing mobility of the world's population, are inadequately performed, if indeed performed at all; that this gives rise to difficulties which often become very acute, creating misunderstanding, fostering racial or social prejudices, and compromising the cause of peace; that anthropology is today the only discipline dealing with social "distantiation"; that it possesses considerable theoretical and practical resources which enable it to train specialists; and, above all, that it is always available and ready to engage in tasks which humanity cannot afford to neglect.[16]

(3) Last, and from the more limited standpoint of this study, it is obvious that the expansion of anthropological museums into laboratories for the study of social phenomena difficult to analyze or, to use a mathematical expression, the "borderline" forms of social relationships, would be the most suitable solution to the problem of anthropologists' professional training. For the new laboratories would permit students to spend their last years of studies as residents or non-residents, under the direction of teachers who would also be resident, as in the case of medical studies. The twofold aspect, theoretical and practical, of the studies would be justified by the new tasks entrusted to the profession. For anthropology would plead in vain for that recognition to which its outstanding achievements in the realm of theory otherwise entitle it if, in this ailing and troubled world of ours, it did not first endeavor to prove its *usefulness*.

NOTES

1. We refer here, of course, to the volume in which this chapter originally appeared.
2. *American Anthropologist*, LIII, No. 4, Part 1 (1951), pp. 465-89.
3. E. B. Tylor, *Primitive Culture* (London: 1871), I, 1.

4. G. Sergi, "Terminologia e divisione delle Scienze dell'Uomo; i resultati di un'inchiesta internazionale," *Rivista di Antropologia*, XXXV (1944-1947).

5. It is in this way that the problem is raised by the Institut International d'Archéocivilisation, directed by A. Varagnac.

6. As envisaged, on the other hand, by the Laboratoire d'Ethnographie Française and the Musée National Français des Arts et Traditions Populaires.

7. Niels Bohr, "Natural Philosophy and Human Culture," *Nature*, CXLIII (1939).

8. Just after writing these lines, we came across very similar views expressed by Jean-Paul Sartre. After criticizing an out-of-date sociology, he adds: "The sociology of primitive peoples is *never* open to this criticism. There, we study *meaningful wholes [ensembles signifiants]*." *Les Temps Modernes* (October-November, 1952), p. 729, *n* 1.

9. Regarding this point, see C. Lévi-Strauss, *Tristes Tropiques* (Paris: 1955), Chapter XXVIII.

10. Pages 188-9. Speaking generally, I should say that all of pages 181-9 of that book would deserve inclusion *in extenso* in UNESCO's Constitution.

11. J. Sutter and L. Tabah, "Les Notions d'isolat et de population minimum," *Population*, VI, No. 3 (1951).

12. See on this subject N. Wiener, *The Human Use of Human Beings* (Boston: 1950).

13. The reader wishing to delve deeper into these remarkable analogies between the social and the natural sciences should consult the excellent book by Pierre Auger, *L'Homme microscopique* (Paris: 1952).

14. With regard to these questions, the reader can profitably consult the special number of *American Anthropologist* devoted to a symposium: "The Training of the Professional Anthropologist," LIV, No. 3 (1952). The problems we deal with here are discussed in that symposium with reference to the situation in the United States.

15. In this respect it will be noted that since 1937 two-thirds of the buildings at present housing the Musée de l'Homme (Paris) have been given over to laboratory work, and only one-third to exhibition galleries. It is this concept—revolutionary at the time—which permitted the establishment of a close association between museographic and educational activities; an illustration of this is the housing, already mentioned, of the Musée de l'Homme and the Institut d'Ethnologie in the same building.

16. Such suggestions are often criticized because they threaten to turn the anthropologist into a "servant of the social order." Even if this threat is real, it seems to me preferable to standing aloof, because the anthropologist's participation results at least in an understanding of the facts, and truth has a power of its own. I hope that the reader will not misinterpret my suggestions. Personally, I do not care for applied anthropology, and I question its scientific value. But those who criticize it in principle should bear in mind that the first book of *Capital* was partly based on the reports of British factory inspectors, to whom Marx in his preface pays a glowing tribute: "*We should be appalled at the state of things at home*, if, as in England, our governments and parliaments

appointed periodically commissions of enquiry into economic conditions; if these commissions were armed with the same plenary powers to get at the truth; if it was possible to find for this purpose men as competent, as free from partisanship and respect of persons as are the English factory inspectors, her medical reporters on public health, her commissioners of enquiry into the exploitation of women and children, into housing and food. Perseus wore a magic cap that the monsters he hunted down might not see him. We draw the magic cap down over eyes and ears as a make-believe that there are no monsters." *Capital*, trans. Samuel Moore and Edward Aveling (New York: Modern Library, 1906), p. 14. The italics are mine.

Evidently Marx had no thought of censuring those "applied anthropologists" of the time for being servants of the established order. Yet they were; but what does it matter to us in view of the facts they uncovered?

Acknowledgments

CHAPTER I, "Introduction: History and Anthropology," first published under the title "Histoire et Ethnologie," in *Revue de Metaphysique et de Morale*, LIV, Nos. 3-4 (1949), pp. 363-91.

CHAPTER II, "Structural Analysis in Linguistics and in Anthropology," first published under the title "L'Analyse structurale en linguistique et en anthropologie," in *Word, Journal of the Linguistic Circle of New York*, I, No. 2 (August, 1945), pp. 1-21.

CHAPTER III, "Language and the Analysis of Social Laws," first published under the same title in *American Anthropologist*, n.s., LIII, No. 2, (1951), pp. 155-63. Reprinted here with slight modifications.

CHAPTER IV, "Linguistics and Anthropology," a paper read at the Conference of Anthropologists and Linguists, Bloomington, Indiana, 1952, and first published in *Supplement to International Journal of American Linguistics*, XIX, No. 2 (April, 1953). Reprinted here with slight modifications.

CHAPTER VI, "The Concept of Archaism in Anthropology," first published under the title "La Notion d'archaïsme en ethnologie," in *Cahiers Internationaux de Sociologie*, XII (1952), pp. 32-5.

CHAPTER VII, "Social Structures of Central and Eastern Brazil," first published under the title "Les Structures sociales dans le Brésil central et oriental," in Sol Tax (ed.), *Indian Tribes of Aboriginal America*, Proceedings of the 29th International Congress of Americanists (Chicago: 1952), pp. 302-10.

CHAPTER VIII, "Do Dual Organizations Exist?" first published under the title "Les Organisations dualistes existent-elles?" in *Bijdragen tot de taal-, land-, en Volkenkunde*, Deel 112, 2e Aflevering (1956), pp. 99-128. The volume was dedicated to Professor J. P. B. de Josselin de Jong.

CHAPTER IX, "The Sorcerer and His Magic," first published under the title "Le Sorcier et sa magie," in *Les Temps Modernes*, No. 41 (1949), pp. 3-24.

CHAPTER X, "The Effectiveness of Symbols," dedicated to Raymond de Saussure, first published under the title "L'Efficacité symbolique," in *Revue de l'Histoire des Religions*, CXXXV, No. 1 (1949), pp. 5-27.

CHAPTER XI, "The Structural Study of Myth," first published under the same title, in "Myth, a Symposium," *Journal of American Folklore*, LXXVIII, No. 270 (October-December, 1955), pp. 428-44. Reprinted here with slight modifications.

CHAPTER XII, "Structure and Dialectics," first published under the title "Structure et Dialectique," in *For Roman Jakobson, Essays on the Occasion of His Sixtieth Birthday* (The Hague: 1956), pp. 289-94.

CHAPTER XIII, "Split Representation in the Art of Asia and America," first published under the title "Le Dédoublement de la représentation dans les arts de l'Asie et de l'Amérique," in *Renaissance* (New York: The École Libre des Hautes Études), Vols. 2 and 3 (1944-1945), pp. 168-86.

CHAPTER XIV, "The Serpent with Fish inside His Body," first published under the title "Le Serpent au corps rempli de poissons," in *Actes du XXVIIIe Congrès des Américanistes* (Paris: 1947; Société des Américanistes, 1948), pp. 633-36.

CHAPTER XV, "Social Structure," was a paper given at the Wenner-Gren Foundation International Symposium on Anthropology, New York, 1952. First published in A. L. Kroeber (ed.), *Anthropology Today* (Chicago: 1953), pp. 524-53. Reprinted here with some modifications.

CHAPTER XVII, "The Place of Anthropology in the Social Sciences and Problems Raised in Teaching It," first published, in French and English, in *The University Teaching of the Social Sciences* (Paris: UNESCO, 1954). Reprinted here with slight modifications.

Bibliography

ADAM, L. Das Problem der Asiatisch-Altamerikanischen Kulturbeziehungen mit besonderer Berücksichtigung der Kunst, *Wiener Beiträge zur Kunst und Kultur Geschichte Asiens*, V, 1931.

———. Northwest American Indian Art and Its Early Chinese Parallels, *Man*, XXXVI, No. 3, 1936.

———. Review of C. Hentze, Frühchinesische Bronzen und Kultdarstellungen, *Man*, XXXIX, No. 60, 1937.

ALBISETTI, FR. C. Estudos complementares sôbre os Bororós orientais, *Contribuições missionárias, publicações da Sociedade Brasileira de Antropologia e Etnologia*, Nos. 2-3, Rio de Janeiro, 1948.

AUGER, P. *L'Homme microscopique*. Paris: 1952.

BALANDIER, G. Grandeur et servitude de l'ethnologie, *Cahiers du Sud*, XLIII, No. 337, 1956.

BALDUS, H. Os Tapirapé, *Revista do Arquivo Municipal*. São Paulo, 1944-1946.

BÄSSLER, A. *Alte peruanische Kunst*, Vol. 2. Berlin.

BASTIDE, R. Lévi-Strauss ou l'ethnographe "à la recherche du temps perdu," *Présence africaine*, April-May, 1956.

BATESON, G. *Naven*. Cambridge: 1936.

BENEDICT, P. K. Tibetan and Chinese Kinship Terms, *Harvard Journal of Asiatic Studies*, VI, 1942.

———. Studies in Thai Kinship Terminology, *Journal of the American Oriental Society*, LXIII, 1943.

BENEDICT, R. *Patterns of Culture*. Cambridge, Mass.: 1934.

———. *Zuni Mythology*. 2 vols. Columbia University Contributions to Anthropology, No. 21. New York: 1934.

———. Franz Boas as an Ethnologist. In *Franz Boas, 1858-1942*, Memoirs of the American Anthropological Association, n.s., No. 61, 1943.

BENVENISTE, E. Nature du signe linguistique, *Acta Linguistica*, I, No. 1, 1939.

BERNDT, R. M. *Kunapipi*. New York: 1951.

———. "Murngin" (Wulamba) Social Organization, *American Anthropologist*, n.s., LVII, No. 1, 1955.

BERNOT, L., and R. BLANCARD. *Nouville, un village français*. Travaux et Mémoires de l'Institut d'Ethnologie, LVII. Paris: 1953.

BIDNEY, D. Review of L. A. White, *The Science of Culture*, in *American Anthropologist*, n.s., LII, No. 4, Part 1, 1950.

———. *Theoretical Anthropology*. New York: 1953.

BOAS, F. *The Social Organization and the Secret Societies of the Kwakiutl Indians*. Washington, D.C.: 1895.

———. Introduction to J. Teit, *Traditions of the Thompson River Indians of British Columbia*. Memoirs of the American Folklore Society, Vol. VI, 1898.

———. The Methods of Ethnology, *American Anthropologist*, n.s., XXII, 1920.

———. Evolution or Diffusion? *American Anthropologist*, n.s., XXVI, 1924.

———. *Primitive Art*. Oslo: 1927; New York: 1955.

———. *The Religion of the Kwakiutl Indians*. 2 vols. Columbia University Contributions to Anthropology, No. 10. New York: 1930.

———. Some Problems of Methodology in the Social Sciences. In *The New Social Science*, ed. Leonard White. Chicago: 1930.

———. History and Science in Anthropology: A Reply, *American Anthropologist*, n.s., XXXVIII, 1936.

———. The Limitations of the Comparative Method of Anthropology (1896). In *Race, Language and Culture*. New York: 1940.

———, ed. *Handbook of American Indian Languages*. Bureau of American Ethnology Bulletin No. 40 (1908), Part 1. Washington, D.C.: 1911.

BOGGIANI, G. *Viaggi d'un artista nell' America Meridionale*. Rome: 1895.

BOHR, N. Natural Philosophy and Human Culture, *Nature*, CXLIII, 1939.

BONAPARTE, M. Notes on the Analytical Discovery of a Primal Scene. In *The Psychoanalytical Study of the Child*, Vol. 1. New York: 1945.

BRAND, C. S. On Joking Relationships, *American Anthropologist*, n.s., L, 1948.

British Social Anthropology; Contemporary British Social Anthropology, *American Anthropologist*, LIII, No. 4, Part 1, 1951.

BRUNSCHVICG, L. *Le Progrès de la conscience dans la philosophie occidentale*. 2 vols. Paris: 1927.

BUNZEL, R. L. *Introduction to Zuni Ceremonialism*. Bureau of American Ethnology, 47th Annual Report. Washington, D.C.: 1930.

CANNON, W. B. "Voodoo" Death, *American Anthropologist*, n.s., XLIV, 1942.

COLBACCHINI, FR. A. A. *I Bororos Orientali*. Turin: 1925.

———, and FR. C. ALBISETTI. *Os Bororós orientais*. São Paulo: 1942.

COOK, W. A. *The Bororo Indians of Matto Grosso, Brazil*. Smithsonian Miscellaneous Collection, Vol. L. Washington, D.C.: 1908.

COOPER, FR. J. M. The South American Marginal Cultures. *Proceedings of the Eighth American Scientific Congress.* Washington, D.C.: 1940.

CREEL, H. G. On the Origins of the Manufacture and Decoration of Bronze in the Shang Period, *Monumenta Serica,* I, Section 1, 1935.

————. Notes on Shang Bronzes in the Burlington House Exhibition, *Revue des Arts Asiatiques,* X, 1936.

CUSHING, F. H. *Zuni Fetiches.* Bureau of American Ethnology, 2nd Annual Report (1880-1881). Washington, D.C.: 1883.

————. *Outlines of Zuni Creation Myths.* Bureau of American Ethnology, 13th Annual Report. Washington, D.C.: 1896.

————. *Zuni Breadstuffs.* Indian Notes and Monographs, Museum of the American Indian, Heyes Foundation, No. 8. New York: 1920.

DAHLBERG, G. *Mathematical Methods for Population Genetics.* London-New York: 1948.

DAVIS, K. Intermarriage in Caste Societies, *American Anthropologist,* n.s., XLIII, 1941.

————. *The Development of the City in Society.* Social Science Research Council, First Conference on Long Term Social Trends. Washington, D.C.: 1947.

————, and W. L. WARNER. Structural Analysis of Kinship, *American Anthropologist,* n.s., XXXVII, 1935.

DELCOURT, M. *Oedipe ou la légende du conquérant.* Liège: 1944.

DESOILLE, R. *Le Rêve éveillé en psychothérapie.* Paris: 1945.

DOBRIZHOFFER, M. *An Account of the Abipones.* 3 vols. Trans. from the Latin. London: 1822.

DORSEY, G. A. *The Pawnee: Mythology,* Part 1. Washington, D.C.: 1906.

DUMÉZIL, G. *Loki.* Paris: 1948.

————. *L'Héritage indo-européen à Rome.* Paris: 1949.

DURKHEIM, E. *Les Formes élémentaires de la vie religieuse.* Paris: 1912.

————, and M. MAUSS. De quelques Formes primitives de classification: Contribution à l'étude des représentations collectives, *Année Sociologique,* VI, 1901-1902.

EGGAN, F. Historical Changes in the Choctaw Kinship System, *American Anthropologist,* n.s., XXXIX, 1937.

————. *Social Organization of the Western Pueblos.* Chicago: 1950.

————, ed. *Social Anthropology of North American Tribes.* Chicago: 1937.

ELWIN, V. *The Muria and Their Ghotul.* Oxford: 1947.

ENGELS, F. *The Origin of the Family, Private Property and the State.* London: 1940.

EVANS-PRITCHARD, E. E. Nuer Time Reckoning, *Africa,* XII, 1939.

————. *The Nuer.* Oxford: 1940.

————. *Social Anthropology.* Glencoe, Ill.: 1951.

FARNSWORTH, W. O. *Uncle and Nephew in the Old French Chanson de Geste.* New York: 1913.

FEBVRE, L. *Le Problème de l'incroyance au XVIe siècle.* 2nd ed. Paris: 1946.

FIELD, H., and E. PROSTOV. Results of Soviet Investigation in Siberia, 1940–1941, *American Anthropologist*, n.s., XLIV, 1942.

FIRTH, R. *We, The Tikopia.* London-New York: 1936.

——. *Malay Fishermen.* London: 1946.

——. *Elements of Social Organization.* London: 1951.

FLETCHER, A. C., and J. R. MURIE. *The Hako: A Pawnee Ceremony.* Bureau of American Ethnology, 22nd Annual Report (1900–1901). Washington, D.C.: 1904.

FORD, C. S., and F. A. BEACH. *Patterns of Sexual Behavior.* New York: 1951.

FORD, J. A. The Puzzle of Poverty Point, *Natural History*, LXIV, No. 9, 1955.

FORDE, D. *Marriage and the Family among the Yakö in S. E. Nigeria.* Monographs in Social Anthropology, No. 5, London School of Economics, 1941.

——. Double-Descent among the Yakö. In *African Systems of Kinship and Marriage*, ed. A. R. Radcliffe-Brown and D. Forde. Oxford: 1950.

FORTES, M., ed. *Social Structure: Studies Presented to A. R. Radcliffe-Brown.* Oxford: 1949.

——, and E. E. EVANS-PRITCHARD. *African Political Systems.* Oxford: 1940.

FORTUNE, R. F. *The Sorcerers of Dobu.* New York: 1932.

——. Arapesh Warfare, *American Anthropologist*, n.s., XLI, 1939.

FRIČ, V., and P. RADIN. Contributions to the Study of the Bororo Indians, *Journal of the Royal Anthropological Institute*, XXXVI, 1906.

GAUTIER, L. *La Chevalerie.* Paris: 1890.

GEISE, N. J. C. *Badujs en Moslims.* Leiden: 1952.

GIFFORD, E. W. *Miwok Moieties.* University of California Publications in American Archaeology and Ethnology, Vol. XII, No. 4, 1916.

——. *Tonga Society*, Bernice P. Bishop Museum Bulletin No. 61. Honolulu: 1929.

GOLDSTEIN, K. *La Structure de l'organisme.* Paris: 1951. Trans. of *Der Aufbau des Organismus.* (*The Organism*, New York: 1939.)

GOODENOUGH, W. H. The Componential Analysis of Kinship, *Language*, XXXII, No. 1, 1956.

GOUGH, K. Female Initiation Rites on the Malabar Coast, *Journal of the Royal Anthropological Institute*, LXXXV, 1955.

GRIAULE, M. *Masques Dogons.* Travaux et Mémoires de l'Institut d'Ethnologie, No. 33. Paris: 1938.

——. Mythe de l'organisation du monde chez les Dogons, *Psyché*, II, 1947.

GUMMERE, F. B. The Sister's Son. In *An English Miscellany Presented to Dr. Furnivall.* London: 1901.

GURVITCH, G. *Déterminismes sociaux et liberté humaine.* Paris: 1955.

——. Le Concept de structure sociale, *Cahiers internationaux de Sociologie*, XIX, n.s., 1955.

HALPERN, A. M. Yuma Kinship Terms, *American Anthropologist*, n.s., XLIV, 1942.

HAMILTON, A. *The Art Workmanship of the Maori Race in New Zealand.* Dunedin: 1896-1900.

HARTLAND, S. *Matrilineal Kinship and the Question of Its Priority.* Memoirs of the American Anthropological Association, Vol. IV, 1917.

HAUDRICOURT, A. G., and G. GRANAI. Linguistique et Sociologie, *Cahiers internationaux de Sociologie,* XIX, n.s., 1955.

HAUSER, H. *L'Enseignement des sciences sociales.* Paris: 1903.

HENRY, J. Review of C. Nimuendajú, *The Apinayé,* in *American Anthropologist,* n.s., XLII, 1940.

HENTZE, C. *Objets rituels, croyances et dieux de la Chine antique et de l'Amérique.* Antwerp: 1936.

————. *Frühchinesische Bronzen.* Antwerp: 1937.

HERSKOVITS, M. J. *The Economic Life of Primitive Peoples.* New York: 1940.

HOCART, A. M. Chieftainship and the Sister's Son in the Pacific, *American Anthropologist,* n.s., XVII, 1915.

————. The Uterine Nephew, *Man,* XXIII, No. 4, 1923.

————. The Cousin in Vedic Ritual, *Indian Antiquary,* LIV, 1925.

————. *Les Castes.* Paris: 1938.

————. *The Northern States of Fiji.* Occasional Publications of the Royal Anthropological Institute, No. 11. London: 1952.

————. *The Life-Giving Myth.* London: 1952.

————. *Social Origins.* London: 1954.

HOLM, S. Studies towards a Theory of Sociological Transformations, *Studia Norvegica,* No. 7, Oslo, 1951.

HOLMER, N. M. and H. WASSÉN. *Mu-Igala or the Way of Muu, a Medicine Song from the Cunas of Panama.* Göteborg: 1947.

HOMANS, G. C., and D. M. SCHNEIDER. *Marriage, Authority and Final Causes, a Study of Unilateral Cross-Cousin Marriage.* Glencoe, Ill.: 1955.

HOWARD, G. E. *A History of Matrimonial Institutions.* 3 vols. Chicago: 1904.

HUNTER-WILSON, M. Witch Beliefs and Social Structure, *American Journal of Sociology,* LVI, No. 4, 1951.

JAKOBSON, R. Remarques sur l'évolution phonologique du russe, *Travaux du Cercle Linguistique de Prague,* II, 1929.

————. Prinzipien der historischen Phonologie, *Travaux du Cercle Linguistique de Prague,* IV, 1931.

————. Observations sur le classement phonologique des consonnes, *Proceedings of the Third International Congress of Phonetic Sciences.* Ghent: 1938.

————. *Kindersprache, Aphasie und Allgemeine Lautgesetze.* Uppsala: 1941.

————. The Phonetic and Grammatical Aspects of Language in Their Interrelations, *Actes du VIe Congrès International des Linguistes.* Paris: 1948.

————, and M. HALLE. *Fundamentals of Language.* The Hague: 1956.

JOSSELIN DE JONG, J. P. B. DE. *Lévi-Strauss's Theory on Kinship and Marriage.* Leiden: 1952.

JOSSELIN DE JONG, P. E. DE. *Minangkabau and Negri-Sembilan: Socio-Political Structure in Indonesia.* Leiden: 1951; The Hague: 1952.

KARLGREN, B. *New Studies on Chinese Bronzes.* The Museum of Far Eastern Antiquities Bulletin No. 9. Stockholm: 1937.

———. *Huai and Han.* The Museum of Far Eastern Antiquities Bulletin No. 13. Stockholm: 1941.

KELEMEN, P. *Medieval American Art.* 2 vols. New York: 1943.

KOVALEVSKI, M. La Famille matriarcale au Caucase, *L'Anthropologie,* IV, 1893.

KRIS, E. The Nature of Psychoanalytic Propositions and Their Validation. In *Freedom and Experience, Essays Presented to H. M. Kallen.* Ithaca, N.Y.: 1947.

KROEBER, A. L. Classificatory Systems of Relationship, *Journal of the Royal Anthropological Institute,* XXXIX, 1909.

———. Review of R. H. Lowie, *Primitive Society,* in *American Anthropologist,* n.s., XXII, No. 4, 1920.

———. *Handbook of the Indians of California.* Bureau of American Ethnology, Bulletin 78. Washington, D.C.: 1925.

———. History and Science in Anthropology, *American Anthropologist,* n.s., XXXVII, 1935.

———. Basic and Secondary Patterns of Social Structure, *Journal of the Royal Anthropological Institute,* LXVIII, 1938.

———. Salt, Dogs, Tobacco, *Anthropological Records,* VI, Berkeley, 1941.

———. The Societies of Primitive Man, *Biological Symposia,* VIII, Lancaster, Pa., 1942.

———. Structure, Function and Pattern in Biology and Anthropology, *Scientific Monthly,* LVI, 1943.

———. *Anthropology.* Revised ed. New York: 1948.

KROEF, J. VAN DER. Dualism and Symbolic Antithesis in Indonesian Society, *American Anthropologist,* n.s., LVI, 1954.

LA VEGA, GARCILASO DE. *Histoire des Incas.* French trans., Paris: 1787.

LAWRENCE, W. E., and G. P. MURDOCK. Murngin Social Organization, *American Anthropologist,* n.s., LI, No. 1, 1949.

LEACH, E. R. Jinghpaw Kinship Terminology, *Journal of the Royal Anthropological Institute,* LXXV, 1945.

———. The Structural Implications of Matrilateral Cross-Cousin Marriage, *Journal of the Royal Anthropological Institute,* LXXXI, 1951.

LEE, D. D. Some Indian Texts Dealing with the Supernatural, *Review of Religion,* May, 1941.

LEFORT, C. L'Echange et la lutte des hommes, *Les Temps Modernes,* February, 1951.

———. Sociétés sans histoire et historicité, *Cahiers internationaux de Sociologie,* XII, 1952.

LEIRIS, M. *Biffures, la règle du jeu,* Vol. 1. Paris: 1948.

———. *Fourbis, la règle du jeu,* Vol. 2. Paris: 1955.

LEROI-GOURHAN, A. L'Art animalier dans les bronzes chinois, *Revue des Arts Asiatiques*, Paris, 1935.

LESTRANGE, M. DE. Pour une Méthode socio-démographique, *Journal de la Société des Africanistes*, XXI, 1951.

LÉVI-STRAUSS, C. Contribution à l'étude de l'organisation sociale des Indiens Bororo, *Journal de la Société des Américanistes*, n.s., XXVIII, 1936.

———. Indian Cosmetics, *VVV*, No. 1, New York, 1942.

———. The Art of the Northwest Coast, *Gazette des Beaux-Arts*, New York, 1943.

———. Reciprocity and Hierarchy, *American Anthropologist*, n.s., XLVI, 1944.

———. The Social and Psychological Aspects of Chieftainship in a Primitive Tribe: The Nambikuara, *Transactions of the New York Academy of Sciences*, Ser. 2, VII, No. 1, 1944.

———. On Dual Organization in South America, *América Indígena*, IV, No. 1, Mexico City, 1945.

———. French Sociology. In *Twentieth Century Sociology*, ed. G. Gurvitch and W. E. Moore. New York: 1945.

———. Sur certaines similarités morphologiques entre les langues Chibcha et Nambikwara, *Actes du XXVIIIᵉ Congrès International des Américanistes*. Paris: 1947.

———. *La Vie familiale et sociale des Indiens Nambikwara*. Paris: 1948.

———. The Tupí-Cawahib. In *Handbook of South American Indians*, ed. J. Steward, Vol. III. Bureau of American Ethnology. Washington, D.C.: 1948.

———. *Les Structures élémentaires de la parenté*. Paris: 1949.

———. Introduction à l'oeuvre de Marcel Mauss. In M. Mauss, *Sociologie et Anthropologie*. Paris: 1950.

———. *Race and History*. Paris: 1952.

———. The Mathematics of Man, *International Social Science Bulletin*, VI, No. 4, 1954.

———. *Tristes Tropiques*. Paris: 1955. Trans. John Russell. New York: 1961.

———. The Family. In *Man, Culture and Society*, ed. H. L. Shapiro. Oxford: 1956.

———. Le Symbolisme cosmique dans la structure sociale et l'organisation cérémonielle de plusieurs populations nord et sud-américaines. In *Le Symbolisme cosmique des monuments religieux*. Serie Orientale Roma, XIV, 1957.

———. Four Winnebago Myths: A Structural Sketch. In *Culture in History: Essays in Honor of Paul Radin*, ed. S. Diamond. New York: 1960.

LEWIN, K. *A Dynamic Theory of Personality*. New York: 1935.

LING SHUN SHENG. Human Figures with Protruding Tongue Found in the Taitung Prefecture, Formosa, and Their Affinities Found in Other Pacific Areas, *Bulletin of the Institute of Ethnology, Academia Sinica*, No. 2, Nankang, Taipei, Taiwan, 1956.

LINTON, R. *The Study of Man.* New York: 1936.

LIVI, L. *Trattato di Demografia.* Padua: 1940-1941.

———. Considérations théoriques et pratiques sur le concept de "minimum de population," *Population,* IV, No. 4, 1949.

LOUNSBURY, F. G. A Semantic Analysis of the Pawnee Kinship Usage, *Language,* XXXII, No. 1, 1956.

LOWIE, R. H. Societies of the Hidatsa and Mandan Indians, *American Museum of Natural History Anthropological Papers,* XI, 1913.

———. Exogamy and the Classificatory Systems of Relationship, *American Anthropologist,* n.s., XVII, No. 2, 1915.

———. Plains Indian Age-Societies: Historical and Comparative Summary, *American Museum of Natural History Anthropological Papers,* XI, 1916.

———. *The Matrilineal Complex,* University of California Publications in American Archaeology and Ethnology, XVI, No. 2, 1919.

———. *Primitive Society.* New York: 1920.

———. *The Origin of the State.* New York: 1927.

———. Notes on Hopi Clans, *American Museum of Natural History Anthropological Papers,* XXX, 1929.

———. Hopi Kinship, *American Museum of Natural History Anthropological Papers,* XXX, 1929.

———. Relationship Terms. In *Encylcopaedia Britannica,* 14th ed. New York: 1948.

———. *The Crow Indians.* New York: 1935.

———. *The History of Ethnological Theory.* New York: 1937.

———. American Culture History, *American Anthropologist,* n.s., XLII, 1940.

———. A Note on the Northern Gé Tribes of Brazil, *American Anthropologist,* n.s., XLIII, 1941.

———. A Marginal Note to Professor Radcliffe-Brown's Paper on "Social Structure," *American Anthropologist,* n.s., XLIV, No. 3, 1942.

———. *Social Organization.* New York: 1948.

———. Some Aspects of Political Organization among American Aborigines (Huxley Memorial Lecture), *Journal of the Royal Anthropological Institute,* LXXVIII, 1948.

MALINOWSKI, B. *Argonauts of the Western Pacific.* London: 1922.

———. *Sex and Repression in Savage Society.* London-New York: 1927.

———. *The Sexual Life of Savages in Northwestern Melanesia.* 2 vols. London-New York: 1929.

———. Introduction to H. Ian Hogbin, *Law and Order in Polynesia.* London: 1934.

———. *Coral Gardens and Their Magic.* 2 vols. London: 1935.

———. Culture. In *Encyclopaedia of the Social Sciences.* New York: 1935.

———. Culture as a Determinant of Behavior. In *Factors Determining Human Behavior,* Harvard Tercentenary Publications. Cambridge, Mass.: 1937.

———. The Present State of Studies in Culture Contact, *Africa,* XII, 1939.

MARTIUS, C. F. P. VON. *Beiträge zur Ethnographie und Sprachenkunde Amerikas zumal Brasiliens.* Leipzig: 1867.

MARX, K. *Capital.* Trans. Samuel Moore and Edward Aveling. New York: 1906.

———. *A Contribution to the Critique of Political Economy.* Trans. N. I. Stone. Chicago: 1911.

———. *Eighteenth Brumaire of Louis Bonaparte.* New York: 1951.

———, and F. ENGELS. *Selected Correspondence 1846-1895.* New York: 1942.

MASON, D. I. Synesthesia and Sound Spectra, *Word,* VIII, No. 1, 1952.

MASPERO, H. *La Chine antique.* Paris: 1927.

MAUSS, M. Essai sur les variations saisonnières dans les sociétés eskimos, *Année Sociologique,* IX, 1904-1905.

———. Essai sur le Don, Forme archaïque de l'échange, *Année Sociologique,* n.s., I. (*The Gift.* Trans. I. Cunnison. Glencoe, Ill.: 1954.)

———. Division et proportion des divisions de la sociologie, *Année Sociologique,* n.s., II, 1924-1925.

———. *Manuel d'ethnographie.* Paris: 1947.

———. *Sociologie et anthropologie.* Paris: 1950.

McCARTHY, F. D. *Australian Aboriginal Decorative Art.* Sydney: 1938.

MEAD, M. *Sex and Temperament in Three Primitive Societies.* New York: 1935.

———. Character Formation and Diachronic Theory. In *Social Structure,* ed. M. Fortes. Oxford: 1949.

———, ed. *Competition and Cooperation among Primitive Peoples.* London-New York: 1937; Boston: 1961.

MERLEAU-PONTY, M. *Les Aventures de la dialectique.* Paris: 1955.

MÉTRAUX, A. *Myths of the Toba and Pilagá Indians of the Gran Chaco.* Memoirs of the American Folklore Society, Vol. XL, 1946.

———. Social Organization of the Kaingang and Aweikoma, *American Anthropologist,* n.s., XLIX, 1947.

MORGAN, L. H. *Systems of Consanguinity and Affinity of the Human Family,* Smithsonian Institution Contributions to Knowledge, Vol. XVII, No. 218. Washington, D.C.: 1871.

MORLEY, A. Doctois Save Man "Sung to Death," *Sunday Times,* London, April 22, 1956, p. 11.

MURDOCK, G. P. *Social Structure.* New York: 1949.

———. World Ethnographic Sample, *American Anthropologist,* n.s., LIX, No. 4, 1957.

MURIE, J. R. Pawnee Indian Societies, *American Museum of Natural History Anthropological Papers,* XI, 1914.

NADEL, S. F. Shamanism in the Nuba Mountains, *Journal of the Royal Anthropological Institute,* LXXVI, 1946.

———. *The Nuba.* London-New York: 1947.

———. Witchcraft in Four African Societies: An Essay in Comparison, *American Anthropologist,* n.s., LIV, No. 1, 1952.

NEUMANN, J. VON, and O. MORGENSTERN. *Theory of Games and Economic Behavior*. Princeton: 1944.

NIMUENDAJÚ C. *The Apinayé*. The Catholic University of America Anthropological Series, No. 8. Washington, D.C.: 1939.

——. *The Serenté*. Publication of the F. W. Hodge Anniversary Publication Fund, Vol. IV. Los Angeles: 1942.

——. *The Eastern Timbira*. University of California Publications in American Archaeology and Ethnology, Vol. XLI. Los Angeles: 1946.

——, and R. H. Lowie. The Dual Organization of the Ramkokamekran (Canella) of Southern Brazil, *American Anthropologist*, n.s., XXIX, 1927.

NORDENSKIÖLD, E. An Historical and Ethnological Survey of the Cuna Indians. In *Comparative Ethnographical Studies* (ed. H. Wassén), Vol. X. Göteborg: 1938.

OLIVER, D. L. *A Solomon Island Society: Kinship and Leadership among the Siuai of Bougainville*. Cambridge, Mass.: 1955.

OPLER, M. E. Apache Data Concerning the Relation of Kinship Terminology to Social Classification, *American Anthropologist*, n.s., XXXIX, 1937.

——. Rule and Practice in the Behavior Pattern between Jicarilla Apache Affinal Relatives, *American Anthropologist*, n.s., XLIX, 1947.

PAGET, Sir R. A. The Origin of Language, *Journal of World History*, I, No. 2, 1953.

PARAIN, B. Les Sorciers, *Le Monde Nouveau*, May, 1956.

PARSONS, E. C. The Origin Myth of Zuni, *Journal of American Folklore*, XXXVI, 1923.

POTTIER, E. Histoire d'une bête. In *Recueil E. Pottier*. Bibliothèque des Ecoles d'Athènes et de Rome, Section 142.

POUILLON, J. L'Oeuvre de Claude Lévi-Strauss, *Les Temps Modernes*, No. 126, July, 1956.

QUEIROZ, M. I. PEREIRA DE. A noção de arcaísmo em etnologia e a organização social dos Xerente, *Revista de Antropologia*, I, No. 2, São Paulo, 1953.

RADCLIFFE-BROWN, A. R. The Mother's Brother in South Africa, *South African Journal of Science*, XXI, 1924.

——. Father, Mother and Child, *Man*, XXVI, No. 103, 1926.

——. The Social Organization of Australian Tribes, *Oceania*, I, 1930-1931.

——. Kinship Terminology in California, *American Anthropologist*, n.s., XXXVII, 1935.

——. On Joking Relationships, *Africa*, XIII, 1940.

——. On Social Structure, *Journal of the Royal Anthropological Institute*, LXX, 1940.

——. The Study of Kinship Systems, *Journal of the Royal Anthropological Institute*, LXXI, 1941.

——. Religion and Society (Henry Myers Lecture), *Journal of the Royal Anthropological Institute*, LXXV, 1945.

——. A Further Note on Joking Relationships, *Africa*, XIX, 1949.

————. White's View of a Science of Culture, *American Anthropologist,* n.s., LI, No. 3, 1949.

————. Murngin Social Organization, *American Anthropologist,* n.s., LIII, No. 1, 1951.

————. Social Anthropology, Past and Present, *Man,* LII, No. 14, 1952.

————. *Structure and Function in Primitive Society.* Glencoe, Ill.: 1952.

————, and D. Forde, eds., *African Systems of Kinship and Marriage.* Oxford: 1950.

RADIN, P. *The Winnebago Tribe.* Bureau of American Ethnology, 37th Annual Report (1915-1916). Washington, D.C.: 1923.

————. *The Road of Life and Death.* New York: 1945.

————. *The Culture of the Winebago: as Described by Themselves.* Special Publications of the Bollingen Foundation, No. 1. New York: 1949.

RAPOPORT, A. Outline of Probabilistic Approach to Animal Sociology, *Bulletin of Mathematical Biophysics,* XI, 1949.

REICHARD, G. A. *Melanesian Design: A Study of Style in Wood and Tortoise Shell Carving.* 2 vols. Columbia University Contributions to Anthropology, No. 18. New York: 1933.

————. *Navaho Religion, A Study in Symbolism.* 2 vols. New York: 1950.

————, R. Jakobson, and E. Werth. Language and Synesthesia, *Word,* V, No. 2, 1949.

REVEL, J. F. *Pourquoi des philosophes?* Paris: 1957.

RICHARDS, A. I. *Hunger and Work in a Savage Tribe.* London: 1932.

————. A Dietary Study in North-Eastern Rhodesia, *Africa,* IX, No. 2, 1936.

————. *Land, Labour and Diet in Northern Rhodesia.* Oxford: 1939.

RICHARDSON, J., and A. L. KROEBER. Three Centuries of Women's Dress Fashions: A Quantitative Analysis, *Anthropological Records,* V, No. 2, Berkeley, 1940.

RIVERS, W. H. R. The Marriage of Cousins in India, *Journal of the Royal Asiatic Society,* July, 1907.

————. *The History of Melanesian Society.* 2 vols. London: 1914.

————. *Social Organization.* London: 1924.

ROBLEY, H. G. *Moko, or Maori Tattooing.* London: 1896.

RODINSON, M. Racisme et civilisation, *La Nouvelle Critique,* No. 66, June, 1955.

————. Ethnographie et relativisme, *La Nouvelle Critique,* No. 69, November, 1955.

ROES, A. Tierwirbel, *Ipek,* 1936-1937.

ROSE, H. J. On the Alleged Evidence for Mother-Right in Early Greece, *Folklore,* XXII, 1911.

ROUT, E. A. *Maori Symbolism.* London: 1926.

RUBEL, M. *Karl Marx, Essai de biographie intellectuelle.* Paris: 1957.

SAPIR, E. *Selected Writings in Language, Culture and Personality.* Ed. D. Mandelbaum. Berkeley: 1949.

SARTRE, J.-P. Les Communistes et la paix (II), *Les Temps Modernes,* Nos. 84-85, 1952.

SAUSSURE, F. DE. *Cours de linguistique générale.* Paris: 1916.

SCHMIDT, M. *Kunst und Kultur von Peru.* Berlin: 1929.

SCHRADER, O. *Prehistoric Antiquites of the Aryan Peoples.* Trans. F. B. Jevons. London: 1890.

SECHEHAYE, M. A. La Réalisation symbolique, *Revue Suisse de Psychologie et de Psychologie Appliquée,* Supplement No. 12, Bern, 1947.

SELIGMAN, C. G. *The Melanesians of British New Guinea.* London: 1910.

SERGI, G. Terminologia e divisione delle Science dell'Uomo; resultati di un' inchiesta internazionale, *Rivista di Antropologia,* XXXV, 1944-1947.

SHANNON, C., and W. WEAVER. *The Mathematical Theory of Communication.* Urbana, Ill.: 1950.

SIMIAND, F. Méthode historique et Science sociale, *Revue de Synthèse,* 1903.

SOUSTELLE, J. *La Pensée cosmologique des anciens Mexicains.* Paris: 1940.

SPECK, F. G. *Family Hunting Territories and Social Life of Various Algonkian Bands of the Ottawa Valley.* Canada Department of Mines, Geological Survey, Memoir 70. Ottawa: 1915.

SPIER, L. The Sun-Dance of the Plains Indians, *American Museum of Natural History Anthropological Papers,* XVI, 1921.

SPOEHR, A. *Kinship System of the Seminole.* Field Museum of Natural History Anthropological Series, Vol. XXXIII, No. 2. Chicago: 1942.

———. *Changing Kinship Systems.* Field Museum of Natural History Anthropological Series, Vol. XXXIII, No. 4. Chicago: 1947.

———. Observations on the Study of Kinship, *American Anthropologist,* LII, No. 1, 1950.

STANNER, W. E. H. Murinbata Kinship and Totemism, *Oceania,* VII, 1936-1937.

STEINEN, K. VON DEN. *Unter den Naturvölkern Zentral-Brasiliens.* 2nd ed. Berlin: 1897.

STEVENSON, M. C. *The Zuni Indians.* Bureau of American Ethnology. 23rd Annual Report. Washington, D.C.: 1905.

STEWARD, J. H. *Basin-Plateau Aboriginal Sociopolitical Groups.* Bureau of American Ethnology, Bulletin 120. Washington, D.C.: 1938.

STEWART, J. Q. Empirical Mathematical Rules Concerning the Distribution and Equilibrium of Population, *Geographical Review,* XXXVII, No. 3, 1947.

SUTTER, J., and L. TABAH. Les Notions d'isolat et de population minimum, *Population,* VI, No. 3, 1951.

SWANTON, J. R. *Social Condition, Beliefs and Linguistic Relationship of the Tlingit Indians.* Bureau of American Ethnology, 26th Annual Report. Washington, D.C.: 1908.

———. *Tlingit Myths and Texts.* Bureau of American Ethnology, Bulletin 59. Washington, D.C.: 1909.

TEISSIER, G. La Description mathématique des faits biologiques, *Revue de Métaphysique et de Morale,* January, 1936.

THOMPSON, D'ARCY WENTWORTH. *On Growth and Form.* 2 vols. Rev. ed. Cambridge, Mass.: 1942.

THOMPSON, L. *Culture in Crisis, a Study of the Hopi Indians.* New York: 1950.

THOMSON, D. F. The Joking Relationship and Organized Obscenity in North Queensland, *American Anthropologist*, n.s., XXXVII, 1935.

———. The Training of the Professional Anthropologist, *American Anthropologist*, n.s., LIV, No. 3, 1952.

TROUBETZKOY, N. La Phonologie actuelle. In *Psychologie du langage*. Paris: 1933.

———. *Principes de phonologie.* French trans., Paris: 1949.

TYLOR, E. B. *Researches into the Early History of Mankind and the Development of Civilization.* London: 1865.

———. *Primitive Culture.* 2 vols. London: 1871; New York: 1958.

VOTH, H. R. *The Oraibi Summer Snake Ceremony*, Field Columbian Museum Publication No. 83, Anthropological Series, Vol. III, No. 4. Chicago: 1903.

WAGLEY, C. The Effects of Depopulation upon Social Organization as Illustrated by the Tapirapé Indians, *Transactions of the New York Academy of Sciences,* III, No. 1, 1940.

———, and E. GALVÃO. The Tapirapé. In *Handbook of South American Indians,* ed. J. Steward, Vol. 3. Bureau of American Ethnology Bulletin No. 143. Washington, D.C.: 1948.

WARNER, W. L. Morphology and Functions of the Australian Murngin Type of Kinship System, *American Anthropologist*, n.s., XXXII-XXXIII, 1930-1931.

———. The Family and Principles of Kinship Structure in Australia, *American Sociological Review,* II, 1937.

———. *A Black Civilization.* New York: 1937.

WATERBURY, F. *Early Chinese Symbols and Literature: Vestiges and Speculations.* New York: 1942.

WHITE, L. A. Energy and the Evolution of Culture, *American Anthropologist*, n.s., XLV, 1943.

———. History, Evolutionism and Functionalism: Three Types of Interpretation of Culture, *Southwestern Journal of Anthropology,* I, 1945.

———. Evolutionary Stages, Progress and the Evaluation of Culture, *Southwestern Journal of Anthropology,* III, 1947.

———. *The Science of Culture.* New York: 1949.

WHORF, B. L. *Collected Papers on Metalinguistics.* Department of State, Foreign Service Institute. Washington, D.C.: 1952.

———. *Language, Thought, and Reality.* Ed. John B. Carroll. New York. 1956.

WIENER, N. *Cybernetics, or Control and Communication in the Animal and the Machine.* Paris–Cambridge–New York: 1948.

———. *The Human Use of Human Beings.* Boston: 1950.

WILLIAMS, F. E. Sex Affiliation and Its Implications, *Journal of the Royal Anthropological Institute,* LXII, 1932.

———. Natives of Lake Kutubu, Papua, *Oceania*, XI-XII, 1940-1941, 1941-1942.

———. Group Sentiment and Primitive Justice, *American Anthropologist*, n.s., XLIII, No. 4, 1941.

WITTFOGEL, K. A., and E. S. GOLDFRANK. Some Aspects of Pueblo Mythology and Society, *Journal of American Folklore*, LVI, 1943.

YACOVLEFF, E. La deidad primitiva de los Nasca, *Revista del Museo Nacional* (Lima, Peru), II, No. 2, 1932.

YETTS, W. P. *The George Eumorphopoulos Collection Catalogue.* 3 vols. London: 1929.

———. *The Cull Chinese Bronzes.* London: 1939.

———. An-Yang: A Retrospect, *China Society Occasional Papers*, n.s., No. 2, London, 1942.

YNGVE, V. H. Syntax and the Problem of Multiple Meaning. In *Machine Translation of Languages*, ed. W. N. Locke and A. D. Booth. New York: 1955.

———. Sentence for Sentence Translation, *Mechanical Translation*, II, No. 2, Cambridge, Mass., 1955.

———. The Translation of Languages by Machine, *Information Theory* (Third London Symposium), n.d.

ZIPF, G. K. *Human Behavior and the Principle of Least Effort.* Cambridge, Mass., 1949.

Index

abreaction, in psychoanalysis, 198; in shamanism, 181

Acoma kinship system, 75

Adam, L., 246, 267

African kinship systems, 64, 303

African Systems of Kinship and Marriage (A. R. Radcliffe-Brown), 303

Agave, 217

age-grades, 105, 121, 125, 130, 148, 236

aikmā, rule of, 125

aimapli, 123

Ainu art, 247

Alaska, 7, 255-256

Albisetti, Fr. C., 127-128, 136, 143, 163

alligator, in Cuna magic, 195

Amazon River, 106-107

America, pre-Columbian history of, 107; representation in art of, 245-266

American Anthropologist, 380

American anthropology, method in, 102

American Indian, art, 248; kinship systems, 64; mythology, 224

ancestors, masks and, 264

Andean civilizations, 106

animism, 19

anthropologist, as "astronomer of social sciences," 378; as historian, 23-24; relationship with linguist, 69

anthropology, xi; American, 102; applied, xv; authenticity in, 366; changes in, 2; and collective phenomena, 18; cultural, *see* cultural anthropology; defined, 18; departments of, 350-351; ethnography-ethnology contrasts and, 354-356; folklore and, 359-360; history and, 1-25, 285-286; isolated chairs of, 349-350; linguistics and, 67-80; meaningfulness in, 365-366; mythology and,

207; objectivity in, 363-364; organization of studies in, 368-371; physical, 351-354; place of in social sciences, 346-379; practical work in, 374-375; psychoanalysis and, 180-183, 198-204; relationship theory and, 95; religion and, 206-207 (*see also* religion); responsibilities in, 369; schools or institutes of, 351-352; social, *see* social anthropology; social science and, 360-363; specialization in, 370; structural analysis in, ix, xiv, 31-51, 288, 295; task of, 363-365; teaching of, 346-379; theoretical and applied, 377-378; totality in, 365; use of term, 359

Anthropology (A. L. Kroeber), 325

Antigone, 214

Antilles Islands, 107

An-Yang excavations, China, 263, 265

Apinayé tribe, 105, 115, 120-121, 129, 144

Araguaia Valley, Brazil, 105

Arapesh tribe, 15

Arawak Indians, 104, 108

archaism, concept of, xiii, 101-117

Argonauts of the Western Pacific (B. Malinowski), 11

Arikara Indians, 236

Aristotelian outlook, 307

Arkansas River, 143

aroetorrari, 109

art, impersonation in, 263; as language, 84; prehistoric, 245-256; split representation in, 245-266; transformation of details in, 247

Ash-Boy, myth of, 226

Asia, split representation in art of, 245-266

Assam, India, 22